42708 -2

PN
4874   Anderson, Jack
A48
A33   Confessions of a
        Muckraker

MAR 3 '82	DATE DUE	
MAR 14 '91		

CONFESSIONS
OF A
MUCKRAKER

CONFESSIONS OF A MUCKRAKER

*The Inside Story of
Life in Washington
during the Truman,
Eisenhower, Kennedy
and Johnson Years*

JACK ANDERSON
with JAMES BOYD

Random House · New York

Copyright © 1979 by Jack Anderson and James Boyd

Grateful acknowledgment is made to Holt, Rinehart and Winston for permission to reprint previously published material from *Drew Pearson Diaries 1949–1959*, edited by Tyler Abell. Copyright © 1974 by The Estate of Drew Pearson. Reprinted by permission of Holt, Rinehart and Winston, Publishers.

Library of Congress Cataloging in Publication Data

Anderson, Jack, 1922–
  Confessions of a muckraker.

  Includes index.
    1. Anderson, Jack, 1922– 2. Pearson, Drew,
1897–1969. 3. Journalists—United States—Biography.
I. Boyd, James, 1929– joint author. II. Title.
PN4874.A48A33   070.4′3′0924 [B]   77-90283
ISBN 0-394-49124-6

Manufactured in the United States of America

9 8 7 6 5 4 3 2

First Edition

To Mrs. Drew Pearson, a great lady

Contents

CONFESSIONS
OF A
MUCKRAKER

1 · The Inspector General

THE IDEA that I would one day tcam up with Drew Pearson began as a bit of escapism, a reverie through which I could almost bridge the distances of space and time between the unreal present in wartime Chungking, high above the Yangtze, and my "real" life, in the future, back home.

I can remember the precise moment the thought was put in my head. I was sitting with press colleagues in our hostel on an ancient hillside. Outside, dusk crept across the China sky like a closing eyelid. A thousand pungent smells from charcoal fires and oil pots filled the night air, and a full moon was rising over the river valley while necklaces of twinkling lights wound around the city of hills swollen far beyond its age-old size by the numberless shanties of refugees.

An impromptu celebration had broken out among us, which had no more cause than that someone had got hold of a bottle of real vodka. The prize was passed from hand to hand, and one by one we began to elaborate our favorite yarns about the grand things we would do when World War II was over. It was a night of intoxication, even for me who did not take a drink, for victory and home-going were clearly in sight and all felt the bubbling ferment of new beginnings.

When my turn came I said I was going to become a top newsman, a famous by-liner, a reporter of national catastrophes and international crises, maybe even a syndicated pundit. One member of our circle—I believe it was Spencer Moosa of the Associated Press—was charitable enough to treat my Walter Mittyisms seriously. "You should go to Washington," he said. "That's going to be the news capital of the world. Why don't you try to get a job with Drew Pearson? He knows his way around the back rooms of Washington better than anyone." I nodded sagely and for the remainder of that night when all seemed within reach, I basked in the self-importance of my partnership with Pearson.

The notion grew on me in the days to come. That Pearson was, as Robert Novak later put it, "the best known, widest read and richest syndicated columnist" did not faze me. I was sure I could construct an appealing résumé, considering that I was only twenty-two. I had served a long teen-age apprenticeship on the Salt Lake City *Tribune*. And was I not a war correspondent? Well, maybe not exactly; I had persuaded a Salt Lake City paper, the *Deseret News*, to arrange for my accreditation in return for stories about hometown heroes gone to war. But I had promoted that fragile accreditation as though it had the full backing of Time, Inc., had managed to get deep into China, had wandered about the interior with a Nationalist guerrilla troop, riding its one horse, and had covered one skirmish, not against the Japanese enemy, to be sure, but rather with a Chinese Communist unit. Drew Pearson would be happy to sign up a fellow like me for his syndicated column, the "Washington Merry-Go-Round."

The aspiration was fed by a singular experience. There was in Chungking a representative from the Chinese Communist Party, which claimed to govern 90 million who were beyond the sway of either Chiang Kai-shek or the Japanese occupiers. He carried a general's title and his name was Chou En-lai. Spencer Moosa permitted me to cover the worldly and wily Chou for the Chungking bureau of the Associated Press.

Chou En-lai established his mission among the submerged masses he claimed to champion. The approach to his modest headquarters led through a maze of slitlike streets that gave off an "overpowering stench of human filth in the open gutters blended with the intoxicating aroma of Chinese foods frying in deep fat with spices." The quotation is from Theodore H. White and Annalee Jacoby's evocation of wartime

Chungking,* as is this description: "A thousand Chungking alleyways darted off down the slopes of the hills . . . some were so narrow that a passerby would catch the drip from the eaves of both sides with his umbrella. . . . The women nursed their babies in the open streets as they chatted with their neighbors; they would hold a child over the gutter to relieve himself.

"The old streets were full of fine ancient noises—squealing pigs, bawling babies, squawking hens, gossiping women, yelling men and the eternal singsong chant of coolies . . ."

In his mid-forties, Chou En-lai had a handsome face, which lingers in my memory for its black eyes and incandescent intelligence. He was slight of build but indefatigable; he affected simplicity but was an elegant man, graceful of movement, accomplished in English and French as well as Chinese dialects, buttressing his arguments with historical and literary allusions that evinced a formidable education. And one caught flashes of a ruthless rationalism that would sacrifice the lives of millions to the triumph of an idea. Walter Robertson, the State Department's Far Eastern expert, described the Chou En-lai of those years as "one of the most charming, intelligent and attractive men of any race" he had ever known. "But he'll cut your throat."†

Even his formulations of official propaganda were artfully plausible, but it was his side excursions that kept me coming back to trespass upon his time. He would expound on the true sources of power behind the façades of constitutions and ballot boxes; on the requirements for a just society in that half of the world where a man counted for no more than an ox, and a woman less; on the ingredients of peace in a world whose balance was fundamentally altered by the re-emergence of Asia; on the tragedy for America as well as for China if we continued to ally ourselves to a Kuomintang which could not win but which could indefinitely prolong China's agony and the world's instability.

Chou En-lai was an unlikely consciousness-raiser for an aspiring newspaperman. Undoubtedly he regarded American reporters as merely ports of infiltration behind the defenses of a nation that had made itself his enemy. Certainly a free press had no place in his domestic scheme, and when he came into his kingdom he would help liquidate the smallest vestige of free expression about basic dogma, not

---

Thunder Out of China (New York: William Sloan Associates, 1946), pp. 10, 6–7.
†C. L. Sulzberger, *A Long Row of Candles* (New York: Macmillan, 1969), p. 1001.

only in newspaper offices but even at the level of the family hearth. Yet for me he brought to life whole realms I had not heretofore pondered. I began to see the world as a network of submerged causes to chronicle, organized frauds to expose, political pretenses to unmask and diplomatic intrigues to dissect.

Those were the realms, were they not, that Drew Pearson moved in, and the suggestion that I seek him out as employer and teacher gave me a concrete objective. Ahead of me stretched an indefinite term of Army service, for I was drafted while in China, but the day came, in early 1947, when I knocked on the Pearson door in Washington ready to present credentials enhanced, I hoped, by a stint on the Shanghai edition of *Stars and Stripes*.

As chance would have it, a vacancy had just opened on the staff; Pearson's reluctant suspicions that a staffman named Andrew Older was a Communist were confirmed after he took the matter personally to J. Edgar Hoover. Older admitted it and had to go, not only because Pearson drew an iron line between Communism and his own liberalism but also because he had too many eager enemies to make himself hostage to an assistant's politics.

I waited by the phone in a Washington hotel room for the great man's decision, and when it came it was with a touch of melodrama —by telegram sent crosstown. I was to report immediately! Whether it was my qualifications or the lack of them that got me the job, I shall never know, for in the interview I found Pearson inscrutable. I suspect that what recommended me was that I was young and apparently scrappy, inexperienced and therefore unconfirmed in error, and willing to work full time for a part-time wage (like many humanitarians, Drew Pearson was a bit on the close side as an employer, a trait I have come to appreciate). Also, I was willing to consider my association as an informal trial run, a condition repugnant to the established professional. All I wanted was an opportunity to get my foot inside the door.

"Relentless rivalry is the lifeblood of the town. Nearly everyone, from the highest to the lowest, is trying to put something over on someone. The vortex of this maelstrom is the Washington press corps. Drew Pearson is the vortex of the vortex." So wrote Drew's former partner, Robert S. Allen, in 1949, during the first years of my apprenticeship. What comes back to me with greatest pungency from those years is the atmosphere of combat, of shooting and being shot at, of exposing villainies and being despised for it.

Our headquarters lurked innocently behind the placid, polished-brass façade of a Federal-style residence at 1313 29th Street on a quiet, tree-shaded corner of Georgetown. It was a rambling old edifice of faded yellow brick, a joint office and home which Pearson had put together by combining two rather small three-story houses and adding, at the juncture, an outward projecting wing of his own design. On one side of this agglomeration reigned the peace and amenity of a proper gentleman's domicile, smoothly administered by a trio of quietly competent servants; on the other, the discordant clangor and ferment of a combination newsroom and spy cell. The office wing had five rooms that housed four secretaries and four reporters ingloriously designated as "legmen." Our quarters had once housed slaves, the boss informed us, with a smiling acknowledgment that the character of the place had little changed.

That some sort of news operation was afoot could be divined from the clacking of a UP news ticker, the clattering of typewriters turning out copy, the continual ringing of ten telephones through the day and far into the night, and those hurried stressful comings and goings that have to do with imminent deadlines. But there was, too, an atmosphere of the clandestine: anonymous phone callers; the mumbo-jumbo of an elementary code we often used because of our assumption that our phones were tapped; the thirty-odd file cabinets that protected our derogatory treasures, standing against the walls locked and portentous; the abrupt breaking off of conversations between the boss and an aide when a second aide approached—for here we kept our sources secret even from one another.

When the static of news ticker, telephone and typewriter fell momentarily silent, the twitter of birds and the hum of bees could be heard from the garden, or perhaps the delicate tinkling of a bell in the residential quarters as the master signaled it was time to clear away the dishes of the main course and bring dessert. A disarming place overall that could have been the residence of a vicar, yet I was conscious, having boned up, that from it had been unloosed an unprecedented array of scoops, scandals and disturbances. There came to mind the 1939 Louisiana exposés that led to the conviction en masse of the state administration. President Franklin D. Roosevelt's Supreme Court "packing" plan and his historic deal with Winston Churchill whereby American destroyers were swapped for British bases reached the world prematurely through the "Washington Merry-Go-Round." The imminence of a German invasion of Russia in the spring of 1941 and the embarkation of the Japanese fleet from its home base in late November were flashed by Pearson. The General Patton "slapping incident," the 1944 proposal to FDR by his envoy at New Delhi that Great Britain be denied postwar control of India, the defection of Russian code clerk Igor Gouzenko and his revelations that a Soviet spy ring was operating in the United States and Canada to steal atomic secrets—all had been first revealed from here, each setting off an international uproar.

There were mementoes around the place of various campaigns and crusades Drew Pearson had instigated, for he differed from other men of the press in that he not only reported news but created it. The motivation behind most of his crusades was his Quaker pacifism and a conviction that peoples must reach out, over governmental barriers, to aid and communicate with one another lest the horrors of the past be repeated.

In the late 1930s he had put aside his Quaker principles because of the overriding peril he saw in totalitarian aggression, and he effectively supported the Roosevelt interventionist policies and the war effort. But at war's end he became plagued with alarming visions—an America permanently militarized, the sweep of Stalinism into Western Europe, a world divided by backward-looking politicians into hostile East-West camps. He had emerged from the war years as the single most influential commentator in the world, and he determined to use that influence.

He became the foremost spokesman of the grass-fire movement to "bring the boys home," which soon built up irresistible heat, causing a forced demobilization whose good and ill effects are still being debated by historians. He conceived and put on the rails the transcontinental Friendship Train, a nongovernment people-to-people phenomenon that whistle-stopped across America collecting donations of food for the war-ravaged populations of France and Italy; under his organizing drive and publicizing flair, the idea generated into a rolling tide culminating in a dozen trains and seven hundred boxcars of food packages worth $40 million (in 1947 dollars). As newsreel devotees of that era will remember, Drew personally supervised shipment of his food overseas and its distribution to the hungry. Roscoe Drummond of the *Christian Science Monitor* judged it "one of the greatest projects ever born of American journalism."

Pearson followed up the Friendship Train by launching other mass efforts: the collection of millions of toys for the children of Europe; the famous letter-writing campaign by Italian-Americans to their relatives in Italy, a factor in preventing a Communist electoral takeover there; the release of thousands of balloons from the borders of Czechoslovakia to be carried deep behind the Iron Curtain on the prevailing eastward winds, each balloon containing a friendly message from the United States. Later on, Pearson the world figure would enter into personal negotiations with Communist dictators for the purpose of easing tensions, the first being his successful effort to persuade Marshal Tito of Yugoslavia to set free Cardinal Stepinac, a coup which Pearson the journalist exclusively reported.

The proprietor of our establishment was thus more widely known than many of the celebrities he wrote about. With his daily "Merry-Go-Round" column and his Sunday-night broadcast over the ABC radio network, the Pearson operation reached an audience of 60 million. The name Drew Pearson evoked the image of the ubiquitous, hyperactive news hawk, with open collar, clipped mustache, the inevitable reporter's hat set back on his head, fast-talking into a mike. So much did his public image fit the mystique of the reporter-sleuth that a comic strip based on his career ("Hap Hazard") was being syndicated in competition with Dick Tracy. No other American had ever had the eyes and ears of so many people for so long a time.

He used this unprecedented access to help what he saw as the humanitarian cause and to hurt those who thwarted it—imperialists, militarists, monopolists, racists, crooks in public and corporate life, all of whom he saw as subverters of the American system and exploiters of the poor. On the attack he was unremitting, and even when not mortally engaged, he thought it salutary that the mighty should be humbled. He often trampled upon the customary immunity granted by the correspondents of that day to the highly placed as regards their private vices, self-indulgences and eccentricities.

Nor did he respect the comfortable gentleman's code by which what was said at private parties or at closed meetings was treated as off-limits to publication. So often did secret conversations at high-level meetings appear in the "Washington Merry-Go-Round" that half of the Cabinet under both Roosevelt and Truman was fearful that the other half was leaking to Drew. Secretary of State Cordell Hull once opened a Cabinet meeting by exclaiming, "Is this for the room or is it for Pearson?" —a remark which was duly published in the column.

And so he had become, as *Time* called him, "the most intensely feared and hated man in Washington." He had put it differently, in a self-assessment written early in his career as the anonymous co-author of a 1931 book on the Washington scene from which the column would take its name: "Because of his independence he is either loved or hated; there is no middle ground of affection where Pearson is concerned."

"A teller of monstrous and diabolical falsehoods," courtly Cordell Hull called him, furthering the Mephistophelian tradition of invective that was to flourish for another quarter century—through Senator Joseph McCarthy's "diabolically clever voice of international communism" to Senator Thomas Dodd's stricken bellow: "He is . . . the Rasputin of our society. Drew Pearson is a liar. He is a monster. Those associated with him are thieves, liars, monsters . . . his business is lying. He is a devil . . . a molester of children . . . What is his strange power in this government?"

Congressman James Mott dubbed him the "polecat of journalism." And Senator Theodore Bilbo weighed in with graphic originality: "He will go down in history as Pearson-the-sponge because he gathers slime, mud and slander from all parts of the earth and lets them ooze out through his radio broadcasts and through his daily contribution to a few newspapers which have not yet found him out."

Yet, damned though he often was, no other commentator could claim a following as massive or as loyal as his. Among the publishers of the Pearson column there were scores, perhaps hundreds, who deplored his philosophy and disliked his opprobrious style, and who would gladly have canceled him had they not feared, based on the experiences of other publishers, that many of his readers would follow him to the nearest competitor. Part of his following, he knew, read him mainly for the titillation derived from seeing the private foibles of the famous made public. But there were many who genuinely admired him, who loved him for his championship of the helpless against the mighty, the duped against the dupers, or who lived vicariously through him as he plagued the great malefactors beyond their humble reach.

Drew Pearson was nearing his fiftieth year and the pinnacle of his influence when I joined his staff. During my first days on the job, the senior staffmen alerted me against stumbling over established taboos: Mr. Pearson did not tolerate certain activities around him, such as smoking; he brooked no insubordination; he did not appreciate questions on how to proceed, expecting his reporters to *know* how to carry out his missions impossible. He could not abide air conditioning, so one must not leave open the door to his den which would let in drafts from the air conditioners in the staff rooms. No one was allowed to use, or even touch, his personal typewriter, an antique portable Corona given him by his revered father in 1922. He required little sleep and was apt to phone his reporters at any hour of the night, as the spirit moved him;

I must learn to come out of a deep sleep instantly and to make a show of alertness, if not joviality, at three o'clock in the morning.

So forewarned, I approached Mr. Pearson with apprehension in the beginning. But the polecat in his lair was disarmingly mild. Sitting behind his paper-strewn desk in a maroon smoking jacket, or in the bathrobe he wore some days until noon, amid pictures and mementoes of his much-loved family, with a black cat named Cinders preening companionably in the out-box on his desk, he appeared not at all menacing. When he arose, he revealed a frame that was tall, trim and well constructed, conveying an impression of considerable physical strength. He had an impressive, high forehead under thinning light-brown hair, and a general look of learnedness that made him seem too dignified and elegant for the rough-and-tumble he in fact relished. The anguished visitor who missed the occasional glint of watchfulness in his blue eyes would likely be lulled by his soft voice, quiet manners and the peaceful gentility of the atmosphere into the comfortable feeling that he was paying a courtesy call on Mr. Chips.

Conversation with him did not flow easily. Despite his prodigious production of the written word and an experience as a public lecturer that spanned several continents and went back almost to his adolescence, he often seemed ill at ease in conversation. He could be a most gracious host, with a disciplined adherence to the ordinary courtesies, but he quickly became bored with small talk. He was a listener more than a discourser. He spoke slowly and would join in intermittently when some subject sparked his interest, then would lapse into silences that could become awkward.

There was a disconcerting drollery about him. He would sometimes introduce a topic with a half-smile, as if it should have a humorous association for his listener. His smile invited a like response, but as he would not elaborate on its antecedent the spark of jollity would fail to ignite, and silence would return.

He was a habitual sniffer. For a long time I sought in those sniffs some clue to his moods and reactions. Did they signify interest? Unease? Approval? Disfavor? But no sniffing pattern developed and they remained inscrutable. During my greenhorn days, a fellow Pearson legman, Fred Blumenthal, would phone me at night, and without saying a word, sniff the familiar sniff a few times while I scrambled about me for a pencil and paper in anticipation of the boss's instructions. Just as I would begin to catch on, Fred would erupt into laughter.

Gentleman-farming in nearby Maryland was his weekend escape; his most contented hours were passed in a rambling stone manor house that overlooked the Potomac River. On several hundred acres, half of which he owned, the other half rented, he supervised the raising of cattle, hogs, feed grains and vegetables. His key product was a by-product, manure, which he marketed with gusto. Savoring the connection to muckraking, he widely advertised "Pearson's Best Manure—All Cow, No Bull—Better Than The Column." On his farms, no field could be plowed, no steer butchered, without his personal decision. So it was at the office; nothing got into the column without passing through his revising hands. He would radically alter copy submitted by his reporters without consulting them, sometimes reversing its intent to suit his own predilections.

When frustrated by staff frailties, he did not shout or pound his desk. His rebukes were nonetheless felt. They came on occasion in the form of the cutting remark, but more often through an almost imperceptible shade of remoteness in his voice. We offending aides would likely be subjected to a calm but encyclopedic interrogatory on our progress in all the minor assignments given us in the past six months, most of which we thought the boss had forgotten or lost interest in as fresh events had pushed more timely matters to the fore.

A term in Drew's doghouse would usually be followed by one of ostentatious favor. He would become contrite, especially if he had indulged in sarcasm, and would try to compensate by awkward displays of kindness.

In the most casual voice he would call upon his legmen to perform the most impossible assignments, without the slightest suggestion how they would go about it. And when upon occasion they achieved the impossible, Drew would feign to regard it as the merest routine. A satisfied chortle was the highest commendation one could expect from him.

The Sunday-evening radio broadcast was the climax of Pearson's week. All day Sunday, while the tension mounted, Pearson and his staff would put together the fifteen-minute broadcast. Details would be hunted down in a frantic race with time, phone calls were under way to all sections of the country, copy would be dictated and revised under the pressure of the moving hand of the clock. Right up to air time he would be on the phone, playing the role of Drew Pearson, psyching himself up for the moment when the signal flashed and he would be on, to sink or swim with: "Good evening, ladies and gentlemen, this is Drew Pearson in Washington."

My first few days on the staff were spent in happy ignorance of this Sabbath regimen. But late in the week he said to me, "Sunday is our big day around here. I'll be needing you all day on Sundays."

I was dismayed. It seemed I must strike out before ever really coming to bat. "I'm sorry, Mr. Pearson," I said. "I don't work on Sundays. I'm at church most of the day."

He said nothing, just let out an abrupt sniff, but what was he thinking? As it turned out, he accepted my Sunday absences. To compensate, I would work into the wee hours of Sunday morning to make sure my contribution to the broadcast was up to date. But I was never to be a part of the excitement and the theater of one of the great broadcast phenomena of the times.

He had come upon the press scene in the twenties, when most Washington reporting consisted of processing official publicity hand-outs and reporting public proceedings at face value, and he had raised a competing standard whereby what an official hid was more news-worthy than what he announced and what he said at closed meet-ings was more significant than his playacting when he was on public display.

"It is the job of a newspaperman," he would insist, "to spur the lazy, watch the weak, expose the corrupt. He must be the eyes, ears and nose of the American people. Yes, the nose is important, for no matter how much stench a newspaperman is exposed to, he must never lose his sense of smell." Or he would say, "I operate by the sense of smell. If something smells wrong, I go to work."

Two faculties mark the true muckraker, he felt: an instinct for penetrating the fraud behind men's pretenses, and a sense of outrage which, though it must grow weary, is ever resilient.

Yet Pearson's general optimism struck me more than his specific skepticism. His preoccupation with scandal never seemed to shake his belief in the basic foundations of the American system. All that was needed for its indefinite improvability, he felt, was exposure of the bad and inculcation of the good. He regarded himself as a part of the system, not as an alienated critic. He even drew up legislation and got his friends in Congress to introduce it. For every rogue he hounded, there was another politician he believed in and with whom he main-tained a lifetime comradeship in arms.

He aimed to reach and influence not only the movers and shakers and the political enthusiasts but what columnist Frank Kent once called "the great rancid mass of the American people." The way to do this, he had decided, was to personalize the abstract, to name actual thieves and perjurers rather than to lament theft and misrepresentation.

He was scornful of the pundits, the pashas of the press upon their lofty heights, who set down great thoughts. "Thumbsuckers," he contemptuously called them. "Write about personalities," he would admonish us. "That's the way to dramatize wrongs. It isn't necessary to put our readers to sleep."

Some of his colleagues thought he dramatized by stretching the truth. He "wrote hard," as they say in the newsroom, overstating his indictments and choosing words in a contentious way that squeezed out every ounce of impact that could be justified by his facts. He was diligent to avoid libel, but he seldom gave targets the benefit of the doubt, "maximizing" his material on the assumption that they were already covering up far worse shenanigans than he would ever get wind of.

A typical column would begin with a hook such as "Although it will be denied" or "Here's the inside story of . . ." Over a period of weeks, daily subjects would include exposés of graft, important and trivial; inside accounts of secret cabinet and committee meetings; predictions prescient and hokey; avuncular advice to the body politic, often in the guise of open letters to his children and nephews; personal reminiscences, historical and sentimental; briefs for liberal legislation; exhortations in behalf of brotherhood, peace and patriotism; malicious swipes at the pomposities of the great or at the antics of boozy Washington wives; thoughtful analyses of domestic politics and international affairs; revelations of the medical ailments, marital crises and emotional quirks of the famous; exclusive interviews with foreign chiefs of state; travelogues of the remote corners of the earth.

Somewhere in this mix was something that appealed to the favorite aspirations, alarums, prejudices or pathologies of a wide array of groups. The anticlerical gentleman who relished Pearson's attacks on politically active Catholic hierachs or the frugal citizen who was enraged by the expense accounts of junketeering congressmen might be bored with his interminable analyses of Balkan affairs or put off by his lobbying for aid to the undeserving poor, but just as such a reader was teetering on the brink of disaffection, up would pop a satisfying item about Father Coughlin's involvement in an alienation-of-affection scrape or an Adam Clayton Powell tour through Paris night clubs with a beauty queen on each arm—the lot paid for by the taxpayers—and the reader's faithfulness in sticking with the column through arid patches would once again be vindicated.

At first I thought it a terrifying responsibility to be obliged, as Pearson was, to put out a new story every day, 365 days a year. How could a man be sure that each day he would come up with something? But it is the genius of nature that it reduces everything, even this, to a supportable routine. When the normal flow of tips slowed, there were a dozen reliable agencies, bureaus and committees whose antisocial proclivities could be counted upon to produce usable copy. In an emergency, several hours spent "under the Dome" on Capitol Hill were almost bound to turn up something sufficiently shabby. When even Congress went dry, Pearson was adept at concocting scandalous stories that had a shocking, novel appearance but which in reality were inevitabilities. Early in 1946 he "disclosed" that 14,000 illegitimate babies had been born to Japanese mothers, fathered by the American Occupation Army. The clinker in that particular scoop was that the U.S. Army at that time had been in Japan only six months. Pearson, sometimes weak on details but with a firm grip on the larger picture, refused to yield to the howls of protest occasioned by what was only, in his view, a technicality; he rode them out, confident that in three or four months his story would be vindicated, which of course it was.

Pearson followed a daily routine that was most intimidating to his staff and would be to any ordinary mortal exposed to it. The combination of home with office establishment enabled him to indulge his appetite for work and his miserliness with time. He would sleep for a few hours at night, get up, pad downstairs in his bathrobe and slippers, type up his latest inspiration or dictate into a machine, go back upstairs and return to sleep, to rise again at six o'clock, pleased with his jump on the day. He liked to phone his targets for crucial interviews before they were awake, assuming that their normal defenses would be down and they might stammer out the truth. Besides, the practice added to his mystique—the menace who never rested.

His killing schedule was made possible by an inestimable gift— which I have tried in vain to cultivate—that of being able to fall asleep at will, anytime, anywhere. In the middle of a conversation, or at his desk, or in someone's waiting room, or while waiting to testify, or on a train, plane, bus or car, he had but to close his eyes and he was gone. A constant traveler, he would meticulously schedule his trips so that he was moving at night, arriving at his destination as refreshed as though he had slept in his own bed. Not a moment of precious working time need be wasted.

He protected his catnaps with an adamancy approaching ruthlessness. Once he was to make a speech in Ogden, Utah, a thirty-minute drive from my hometown of Salt Lake City. Arrangements were made for my father and mother to pick him up at the Salt Lake City airport and drive him to Ogden; this would give them a chance at last to meet the great man and to hear from his own lips glowing accounts of their son. Excitedly they awaited Drew, but no sooner had he shaken hands and entered their car than he fell into a sound sleep, not to awaken until the car stopped at the door of his speaking site.

It was required that a secretary be in the office at seven so that Drew's overnight dictation and rough drafts could be cleanly typed for his editing at eight, at which time he would make his formal entrance.

In the evening, as the last of the daytime regulars was leaving, Joseph Canty would check in to begin his nighttime stint at indexing the files, keeping the books and answering the phones. Canty, a night owl, often worked into the early hours, leaving just before Drew's predawn visitations, giving the Pearson offices a near round-the-clock operation that was pleasing to Drew's aspiration toward omnipresence and tight security. The files, always locked, were seldom left alone. For cat burglars and government bag-job artists, it was a tough joint to crack.

Drew entered fully into the conspiratorial spirit of the world he moved in. He would keep his sources and his "finds" from us, even concerning stories we were working on, and sometimes would assign two of us to pursue the same story, without either of us knowing the other was on the trail, until we began to stumble over each other. In the meantime, when we separately checked in each night with our discoveries, he would mystify us with his own knowledge of the case, not telling us he had just gleaned it from our unknown partner. This fostered his image as the omniscient sleuth, an image that grew more and more important to him as his responsibilities as executive and celebrity progressively removed him from the scene of actual investigative reporting.

The telephone was our life line. Though we were flooded with calls from cranks and people with insignificant information, our orders were to treat incoming calls with utmost seriousness. The tipster, Drew knew, has to screw up his courage and nerve to a high point, often requiring weeks of thinking about it to make the initial phone call; if he doesn't get through, he may never try again. The sound of a ringing phone, however faint, set off an automatic alarm somewhere in Drew's machinery. To his wife Luvie's great consternation, he could not resist going to the phone, even from the dinner table. Two of his great exposés, he would point out—the May-Garsson war frauds and the grain speculations of Senator Elmer Thomas—originated in calls he took at dinner time.

It would have been a shame if during those years our phones were *not* being tapped by someone, for we always assumed they were and went to considerable trouble to circumvent the tappers. Whenever a tip of real potential came in on the phone, we would have the caller sign off and arrange to call him back from a "safe" phone. When Drew called me with something sensitive to impart, he would rhythmically strike the receiver with a pencil, on the theory that this constant tap-tap would scramble the reception of his interceptors. Twenty years too late to matter, I learned that if indeed Drew's phone *was* tapped, his scrambling remedy, alas, had had no effect except to prevent me from understanding what he was saying.

That his success and power rested in large measure on the practiced impugning of others confused me, at first, in identifying the true wellspring of his career. I hesitated to use the word which day-to-day contact with him suggested—idealism—for I could not at once reconcile idealism with his guileful mastery of the jugular arts. But idealism is what it was. When I think about Drew, now that all is said and done, this is the word that comes first and rings truest.

He wanted right to be done; that was the signal beaming steadily from him. He wanted to do good, not in the vague, sporadic, well-intentioned way of the half-committed, but precisely, continually, rigorously, and above all, effectively. He believed that he had a responsibility to do good—that he owed it—to justify the undeserved good fortune that had attended him from birth: the love and care of adored parents; the Quaker faith; a decent education made possible by the sacrifice of parents, teachers and unknown donors; the genteel poverty of a professor's son that permitted him vision and access without robbing him of the need to strive; and the boundless opportunity America had offered him.

When he first appears in the remembrances of relatives, as a boy, he is shepherding his younger brother and sisters, trying to fill the gap caused by the frequent travels of his father on the lecture circuit. As a student, his commitment can be measured: winner of the highest scholarship in each of his years at Phillips Exeter Academy; class valedictorian at Swarthmore College, and editor of its yearbook, *Halcyon.*

At twenty-one, right after World War I, he undertook two years of service in Yugoslavia with a contingent of the American Friends Service Committee to work among starving, typhus-ridden refugees in a devastated area where 1.5 million people had already perished. Even as a young man, Drew was not interested in mere gestures. His biographer Oliver Pilat has written of this period: "Others in the unit found the primitive conditions unbearable. They resigned and went home. Within a few months young Pearson was asked to assume command of the unit . . . He grew a rather frail mustache in an effort to look old enough for the responsibility entrusted to him.

"The European headquarters of the American Friends Service Committee in Vienna received impressive reports on Drew's performance. He had shared his personal rations of bully beef and beans with the starving peasants when he first arrived and had performed other 'sacrificial acts.' References were made to him as 'the Saint of the Serbian Mountains.'

". . . as unit chief Drew worked harder than anybody else. . . . he had no diversions. Night after night he could be found in his tent moving from one troublesome detail to another as if, in a friend's phrase, 'each was a newspaper deadline.' "*

Under his unsparing drive, refugee barracks and a hospital were erected. Fields were plowed and sown, and a ruined hydroelectric plant restored. In time, three villages were constructed. The villagers named one of them Pearsonovatz.

The young man of Swarthmore and the Serbian mountains was still visible in the Pearson I met in his middle age. The scope of his concern had enlarged from his family and a few Serbian villages to the nation at large, and in a true sense, the world.

Stingy as he was with every minute of his time, he nonetheless devoted large portions of it to charitable works. As a political progressive, however, he believed that the mass afflictions of mankind could not be dealt with by private philanthropy alone. He saw Bad Government as the cause of many of those ills, and Good Government as the cure for many others. Given his nature, he was at all times up to his ears in politics.

In his early years as a reporter he chafed under the restrictions of the

Drew Pearson: An Unauthorized Biography (New York: Harper's Magazine Press, 1973), pp. 59–60.

established press—of covering only what he was assigned, of getting into print only what passed the censorship of cautious superiors, of being read only by the readers of one newspaper. He was fired from the Washington bureau of the Baltimore *Sun* when it was discovered that he had temporarily escaped his confinement by anonymously co-authoring two books written in the wide-ranging accusatory style he preferred. The books—*Washington Merry-Go-Round* and *More Merry-Go-Round,* collaborations done with Robert S. Allen—were so successful that he and Allen received an offer in 1932 to do a syndicated column that would appear in several papers.

It was then that Pearson began to conceive of a column such as had never been seen before. It was just a dream at first, of a column that would appear not in several papers, but in several hundred. It would be read not only by intellectuals and liberals and political enthusiasts, but by great numbers of ordinary people running into the tens of millions who would be attracted by a formula that contained something for everyone. It would specialize in the butchery of sacred cows in papers which, elsewhere in their pages, held them sacrosanct: Presidents, charismatic generals, jingoes, supercops, noted divines, corporation heads. Though it would be ever on the attack, it would escape the conforming fetters of editors, publishers and lawyers; he would have but to think a thought or unearth a crime and it would be read coast to coast and border to border.

It would escape from the strictures that news must be novel and timely; if a proposal or a charge did not "catch on" right away, the column of his dream would keep repeating and embroidering it until it did. It would day by day champion the cause of the abused against every form of institutionalized greed and violence. It would elude the traditional canons of propriety; if a target senator's voting record or his bribe-taking didn't defeat him, then the column would placard his drinking, womanizing, loafing, junketeering, even his senility. It would have the power to launch political careers and end them, force prosecutions, popularize panaceas, block confirmations of high officials, switch votes on legislation, make the unthinkable thinkable, rouse the public against abuses and create a favorable climate for reforms. And it would so entrench itself with readers and editors that it could survive espousing the most unpopular cause or making the most spectacular mistake. It would be a voice that could not be silenced.

Such was the dream. Its fulfillment in every detail was the great and unique labor of Pearson's life. Under its goad and burden he would grow unutterably hard beneath the still-gentle exterior—not the hardness that has to do with callousness or indifference or selfishness, but the hardness that steels the good man to do that which must be done.

To gain the independence to expose, condemn and exhort without censorship, he must carve out something that did not then exist, the capacity to leap over the half-dozen hurdles that stand between an accusatory reporter and the reading public—editors, publishers, advertisers, distribution syndicates, libel lawyers and pressure groups—all of whom sought at times to exercise veto power over disclosures that were damaging or offensive to the interests they represented.

In one sense Drew Pearson's career can be seen as a quest for alternate ways to reach the public, so that if one was closed off, he could strike through another. As a young reporter, he turned to the writing of books because in them he could expose and lampoon targets in a way that was taboo in most papers. The undertaking of a syndicated column was another way to outreach the censors in that, though a local editor could blot him out in one place or on one issue, he would "get through" elsewhere.

The syndicate which distributed his column to the various newspapers, United Features, could of course censor it at its source, and sometimes did, rather than risk libel action or other unpleasant repercussions from offended targets. Whenever that happened, Pearson would not accept it, as other columnists would. Infuriated, he would often wire copies of all suppressed material to all his subscribers at his own expense, and he would always make it a point to row with United Features, hoping to make them gun-shy eventually.

A prime motivation for expanding into radio broadcasting was that it added a new and massive delivery system to his arsenal for penetrating the various defenses against his column, especially local and regional defenses.

Other incendiary columnists of the day, such as Walter Winchell and Westbrook Pegler, entered into formal agreements guaranteeing that their syndicates would pay all libel judgments; this removed the columnist from liability but it also put him into his syndicate's hands, for it strengthened the syndicate's right to censor material that might result in litigation and gave it the right to dictate settlements calling for retractions or other backdowns by the columnist. Pearson would have no part of such an arrangement. Nor would he take out libel insurance; his policy was to fight all libel suits himself, to the bitter end. This defense cost him hundreds of thousands of dollars in legal fees;

and worse, he always lived with the fear that a multimillion-dollar libel judgment would wipe him out altogether, but he accepted that fear as the price of independence. Over the years he was sued hundreds of times, for an aggregate amount of more than $200 *million;* he lost only once in court, paying a $40,000 judgment to Norman Littell.*

If a subscribing newspaper was sued because of a Pearson column, Drew would undertake the paper's defense, too. Editors around the country knew this, and as years passed without Pearson's ever losing a suit, each victory strengthening his legend of invincibility, most of them ceased to censor his column for libel or even to ask him for proof of his charges, and instead printed the column automatically.

When the dominant newspaper in an area canceled the column, as occasionally happened, he would try to sign up the nearest competitor, an increasingly effective tactic as the column grew in popularity and became a real factor in circulation competition. When the nearest competitor would not have him, or when there was no competitor, Drew was not stopped. He would go to all the weekly papers in the area, offering a weekly digest of the punchiest segments of the daily columns at practically no cost to the papers. Nothing gave him more satisfaction than to circumvent a publisher who sought to shut him out.

As he grew in papers and power, he left the giant United Features Syndicate in favor of a small one, Bell-McClure; there he was the star performer and could exert overpowering leverage in any censorship dispute with the owners. Later he became an owner himself, purchasing a one-third interest in Bell-McClure.

He had broken out. Editors, advertisers, publishers, syndicate, network, libel lawyers, pressure groups, bands of conspirators could harry him for a time and shut off one or another of his many outlets, but that was all. Whatever he typed on his portable Corona on those predawn, slipper-clad forays to his den, whether utopian scheme or scurrilous attack, would shortly be read at breakfast tables and on subways in every pocket of the country.

Though his choice of foes was rooted in political and moral principles over which he anguished, he was not a reluctant warrior, once committed. He was, I came to believe, one of that tenacious breed for whom nothing produces so much exhilaration, zest for daily life, and all-round

---

*Littell was a corporate lawyer who had been Assistant Attorney General under FDR, then consultant and adviser to foreign embassies in Washington. Pearson maintained he should be registered as a foreign agent—one reason for the suit.

gratification as a protracted, ugly, bitter-end vendetta that rages for years and exhausts both sides, often bringing one to ruin. My years with Drew were to be dominated by these contests, which form the main burden of this book; two of the milder ones were nearing decision when I joined him. One was the struggle with John P. Monroe, a Washington influence peddler whom Drew had roughed up, in a preliminary way, by publishing accounts of his lavish entertainments of high government officials, replete with what were then called "party girls." Stung unto rashness, Monroe sued Pearson for $1 million, charging defamation of character.

Drew suspected Monroe of worse offenses than he had yet uncovered and determined to nail him for black-market violations of the postwar economic controls. Requiring someone unknown in Washington, Drew hired a young New York investigator named Sidney Baron, who, posing as a prospective buyer of beef at over-the-ceiling prices, wormed his way into Monroe's circle. I was assigned to aspects of the Monroe story, but Drew did not tell me about Baron. The infiltration satisfied Drew that Monroe's establishment, located in a palatial residence which we would later dramatize as "the House on R Street," was a headquarters not only for entertaining procurement generals and Cabinet members but for black-market operations as well.

In time, Drew brought in the FBI. Through Baron, the Bureau planted one of its agents on Monroe, posing as a New York fur dealer. Out of this cooperation came indictable evidence of eight separate black-market transactions—and a series of "House on R Street" stories, reported exclusively by the "Washington Merry-Go-Round." Monroe was prosecuted, convicted and went to jail, and the defamation suit fell apart in his general demise.

And there was the case of General Patrick Hurley, tycoon, Secretary of War in the Hoover Administration and later an ambassador under FDR. Hurley became incensed over Pearson's barbs about his vanity, one being that he practiced his entrances and exits before a mirror. They appeared in the book *Washington Merry-Go-Round,* and when Drew's co-authorship became known, Hurley had a hand in getting him fired from the Baltimore *Sun.* Over the years Drew kept a hostile eye on Hurley, lampooning him at every opportunity. Almost two decades after the *Sun* incident, when Hurley ran for election to the United States Senate in New Mexico, Drew went out there at the peak of the campaign, and over a statewide radio-network program which he paid for himself, mounted a scathing, documented attack on Hurley's public career which helped to defeat him.

His mission being what it is, the muckraker must expect, though of course he does not, to be widely reviled, especially by the highest authorities of the state. He becomes aware that he survives only because of the thin protective shield of the Constitution and an inconstant public sentiment that he is of some vague use to society. By the time I met Drew Pearson, three Presidents—Hoover, Roosevelt and Truman—had tried at one time or another either to furtively suppress him or publicly discredit him.

In wartime, when government secrecy is invested with the halo of national survival, and public tolerance for dissent is at low ebb, the controversialist operates at particular hazard. During World War II, Drew's exposés of diplomatic intrigues, military fiascos, and waste and profiteering in the war effort made him vulnerable, for he could be prosecuted under cover of national security. And so it was that General George C. Marshall, the organizer and director of American armies around the globe, was approached with the suggestion that leaks to Pearson about military affairs had become intolerable and that this was the time to move against him.

"No," said Marshall. "Pearson is my best inspector general."

Pearson was proud of that anecdote, and it captured the fancy of his staff. As the inspector general's adjutants, we cruised the continent, conscious of great obstacles and dangerous enemies but aware, too, of our own fire power. Our leader was believed in the land. Six hundred and twenty-five newspapers published our findings each day, two hundred and twenty-five radio stations broadcast them each week; our infiltrators were in every important department of government, even the FBI; key figures of the establishments hostile to us were secretly on our side. We were ring-wise, courtroom-wise, and had the élan that comes from habitual victory. Ahead of us lay an inexhaustible cornucopia of evils to fight and follies to stumble into. Heady days.

2 · A Mormon in Gomorrah

I WAS A laughably naïve Sherlock Holmes to be let loose on the nation's capital. To a newcomer whose mores had been formed in an austere Mormon family, the tone of political Washington caused something of a culture shock.

There was, for instance, the matter of public intoxication, even brawling, on the part of dignitaries. I read in the newspapers one day that the executive director of the Democratic National Committee had been arrested while traveling in New England, dragged into a police station and booked for drunk driving. I assumed it would ruin his career, as it certainly would have back home in Utah, and commented to my office mates what a shame it was that a public leader would forfeit his position and bring such grief and humiliation on himself and his family. But they informed me that in Washington such a lapse was not taken seriously and that no harm would come of it.

Soon after, I learned from Drew Pearson that Secretary of the Interior Julius Krug had keeled over while making a luncheon speech, still whoozy from his revelings of the night before. He had a reputation for such excesses, and he was not alone in the Cabinet; according to the Pearson pipeline the guzzling of Treasury Secretary John Snyder had gotten out of hand and was causing concern in the Truman White House.

The thing seemed to be endemic, even epidemic. Around about this time a great party was given for two thousand of the "in" people of the capital by Congressman Frank Boykin. The after-dinner remarks were delivered by Chief Justice Fred Vinson of the Supreme Court. As the eminent jurist, a mournful-looking man, began declaiming, an inebriated congressman from Missouri named Dewey Short arose and shouted scurrilous epithets at Vinson, who now began to look even more mournful. For a while Short's abuse of the Chief Justice was indulged as apparently within the tolerable limits of conduct at such affairs. But then, as Vinson's distress became acute, Washington's Chief of Police Robert Barrett stepped forward. The chief was liquored, too. He tried to silence Short by diplomacy, but failing, began punching him, in a bravura display of concern for the dignity of the Chief Justice. Fellow officers restrained Barrett and he was led away; Short subsided; the Chief Justice went on with his address.

Again the Democrats were gathered in celebration, this time at a party hosted by the Democratic National Chairman, Senator J. Howard McGrath, soon to become Attorney General of the United States; most of the reigning officialdom attended, including President Truman, but their presence had no inhibiting effect. By midnight the scene was almost indescribable. Women of mature years were shining up to young men. Some party stalwarts had passed out altogether; others were vomiting in corners. The management of the hotel, taking it all as a matter of routine, stood at the rear, professionally assessing the damage and laying plans to replace the carpets and other furnishings in time for a convention scheduled for morning.

Even Republicans, supposedly of graver disposition, were caught up in the whirl. One of my earliest recollections of Washington is of a tragicomic speech by Michigan Congressman Fred Bradley, protesting that all the wining and dining was getting him down. "Banquet life is a physical and mental strain on us hardly imaginable to the folks back home," said the distraught Bradley. "The strain is terrific." He was dragooned into attending altogether too many parties, he complained; but his appeal for fewer invitations was greeted with guffaws. Three weeks later Representative Bradley, age forty-nine, dropped dead. The official diagnosis was heart failure.

Other customs of the capital were startling to an outlander. I found, for instance, that many a large financial undertaking was consummated in cash—that is, with envelopes filled with greenbacks, a curious medium for honorable transactions of any size.

Many of the bulging envelopes contained "campaign contributions," an all-purpose phrase that covered a multitude of purposes. Most of the forty-eight states had laws requiring some kind of disclosure of such gifts so that the voters could find out who was supporting the candidates, how much money they took in, and what they did with it, but the federal politicians had long ago carved out the District of Columbia as a disclosure-free haven for political gifts. The capital thus became a mecca for unsavory contributions from all over the country. Cash was preferred, with no records left lying around to cause later embarrassment. The receivers of such gifts were restrained only by their conscience as to whether they actually used the money for campaigning or for more personal purposes.

Theoretically, one group of Washingtonians, the members of Congress, were required to report all donations they received to the Chief Clerk of their respective bodies. But almost none bothered to do so. Instead, most members handed in fabricated reports that listed only a fraction of their actual receipts. It was an open scandal that everyone condoned.

A few years after my arrival in Washington, a conscientious congressman from my native Utah, David King, wept softly as he described the frustration of running for office. It was almost impossible to become a lawmaker, he told me desperately, without first violating the law, for the first official act of almost every member of Congress, he said, was to sign a falsified report on the money he had raised and spent in his campaign. Members were confident there would be no investigation of their reports by the Chief Clerk, who was their employee, and no prosecution by the Justice Department, which was becoming more and more politicized. They were entirely right. As of 1947, despite literally thousands of violations, there had never been a single prosecution under the 1926 Federal Corrupt Practices Act. Another twenty-two years would pass before the law was enforced for the first time.

The milk of human generosity overflowed in Washington. I had always assumed that respectable persons did not accept as gifts those personal items that everyone is expected to provide for himself and his family. But whenever the Drew Pearson organization started to scrutinize some official, we usually found out, incidentally to our main purpose, that he and his family were inveterate takers of gifts from "old friends" who almost always happened to want something from the government. Furniture, appliances, home renovations, liquor, cosmetics, hotel accommodations, ocean-liner tickets, even groceries and suits of clothes were regularly turning up on the doorsteps of fortunate officialdom. Apparently no need was left unmet. I once ran across a representative of International Latex who, while making his rounds of senatorial offices, would ask the office girls for their bra and girdle sizes; the young ladies would turn in their intimate measurements to this obliging stranger, who, on his return trip, would hand out dainty packages of support garments.

Interior Secretary Julius Krug, a man of parts, was an indefatigable recipient. One of my early recollections is learning that a lobbyist was providing Krug, a favorite target of Drew's, with the attentions of young lady companions. This was a growing service industry in Washington. The girls were prize specimens and were awarded in accordance with an intricate hierarchical system. A certain level of official—say, a junior congressman—was entitled to what were called "$50 girls," who, I reasoned, must be extraordinary creatures, for $50 was my weekly salary. Imagine the astonishment of a struggling newsman (me with my ear pressed against the door of the opulent life) when I found out that a Secretary of the Interior was entitled to $200 girls! It should be said for Krug that he did not, amid the distractions of his deluxe revels, forget his wife. He saw to it that his lobbyist friend provided her with free nylons.

The first beat assigned to me was Congress; it became a baffling source of mystery and dismay. I had no background for the assignment beyond a high school class in civics, and I expected the boss to take me aside and share with me his secret sources and tested methods. Instead, he put me in the hands of the reporter I was replacing, who, understandably enough, escorted me up to Capitol Hill, introduced me to the first congressman we encountered and left me to sink or swim.

The startled congressman, Norris Poulson, was a freshman from California who rather hoped, because of my Drew Pearson credentials, that I could tell *him* what was happening in the back rooms. I next called upon Senator Homer Ferguson, who, unbeknown to me, disapproved of Drew and had nothing to confide to one of his snoops. Choosing at random, I sidled up to a congressman named Fred Crawford, who did not wait to hear my first question but began berating me for Drew's sins.

I gave up the quest for guidance and plunged into the pursuit of stories. A dispute of the day involved Senator Kenneth McKellar of Tennessee, and I sought out his office hoping for an interview. I knew something of his great power, for he was the dean of the Senate and the chairman of its most potent committee, Appropriations, but I did not know of his fabled ill temper or his violent hatred of Drew Pearson; the Tennessee Democrat had long been the prize exhibit in Drew's "Old Codger" campaign against the inanities of the seniority system, which automatically vested a peculiarly arrogant and arbitrary power in what Drew regarded as obsolescent reactionaries.

Had I consulted my office, I would have been shown a thick folder on the Pearson-McKellar warfare, whose highlight was a one-hour extemporaneous flogging of Drew delivered under the immunity of the Senate floor in response to a column charging McKellar with having attacked a fellow senator with his pocketknife. Though impelled by wrath, McKellar aimed at art and many felt he achieved it, including Drew, who reprinted as much of it as would fit into a column. While finding his range, McKellar fired off the lesser and obligatory calumnies, calling Pearson a "dishonest ignorant corrupt and groveling crook." But it was the hues and gradations of Pearson's falsity, its natural and acquired characteristics, that McKellar wished to delineate to his visibly appreciative brethren: "He is a natural born liar, a liar by profession, a liar for a living, a liar in the daytime, a liar in the nighttime . . . He is an ignorant liar. A pusillanimous liar. A peewee liar . . . a revolving, constitutional, unmitigated, infamous liar."

Innocent of all this, I sat in McKellar's reception room and he, unaware of my affiliation, received me. All went well till I mentioned whom I worked for. Instantly the aged figure before me, the shriveled ruin of a once impressive specimen, was consumed by a sputtering rage. His lined, ancient face flamed purple with life, his mouth became contorted, as if my presence, or even existence, were an intolerable affront. He lurched at me, out of control, rasping out objurgations and pummeling me with frail fists that landed like small pillows. Startled, wounded in spirit, but above all fearful that the old termagant would burst and expire before I got out of there, I fled awkwardly through the nearest exit.

Clearly, I faced unusual obstacles and must take a new tack. I would compensate for inexperience and unpopularity by doggedness. I haunted the Capitol, prowling relentlessly if aimlessly through its endless halls, my nose buried in congressional reports and directories. Wherever there was an open door I would drop in on meetings of the most obscure committees, and I would sit dutifully in the House and Senate press galleries through rounds of speeches that no seasoned correspondent would suffer. I was determined to catch up through a process of indiscriminate absorption, and though my employer must have been appalled at some of the obscure gleanings I brought him, there is something to be said for approaching Congress from the bottom up.

Acts of Congress, amended and improvised as they often are during chaotic floor sessions, are seldom precise or entirely self-explanatory and must often be administered and adjudicated in light of what was said in Congress when the bill was debated. But when in idle moments I read the official record of events I had witnessed the day before, I often found that history had been the victim of instant tampering. The hometown editor would never see those statements that revealed his congressman to be an ignoramus, for they had been mysteriously excised. The eloquent speech that ran for five thousand words in the *Congressional Record,* and which might four years hence sway the decision of a judge—especially because it immediately preceded the vote and had not once been challenged during delivery—had in fact not been delivered at all, but rather been submitted to the Clerk's office two hours after the vote was taken by a senator who had not attended the debate.

Inquiring into this metamorphosis, which changed absentees into prime movers and verbal clubfoots into gazelles, I found that a Solon, after participating in debate, could go back to his office, send for the transcript and revise it at his leisure, or better still, have one of his aides revise it—here, changing "no" to "maybe"; there, adding a literary curlicue or reversing bogus arguments that he had somehow gotten backwards during the original debate.

This does not mean that there were not many members of Congress who left the record unaltered and stood by exactly what they had said, but it does mean that distortion of the official record was widespread, was systematized, was known to all and protested by almost none, and therefore represented the conscious will of the Congress.

In poring over the rules that govern the Congress, I noted a provision requiring that if a member is absent when the body is in session, he forfeits his pay for the period of his absence. To gain exception from this penalty, he must be formally excused by the membership on the grounds that demonstrable official business requires him to be elsewhere.

Having grown used to peering down from the press gallery at rows of empty seats—the absentee rate ranged from 90 percent on days when there was debate but no quorum calls to about 30 percent when there were regular roll calls—I searched in vain for any instance of members having their pay docked as required by the rules. Once in a great while some member would request permission to be absent on official business, but 99 percent of absences were unauthorized. The lawmakers simply ignored their own laws.

The House of Representatives in those days regularly featured an unedifying spectacle called "the teller vote." On a teller vote, instead of individually answering "aye" or "nay" to the roll call, the members would get into one of two lines and be counted by a teller as they trooped by. There was thus no record of the way an individual member voted. Defenders said the teller system saved time, though they opposed the installation of an electronic system that would have saved far more time while recording each member's vote, for the sake of posterity and the scrutiny of his constituents. Sometimes, after the result of a teller vote was announced, there would be a challenge from the losing side, a challenge sufficiently strong to require that the vote be taken over, this time by a roll call. On some of these occasions, forty to eighty members would switch their vote to the reverse of what it had been when the voting was anonymous.

A web of concealment overlaid Capitol Hill that I found hard to reconcile with the forthrightness expected of public trustees. Senators were provided with staffs, paid for by the taxpayers. But they refused to publish the identity or the salaries of these public employees, giving rise to speculation that they were larding their payrolls with wives, sons, nephews, uncles, cronies and creditors, speculation which all too often proved justified whenever the secrecy was penetrated.

I was instructed to keep an eye out for nepotism scams, a periodic feature of the Pearson column. We used to give awards for assiduity in getting relatives on the federal payroll. During my first season on the Hill, the champ was Congressman Gene "Goober" Cox of Georgia. The crusty, countrified "Goober" had his wife and son on his Washington payroll, and a sister drawing pay in his congressional office back home. This count would have made him only one of many contenders, but here he began to draw away from the field. Cox had installed his brother as postmaster of Donalson, Georgia, and a sister as postmistress of a neighboring town. A brother-in-law was the assistant House bill clerk, and a nephew was bedded down in the Agriculture Department.

This was as far as we could lift the veil on "Goober's" family placement service. Likely there were other Coxes spotted throughout the public service, but even if not, these eight collected enough from the taxpayers to make the Coxes the most prosperous family in their neck of Georgia.

It was not just this succession of tawdry occurrences that pointed to something amiss. A plenitude of criminal proceedings enlivened my early weeks in the capital; no fewer than seven unrelated prosecutions against officeholders were in various stages of progress. And when I recalled that only 3 percent of all criminals are found out and brought to trial, and considered the special difficulties of detecting the gossamerlike crimes of politicians and the advantages they have over ordinary felons in avoiding prosecution, I began to visualize the hidden battalions which these seven represented.

During my first three months on the job, the trial of Congressman Andrew Jackson May, the once mighty chairman of the House Armed Services Committee, held center stage. He was accused of selling his office, of taking at least $50,000 in bribes in return for aiding the Garsson brothers, two military-equipment contractors, to obtain $78 million in contracts. Day by day, as the heavyset May tried to appear above it all, the trial brought out chicaneries of unbelievable magnitude and pettiness, all of which I studied with particular interest, for Drew Pearson had exposed the May-Garsson alliance and had forced it to trial in the period just before I joined his staff. On July 7, 1947, May and the Garssons were found guilty; all were sentenced to prison. For a Pearson reporter, the trial was a sort of badge of lethal authenticity. It was also an unsettling experience, for it brought home the realization that at the end of a successful investigative story, when the exhilaration of the chase is over, comes the ruination of several lives, including those of innocent people, such as family members.

I did not know what to make of all this, confounding as it did my boyhood visions of heroic figures in marble halls. I realized that all these untoward incidents did not add up to an indictment of the majority here. On the contrary, I was daily observing, if from afar, leaders of branches and agencies of the government who were obviously men of impressive ability and decorum. Yet, in the minority or no, shabbiness in things small and large was so widespread, so confidently strident, that the majority was resigned to it—as to a power so significant and entrenched that it must be appeased except in the most flagrant instances or in cases that were exposed to the public. That was my first conclusion about Washington.

. . .

One night in the early weeks of my apprenticeship, Drew Pearson received a phone call from one of the innumerable friends who made up his nationwide network of tipsters. The caller was Lawrence Durbin of Lima, Ohio. His purpose was to alert Drew about an Ohio congressman, Robert Jones, who was about to be confirmed as a member of the Federal Communications Commission. It was an open secret around Lima, said Durbin, that the congressman had once been a member of the local branch of the Black Legion, a Ku Klux Klan offshoot whose members wore black instead of white hooded robes. Jones had been launched on his political career by the Black Legion, Durbin alleged, and had continued to draw support from organizations that were overtly anti-Semitic, anti-Catholic and anti-Negro.

It was the sort of tidbit that made Drew's mustache twitch. In 1946 he had embarked on a crusade to deflate the postwar revival of the Klan. He had succeeded in so provoking the Grand Kleagle of All the World that the Kleagle had challenged Pearson to come out in a public place and repeat the attacks he had been making on the Klan from the safety of his guarded radio studio. Drew at once offered to go to Atlanta and broadcast from the steps of the state capitol. There, on July 26, 1946, ringed by the state militia, while listeners wondered if at any moment they would hear gunfire, Drew scarified the Klan for half an hour. Thus had he made himself a personification of the anti-Klan cause, to whom small men from small towns could come in hope and confidence.

"What proof do you have of Jones's membership?" Drew asked Durbin. It was common knowledge, Durbin responded, among hundreds of people around Lima. He also had access to a specific exhibit which had been lying around for nine years. It was an affidavit signed by the erstwhile local commander of the Black Legion, who had gone to seed but was still around, stating that he was present in 1934 when Jones was inducted into the organization. With digging, Durbin promised, other witnesses could be found.

Drew went to his haphazard files and pulled out a folder on Jones. It held partially corroborative, though inconclusive items. There was a message of greeting from Jones to a rally staged by the racial hatemonger Gerald L. K. Smith. There were a series of statements made by Jones and republished approvingly in the house organs of William Dudley Pelley and William Kullgren, pro-Fascists and anti-Semites who had been indicted for sedition during the war. The Jones statements themselves were not bigoted or seditious, merely isolationist, but their recurring appearance in the journals of the far right showed Jones to be a favorite of elements whom Drew despised.

The next morning Drew had his staff check whether Jones had ever publicly disavowed the use of his name and statements by the hate organizations that had embraced him. Other public figures who were in coincidental agreement with the ultraright on some issues had done this, to keep their good name from being exploited for murky purposes. But Jones, it turned out, had not. Next Drew called Durbin, had the affidavit read to him and got a promise that it would be put in the mail to him immediately.

Jones had been named as a Republican member of the Federal Communications Commission; he was sponsored by Republican congressional leaders and appointed by a Democratic President; thus he had the support of both parties and had no opposition. The nomination was to be acted upon the following day by the Senate Commerce Committee. Almost a dozen congressmen were scheduled to appear in Jones's behalf; there were no adverse witnesses; everything was sewed up.

Drew had no time to investigate further, nor to function through the column, which went through a four-day pipeline (i.e., the journey of the column copy from Pearson's office to the syndicate and, by mail, to the 600 newspaper outlets, the last stage being publication). Nor could he take up his microphone, for his radio broadcast was on Sunday and it was only Thursday. So he acted in two nonjournalistic capacities, as was habitual with him—that of back-room manipulator and public figure. Calling a friendly member of the committee, Senator Edwin Johnson, a big, bluff Colorado Democrat, Drew outlined the case against Jones and arranged to testify the following morning in opposition to him.

The decision underlined a number of traits I had begun to notice in my boss, traits which alternately alarmed and filled me with admiration. He appeared reckless to me if not irresponsible, for throwing himself so hastily into the breach, for his information was flimsy and unsupported. Wasn't it ill proportioned for Drew, I wondered, to risk a public humiliation that would weaken him in more important battles, merely to stop an unknown from getting a secondary post? And inordinate to attempt the derailment of a man's career because of a youthful association, long in the past? And unseemly for a journalist to make himself a direct antagonist in a matter of this kind, instead of remaining an unembroiled reporter of the facts? The questions would recur again and again over the years, and a quarter century of wrestling with their pros and cons would not completely resolve them.

Drew did not deign to explain his rationale to junior staff members. I could surmise some of it. At this stage of his career he had come to trust his judgment, his instinct, his experience when the documentation was weak—his judgment of the reliability of an informant who had recollections but no documents, his instinct as to what was the probable truth, his experience of the pattern, seen so many times before, that could be envisioned from a few puzzle pieces. He hated to make mistakes but he had been right so many times that he was not afraid to risk being wrong, or rather, he would not allow himself to be immobilized by that fear. And so it was that he set off on the morning of June 27, 1947, as he had on so many thousands of mornings, to slay a dragon, this time a small one named Jones.

The Jones nomination was being processed by a three-man subcommittee of the Senate Commerce Committee, presided over by Maine Republican Senator Owen Brewster, who was committed to pushing it through successfully. It was a fateful circumstance that dealt Brewster this routine assignment. Though Drew had begun to regard Brewster as too close to Pan American Airways, a Pearson villain, he had never really tangled with Brewster. The few mentions of Brewster in the column over the years had been limited to a mixture of mild praise and mild criticism. Now the two would meet as adversaries prematurely, over an issue that a few days before had meant little to either.

Six congressmen testified in support of Jones in rapid succession, then Drew was called and put under oath. He was appearing, he said, not as a columnist but as a person with a professional interest in the broadcast industry, over which the FCC ruled. As a radio commentator he had a vital interest in a commission that upheld freedom of speech to the furthest limits; as an applicant for a radio-station license in Baltimore he wanted a commission that was impartial in its license awards. He had reason to doubt that Jones, on his past record, believed either in freedom of speech or in impartial licensing.

Then, in a soft voice, stated his main premise: "The FCC must uphold the rights of all sides in political debates, all religions, all races . . . whoever is appointed should be free from any taint, remote or otherwise, of religious, racial or any other prejudice."

Brewster broke in, "Is that not a rather high order?"

"I don't think so," Drew answered.

Then he turned his guns on Jones, who was present in the hearing room. "Jones has been identified—politically and perhaps personally—with one of the most anti-Semitic, Fascist-inclined political schools in the country, namely Gerald L. K. Smith." Drew went on to list the rightist organizations that featured Jones's pronouncements. Then he said that according to information contained in an affidavit he expected to receive and turn over to the committee before day's end, Robert Jones had been a member of the Black Legion—and with a Pearsonian flourish, he added that Jones had been inducted into the Legion in the basement of the home of Bert Effinger, the Legion commander in Lima.

Senator Brewster probed for the soft spot in Drew's argument. Even if what he said about Jones was true, would he have disqualified Supreme Court Justice Hugo Black, one of Drew's liberal heroes on the Bench, because in his youth he had joined the Ku Klux Klan?

Drew replied that Black had expiated his Klan connection by a long and honorable record, but that Jones's record merely emphasized his. "You can forgive a man for the mistakes of his youth . . . But I want to go on to read the record of some of the men who have used Congressman Jones, supported him, quoted from him, apparently agreed with him quite recently . . ."

But didn't Jones have freedom of speech too? Didn't he have the right to state his views on public issues without being persecuted for them years later?

Drew answered, "While I would champion his right to say what he thinks, I would challenge his right to sit on a quasi-judicial body which has to pass upon the most important liberties we have."

Senator Homer Capehart, the rotund Republican from Indiana, was less philosophical in his questions than the wary Brewster. Drew's charges were unproved hearsay, Capehart grunted.

Drew replied, in effect, that the committee had the duty to consider complaints against the nominee; these complaints did not have to be proved; a private citizen did not have the facilities for that. It was up to the committee, with all its powers, to investigate and ascertain the truth of serious charges. Drew had shown that there was smoke there; the committee should now find out whether or not there was a fire. Thus Drew sought to separate the role of Pearson the journalist from Pearson the citizen.

Congressman Jones, age forty, immediately presented himself before the committee, took the oath and said, "I brand the statements made by Andrew Pearson . . . as unmitigated lies."

His categorical vehemence was disturbing. There are all kinds of weaselly, ambiguous ways to slink away from a charge, but Jones had not taken any. His head-on denial made the exchange a big news item. Overnight, the matter became a major challenge to the credibility of Drew Pearson, to be decided in the forum where he had more enemies than anywhere else.

I was summoned from the catacombs of the Capitol for a hasty, hallway huddle with the boss. He greeted me with a quizzical, sheepish grin, an aspect of his attitudinal repertoire I had not before noted. Later I would come to recognize it as an apologetic grin, which meant he was about to confess to some inadequacy or invite me to help him bail out of a leaky accusation.

He was in something of a predicament, he began, almost inaudibly. His charges against this fellow Jones were under fire, and they had the status of only hearsay unless we could find eyewitnesses and produce them before the Senate. How would I like that assignment?

I was on the next train for Lima, fretted with dawning misgivings. It stood to reason that the only people who could identify Jones as a Black Legionnaire were other members. But they were sworn to secrecy and prone to violence, especially where nosy strangers were concerned. Any member who fingered Jones not only would have to reveal his own membership but would expose himself to reprisals. Against these obstacles I was armed only with the names of Bert Effinger, Lawrence Durbin and the local CIO leader in Lima, Joe Emmons.

Drew had been most solicitous in advising me in detail on the best travel schedule to Lima, but he offered scant suggestions on what I should do after I got off the train. I had imagined all along that there were secret stratagems for cracking a story, patented ruses by which a master reporter penetrated the impenetrable, and that from Drew Pearson I would learn them. But as the train rumbled at dusk through somber-looking stretches where lived the black-hooded Klansmen— counties with names like Stark, Shelby and Allen—it was borne in on me that there were no magical ways. There was only shoe leather, an untiring larynx, a folded sheaf of notepaper, and an amalgam of gall and hope.

From Durbin and Emmons I got some names of people who ought to know about Jones and the Legion, if they would only talk. And Emmons provided me with a car and a driver who knew the outlying roads.

As a Mormon missionary, tracting in Baptist country, I had learned to gentle the hostile householder who did not want to hear about salvation from a nineteen-year-old door-to-door evangelist. Black Legionnaires could be no more impervious than hard-shelled Baptists. So in my quest for repentant legionnaires, I put on my best missionary manner.

At such public houses as the countryside offered, I would strike up one-sided conversations with taciturn natives and work around to bygone days: "Say, wasn't the Black Legion pretty strong around here then?" From fragments of conversations a portrait of Jones emerged that helped me concoct an effective tactic for de-hooding him.

Jones had joined the Black Legion in 1934 at the age of twenty-seven. He was then about to run for county prosecutor, an important post in the local power and patronage structure. Lima had over six thousand Legion members and was instrumental in electing Jones. As time passed, however, wider vistas beckoned the young prosecutor; from his perch at the pinnacle of Allen County he began to aspire to a grander jurisdiction—the Fifth Congressional District of Ohio. But Ohio at large had its share of Catholics, Jews and Negroes, so Jones began quietly to put distance between himself and his hooded brothers. He ceased to attend their functions, took legionnaires off the county payroll, and whenever the matter of his old association arose, he denied that he had ever had anything to do with the Legion.

There were bound to be stalwarts around, then, who were unhappy with Jones not because he was a Klansman, but because he had disparaged his old friends. Underneath the black robes of many a legionnaire, moreover, beat a Populist heart. They were against the banks and the utility companies Jones had championed in Congress. Here were exploitable openings. I now asked for information on Jones, not to expose a bigot, but to punish a backslider. Joe Emmons, the CIO chief, was of critical help now. Under his auspices, instead of appearing as a suspect outsider, I was able to approach the pro-Labor Klansmen as a vouched-for friend.

By the end of my third full day in Lima I had located a half-dozen persons who had identified Jones as a legionnaire from personal knowledge. I persuaded three of these—the most important three, who had presided at various stages of his induction—to give public testimony. Virgil (Bert) Effinger, the "grand old man" of the Lima Legion, had conducted in his own basement not the initiation, as Drew had testified, but the "investigation" of Jones, wherein he was found worthy.

Glenn Webb and Frank Barber had administered the two-stage oath, which was quite an elaborate affair. Jones, bareheaded and in ordinary dress, had been led by robed and hooded figures to the center of a clearing, before fifteen hundred onlookers. With a loaded revolver held to his back, he knelt on one knee, hand over heart, and swore undying fealty to the Black Legion and its patriotic principles.

My missionary experience had taught me that deep in the souls of most people lurks a compulsion to talk about themselves, to confide in someone their darkest secrets, to spill what they know—against their own interests, even against their fears. It is as though by retelling their experiences to an appreciative listener, they are showing an otherwise indifferent world that they, too, have trod the earth, have coped, have counted, have played a role.

I found that former Black Legionnaires, if approached properly, were no different from the errant churchgoers and faithless husbands of my missionary days. But it is also true that those who give incriminating interviews, like those who impetuously sign installment purchase contracts, tend toward remorse on the morning after. So I would stick to an informant like adhesive, trying to work up his salient reminiscenses into a written statement, and if he showed the slightest receptivity, never to leave his side until he had signed his name to it. In the case of our prize witness, Frank Barber, who was articulate and who held a semireputable position as part-time constable of the hamlet of Beaverdam, Ohio, I recall that I got him into an automobile in the middle of the night and rode the back roads until I could find and awaken a notary public to duly attest Barber's statement.

Drew Pearson, who had been subdued in an uncertain limbo for days while Jones with ever more strident innocence took shots at him, was mightily pleased. He immediately turned over the affidavits of Effinger, Webb and Barber to the Senate committee, arranged for them to be subpoenaed, trumpeted abroad their confirmation of his original charges and instructed me to shepherd them all back to Washington. This was a risk, albeit necessitated by the untenability of Drew's exposed position, for it locked us into place when our investigation had just begun and gave our adversaries an advance look at our cards.

For a day or two, Congressman Jones wilted under Drew's fresh onslaught; he was now in danger of being exposed not just as an ex-Klansman, which could, after all, be ridden out, but as a perjurer before the committee, which could not. But then, with that incomparable resilience which marks the true office seeker, he bloomed anew, denouncing the affidavits as "vicious lies" inspired by a vile and unholy duo, Pearson and the CIO.

The witnesses and I self-importantly boarded the train to Washington. Only one trifling cloud glowered over my self-congratulation. In the close quarters of a Pullman car, my companions exhibited certain disquieting characteristics I had dismissed out on the hedgerows—an occasional glitter of the eye, a gutteral note when taken in mirth, a venality of idiom—that were not altogether compatible with reliability.

Webb was clean-cut enough and could have passed as, at least, a used-car salesman. But Barber, with a tousled gray head that hung forward, eyes that occasionally gave off a cold glint through wire-rimmed spectacles and a habit of ruminatively extruding his lower lip, had about him an aura of a gory, combative past. As for Effinger—he looked just like Victor Jory playing a fugitive moonshiner, with his hooked nose, a thin straight line for a mouth, and burning eyes that periodically glazed over as he withdrew into uncommunicative reveries.

True, they were not your usual witnesses before Senate committees, but authentic men of the burning cross were not supposed to be respectable citizens. That was our point about Jones, wasn't it? Buoyed by such sophistries, I began to bask in a glow not unlike that which must have exhilarated the great Frank Buck as, confounding all odds, he neared home port with one of his marvelous menageries.

No sooner were our witnesses installed in the Mayflower Hotel than Drew took the offensive. On his Sunday-night broadcast he attacked the committee Republicans for plotting to rush through the Jones nomination. Then he introduced "the chief of police of Beaverdam, Ohio, a very solid citizen, Mr. Frank Barber," who gave the nation his eyewitness account of Jones's ordination. Barber took to the microphone well and was quite convincing.

The next morning Drew and I escorted our witnesses to the hearing room, which was located in the Capitol, close to the Senate floor. The place was crowded with newsmen and sightseers drawn by the publicity. Drew wore an air of pious magnanimity appropriate to him who is about to be vindicated. The doughty Jones, too, was much in evidence. From an impassive face that betrayed no glint of recognition, he intermittently flashed the evil eye upon his nervous ex-comrades. On the rostrum, where at the first session there had been only three senators, there were now six.

Chairman Brewster brought the hearing to order. Brewster was the author of the day's scenario, but as is often the case with astute men of power, it was his style to work through others. His instrument on this occasion, whom Brewster had anointed to confront the terrible columnist, was Homer Capehart.

For men who had not beheld Senator Capehart before, he presented an especially disturbing apparition. Obese and rumpled, he was scarcely able to squeeze into his chair, and once wedged into it, would balloon out over his diminutive Senate desk like a cartoon caricature of glutted error triumphant. The eyes in his round face were small, or perhaps they only seemed small, encroached upon as they were by great cheeks tending to the rubicund. Chaotic wisps of thinning hair completed the general picture of dishabille. His voice was of an extraordinary resonance and power, sonorous but primordial, a voice such as is seldom heard on earth, such as one expects to hear call sinners to the Last Judgment.

Capehart had all the equipment necessary for a great orator save the conceptual. He had little sense of rhetorical symmetry, and as soon as he was well launched, would begin to double back on himself, igniting audiences to a fever of expectation only to douse them with appalling anticlimaxes. It was his facial expression that was his most arresting feature—a look of baffled disgruntlement, of uncomprehending exasperation over the inability of others to see those simple truths that were so clear to him. He had a penchant for simple solutions to vexing problems to which there were no solutions. Each year, for instance, he would offer an amendment to abolish the farm program in favor of a homemade concoction of his own. Despite his grandiloquent appeals, it would always be defeated by votes in the order of 80 to 1, whereupon he would wander incredulously about the antechamber, shaking his head at the folly of men, submerged in a gloom wherein he seemed not to hear his colleagues' inevitable jibes: "You can't win 'em all, Homer."

But this man of heroic girth and discordant talents was a sharp interrogator, and he relished, or at least seemed to on this day, the role of hatchet man. As the hearing opened he went to work immediately on victims already half mesmerized by the sight and sound of him. What followed is, over the void of thirty years, still mortifying to recollect. Five minutes into the hearing I began to apprehend that the Brewster committee, far from being pleased that we had done its work for it, had in fact laid an ambush for us.

The first witness, Bert Effinger, was scarce into his opening sally— "I know this man, Bob Jones, was taken in at the Tapscott Farm"— when Capehart was upon him, brandishing court records which showed that seven years earlier, Effinger had been convicted and sentenced to jail for perjury and contempt of court for making false charges against a judge. At this the seventy-four-year-old Effinger, who had seemed a veritable lion in Lima, deflated before my eyes into a poor lost lamb. Worse, I noticed Glen Webb, our second witness, sag a bit, as if the air were leaking out of him.

Capehart demanded details on the Tapscott Farm affair. "I don't remember now," said Effinger. "I didn't see Bob Jones go in the Black Legion, and I don't remember that he did now. I can't remember it. If he did, I don't remember it. Maybe he did. I do not know whether he did or not."

No matter what was asked him, Bert would say that he couldn't remember. His wife had told him back in Lima to stay out of it and say nothing or he'd get in trouble. I had persuaded him otherwise, but what did I know, in my callow self-assurance, of the dark, residual powers of wives?

Q. Did you come [to Washington for the hearing] by way of automobile or in a bus?
A. I have forgotten how I came.
Q. Whom have you discussed this with in the past few days?
A. I don't know who I discussed it with. I don't know anybody.

Senator Brewster took over from Capehart and returned to the perjury conviction.

Q. Do you recall that episode?
A. I do not.
Q. Would you like to examine this [document] and see whether it would refresh your recollection?
A. No, sir. Because it would not.
Q. Do you recall whether you ever . . . served any time in jail?
A. I don't remember.

While the remains of Effinger were being assisted to the rear, I rallied my remaining witnesses with whispers and nudges of encouragement. Glen E. Webb was next on the stand. Let me say of Webb that he was game. He had brought his wife with him from Lima to watch him testify and he stuck doggedly to his affidavit: "I initiated Robert Jones into the Black Legion on the Tapscott Farm east of Lima, Ohio.

Robert Jones kneeled before me where I could see him face to face, with a gun at his back according to our ritual, as he accepted the oath of obligation."

Capehart did not wish to pursue the matter. He had another dossier in hand, and from it he ominously drew out a document and began reading from it with a voice that seemed to issue from an underground cave. It was a confession, signed many years before, by Webb, in which he admitted to having forged nineteen payroll checks. Webb agreed that it was his confession, all right, and after that it didn't matter much what he said. The audience was atwitter; from the ranks of the press I could overhear unkind cuts about the quality of our testimony.

One hope remained—our weekend police chief and pensioner, Frank Barber. But what had they dug up on him? Lesser men, viewing the wreckage of their predecessors, would have fled from the stand, but Barber summoned up at least a show of equanimity. He possessed that quality of inner assurance often seen in bumpkins, caused perhaps by the happy lack of a sense of scale. To him, the world of Beaverdam, Ohio, contained all the essential elements of the most cosmopolitan and wicked of world capitals; having survived to old age the trials and vicissitudes of Beaverdam, he reckoned that he stood on equal footing with any man, if not higher.

Questioned on the details of the oath he said he had administered to Jones, he answered repeatedly that while he could not reveal the secret words, he was sure that the oath was no mystery to the committee, since some of the members had undoubtedly taken the same oath —a diversion the committee was, or at least seemed, unwilling to get into.

Examined for evidence of animus against Jones, he said, with just the right rhetorical flourish, "I am not opposed to him. I am here to tell the truth, sir. Maybe I can help Mr. Jones." And he went on to affirm that a conscientious Black Legionnaire who lived up to his oath was qualified to be not only FCC commissioner but President.

Plumbed for admissions that he was in the pay of Pearson, he responded to the question of who was paying the bills he was running up at the Mayflower by declaiming grandly that no one had paid them yet, but that since he had been invited to journey to Washington by the government, he assumed his bills would be paid by "the United States."

Then Senator Capehart, beaming triumphantly like Quasimodo upon discovering the molten lead, opened up the demolition effort by introducing records showing that Barber had, on the previous Fourth of July, set up a speed trap outside of Beaverdam and arrested eighty persons, fining them each $3. The implication of Capehart's questioning was that Barber was guilty of making false arrests in order to pocket the fines, but Barber stoutly demurred. He was just doing his duty; the fines had all been turned in to the county judge. Let the committee check his honor's records.

When Capehart backed off, hope kindled anew in our ranks, and it grew as Barber authoritatively described Jones's induction and his faithful attendance at Black Legion functions. But how could Barber be so sure it was Jones he had inducted, in the dark, among hundreds of people? Why, he had shone a flashlight in Jones's face, part of the ritual. And he had known "young Bob Jones from boyhood," just as he had known his father before him, "Jink" Jones, who was a prominent member of the Ku Klux Klan.

Reminiscenses poured out of the voluble constable; he was convincing; he made all the right moves. The audience was murmuring; the scribes were writing. For the first time in a hour, I dared look over at Drew.

Then Capehart drew out yet another file. He began reading affidavits given twenty-five years before by Barber's wife, mother, father and sister—all to the effect that Barber was insane and ought to be locked up. The senator held up another document in his pudgy hand. "I hold a medical certificate and commitment papers of where you were committed to the hospital for the insane in Ohio . . ."

"Yes, sir," said Barber, "that is true. I was sent there through a frame-up . . ."

Capehart continued remorselessly, citing records that Barber had made homicidal and suicidal threats, had chronically complained to the authorities of being persecuted, had been in jail six times. What about it?

"I was in jail in Hammond, Indiana, for shooting a guy," Barber volunteered.

"Yes," said Capehart, ". . . you have quite a record here—shooting a man in Hammond, in jail six times, confined to the insane hospital in Ohio, and then you arrive in Washington and go on a national radio hookup."

"Well, sir," replied Barber, "I have always tried to be a law-abiding citizen. You can't find a thing in any of those cases but what I wasn't justified in doing."

I could take no more. I was to follow Barber on the stand, and as shambles descended upon our cause I went out into the hall to review my points away from the distraction of falling bodies. At least one reporter I passed was wrapping it all up in an envenomed lead: "Pearson and his legman, Jack Anderson, at last produced their much heralded witnesses—a perjurer, a forger and a lunatic."

I planned to be a model of decorum and respect, to testify in a soft-spoken but meticulous manner. This seemed the proper demeanor to assume before a high tribunal by a twenty-four-year-old legman upon whose legitimacy a dubious light had been cast. But more than that, I had been brought up to regard the Constitution as a divinely inspired document, literally, and to look upon its protectors—as I assumed Presidents and senators to be—with the same reverence that was due the Apostles of my Church. Such was the hold of that belief upon me that my observations of senators in the flesh had not quite undermined it. I was in the ambivalent posture of an aborigine toward the witch doctor in the sixth month of a drought—dashed but not yet disaffected, still inclined toward propitiation, still willing to believe that the weirdest of gyrations and incantations somehow play a part in the divine scheme.

When it was almost time for me to go on the stand, Drew approached me in the hall. "Jack," he said. "I want you to go in there and rough up the committee."

I was stunned, and more important, scared. I mumbled something about wouldn't it be better to make a respectful, reasoned presentation of the—

"No!" He was seething, or as close to it as he ever let himself get. "You've got to raise hell with them. We can't let these hypocrites pee on us like this, Jack."

You should never do that to an employee who is about to testify for the first time. I groped toward the witness stand with my stomach sinking into infinity and my mind a blank. Gone were my rehearsed arguments. Above bulked the implacable Capehart. Ahead, I was sure, was a debacle and probably jail. Certain I was that the United States Senate would not tolerate a contumelious pip-squeak; I would be marched out in handcuffs, and a photograph of my disgrace would appear in the Salt Lake *Tribune*. Worse, I could not focus on what I should say, so alien was the role assigned to me. But indignation is the greatest of mobilizing forces. After feeding for a few moments on the callous dismantling of my Lima investigation, I found that a rising anger gave me the mood and the words.

Upon being sworn, I began blathering immediately and had to be called to order. Capehart started asking me questions about my residence, place of employment, etc.—a routine designed to establish at the outset the subservient place of a witness before a senator. When he suggested that there was something questionable about my trip to Lima, I spoke up: "I went down there to conduct an investigation, Senator, that I think *you people* should have been conducting."

"We will be the judge of that," the organ intoned.

Then, closing my eyes and jumping in, I charged the committee with attempting a whitewash and holding a bobtail investigation. "The committee is doing its best to confirm this man in a hurry," I piped.

Capehart's usual expression of incredulous disconsolation deepened, as if, in addition to encountering flummery, he had also been affronted with a bad smell. Proof, he demanded. "PROOF!"

The sheer vocal power of the man almost withered me. But not quite. "Well, sir, let me ask you," I said. "Did you intend to go down there? Did you intend to send somebody there?"

"I am not a witness here. Answer the question."

Before I was aware of it, Capehart was dismissing me from the stand. I was suspended momentarily between a sensation of relief and the feeling of Drew's censuring eyes upon my back. I insisted upon being heard further, and Capehart acceded.

I began to paint what I hoped was a compelling picture of gumshoeing around Lima, of all the little people who were willing to tell me personal recollections of Jones's days in the Black Legion but who were afraid to sign affidavits, and of how right they had been to fear reprisals. I named six of them and challenged the committee to interview them for proof that Jones had lied to the committee. I expressed curiosity over the source of the committee's files on the Lima witnesses and hinted that the committee was in collusion with Jones both in discrediting them and in refusing to conduct its own investigation on the scene. I was under way.

The invention of the microphone has had a pernicious effect on the American character. Sixty years ago most Americans were suitably humble about speaking in public; now we are a nation of curbstone pundits and incipient mob orators. Hold a mike in front of an otherwise reticent man, let him hear the magnified sound of his own voice, and he suddenly feels competent to pass judgment on any subject before a network audience of 60 million souls. Something of that presumption overcame me as I heard my words bounce off the rostrum. The erstwhile Apostles had been diminished to miscreants to be lectured. It was their questions, not the witnesses who had failed, I said. Perceiving that it was impolitic, in the limited time available, to try to mount a defense of perjury, forgery or armed assault, I seized upon Barber's role as traffic cop.

Why, I demanded to know, had this committee maligned Chief Barber for such an extraneous and laudable act as making speeding arrests on a day of peak auto fatalities? What was the matter with traffic safety? Shouldn't he enforce the law? I was now in full flight, and I could hear myself exclaiming, as though it were another person, "Barber was out there trying to do his duty . . . and I think that the subject before the committee, Senator, is Mr. Jones's background and not Mr. Barber's or Mr. Effinger's or Mr. Webb's. I think you should have dealt with what they know about Jones rather than—" The gavel was pounding; senators were heading for the door; Capehart had adjourned the hearing.

However poorly my diatribe may have been received elsewhere, it made a big hit with Drew and his top assistant, Dave Karr. With handshakes and backslaps, they escorted me out of the hearing room as though I were a victorious boxer. I had held up my end of the coffin.

Senator Brewster declined to pursue my leads or to investigate Jones further, contending that his detractors had been totally discredited. And such was our disarray and Brewster's control over the proceedings that there was no effective challenge to his decision. Congressman Jones's nomination was whooped through the committee and then the full Senate by unanimous votes, a pointed humiliation for "the nation's most influential journalist."

One does not provoke and then lose such a battle without suffering reprisals. In years to come, Commissioner Jones, henceforth a power over the broadcasting industry, would join with other Pearson enemies in a concerted effort to drive him off network radio. And in the immediate aftermath of the hearings, bileful newspaper editorials assailed us daily, followed by magazine appraisals—*Time, Newsweek,* the *Saturday Evening Post*—the unifying theme of which was that Drew Pearson and his grubby legman had been shown up for their reckless reporting.

In retrospect, it was not an auspicious debut for me. But at the time

I was oblivious. Nature grants to the young man an astigmatism that hides from him the likelihood, or even the possibility, that he has made an ass of himself. Were it not so, repeated mortification would soon geld him of his bounce and resilience; he would cease to woo, to strive, to boast, to dream vaulting dreams and to follow lures his prudent elders disdain. Far from being chastened by the routing of my witnesses or the 90-odd to 0 vote against us by the world's greatest deliberative body, I looked on my Lima effort as a tour de force which only unkind circumstance prevented from being a Steffensian triumph. I attributed the bad notices to the envy that anonymous, one-lunged creatures of editorial offices must bear toward gazelles like Pearson and me who get to leap and pivot across the public stage. Had not truth, however poorly packaged, been on our side? And when the gavel ended the episode, had I not faced down the senators? However flawed my assessment, I drew from it valid insights which in the long life of jousting with Congress that lay ahead of me would prove almost infallible guides.

Senators, on the showing I had seen, were a duplicitous but rather timid lot. That is to say, they were ambivalent toward objective truth but cautious in their derelictions, a contradiction arising no doubt from their dependence every six years on public favor. As they were partisans, and more akin to mercenaries than to seekers after truth, their investigations and hearings were governed not by equitable and constant rules and procedures that seek the whole truth, as in a court trial, but by prejudicial and arbitrary ones designed to exclude that which would endanger their predetermined verdict. How else could it be explained that their most controversial probes were periodically truncated by closed-door, faction-ridden votes over who would testify and which evidence would be excluded?

But democracy had made its inroads into the Star Chamber. No senator dares to be known as a rigger and a finagler; if a bad enough stink is made over his suppression of evidence, he will quietly disengage himself from the battle and often turn up on the side of justice. During my tirade against the committee, I got the scent of their arrogance dissolving, their alarm mounting, as they hurriedly adjourned and retreated to their cloakroom. It was too late then, and our improvised case too ludicrously bungled, and the public too little interested, for us to carry the day. But I glimpsed the vision of how easily, under different circumstances, we could have turned the tables.

I would run on about it to Drew, with the fever of discovery that burns in youth when it stumbles upon old truths. Drew was, at that moment, being pressed by Howard Hughes for advice on how to deal with a hostile probe into his affairs by none other than Senator Owen Brewster, and I soon found myself collaborating with the Ultimate Tycoon in one of the great square-offs of Senate history.

3 · Brewster at
the Brink

For Senator Owen Brewster, opportunity stood at flood tide in the summer of 1947. He had spent a dozen frustrating years as a viewer-with-alarm for the Republican minority; now the levers of power had at last been placed in his hands by the GOP congressional sweep of 1946. He found himself chairman or number-two member of several key committees of the Senate. He was confident he knew how to use that power to advance his career, his principles, his party and the financial interests that supported them all.

Brewster was in his fifty-ninth year when the long winter of Democratic congressional rule ended; and he had played a role in the coming of spring. Over the years his intelligence and industry had won him an influence beyond his rank on Senate committees of vital interest to big business—the Finance Committee, which levied and forgave taxes; the Commerce Committee, which bestowed subsidies and monopolies; the Committee on Naval Affairs, from which flowed vast industrial projects. Brewster had put his growing importance to businessmen at the service of his party by raising large campaign contributions for GOP Senate candidates from them—Drew called him a "bag man"—and in recognition of this he was soon to be named chairman of the Senate Republican Campaign Committee.

Similarly, he had devoted his considerable analytical and forensic talents to discrediting the Democratic presidency. A year earlier, in 1946, he had shone as the minority scold on the joint congressional committee to inquire into Pearl Harbor, using those widely followed proceedings to blame the late President Roosevelt, whose image was still the chief asset of the opposition party, for the unpreparedness that led to the destruction of the Pacific fleet. And now he was a leader of the majority, with power to direct and orchestrate events. Deftly had he used this power in the almost effortless humiliation of the despised but feared Pearson; and while the plaudits of the Republican cloakroom were still ringing in his ears, he unveiled to colleagues a breath-taking political offensive compared to which his routing of the muckraker had been a minor ambuscade. As chairman of the Senate War Investigating Committee—the post that had catapulted Harry Truman into the presidential succession—he was preparing a whole series of probes into putative wartime bungles and scandals that figured to tarnish the Roosevelt-Truman image by the following year's presidential election. To lead off, he directed that public hearings be opened into accusations that President Roosevelt had overruled his military experts twice during the war in order to hand out fat war contracts to Howard Hughes, a financial benefactor of his son, Elliott—contracts on which $40 million had been squandered without delivery to the government of anything.

Ralph Owen Brewster (he disliked "Ralph," so it was seldom used) possessed what seems in retrospect a refreshing partisanship, a rousing hatred for the other side and all its works that evokes nostalgia in these tepid days of the nonpartisan politician who is for himself alone and who takes no risks and suffers no discipline for the party weal.

To many politicians, then as now, the mere winning and holding of office, with its appearance of success and importance, are sufficient ends in themselves, but not to Brewster. In his youth he had been a two-term governor, ruling through a cooperative legislature of his own party, and he knew what power was, and wherein lay its source. Through the bleak thirties and forties he had chafed under the impotency of holding office without power; he had learned the futility of winning individual victories in safe Maine while across the nation his fellow partisans went down. Power came from *party* victories; it came to those few who earned party leadership by toiling and scheming and risking unpopularity, even notoriety, in the party's behalf; and it came in its plenitude only when a presidential victory crowned party control of the Congress.

Grim things must be said and done to bring down a Democratic President, and Brewster was willing to do them, for taking the presidency was the desideratum that led to the grand consummation of politics as he saw it: the booting out of all Democrats not cemented to their chairs by dubious civil service laws; and the capture of their financial-support system by scourging from the trough all the "Democratic" corporations, lobbyists and lawyers who now fattened there. Conspicuous among these was Howard Hughes, an adept at devouring air routes and contracts at the expense of deserving Republican contributors close to Brewster's heart.

During the Pearl Harbor inquiry, the Maine senator had led a successful effort to gain committee access to the Roosevelt presidential papers stored at Hyde Park. Among those papers he had come upon links between the Roosevelt family and the Hughes contracts. Thus he could now serve multiple ends with one investigation—the discrediting of a sanctified Democratic regime, its potent mythology and its survivors, and at the same time, the crushing of a menace to friendly business interests.

Brewster was a hardened veteran of congressional investigations, and he recognized that this one had the basic ingredients of a blockbuster. During the height of the war Howard Hughes, then in his middle thirties, was awarded two contracts, of $18 million and $22 million each, to create and build two revolutionary aircraft—a giant *plywood* cargo seaplane that could fly the Atlantic carrying thirty-five tons of men and weapons, and a super photo-reconnaissance craft fast enough to end our marked inferiority to the Germans in that area. Years passed; the war ended; the postwar era entered its third year. Yet neither contract had been fulfilled. The reconnaissance plane was still being tested; the monster cargo craft had never flown; the prototype was laid up like a beached whale in one of Hughes's mammoth hangars. He allowed an occasional photograph of it, from a distance, perhaps to keep alive the hope that is said to spring eternal.

Boondoggles of such magnitude are good for evanescent headlines, but if they are to really stick in the public craw, two considerations are usually necessary: the fiasco must occur under high auspices, and the target chosen for disgrace must posses in his person, his milieu or the whimsicality of his offense, a titillating potential, a certain oomph capable of kindling prurient public interest. The first condition was met when Brewster discovered that both contracts had been ordered over the objections of regular procurement channels, through the intervention of the Roosevelt family—FDR himself in the first instance, joined by his son Elliott, then an Army Air Force colonel, in the second. No auspice could have been more satisfactory.

And as a target, Hughes had star potential. Had he been merely an airline president and manufacturing mogul, even the evaporation of 40 million of the taxpayers' dollars would not have long sustained the public's imagination, for citizens and media take little interest in boardroom nonentities. But Hughes was more than an industrial magnate. He was a bachelor, young, tall, dark and by some lights handsome. He was rich beyond comprehension—worth, as near as could be figured, $150 million (back when money was worth several times today's valuation). He had won fame as a test pilot and a movie producer. He was widely suspected of innumerable intimacies with women of beauty. He knew the power of an idea whose time has come, and in his movie *The Outlaw* he had dared to unloose upon the world Jane Russell's bosom —as it turned out, a cultural breakthrough of revolutionary proportions which created a stir so visceral that public entertainment has never been the same since, and thirty years later Miss Russell commanded huge fees for exhibiting brassieres on television commercials. Better still, Hughes, even at that early stage of his life, was already known to be quirky and reclusive, thus offering the public an aura of personal mystery and privacy which the Brewster hearings promised to violate.

The hand of meticulous planning was visible in the prehearing manipulation of the press via daily leaks from the Brewster committee, leaks designed both to build public interest in the coming hearings and to prejudice the public before the hearings began. Among the first titillators were accounts of racy parties thrown for government officials by Hughes's Washington operation. "Softening-up parties" they were called—glittering oases amid the browned-out austerity of wartime. Champagne flowed, movie starlets swam in the apparent nude, and solicitous young models, whom Hughes paid $200 per party, circulated, "entertaining" the more adventurous guests. The regulars at these affairs included redoubtable Julius Krug, then chief of the War Production Board and now Secretary of the Interior; high military procurement officers; and a veritable penful of congressmen, such as uncontrite Democratic Senator Mon Wallgren of Washington, who quipped, "If those girls were paid two hundred dollars, they were greatly underpaid." Even more expansive delights were available to key procurement personnel. One Air Force colonel, for instance, was treated to a $1,000 New York weekend by Hughes's lobbyists.

Shots of the Hughes hostesses in scanty attire appeared every day in the papers as illustrations of how, under the Democrats, the war was won. To the relatively parched electorate of those days, this was pulse-quickening stuff, and Brewster's committee publicists capitalized on it by promising a sordid extravaganza of "broads, booze and brass."

The stage was thus set for the dragging on of the martyred President. FDR, it was revealed, had personally ordered, over the objections of the Joint Chiefs, the funding of the plywood cargo plane chimera and had reinstated it after it had been canceled for nonperformance—in both instances at the instigation of one of his top administrators, Jesse Jones, who when not in government was the banking partner of a Hughes functionary in Houston, Noah Dietrich.

The genesis of the second contract—for the reconnaissance plane—featured even juicier oddities. Despite a major promotional effort by Hughes, his contract bid had been rejected by Air Force procurement officers. Suddenly Elliott Roosevelt was called home from his combat post in the Mediterranean and superimposed on the procurement office, with plenipotentiary power to select the photo-reconnaissance plane contractor. Within a fortnight, young Elliott reversed the previous decision and pushed through the award of a $22 million contract to Hughes, whereupon the providential visitor returned to the front.

But not before leaving behind a trail of indiscretions that remained warm long after the war ended and the contract flopped. While Colonel Roosevelt was deciding between Hughes and his competitors he had permitted himself to be treated to a considerable spree by Hughes factotum Johnny Meyer, the recruiter of girls for those celebrated parties. Committee investigators toted up $5,068 in night-club and hotel bills that Meyer had picked up for young Roosevelt. More felicitously, Meyer had introduced the actress Faye Emerson to Roosevelt, and had bankrolled segments of their subsequent coast-to-coast courtship and honeymoon. No detail was too trivial or intimate for the Brewster investigators to publish; e.g., Meyer had furnished, for the shapely Emerson legs, $132 worth of war-scarce nylons. The picture was thus made vivid—here was the son of the President of the United States, in the middle of a war of survival, with Hughes nylons hanging out of his pocket, a Hughes-introduced beauty on his arm, a Hughes procurer picking up his night-club and hotel bills, while the prodigal son was in the process of rejecting the bids of competitors and awarding a multimillion-dollar contract to Hughes that four years later was still unfulfilled.

The accomplished hatchet man strives to induce a pig-pile effect, under whose grunts and stench his victim will be smothered beyond retrieval before a defense can be entered. And so Brewster now announced that one Harriet Applewick, a Trans World Airlines stewardess, had refused to fly on Hughes's plane anymore because of his persistent carnal advances. Moreover, said the committee, Hughes had dropped out of sight, and his sidekick Johnny Meyer had disappeared without a trace somewhere in Patagonia, in the remote regions of the southern Argentine. Emboldened by such headlines, defamers began to come out of the woodwork. In New York City a night-club cigarette girl named Patricia Miles noticed Meyer's picture in the paper and immediately filed a $25,000 paternity suit. For more than a year, Miss Miles alleged, she had "visited" the resilient Meyer in his hotel-apartment three or four evenings a week. When she at length told him she was pregnant, Meyer had characteristically vanished, leaving her to cope as best she could.

At Pearson headquarters we watched Brewster's evisceration of Hughes with a sort of glum admiration. Ordinarily the Hughes-type exposé, with its mix of dubious war contracts, tawdry lobbying, First Families in dishabille and tycoons on the run, was Drew's cup of tea, the kind of story he all but owned the copyright on. Normally we would by now have had a pipeline into the committee, would have opened up other sources, and would already be filing exacerbating columns.

But this time Drew held back. For one thing, he was damned if he would run with Brewster, whom he had marked down for condign punishment, a sentence not to be stayed merely because Brewster was temporarily masquerading in the Lord's livery. For another, from the first whiff the whole thing had smelled to Drew of Pan American Airways, the chief beneficiary of a Hughes downfall and an enterprise known to have an intimate relationship with Brewster.

It so happened that Pan American was to Drew the archetypal corporate ogre. Since the 1920s he had been berating Pan Am as a greedy octopus fed by taxpayers' subsidies and protected by exclusive government franchises. It represented to Drew one of the most pernicious of political evils—the corporation that grows rich through government intervention while all the time influencing the political process to encourage yet more intervention.

At that very moment, in fact, Pan Am was making its boldest bid to have the United States set it up as an official worldwide monopoly. Its plan was known as "the chosen instrument" concept, under which Uncle Sam was to sponsor and subsidize one airline which was to carry all American traffic overseas; no new competitors would be allowed and all existing American carriers with overseas operations would be forced either to merge them with "the chosen instrument" or to shut them down. Such a behemoth, so Pan Am's argument went, would be able to overwhelm the new foreign airlines which had begun to rise out of the war's rubble and thus would dominate world air commerce in the interests of the United States. It was presented as a matter of national interest, of America being number one; it was not mentioned that only Pan American Airways was at the moment large enough and sufficiently established around the globe to assume the chosen-instrument role.

Was it not curious, we thought, that legislation to enact this plan into law had been introduced by Senator Brewster, who had lined up ten members of his Commerce Committee in its support and was on the verge of pushing it through? And was it not equally suspicious that Howard Hughes was the major obstacle to that legislation?

Hughes's Trans World Airlines was the only U.S. overseas carrier big enough and politically connected enough to endanger Pan Am's scheme. During the latest contest for government-awarded overseas air routes, an arena long dominated by Pan Am, Hughes had shown his muscle by carrying off Paris, Rome, Cairo and other world capitals. Little wonder that Pan Am, suddenly exposed to the headwinds of competition, was broaching a final solution to it. We suspected, therefore, that the effort to reduce Hughes to an object of public ridicule —emanating as it did from Brewster—was rooted in something more substantial than indignation over two World War II contracts that had gone sour.

Moreover, the closer we looked into those contracts, the less they resembled frauds, taking on instead the appearance of chancy wartime measures that failed but which were conscientiously undertaken. Against the $18 million the government lost on the cargo plane, Hughes had dropped $7 million of his own money. And he had spent $5 million of his own in developing the reconnaissance plane before he went to the government for a contract, money that he never recovered. If this was war profiteering, where was the profit?

The cargo-plane idea had been the brainchild of the great industrialist Henry J. Kaiser, builder of the Grand Coulee Dam, who had enlisted Hughes to design and build it. It was a companion scheme to Kaiser's equally fantastic proposal to build prefabricated merchant ships on an assembly line, vessels that could be welded together, thus reducing construction time from months to days. Both were desperation attempts to deal with the grim fact that in 1942 German U-boats were sinking 700,000 tons of Allied shipping each month, twice as much as we were building, a ratio that, if not altered, would with the precision of mathematics soon knock us out of the war. Any shipbuilding expert could tell you that boats slapped together like this, if they could be built at all, would never survive the tempests of the North Atlantic, just as everyone knew that 200-ton plywood crates could never fly through its savage storms. But Commanders in Chief exist to overrule such cautions and to take the gambles that must be made. The Liberty-ship panacea worked and saved the war effort; the cargo plane failed, and lost some money.

So, too, the contract for the photo-reconnaissance plane, the F-11, had some earmarks of credibility. That it was a legitimate endeavor and not a rip-off was attested to by one salient fact: Howard Hughes flew the plane on its maiden test flight and was almost killed in its crash. After he mended, he redesigned the F-11 and test-flew it again, this time successfully. At the present moment, it was almost ready for delivery to the government. Better late . . .

What tarred the F-11 failure, of course, was Colonel Roosevelt's having been mysteriously insinuated into the decision-making process with extraordinary powers, and his acceptance of a bit of *la dolce vita* from Hughes while making a decision in Hughes's favor.

On the first point, young Roosevelt was not an illogical choice to break the decision-making bottleneck; a decorated combat flier of photo-reconnaissance aircraft, a wing commander, he was an expert on the deficiencies of existing reconnaissance planes. But there was no way to put an acceptable face on the favors. One could understand a flier home from the dreary front hankering for a little spree and delighted to have a Johnny Meyer around; one could understand a Roosevelt assuming that no one would feel he could be bought for entertainment tabs; one could make allowances for the disoriented climate of wartime encounters. Still and all, it was wrong, reckless and discreditable for both Hughes and Roosevelt, and dearly were they now paying for it in public abuse. But did it lead to a corrupt decision in Hughes's favor?

We were willing to give him the benefit of the doubt. Roosevelt knew that after making his choice, he would be returning to combat where he and his comrades would continue to risk their lives in deficient planes until the replacement he had chosen was available. Would that all contract awards faced an equal test of sincerity!

My mentor's sympathies, then, lay with Hughes, but Drew felt stranded in an unsatisfying posture. It was his nature to want to play an important part in the great political brawls of the time, to put his mark on them, to help shape their outcome toward the benefit of his causes or the distress of his foes. Yet he would not take Brewster's side and could not take Hughes's. For though Hughes was probably the victim of an unsavory gang-up, his own conduct in the matter was too shabby to defend and he was not even making a fight of it himself. Grumbling at each day's leaks, Drew held back, watching the thing spin, looking for a handle to pick it up by.

At this point in his disintegrating fortunes, Howard Hughes phoned Drew from one of his West Coast redoubts. He had long considered Pearson to be journalism's leading molder of public opinion and the man most knowledgeable about the Byzantine twists of conspiratorial Washington. And since Drew's animus against Hughes's tormentors was clear, there was a mutuality of interest present that encouraged him to seek Drew's help and advice.

In the manner of cornered men whose expense accounts have already been made public, Hughes admitted to misdemeanors but pled innocent to felonies. He had indeed wined and wenched government officials and military brass, sometimes to excess. It was necessary, he said; his competitors did it, and as a relative newcomer trying to buck long-entrenched interests and liaisons, he had to play the game in order to get a hearing on his proposals. He had never looked on aviation as a moneymaker, he insisted; he was in it because he had a passion for it. He yielded to no man in his mastery of the dark arts of making money, as the astronomical profits of his other businesses showed, but in aviation, he had lost $14 million in thirteen years.

Then he got to the nub: three months before, Brewster had attempted to lobby him in behalf of Pan Am, he said, and having failed, they were both out to destroy him. Pan Am had put great pressure on him to merge Trans World with Pan Am and co-sponsor the chosen-instrument plan. Brewster himself had told him at the Mayflower Hotel that the probe would be dropped if he joined forces with Pan Am. Hughes had asked for thirty days to think it over, and while he dickered with Pan Am the investigation had lain dormant; when he finally rejected their offer, it was revived with a vengeance.

Hughes had a deal to broach to Pearson, although it was not tendered so indelicately: he had hired top investigators and ex-Senate staffers to put Brewster under the microscope and keep him there; what they came up with he would share with Drew; he would appreciate Drew's counsel and the sharing of information Drew might have. Drew translated this to mean that Hughes was dredging up muck on Brewster and wanted him to publish it, a proposition that delighted Drew, for he had no scruples about sources, or about hidden alliances with people he was reporting on, as long as the information itself was reliable.

Regular communication began between the two. Drew would take down Hughes's information and pass it on to me to check out. It involved small but compromising favors Brewster had accepted from Pan American, legislative errands he had run for them, back-scratching friendships between Brewster and Pan Am officials. There had also been potential scandals involving Pan Am which the Senate War Investigating Committee staff had investigated before Brewster's take-over as chairman but which he had then put the lid on. One by one, the leads checked out as accurate.

As for Hughes's version of his troubles, Drew accepted it in the main, for it confirmed his own hunches. And it was a matter of record that Brewster had discussed with Hughes the "chosen instrument" bill, for shortly after the meeting Hughes had described to Drew, Brewster had told *Aviation Week* magazine that Hughes was now moving toward support of the bill. For Brewster to have discussed his pet bill with Hughes while holding an investigation over him was akin to blackmail, even if Brewster had not been as direct as Hughes alleged. Anyway, it was not necessary to be *for* Hughes; it was a matter of whom to be against—Hughes-TWA or Brewster–Pan Am. For Drew the choice was foreordained.

We were preparing several helpful columns, Drew told Hughes, but Hughes was mistaken if he thought he could wage this battle through such surrogates as columnists, lawyers and PR men. This was not one of those Washington winds that could be ridden out by lying back while it spent itself, Drew said. Hughes was up against both Pan Am and the Senate elders; they had the machinery, the ammunition and the know-how to keep the thing going while he was pounded into the ground. He would have to come out of seclusion and beard the lions personally. The basic ingredients of public sympathy lay on his side, Drew said, if he would come out of his shell and summon them forth.

"What do you suggest?" asked Hughes.

Well, it was a matter of attitude, of élan, of image, Drew said. He had been discussing the question with an associate, Jack Anderson, who had recently tangled with Brewster and his Senate satellites; Anderson would call him.

Marvelous are the ways of democracy. Only three months after Drew Pearson had hired me off the street with little to recommend me but somewhat watered credentials as a "war correspondent," a smattering of Chinese slang and a certain bravado, I was to advise the notorious Howard Hughes on large affairs of state. As I think back on it, I do not recall being overawed. I was happy to help the fellow out and intrigued over the availability of such a prominent guinea pig for the testing of my theories.

Phoning Howard Hughes was an elaborate process, even in those days, even at his request. First you obtained the various phone numbers of his peripatetic secretary, Nadine Huntley. Then you called Miss Huntley to make an "appointment" to call Hughes. If your audience was granted, she would call back to give you a phone number and a time to make your call. You called at the exact minute, and he would be there. His explanation for this regimen was that impaired hearing required him to be at a specially equipped phone.

His voice had a touch of Texas in it, was pleasant but precise. His first rule of conversation was to dispense with all amenities and proceed immediately to the point. What did I think he ought to do?

I stated my basic theory of senatorial behavior: senators are great bullies but poor fighters; they are occupational cowards, or rather, victims of excessive caution. They could be fearsome infighters when the public wasn't watching or when their victim was a pushover, but they would run from a donnybrook of uncertain outcome, for they were in the popularity business. I offered to cite chapter and verse, but Hughes pressed me on to my conclusions, which were, in substance, that since he could never effectively defend his lobbying tactics or get far on his contract performance, and since any attempt to do so would only put him right where Brewster wanted him, his salvation lay in turning the hearing into a free-for-all that would scare off the senators.

And how was he to do that?

By charging that he was the victim of a crooked cabal; by clamoring that the hearings were being rigged against him; by demanding fair, American procedures—like the right to cross-examine his accusers and call his own witnesses. An attack a day on Brewster and on un-American procedures—that was my formula.

But wouldn't that unite the senators behind Brewster and against him?

That was the hazard he must risk, I advised cheerfully. The fair-play appeal would unnerve them, I theorized, and the idea that Brewster might be leading them all into a swamp would cause them to back off a bit. And once Brewster began to lose control of the committee and the bickering started, the hearings would fall apart. You have to have unity to frame a man.

Hughes thanked me, remaining noncommittal; we would talk again by phone, he said, and would meet soon.

At about this time a source within the Brewster committee provided us with a preview of the public hearings, then a week off: the Senate's largest and most ornate facility, the Caucus Room, would be the setting, and accommodations had been made for a record number of reporters, broadcasters, news cameramen and klieg lights. Brewster would not preside, having picked a protégé for that role, Republican Senator Homer Ferguson of Michigan, a former judge and law professor with a white judicial mane and no visible connection with Pan American. Leading off as witnesses would be such headline-assuring heavyweights as Henry J. Kaiser, Jesse Jones and Undersecretary of State Robert Lovett. These were men of gigantic affairs, and their participation would lend an aura of a grand inquest to the extravaganza; through this glittering sounding board would be broadcast the story of FDR's overruling of the Joint Chiefs, of procurement regulations violated, of vital war material wasted, of nonperformance rewarded. The bibulous Julius Krug, who as War Production chief had signed orders making large sums available to Hughes, would then be brought on, to be grilled about the girlie parties and other facets of the Hughes formula for doing business with the United States. Then would come Johnny Meyer to explain the $164,000 he ran up in entertainment expenses in advancing Hughes's interests; Meyer was still at large, reportedly near Cape Horn, and if he could not be intercepted and produced, his account ledgers would be, along with the aqua-chorines and the $200 hostesses, who could substitute for him. Then the Roosevelt scion would be called and confronted with his peccadilloes. Thus all the salacious items that had heretofore been leaked out would be rerun in magnified form, day by day. At the end of the line, according to the Brewster scenario, after the last accusation had been dramatized and the final scurrility elicited, what was left of the once haughty Howard Hughes would be led in, under subpoena, for the *coup de main*.

With the Brewster juggernaut rolling apparently unopposed, the danger as Drew Pearson saw it was that editorial and public opinion would solidify on the committee's side before the Hughes defense could be uncorked. Drew was determined to forestall that, but if he was to do so, he must jump off immediately, and here our logistical problem was particularly troublesome. Four days elapsed between our issuance of a column and its publication. During the gap, the posture of something as chaotic and incendiary as an unfolding scandal could turn upside down. By the time our early columns reached the public, Hughes might have come on strong, dallied desultorily or blown up altogether. It was as though we were commanding one wing of a pincer attack in ignorance of tomorrow's weather, the gas supply and the intentions of our coordinate wing. Drew therefore drew up a plan that would be serviceable in all eventualities.

He took his cue from a proverb often quoted in Washington circles: "The perfect is the enemy of the good." He would praise Brewster faintly for revealing to the public the motes in Hughes's operation while challenging the senator to expose the beams of larger offenders, too, chief among them Pan American Airways. When Brewster declined, as he surely would, the column would damn him, with a daily heightening emphasis, for destroying what could have been an exemplary investigation by covering up for his corporate friends and using his public office to aid them in what was essentially a corporate fight for air routes and air-mail contracts.

Seven columns and two network broadcasts, based in part on the Hughes information I had verified, were prepared and scheduled to bombard the public over the twelve days during which the contest would likely be decided in the Senate Caucus Room. We opened on soft shoes as the hearings were getting under way:

"Senator Brewster has performed a useful service in bringing out the bizarre night-club parties, the Hollywood lovelies and other allurements used by airplane manufacturer Howard Hughes to cozy up to government officials. However, the big question is, will Brewster's probe go far enough?"

Other lobbying offenders were listed. "But the most successful of all —far more successful than the obtuse lobbying of Howard Hughes—

was that of Pan American Airways. If Senator Brewster went into these lobbying set-ups, especially the amazing ramifications of Pan American Airways, he would be doing a great service to the country."

The following day the column was still friendly, praising "hard-hitting GOP Senator Owen Brewster of Maine—tough, shrewd, an old hand at Senate investigations." But as the days passed, the man from Maine would be found wanting: "Brewster is known as the best friend Pan American Airways has in the Senate."

In print and on the airwaves, Drew hammered away at one theme: don't be deceived by the splashy headlines; behind them was a "desperate struggle between two great airlines for the most lucrative travel routes in the world"; in that struggle, Owen Brewster was "Pan American's chief congressional spokesman."

Brewster denied any "connection" to Pan Am, a predictable denial which phase two of our prepackaged attack was aimed at. Here again, the information provided by Hughes was invaluable. The "chosen instrument" bill Brewster introduced *had been drafted by Pan Am's lawyers;* Pan Am had flown Brewster on its "special plane N.C. 4000" to the North Carolina home of his predecessor as Senate Commerce Committee chairman, Senator Josia Bailey, to try to persuade him to come out for that bill; Pan Am occasionally flew Brewster to Maine and to his favorite watering spot, fashionable Hobe Sound, Florida, where he stayed free of charge at the vacation hideaway of Pan Am Vice President Sam Pryor, the Republican national committeeman from Connecticut.

Drew had a cooperative friend on the Brewster committee, Senator Claude Pepper, the liberal Florida Democrat. Our column was almost the lone pro-Pepper voice in Florida's conservative press, and Drew, always an unabashed caller-in of debts, day by day nudged Pepper toward leading a Democratic attack on the way Brewster had stacked the probe against Hughes. Gradually Pepper warmed to the task. On the day one of our columns appeared describing the secret residences and apartments maintained by Pan American for the quiet entertaining of government dignitaries, Pepper interrupted the hearings to cite these items and to demand a committee probe of Pan Am. And one afternoon Pepper went to Brewster's private office to complain of improper anti-Hughes leaks by the committee. He found Brewster closeted with Sam Pryor and Pan Am's publicity agent, Julius Klein. Pepper told Drew, and that item went right into the next column.

In such manner, before the hearings reached their critical phase, we prepared most of our case and put it into the pipeline, scheduled for delivery on doorsteps and in living rooms during unknowable days ahead when the anti-Hughes tide should be cresting. To millions of readers and listeners, to senators, to editorial writers and commentators, our columns and broadcasts would at the least be daily reminders that the attack on Hughes, however overwhelming, was suspect in that those who sponsored it stood to gain from his destruction and had sinned perhaps more than he.

We hoped, thereby, to provide a brief stay of execution, to help keep opinion fluid until the defense could be heard, but only Hughes could make that defense and he was in hiding, his plans as inscrutable as ever.

Somewhere within the golden belt that encompassed Los Angeles and Las Vegas, inside the cranium of the reclusive celebrity who was vainly sought by hordes of newsmen and photographers, a most formidable brain and will were functioning twenty hours a day. Howard Ribard Hughes was a man consumed by an inordinate drive to achieve and dominate which the current crisis had stimulated to a feverish pitch. Almost ceaselessly, he sifted and mulled the steady stream of intelligence and advice that poured into his nomadic command post from investigators, public relations men, lawyers, corporate associates, friendly reporters and beholden politicians; always the intelligence brought some new alarum, the advice that he make prompt public rebuttal to the attacks that were piling up hour by hour, but always the decision that emerged at the end of each twenty hours was unchanged —watch and wait.

I would have been distressed at this apparent passivity had I not caught occasional glimpses of a subterranean operation that was anything but passive. Hughes had sent out private detectives who were invisibly dogging Brewster and his links with Pan American; the tycoon had gained entrée to the enemy's information, at least its old information, by quietly engaging as attorneys the former chief counsel and associate counsel of the Senate War Investigating Committee, Hugh Fulton and Rudolph Halley; his operatives had penetrated even into Brewster's household, co-opting a former maid and pumping her for even the minutiae of Brewster's domestic routine.

Painstakingly he assembled and weighed this input of information and pieced it into his emerging plan, letting some of it out through us, some through others, retaining some for his own use. A man at once driven and self-contained who always worked at top capacity, Hughes was not to be hurried or interrupted. He was a perfectionist, and perfectionists get that way by taking their own good time.

On July 28, 1947, as the Washington hearings opened in public session, Hughes finally broke his public silence by issuing an "open letter" in California to Senator Brewster: "Since you think it is so horrible for anyone to accept my hospitality, why don't you tell about the $1,400 worth of airplane trips you requested and accepted from me? . . . Why not tell that this investigation was really born the day that TWA . . . first challenged the theory that only Juan Trippe's great Pan American Airways had the sacred right to fly the Atlantic?"

To *Time* magazine it seemed pique: "The inscrutable Mr. Hughes, who had been ignoring the whole thing in Hollywood, suddenly got mad." But in fact, there was cold calculation behind it. Like the sudden flash and thunder of artillery that finally breaks the waitful silence, Hughes's statement heralded a general attack; he had taken the offensive.

Immediately thereafter another epistolary salvo exploded, this one containing an intractable word that put it on the nation's front pages. Brewster, Hughes charged, had tried to "blackmail" him into merging TWA with Pan Am by offering to call off the present investigation if he agreed. The offer was made during a luncheon in Brewster's apartment at Washington's Mayflower Hotel in February 1947. "The committee," Hughes charged, "is being used as a blackmail weapon."

Each day now brought a new Hughes counterattack; one day an "open letter" would charge that "Brewster has been carted all over the country as the free guest of Pan American Airways in their luxurious, private executive airplane"; the next, Hughes would demand that the Attorney General investigate the relationship between Brewster and Pan Am, and that Brewster be required to step down and testify under oath, at his own hearings, as to the Hughes accusations. His statements were tightly crafted so that almost every sentence contained compact epithets of the kind irresistible to news editors:

"Senator Brewster, well known as *the mouthpiece for Pan American Airways,* has misused his high powers as a Senator to try and *blackjack me into a merger* . . . and to stage a *three-ring publicity circus* for his own personal gratification." The long silence with which Hughes had endured savage punishment had created almost a public hunger for his response and enabled him now to attack daily without seeming pugnacious or vindictive.

The press was eating it up; the prime anti-Hughes testimony in the hearing room was being countered by ex parte press releases from somewhere in California, for example: "It is a sad situation when a U.S. Senator has to drag a lot of innocent girls into a congressional hearing in order to achieve personal publicity."

During these days I tried to probe Brewster's strengths and weaknesses with something of the objectivity of a pug studying the ring habits of his next opponent. I looked first for those personal weaknesses that Drew had taught me to cherish in an adversary: overweaning vanity, bumbling pomposity, addiction to creature comforts, a tendency to alcoholic indiscretion, the heedless pursuit of venery.

I found nothing. Brewster was unpretentious of manner and disciplined in utterance. He did not drink at all, or even smoke, and in his relations with the habitually exploited Capitol Hill secretary, I found no departure from the most punctilious code of chivalry. His daily routine was a rigorous model of hard work; his life at home was frugal. Even his two culpable indulgences had a saving grace about them: the corporate plane rides were no doubt prized for the working time they saved him, and when he occupied Sam Pryor's Hobe Sound lodge for Thanksgiving vacations, he brought his own turkey and cleaned the place up afterward. As far as our spies could ascertain, his nightly revels at his Mayflower Hotel apartment were confined to doing his laundry; nylon wash-and-wear shirts had recently been introduced and Brewster had purchased one; each night he washed out his white shirt, hung it up to dry and the next morning put it on again, ready to face, impeccably, the Washington power structure. Such men do not make easy opponents.

It was Brewster who showed me the advantages of being born ugly. Ugly he was—billiard-bald on top, cheerless-eyed, meaty-lipped, an appearance dark and gloomy. For him, the ballot box would have seemed the least likely springboard to success. Yet he had carried his unfair burden up through the Maine legislature to become governor of his state, and then congressman, senator, chairman and a power in national Republican councils. This had to bespeak the inner superiority that unkind fate can nurture—the compensating enlargement of brains, tenacity, guile, fortitude. On the hard testing ground of numberless speaking halls, committee chambers and smoke-filled rooms, he had somehow managed to warm the chill his visage cast, to triumph over his physiognomy through the qualities he brought to the lectern and the conference table.

It was, then, a man long ago stripped of illusions who now assessed the first rounds of his confrontation with Hughes, and according to our sources, found the results mixed. His hearings were easily the biggest news event of the year. The testimony was going as expected. Kaiser had tried to defend Hughes's performance, but what came through was Hughes's stand-offishness in doing business—even Henry J. Kaiser had trouble getting to see him. The generals and colonels established, as expected, that the Hughes contracts had been politically imposed on them outside procurement channels, and that in the construction phase, Hughes had been the only defense contractor in the entire war effort to be freed from strict day-to-day government supervision and accountability. The civilian heads of wartime production duly excused themselves from responsibility for the contracts on the ground that President Roosevelt, and later his son, had made the decisions; the details of those contracts had been bared, showing, for instance, that even if the Air Force finally received delivery of the cargo plane, Hughes would remain the actual owner for four and a half years, during which time the government must lease the plane from him at $37,500 per month plus extras, a sum that could theoretically mount up to over $2 million. And now the disreputable Johnny Meyer, having at last surfaced in Paris, was on the stand and had begun to confirm chapter and verse the "broads, booze and brass" tactics by which Howard Hughes had subverted the war-procurement apparatus.

Two days of Meyer's testimony made it manifest why Hughes had tried to hide the stout, cherubic, forty-one-year-old quipster. The comical irrepressibility that made Meyer a valued court jester also made him a damaging witness. Instead of obscuring his services to Hughes as procurer, party thrower, spree-bankroller and check grabber for wartime officialdom, Meyer took a craftsman's pride in amplifying the finer points of his trade. What was wrong, he burlesqued in mock dudgeon, with inviting girls to parties, giving them fine presents and paying them properly for their services?

The committee established that on the day Colonel Roosevelt certified that only the Hughes F-11 could meet Air Force requirements, Meyer had launched him on a $1,500 night-clubbing weekend,* and that Hughes interests also paid for Roosevelt's wedding breakfast and honeymoon flight. But Meyer vouchsafed that this was no big deal. Roosevelt, he said, was "only one of a thousand and one" military and

---

*Roosevelt stoutly contested this, testifying he had paid some tabs in Meyer's presence and showed that Meyer had unfairly attributed some expenses to him when he was not present.

government officials he had entertained for Hughes, not one of whom had ever volunteered to pick up a tab "during my entire war."

A commander less perceptive than Brewster would have exulted in such clockwork progress and basked in the daily headlines his blueprint unfailingly produced. But he cautioned intimates that despite the devastating testimony, the atmosphere of rout had not developed.

Refractory elements of the press, Brewster complained, were successfully promoting skepticism about his motives, and many a man in the street seemed perversely to identify with Hughes; the mail showed this, as did the unprecedented clamor from the public to find out when Hughes would testify and how to gain admittance. Brewster was realistic enough to acknowledge what few men would: that he himself was the obstacle, that his credibility was suspect. He foresaw that distrust of him could be promoted by Hughes and his press allies into a stumbling block on which his whole enterprise might fall. Underneath his mousy exterior, Owen Brewster was a gambler, resigned to the taking of risks to gain the ends of power. And so he now announced a renunciation of privilege unknown in the history of Senate investigations.

In the interests of truth and fair play, he said, he would give up his immunities and rights as a senator and committee chairman and take the stand as a "plain citizen" to testify on the Hughes accusations against him and subject himself to interrogation. And he waived his right to examine Hughes. Heretofore an investigating senator could say anything, true or false, with legal impunity and was inviolable to questioning of any kind, from any quarter.

Moreover, Brewster invited the Attorney General, an agent of the Administration he sought to destroy, to investigate Hughes's charges against him. If he had tried to blackmail Hughes, Brewster asked, why had Hughes concealed it for so long, only to allege it now when he needed to divert the public from the facts? Was that the action of a believable man? "One does not wait six months when a blackmail charge is involved."

These were grand gestures, and Brewster now moved to complete the turning of the tables of imagery. The committee unilaterally canceled its previous arrangement with Hughes, under which he was to testify a week hence, and issued a subpoena commanding him to appear at the hearing room within sixteen hours for public testimony. If Hughes appeared, his free ride on the wings of hit-and-run statements was over, and he would be clamped under the crippling restraints of proof, cross-examination, perjury action. If he did not appear—and the man had thus far exhibited an almost pathological reluctance to testify —he would become a fugitive from justice, pursued by federal agents, a sorry contrast to the forthcoming Brewster.

But there was a small-print calculatedness in all that Brewster did, even in his grand gestures, or rather, especially in them. He would testify *after* Hughes, when he would know the extent and the limitations of Hughes's information; he would be questioned only by committee members, who were either indebted friends or colleagues bound by the ancient courtesies and current expediencies, and removing almost the last element of chance, he had entered into an illicit arrangement with a Washington police official to bug the rooms and tap the telephones that Hughes and his entourage would use when they came to Washington.

On the radio, a confident Brewster taunted Hughes to come forward. "I want to see the whites of his lies," he said.

4 · The Summertime of Howard Hughes

"I AM NOT going to be intimidated or made to jump through a hoop."

With these words, and an insistence on the original arrangement that he appear five days hence, Howard Hughes defied the Brewster committee; before its subpoena could be served he went into hiding, an exercise at which he had no peers. At the committee's direction, an army of U.S. marshals was deployed across the West Coast, ordered to hunt Hughes down and bring him to Washington, in handcuffs if necessary.

In a society accustomed to instant, intensive media coverage of celebrities embroiled in public disputes, no recent photo or newsreel spot of Hughes had appeared; his voice had not been heard on the radio; none but insiders knew where he was at any given moment. Advisers cautioned him that he thus played into Brewster's hands; at what cost can the chief officer of four great corporations conduct himself like a fleeing felon? But he replied that the fullness of time was not yet at hand.

When it served his purpose, he materialized briefly to chosen newsmen as a voice on the phone or as a name on the press statements he continued to promulgate from hiding. And in one such dispensation, he explained his rationale to Drew.

We had been right, Hughes said, in counseling a brass-knuckles counterattack on Brewster and Pan American, and in our emphasis on the decisiveness of his personal role. The chief weapon in his arsenal was bound to be his own appearance before the committee, he said. He was gambling everything on it, and all his schemes were orchestrated toward making it a climactic event. Up to a point, the vanishing act should whet the public's appetite for his ultimate appearance without dampening the sympathy that all sources agreed was growing. And it was crucial to the mystique he was developing—of the lone, mysterious hero riding into the lair of devious enemies—that the clowns be cleared from the stage before he made his entrance. Brewster's plan was to trivialize him, he said, by plunking him down at the witness table side by side with the tawdry Meyer, the indiscreet Roosevelt or some garrulous tart from one of his parties.

So he was waiting out the committee. His men were keeping tabs on the subpoenaed showgirls and he would be tipped if any were called. The committee would soon use up Meyer and Roosevelt, for it had to put on its show every day. Hughes did not mention a key motive we learned of later: no one on the committee seemed to have noticed a little technicality—Johnny Meyer's dog-eared subpoena had almost run out. The moment it did, his flight to parts unknown would begin.

And there was yet another reason for delay. While the Brewster committee each day was eliciting testimony that disparaged Hughes's F-11 as a $20 million fiasco born of political favoritism and mismanagement, back in Culver City in a guarded hangar at the Hughes aircraft plant, mechanics and engineers were working nonstop on the plane to get out the last bugs. The Pentagon was now ready to accept delivery. But Hughes calculated that with a few modifications, the F-11 stood a chance of breaking the world's speed record for a cross-the-continent flight. What if he were to make such a flight on his way to testify?

While the mechanics toiled, and Meyer's subpoena ran, Hughes continued to hide out. Instinct told him that the public, which does not like to see the government pushing people around, was tickled by his defiance and the committee's inability to find him. An invisible tide runs in these affairs and Hughes had divined, during his nocturnal perambulations between Los Angeles and Las Vegas, that it had stopped running against him and was almost ready to turn.

I remember a morning when a ripple of excitement went through the capital city as the Washington *Post* placarded: HUGHES PLANS RECORD-MAKING TRIP TO HEARING IN CONTROVERSIAL PLANE.

A furor ensued, which further dramatized Hughes's coming. The Army Air Force, which was at long last about to take possession of the F-11, protested the plane-endangering flight. When the government's contract with Hughes was reviewed, it showed that Hughes, who was as much the wizard at contract drafting as at plane designing, had complete control of the craft and could test it in any way he chose. But with uncharacteristic affability, Hughes bowed to the Air Force. "Too much taxpayers' money has already been wasted on promoting these hearings," he said.

It was my private theory that Hughes, deciding that the plane wasn't ready, after all, for a record attempt, leaked out the story of his flight plans in order to provoke the Air Force protest he was sure would come; then he magnanimously relented, leaving the impression that, but for governmental jitters, the F-11 could have done it.

In any event, the dispute gave his entrance almost as much drama as a record flight would have. He announced he would wing to Washington in his converted B-32 bomber. At appropriate stages of his flight, the wire services flashed press and radio bulletins of his progress. Thus, to the consternation of committee Republicans, he arrived in Washington not as a shady suspect under subpoena, but as a figure of excitement and mystery, a lone eagle, come in the folk-hero tradition.

On the evening of Hughes's arrival I was invited to confer with him in his hideaway suite in the Carlton Hotel. I drove toward the hotel aquiver with expectations both innocent and concupiscent. To sit down with the great man as a counselor on the eve of mortal combat, to add my footnote to the drama of state that would open on the following day were exciting ego-puffing prospects for a novice reporter. And I was not unmindful of all those stories about the party girls who surrounded Hughes. I entered the Hughes suite, erect and grave as one conscious that he walks upon the stage of history, yet casting furtive glances in search of voluptuous shapes reclining in wanton attitudes. Alas, there were none—only an aide in business suit scurrying about as if under great pressure.

Hughes soon emerged briskly from his inner sanctum, tall, lean, dark, a bit heavy-lidded. After a terse greeting he led me back to his room and motioned me to a chair. The unspoken relationship between us was that of allies, co-conspirators, rather than reporter and subject. He handed me a folder that contained the most recent gleanings of his intelligence operation, and I passed on whatever my recent scrounging among Senate sources had turned up—that Brewster, for instance, was planning to have Meyer recalled after Hughes began testifying. I again pressed my view that a combative strategy would be best.

Hughes ingested all I had to say as if a mechanical monitor were measuring it against other input of a confirming or conflicting nature and making the necessary adjustments. Of all the prominent figures I have observed since then, only John F. Kennedy equaled Hughes in his quick and incisive grasp. But Hughes was a distracting listener, alternately brooding and fidgeting, hitching up his socks, drumming his long fingers on the armrests of his chair. I recall most of all the pressure of his searching gaze—dark eyes that were sharp but cold, seeming to lack the faintest sparkle of frivolity.

He discussed concisely the origins of his troubles with the government, using me, I thought, as a sounding board for some of the testimony he planned. He mentioned his early achievements in aviation and complained how, despite them, he found door after door closed by those who seemed to instinctively fear and resist him as a difficult loner, an outsider.

After his 1937 record-breaking transcontinental flight in a plane he had designed and built—and which *Jane's Fighting Ships* judged "the fastest and most efficient plane in the world"—Hughes had submitted the plans to the Army, confident he was presenting a sudden opportunity for air supremacy to a disarmed nation.

"They turned it down," said Hughes, suddenly animated, as though still incredulous over a shock he had lived with for ten years. "They said they couldn't use a cantilever type plane. Nowadays that's all they do use." The Japanese eventually learned enough about the plans, Hughes said, to develop the Zero from them. He had swallowed his resentment and had designed a two-engine pursuit ship, then a novel concept.

"The Army made me wait four months for a decision while Lockheed was preparing a competitive design. By a strange coincidence, Lockheed turned up with a two-engine design like mine, and the Army took theirs. It became the P-38 and it made Lockheed what it is today."

His penchant for secrecy became an obsession, one he pounded into his subordinates, with sometimes adverse consequences. One day when Hughes was away, an Air Corps general arrived unannounced at the Hughes plant to examine his latest project. Hughes's aides refused to unlock the hangar for him, leaving him red with rage and thenceforth implacable in his hostility. "When they turned down my two-engined pursuit job, I backed into my shell and determined to build, with my own money, a plane so sensational they couldn't turn it down."

An enigma surfaced here—a love-hate relationship; Hughes was patriotic, after his fashion. He regarded himself as a valuable national resource, but one that was underutilized due to the obstructionism of nonentities. To the extent that the U.S. government was a symbol and representative of America, he revered it and ardently wished to serve it. And he was wedded to it by less idealistic bonds: only a great government could use and afford projects of the magnitude that particularly fevered the Hughes imagination. But "the government" as a flesh-and-blood organization seemed quite another matter—a great blob seething with chicaneries, bogged down in trivia, lacking elementary perception, coveting small graft and large attentions—a sorry Balkanization he scorned and distrusted.

He responded to the bureaucratic freeze-out in a way congenial to him—by designing structures that would overcome governmental resistance without unduly discommoding his schedule. He developed bridges that spanned the bureaucracy, such as Jesse Jones. And he established an apparatus calculated to sate the appetites of officialdom —psychic, culinary and libidinous. To run it, Hughes said, "I brought Johnny Meyer over from my movie operation—to be a company gladhander, entertain visiting nabobs, and so on. I didn't bother with that sort of thing . . . I had too many important things to attend to."

Meyer had humanized Hughes's forbidding image. "Don't underestimate Johnny Meyer," said Hughes. "Did you know that he soon made himself welcome at Hyde Park and at the White House?"

He detested the lobbying tactics he had to stoop to, he said, but he had been driven to regard them as the tariff charged for doing business with the government. "Before Meyer started operating, I couldn't get to first base with the Army . . . Noah Dietrich will testify that General Echols told him personally he would do no business with me—because of personal dislike. Think of it—in the middle of a war, with my plant idle! Why? I didn't extend the hospitality they got from the other companies."

When he did get contracts by going over and around the military bureaucrats, they retaliated by denying him material allocations.

"I wound up in the tightest part of the war with two plane contracts and no priorities. Under those circumstances I couldn't deliver, and no one else could have. You heard Kaiser on the stand, didn't you? He said it was 'a beautiful frame-up' to kill the Hercules [the wooden flying boat] program. And it succeeded."

Both aircraft were now almost completed and ready for delivery,

Hughes said. "The Army wants to take delivery of the F-11 right now, and if the Hercules doesn't fly within ninety days, you have my word that I'll leave the country and never come back."

Hughes was on his feet, his willowy figure pacing the room. He defended the terms of his contracts, pointing out that neither was on a cost-plus basis under which the government pays for mistakes or mis-estimates. "I take the loss," he said. "The only thing I've been tough about has been the question of control—control of how my creations are designed, built and tested. That used to be called artistic integrity, but now they paint it as shysterism."

There was a black edge to his combativeness. "I've seen the seamy side before, a lot of it, but until now I didn't think it was possible that Americans in high office would try to destroy me or any other man just for politics, just for contracts and air routes. And if someone did try, I didn't believe our system would permit it to happen. But it does permit it. However things come out this week, I'll never be able to think of this country in the same way again."

I did not then try to reconcile the two sides of Howard Hughes— the cool suborner of officials who could talk so movingly of the American way, of disillusion, even of despair, while at the same time stalking his foes with almost every weapon that money, stealth and ruthlessness could command. Over the years, as his tendencies toward withdrawal, secretiveness and remote manipulation of politicians grew to ultimate proportions, I would think back on this night, reflecting what a fearful thing it is to strip away the remaining illusions from an iron-willed genius who precariously, like Janus, faces toward both idealism and cynicism, service and rejection.

But at that moment in the Carlton Hotel, I felt only a surging excitement at what I thought I saw—this reclusive and autocratic man in the process of rising up out of himself to tomorrow's occasion that would demand of him everything he instinctively resisted and despised: to come out of his eerily controlled world; to put himself on public dispay; to swap harangues with politicians, to ham it up and demagogue it in the manner of those he disdained; to personally woo his fellow-men after he thought he had risen beyond their claims on him.

"Apparently the entrance is about to be made." Sarcasm curled the voice of the temporary chairman, Homer Ferguson, as he reassured the apprehensive multitude that the star witness would show, after all. Three quarters of an hour before, the grand inquisitors of the Senate, armed with the combined powers of prosecutor, judge and jury, had entered the packed Caucus Room and had taken their seats on the dais, their bearing full of the aplomb of men who move familiarly in a world of marble floors, lofty ceilings and massive cut-glass chandeliers that on quieter days could be heard to tinkle exotically.

On the Republican side of the long mahogany table sat five of the most aggressive partisan investigators ever to arraign a malefactor in the Senate: Owen Brewster, Homer Ferguson, Harry Cain, John Williams and Joseph McCarthy. On the Democratic side, only the flamboyant Claude Pepper was their match, the rest—Carl Hatch, Herbert O'Connor, J. Howard McGrath—were breeze-testers of a more cautious demeanor. The senators looked out upon an empty chair where Howard Hughes was supposed to be and upon fifteen hundred sweltering spectators who jammed the place to the window sills, ringing the walls three-deep with standees. For them, and for the record turnout of reporters present, Ferguson's announcement recharged the wilting mood of high anticipation.

Hughes's tardiness seemed to me part of the psychological warfare by which he had from the beginning sought to even the odds. Each passing moment of affront reduced the magisteriality of the tribunal even as it magnified the importance of the accused. For almost an hour all necks had intermittently craned toward the entrance, and by now it was manifest that Howard Hughes was the attraction for whom the throng had braved the stupefying heat of a Washington August, the prize for whom the unlit klieg lights waited, and the six motion-picture cameras, and the unfamiliar apparatus that would for the first time televise a Senate hearing—to five thousand pioneer viewers in Washington and New York.

From the great oaken doors of the Caucus Room, a line of those hopeful of gaining admittance stretched along a long corridor, down a winding marble staircase worn at the middle of each step by the tread of millions of feet, across a rotunda and out into the street. Applause could now be heard rippling toward us along that line, growing ever louder until in a contagious instant it swept across the Caucus Room as Hughes entered. His floodlit head, surprisingly youthful and agreeable for the sins it reputedly bore, towered above the surrounding policemen who held back the crush of admirers and cleared a path for him to the witness chair. He waved acknowledgment while averting his face from the crowd, as though determined to play his role but wincing at the prospect.

However friendly the momentary sentiment of transient spectators, however artfully Hughes had thus far manipulated public opinion, he was at last where Brewster wanted him—alone in the witness chair, delivered up to his enemies, in constant jeopardy. This was the bullring era of congressional investigations, and the witness was the bull, foredoomed to destruction by an almost ineluctable process. On the other side of the Capitol the butcheries of the House Un-American Activities Committee were then at their goriest, under Chairman J. Parnell Thomas. During the previous month or so, a herd of Hollywood screenwriters, accused of no crimes but burdened with left-wing associations, had been pushed one by one into the arena, under the same cameras that rolled now, and cut down by the swords of pear-shaped matadors who ran no risks. The same process was incubating in the Senate and would shortly become personified in one of the Brewster committee members who now stared down appraisingly at Hughes—Republican Senator Joseph R. McCarthy of Wisconsin.

The rules under which the Red hunters and crime busters of the late forties and early fifties would flourish were already well entrenched when Howard Hughes was administered the oath by the handsome young committee counsel, William P. Rogers, later to become Attorney General and Secretary of State. As long as Hughes sat in the Senate Caucus Room, his rights as an American were in suspension. The lawyer at his side could play no role beyond advising him on whether to take the Fifth Amendment—no alternative at all for an executive upon whose credibility rode vast government and corporate enterprises. His other choices, once the questions started coming, were rather grim, assuming that the documents piled in front of Rogers contained even a modicum of culpable behavior on Hughes's part. If he told the truth, he might indict himself; if he remained silent, he could be prosecuted for contempt of Congress; if he dissembled, he could be jailed for perjury.

Nor were any of the standard protections of Anglo-American jurisprudence available to the witness. No formal indictment or bill of particulars limited the field the senators could gallop in. No rule of germaneness, no requirement that a proper legal foundation be laid shielded him from fishing expeditions into any aspect of his life. No innuendo or fabrication, however preposterous, could be stricken from the record—for the cameras and microphones that would be banned from a courtroom transmitted instant records that were ineradicable. The witness could not in any systematic way refute what was alleged, for he could neither cross-examine those who testified against him nor bring forward his own witnesses to present his side. Even the tradition of solemnity and decorum that assures the courtroom defendant an unharassed opportunity to marshal his thoughts was absent here. The witness sat in an arena atmosphere, complete with cheers and boos, under the punishing glare of klieg lights, exposed to the random approach of any onlooker or reporter; a decade before, in the very spot where Hughes now sat, an impudent photographer had stripped the legendary financier J. Pierpont Morgan of his shield against the world —his austere air of gravity—by thrusting a circus midget on his lap while flash bulbs popped for the gratification of the nation's egalitarians.

But Hughes carried invisible extralegal armament, and his consciousness of it made him appear miscast in his assigned role of victim. He had entered the room with the demeanor of one who had come to even scores, and as he settled grimly into his chair he fixed upon the tribunal a black look, a stare of long-simmering anger. A senator seeing that look might begin to question the notion that Hughes was a dismissible playboy, might be moved to assay the possible cost of making an enemy of this "eccentric" magnate who controlled $150 million.

In his right hand Hughes held an apparatus by which a hearing aid was wired into the loudspeaker system—a device he would characteristically use to tune out as well as tune in the committee—and now he held it to his ear and nodded to the committee that he was ready to proceed.

A hush fell over the great room as all strained for Hughes's words: "I have made certain accusations to the press. I stand on them. Senator Brewster, I understand, has said he would like to hear me repeat them under oath. I think Senator Brewster should take the stand. Allow me to cross-examine him and bring in witnesses."

Hughes spoke in an authoritative, matter-of-fact tone as if unaware he was demanding the instant repeal of a century of Senate procedure. When the chairman hesitated and began to confer with colleagues instead of promptly ruling Hughes out of order, I recalled Drew's words: "They look invincible up on their rostrum, but with all their powers they are still just worried politicians in a free country. When the public is really watching them, they don't dare turn down a challenge to be fair."

Ferguson ruled: "The subcommittee won't let Senator Brewster cross-examine you or let you cross-examine him. You and the Senator may each submit written questions to this committee. The subcommittee feels that Senator Brewster should have only the same privileges that you have."

"And I want only the same privileges as the committee," responded Hughes. "Any questioning of me by the committee is itself in the nature of cross-examination, if it's unfriendly." He repeated his demand to interrogate Brewster and asked: "Will I have the right to call other witnesses?"

"We will rule on that when you request witnesses," Ferguson answered, obviously on the defensive.

Having dramatized his complaints and brought the committee to the edge of a partial surrender of control over the hearings, Hughes agreed to proceed with his statement. His opening salvo made it clear he was taking the position that he was there to *make* charges, not answer them.

"I charge specifically," he said, "that during luncheon at the Mayflower Hotel in Washington in the week beginning on February 10, 1947, in the suite of Senator Brewster, that the Senator told me in so many words that if I would agree to merge TWA with Pan Am and would go along with his community airline bill, there would be no further hearing in the matter." And then he sat back as though he had said all there was to say.

"Proceed," directed the chairman.

"I've made my statement," said Hughes. "I told you what took place."

"Is there anything else you wish to discuss?"

"No. I thought Senator Brewster would want to talk after that."

I was sure Ferguson would pointedly ignore Hughes's attempt to dictate committee priorities. He could not permit the first day of the Hughes testimony, the most formative day as far as molding public opinion was concerned, to yield up the impression that Brewster, not Hughes, was the defendant. He could not permit Hughes to establish, procedurally and in the public mind, that this was a dispute between Brewster and Hughes rather than an examination by the Senate into influence peddling, waste of public monies and nonperformance on contracts by Hughes. This was the day, above all days, when they had to force some admissions from Hughes. Surely Ferguson would launch into the examination which the committee had been preparing for months. But instead he turned to Brewster and asked, "Would the Senator like to testify?"

In such a situation, the demands of political *machismo* left Brewster no choice. "I certainly would," he declared emphatically, and he came down from the committee bench to take the witness chair as Hughes vacated it—a symbolic turnabout.

Brewster wore a dark pin-stripe suit and the mien of a confident, reasonable man; he was appearing before friends, on a familiar battle-ground, doing what he did best. Quickly he traced his version of the investigation. Suspicion about the Hughes contracts, he said, had first arisen during the days when Senator Harry Truman was chairman. Information was then collected. The committee had been patient, giving the contracts time to be vindicated. They had not been, Brewster said. The issue of these hearings, from which they must not be diverted, was nothing but this: "Why, two years after war's end, had not the government gotten anything out of the eighteen million dollars invested in the cargo plane, and only one usable aircraft for the twenty-two million dollars poured into the reconnaissance plane?"

Brewster turned to the Hughes charges against him. It was not he but Hughes who had suggested that Brewster fly on the Hughes plane, Brewster said. It was Hughes, not he, who had raised the questions of TWA merging with Pan Am and of TWA supporting the "consolidation bill." Brewster had first met Hughes only two days before the alleged blackmail threat was made, when Hughes came to Washington to appear before the committee in executive session.

"It is inconceivable to me," Brewster said, "that anyone would seriously contemplate that anyone who has been in public life as long as I have—in the state legislature, as governor, in the House and Senate —could, on such short acquaintance and in one short meeting, make so bald a proposition as he describes. It sounds a little more like Hollywood than Washington. No one of any competence or experience could make such a proposition. I can assure you I never did."

Brewster was scoring, I thought. It *did* seem unlikely that a cagey old survivor would, at a first private meeting, make a bribe offer to a dangerous stranger like Hughes. The Maine senator now rose to what was for him a peak of emotion as, his resonant voice thick with resentment, he told a tale of seeming treachery.

Not long after Brewster had revived the Hughes inquiry, he received a strange visit from Hugh Fulton, the just departed chief counsel of the Senate War Investigating Committee. Fulton had run the committee staff from the Truman years until the Republicans had taken over the committee and had installed their own man, George Meader, as chief counsel. Fulton raised the question of the Hughes probe, Brewster testified, and told him to beware of it because it might turn out to be "a hot potato . . . that I might regret." Smelling a rat, Brewster called in his secretary so she could take down his reply to Fulton (such preposterous scenes were sometimes necessary in the days before hidden tape recorders). Nothing would induce him, Brewster told Fulton, to stray from his duty.

Fulton withdrew, but two weeks later he was back, this time to talk to Meader. Fulton was now working for Howard Hughes, he jauntily announced; moreover, the former assistant counsel for the committee, Rudolph Halley, was now working for Hughes too! (The passage of thirty years has not dimmed for me the brazen audacity of that act by Hughes; it was almost as though Richard Nixon, just before the impeachment hearings, had hired John Doar and Albert Jenner as his lawyers).*

Brewster continued his story: Fulton told Meader that if Brewster was to bring his investigation of Hughes to a showdown, Fulton and Halley would be in it on Hughes's side . . . "with brickbats flying." There was only one way to interpret this, Brewster felt. Fulton was threatening to use against the committee and himself all the confidential, embarrassing information an insider could pick up over a period of years. Fulton then advised Meader not to use his prerogative as chief counsel to advise the committee as to whether the Hughes probe should be proceeded with; stay out of it, Fulton continued; leave the initiative to Brewster. (Apparently Fulton had been unimpressed with Brewster's little lecture to him and the stenographer, and had assumed that, gestures aside, his "hot potato" message to Brewster would prove sufficient.)

"That reveals pretty clearly that they were seeking to lay a trap for me," Brewster said, his voice breaking. He stopped for a moment, seemingly fighting off tears, then continued, "I promptly appointed a subcommittee headed by Senator Ferguson to handle this matter and let the chips fall where they may. I cannot and will not yield to a campaign of this character."

As Brewster concluded his statement, the Senate tribunal showed seven faces that were studies in sympathy, or at least six; Pepper's

---

*Fulton defended the switch quite arrestingly: an investigating committee, he pointed out, is supposed to be an impartial fact-finding body, not a legal adversary; therefore the conflict of interest question could not arise, since the committee's only legitimate interest was in finding the truth.

lineaments, behind the cover of his great bulbous nose, were unreadable. Hughes, who had taken up position in the press row behind Brewster, where he loomed above the scribbling reporters like a dark cloud, would regularly shake his head as Brewster recounted his version of events, and on occasion, would snort disbelievingly as though Brewster had exceeded the limits of falsehood allowed even a senator.

A brief and circumspect questioning of Brewster by Chairman Ferguson reinforced Brewster's contradictions of Hughes's testimony. Ferguson turned to Hughes and asked him if he had any questions.

"Between two hundred and five hundred questions, just about."

"Then put them in writing and I'll ask them tomorrow," Ferguson replied, and gaveled the hearing into recess.

That night I again called on Hughes in his hotel suite and found him satisfied with his day and impatient for the morrow. He was pleased with the lionizing sentiment of the spectators, and he noted the caution with which the senators treated him. These were evidences that our strategy was working, we agreed. He had the feel of things now, and his native contempt for politicians was enhanced by the ease with which he was beating them at their own game. Tomorrow he would step up the pressure, whip up the crowd more, rip into the committee more aggressively.

So it was that on the following morning Hughes returned to his attack on Brewster and the committee leadership with an enhanced truculence. His theme of the day was: "Senator Brewster's story of yesterday is a pack of lies. I can tear it apart if given the opportunity."

He demanded that opportunity repeatedly, drawing applause from the spectators; Chairman Ferguson repeatedly refused. Hughes and his staff had overnight submitted written questions, which, in accordance with the procedure established as a concession to Hughes, were now to be asked of Brewster by the chairman. But Hughes now attacked the procedure, reasserting his right to personally conduct the cross-examination and charging the committee with having slipped his questions to Brewster in advance of the hearing.

"You told me yesterday that I would be allowed the same privileges as Senator Brewster. Are you now prepared to hand to me in advance the questions that your men on the committee are going to ask me?"

When Ferguson demurred, the crowd hissed. Hughes, looking up into the jaws of his judges, pressed his attack on them. The committee, he charged, had mysteriously dropped an investigation into a wartime Pan Am contract for a photo-reconnaissance plane, the F-12—the performance of which was "less fortunate" than with his own F-11; how could they explain this? Why had not the committee followed its staff recommendation to investigate the profiteering arrangements made by Pan American with the government for building South American airfields during the war?

"Where did you get this information?" snapped Ferguson.

"I obtained it from Mr. Fulton. I believe it was under his jurisdiction when he was with the committee."*

With this committee-sobering testament to the authenticity of his data, Hughes returned to the attack. How could they explain why the investigation of him, after laying dormant for years, had been "suddenly reactivated" when Brewster became chairman, after the TWA–Pan Am merger had been rejected, and after the rejection of Brewster's proposition to him? "There's too much coincidence in all this," he thundered. And again the crowd applauded.

From attack, Hughes went to ridicule. Pan Am President Juan Trippe always spoke of Brewster "as though he worked for him." Hughes challenged the senator to repeat under oath that morning the statement he had made to the press a week before about Harriet Applewick, saying he had affidavits which would prove Brewster had lied.

Chairman Ferguson, a former judge and prosecutor, presumably had experience in putting down an unruly witness, but he seemed unhinged by Hughes, as though he were staring into the mouth of an erupting volcano. He invited Senator Brewster to return to the stand and began to put to him the written questions of Hughes in a listless, deferential manner, stressing several times to Brewster that the questions were not his but Hughes's.

Q: Is it true that you are a close personal friend of Sam Pryor [the Pan Am vice president]?
A: It certainly is. We have a close and very gratifying personal relationship.
Q: Have you ever accepted free airplane trips on Pan Am's special private airplane?
A: I have.
Q: Did you ever accept transportation to Raleigh, North Carolina?
A: I did.

*Fulton, responding to criticism for providing Hughes with "confidential information" was equal to the task. "What's confidential," he said, "about the fact that Pan Am held up the United States in its hour of extremity?"

Q: What was the purpose of your business there?

A: I went down to confer with Senator Bailey [then the Commerce Committee chairman] about the Community Airline Bill.

In similarly laconic fashion Brewster admitted to having a social relationship with Juan Trippe; to having accepted small gifts from Pan Am personnel; to having been flown to Florida on Pan Am's plane; to having twice vacationed at Pryor's retreat at Hobe Sound.

Brewster would put the most natural face possible on his receipt of favors from Pan Am, minimizing their value and frequency and attributing them to personal friendships that had nothing to do with politics, investigations or legislation, whereupon Ferguson would go on to the next written question without probing the implications of the previous answer.

Even so, I thought, the answers were damaging to Brewster and the committee leadership. Hughes's network of private eyes, former Brewster menials and ex-committee lawyers had done its work. Here was Brewster, the instigator of the Hughes investigation, confirming a series of cozy relationships with the entity that stood to gain the most from Hughes's disgrace. Here was the sponsor of legislation that would, in effect, give Pan Am a world-wide air monopoly, enforced and subsidized by the United States, admitting to being flown about by Pan Am on a lobbying mission for that bill. It did not matter that the known favors were modest; the news leads for the day were bound to read: "Brewster admits taking favors from Pan Am."

But with the true warrior's striving for overkill, Hughes was dissatisfied, or at least he feigned dissatisfaction. Repeatedly he broke in to upbraid Ferguson for failing to follow up Brewster's admissions with sharp interrogation. Taking their cue from Hughes, the spectators became increasingly demonstrative, cheering Hughes's sallies, hissing or booing at Ferguson's refusals to turn the questioning over to Hughes —demonstrations which Hughes encouraged by turning to the crowd and saying, "I want to say I thank you people who want to see fair play in this hearing."

At one point a red-faced Ferguson ordered the room cleared of demonstrators.

"Who is to be removed?" asked the police squad leader.

"Whoever demonstrated," said Ferguson.

"Well, Senator, I guess that's everybody," responded the cop.

The police laid hands on the nearest bodies, whereupon a melee broke out as spectators rallied to the defense of their fellows. Above the tumult the voice of a young college student rang out: "I speak for the audience. We will be quiet. As American citizens we would like to hear this because—"

Guards pounced on the student. Ferguson surveyed the mounting chaos, and perhaps anticipating the predictable press coverage should he ban the public, suffered a failure of nerve. "Don't put him out," Ferguson ordered. The general eviction order was withdrawn and quiet was restored.

When Ferguson asked Hughes if he had any more written questions, Hughes announced a boycott of the procedure: "I have other questions, but there is no use submitting them in this manner. Brewster's answers have been evasive and in many cases he gave no direct answers at all. He was never challenged. I shan't submit any further questions in this way." So ended the first phase of the duel Hughes had derailed into what the New York *Times* called "a kind of forum and under circumstances without known parallel in American history." The committee had been glimpsed in futile disarray, while an artful bit of Hughes imagery, in his morning statement, had caught the media fancy.

"One of us must be telling something here which is not the truth," he began. "Nobody kicks around in this country without acquiring a reputation, good or bad . . . I may be a little unkind in what I have to say . . . Brewster has been described to me as clever, resourceful, a terrific public speaker, able to hold an audience in the palm of his hand, one of the great trick-shot artists in Washington.

"I am supposed to be capricious; I have been called a playboy; I have been termed eccentric. But I don't believe I have the reputation of being a liar. For twenty-three years nobody has questioned my word. I think my reputation in that respect meets what most Texans consider important."

For the committee majority, the probe stood at a critical juncture. Brewster had been compelled to lend himself to Hughes's characterization by admitting he could not substantiate his charge regarding Harriet Applewick, and by withdrawing it under Hughes's challenge. The Republican committee members, plainly disturbed at the tide of events, bored in now in an attempt to dissipate the aura of authority and forthrightness that had enabled Hughes to dominate the hearings. Why, he was asked, if his story of Brewster's blackmail attempt was true, had he not reported Brewster to the authorities immediately? Why had he gone along for a time with the alleged blackmail?

"I don't know that anyone who gives in to blackmail is guilty of anything in thus eliminating what is an illegal threat to him."

Why did he bring it up now then?

"Because I have nothing to lose now. My reputation has already been ruined. I might as well lay my cards on the table."

What did he have to say to the charge of the Army colonel who testified that Hughes's cargo-plane performance was negligent, that in four years at the airplane plant, the colonel saw Hughes only once?

"I can only tell you that I designed every nut and bolt that went into this airplane. I designed this ship to a greater degree than any one man has ever personally designed any of the recent large airplanes . . . I worked eighteen to twenty hours a day for six months to a year on this plane. And with my other work on the XF-11 and other war work, my health was so broken down that I was sent away for a rest of seven months after the war ended . . ."

Almost always the answers came like a rifle shot, usually with a vehement ring of truth, often with an eloquence that put a period on the subject. Ferguson at one point said to Hughes, "You're a hard man to be nice to." What he probably meant was that Hughes was a hard man to confound; and by these men, during this week, he was not to be confounded.

Even the most promising of the committee approaches—the exploitation of Johnny Meyer—turned into a demonstration of the committee's futility. The time came for the recall of Meyer to share the witness stand with Hughes. But Meyer was nowhere to be found. Unwatched, his subpoena had expired, and the moment it did he had disappeared.

"Do you know where Johnny Meyers is?" a bristling Ferguson demanded of Hughes.

"Do you mean Johnny Meyer?"

"Meyer or Meyers, where is he?"

"I don't know."

"Well, he was supposed to be here but I'm informed he cannot be located."

Laughter swept the Caucus Room.

"This is nothing to laugh about," shouted Ferguson, the strain apparently beginning to tell on him.

"Somebody laughed behind me," said Hughes, relaxed and smiling a mocking smile.

"You laughed, too!"

"Laughter is contagious."

Ferguson continued to press. "He is in your employ. You knew we hadn't finished with him."

"I have twenty-eight thousand employees, and I can't know where all of them are all of the time."

"Will you see that he is here at two P.M.?" Ferguson demanded.

Hughes sat silent for a moment; then, confident of his ascendancy, he answered with cold insolence, "No, I don't know that I will. Just to put him up here on the stand beside me and make a publicity show. My company has been inconvenienced just about enough . . ."

Ferguson warned Hughes he was on the edge of contempt of Congress. "Will you bring Mr. Meyer in here at two P.M.?"

Hughes called his bluff. "No. No, I don't think I will."

The two glared at each other. Ferguson ordered that another subpoena immediately be served on Meyer—if he could be found.

There had been a moment when Chairman Ferguson almost recaptured the initiative and control that had unaccountably been snatched from the committee. Accusing Hughes of manufacturing the "Brewster-Hughes controversy" in order to keep his contracts from being brought before the public, Ferguson had argued that the issue was one of equal justice against the power of wealth, public order against anarchy.

"What you are doing here clearly indicates that you are trying to discredit this committee so that it cannot properly perform its functions. The integrity of the United States Senate is at stake. I speak for the Senate. If you believe that because of your great wealth and access to certain publicity channels you can intimidate any member of the committee, you are mistaken—and that's final."

For the first time, the applause went to Ferguson. It was a moment when the pendulum might have swung. But before Ferguson and his allies could wrap themselves too snugly in the institutional pride and solidarity of the Senate, the alert, irreverent Pepper punctured the spell by asserting that Ferguson did *not* speak for the Senate, not even for the Democratic senators on the committee. "You've been carrying that speech around in your pocket since yesterday, Homer, waiting for an excuse to make it."

The breakup had begun. The Democrats, looking for respectable reasons to defect, had found them in Hughes's striking performance, Brewster's several admissions and Ferguson's ineptness in the chair.

The network radio news shows reflected the degree to which Hughes had turned the hearings on their head. The instigator of it all, Senator Brewster, had begun to assume the aspect of a helpless victim, complaining in an interview that Hughes "has set out to destroy my usefulness as chairman of the Senate War Investigating Committee and as a member of the Senate Interstate Commerce Committee."

The respected ABC commentator Erwin D. Canham warned that in two days Hughes had brought the committee to the brink of destruction: "Rarely, indeed, has a witness been able to put a Senate committee member on the defensive. Rarely has a witness talked back, or asked questions back. But that is what happened today and yesterday in Washington . . . The institution of Senatorial inquiry hangs in the balance and needs to be rescued." Canham urged the committee to broaden its probe to include other companies and other individuals. It must reform its conduct and show that it could act "judicially, impartially, non-politically" in order to "save itself and the useful institution of Senate inquiry."

A spate of newspaper editorials echoed Canham's concern. But the committee was not to save itself. The astonishing turnabout in the roles of victim and executioner only grew more apparent. Each morning Hughes would appear in the crowded Caucus Room, buoyed by the applause from the constant line that now extended through three long corridors. Each day the senators more and more resembled straight men—listless foes who despaired of the battle but knew not how to end it, covert allies who now floated sweetheart questions.

Always the audience hung on his words, words I had heard before—about his trail-blazing planes of the past; about the Jap Zero and the P-38; about how he persisted in pressing new ideas on the brass "because I wanted to design and build something for the Army. I wanted to contribute something"; about how the bureaucrats cut off his materials; about how, aside from the two contracts in question, the Hughes enterprises had delivered $200 million worth of material to the war effort while making a lower profit than before the war or now.

When he talked of his creations, as Claude Pepper encouraged him to do, it was a suddenly different Hughes speaking. The scales of bitterness had fallen from his eyes. At one point he described his great Hercules as it then stood at the Culver City plant, ready to be tested, in that relative infancy of the air age: "Imagine . . . an airplane five stories high, longer than a city block, with a wingspread of 310 feet, a wing area three times that of any plane ever built . . . a plane that weighs 200 tons, with eight engines, each of 3,000 horsepower . . . with controls so complicated that, for the first time, human hands cannot control them . . ."

He had designed electrically powered controls that made the advent of such giants of the air possible, had grappled as no one had before him with the question of the "size barrier" in aircraft—the maximum possible size at which it is practicable to build a plane. He promised that the plane would fly, but even as it stood, he said, the research breakthroughs and what they meant to the future of aviation already dwarfed any money the government had spent or that he had spent.

It was this Hughes—the Hughes of vision and risk—that had gotten through to the public, something transmitted in his appearance and demeanor, conveyed not only through his natural mastery of imagery, but through the basic facts of his life. He was seen, as he had planned to be seen, as a genuine protagonist being harassed by a bunch of corporate and political trimmers and potbellies. As columnist Marquis Childs put it: "The contrast between Hughes and the Senators could hardly be sharper. It is youth vs. age. Hughes stands for new ideas, for experiment, adventure. He has repeatedly risked his life in testing his own ideas."

His Senate opponents were men less inclined to taking risks than to cutting losses. And so the morning came when Hughes arrived for his day on the stand, a 400-page statement under his arm. But there were no senators, for the hearings had abruptly been canceled at a midnight meeting. Two official reasons were given for scuttling them: the inability to locate Johnny Meyer, and unidentified demands on the senators' time.

Ferguson would that day enter Bethesda Naval Hospital, ostensibly for treatment of "piles." Brewster was already on his way to Dexter, Maine, and in an interview en route, he extended half an olive branch. Hughes had not intended to defraud the government, Brewster granted, but he had "unwittingly cost his country millions" because of a "mania for perfection." Hughes, said the fleeing senator, was "a sort of mad genius, an insane perfectionist, a potential Michelangelo in his field."

A sense of shock pervaded the Caucus Room. Veteran reporters could recall no precedent for a Senate cave-in of this kind, with so much unresolved. For a while Hughes sat in his witness chair, symbolically posed, staring at the empty chairs of the tribunal. Then to the reporters and admirers who crowded in on him, he gave a final abrasive statement:

"It was obvious from the time I first walked into this room that the public and the press were on my side. As soon as Brewster saw he was fighting a losing battle against public opinion he folded up and took a run-out powder . . . There was no reason for the other Senators on the committee to stay here and fight his battle for him if he was too cowardly to face the music."

His exit from the Caucus Room was barred by a cheering horde of autograph seekers whom he forbearingly indulged for the last time. When he finally reached the street where his limousine waited, the windows of the Senate Office Building above were crowded with waving spectators.

He climbed into his limousine, which glided off and swiftly receded down Constitution Avenue.

Eleven weeks later, on November 2, 1947, Hughes piloted the giant Hercules at Long Beach, California. It rose a short ways above the water and flew across the bay, astonishing onlookers with its size, which dwarfed anything ever before seen in the air (its wingspan was 60 percent greater than today's Boeing 747). After flying for a short distance, Hughes brought the plane down. It was returned to its hangar, where it would be kept in secret, lacquered splendor until the death of its creator three decades later.

Like the reserved gentleman he was in his private capacity, Drew Pearson did not put on display the alternating elation and anguish that is the lot of the perpetual aggressor in a lifelong war of many fronts. But for a while after the Brewster debacle, his enigmatic features betrayed an only partly concealed air of delight. Those on his staff noticed it in his inward half-smile as he passed preoccupied through our rooms, in the ruminative chuckle that now and then reached us from behind the door of his sanctum, and in the fragments of badinage we overheard while standing before his desk as congratulatory telephone calls came in.

But there was one drop of wormwood in the cup of celebration. Had Senator Brewster been close to an election, the odium that now attached to him might have been insurmountable, even for the leader of the one political party in a one-party state. But in fact he had five years to serve before again facing the voters—plenty of time for even the most acute embarrassment to dissipate and become blurred in the mists of the ill-remembered past.

In the years that followed, Brewster acted as one determined to keep a low profile, and above all, to avoid any activity that might recall to public mind his embarrassment. When, three months after its helter-skelter flight from the Hughes hearings, the Brewster committee reassembled to give that inquiry a brief formal burial, Brewster was safely in Europe. And for eons thereafter, he walked softly and spoke amiably. He shelved the series of investigations with which he had once planned to harry the Democrats right up to the 1948 presidential election; his stellar vehicle, the Senate War Investigating Committee, fell dormant and was in time disbanded.

But Pearson, who well knew how politicians count on the short memory of the public and who therefore conducted his adversary campaigns in terms of decades, was bound that when Brewster came up for re-election in distant 1952, his ignominy should still be fresh and green.

We were directed to keep a sharp eye at all the usually productive keyholes. Bombshells were not required; anything reasonably grubby would serve to perpetuate Brewster's murky image, but for the longest time luck withheld from us even its smallest favor. We would develop an entrée to closed-door hearings at which Brewster presided, only to learn that he was leaning over backwards to be fair. We would open up an inside line on the conduct of a group of junketeering senators that included Brewster, only to find that while colleagues were succumbing to the temptations of Paris and Rome, Brewster was working remorselessly at the public business. We would check the Washington air terminal where the private and corporate planes landed; other senators would depart and arrive on the planes of firms doing business with the government, but Brewster was nowhere to be seen, and we even got a discouraging report that he had taken to driving back and forth to distant Maine. But Drew remained patient, printed the favorable accounts, and with his muckraker's faith in the incorrigibility of the public malefactor, waited confidently for the surfacing of misconduct that was, he was sure, not absent but only concealed.

At length, on one of his hard-working trips abroad, this one to Spain, Brewster permitted himself the indiscretion of being accompanied by a lobbyist and by a member of the House of Representatives. They were Charles Patrick Clark, the Washington agent for Spain who had lately received $300,000 in fees for promoting U.S. aid to Dictator Franco, and Democratic Representative James Keough of New York who, after ten years as an unknown congressman of parochial horizons had, under Clark's tutoring, emerged on the international scene alongside Brewster as a leading congressional advocate of aid to Franco.

One night as the trio moved across Spain by rail, the trousers of the Honorable Keough were snatched from his sleeping compartment. In the ensuing hubbub it was learned that one of the pockets had contained a $5,000 wad of bills. They weren't Brewster's trousers, of course, but the incident lent an unedifying cast to the trip.

I was assigned to keep close tabs on Clark. For a time I loitered about his habitats, discovering nothing in particular except that he employed a most attractive young secretary. I ingratiated myself with the lady. The veil of time, perhaps mercifully, leaves me no recollection of the particular sheep's clothing in which I approached her, but by some means I led her to confide two tidbits from the small store of sensitive information the prudent Clark had made her privy to. Clark had begun calling on Brewster regularly at his Mayflower suite to play gin rummy, a curious lapse in the senator's no-nonsense Puritanism. And Clark always went to the card table with a fat wallet—just before one such game, his secretary cashed a $1,000 personal check for him at the cashier's office of the Mayflower. Keough's trousers and the gambling with Clark weren't much, but Drew considered them serviceable pieces of the mosaic he was constructing.

Three years passed on such thin fare. Then, in June 1950, an old skeleton, or at least the faint rattle of one, was found in Brewster's closet when it came to light that a Washington, D.C., police lieutenant named Joe Shimon had tapped the telephone and bugged the suite used by Howard Hughes during the 1947 hearings. Although no one accused Brewster of involvement, this was Drew's immediate assumption and he set about to keep the incident from sinking from view. Privately and publicly, through manipulation and accusation, Drew pressured the Congress and the Justice Department to conduct an official probe. None of the appropriate committees—those charged with oversight of congressional misbehavior, or civil rights violations, or crime in its various aspects—was prepared to investigate a colleague. But Drew persuaded the sometimes receptive Senator Pepper to convene a subcommittee of the obscure District of Columbia Committee, on the premise that it was probing not Brewster, but the Washington police department. And sure enough, a few subpoenas and interrogations under oath of D.C. police officers revealed the following:

1. Brewster had requested the Washington Police Department to assign to him Lieutenant Shimon, the department's wiretap expert.

2. Shimon had received "expense payments" from Brewster's secretary—a violation of police regulations.

3. In setting up the tapping and bugging operation, Shimon had instructed the three cops who manned the equipment to listen particularly for references to TWA or anything about airlines.

4. The eavesdropped information was transmitted to one Henry Grunewald.

5. Shimon was seen on one occasion receiving a $1,000 cash payment from a man fitting the description of Grunewald.

For a time our attentions were concentrated on this Grunewald and on establishing a connection between him and Brewster. "Henry the Dutchman" he was called in the lobbying community, and even in that Florentine circle he was considered a man of mystery and complexity —the sort who amassed $223,000 in gambling winnings one year and declared it on his income tax—but under the whimsical heading of "brokerage fees and commissions."

We learned that Grunewald was often seen entering Brewster's office, that the senator called him "Henry," that it was Henry who had brought William P. Rogers to Brewster when he was looking for a chief counsel for his Senate War Investigating Committee.

We extrapolated that Grunewald was probably supervising the wiretap operation, paying the tab, and transmitting the information to Brewster so that the senator's participation would not be direct. This deduction was strengthened when it was later established that Brewster used Grunewald to distribute campaign funds that he did not want connected to the Republican Senate Campaign Committee. Senator Pepper issued a subpoena for Grunewald, but of course he could not be found. Days passed. Drew felt that the committee was insufficiently aggressive in finding him, and gave me the assignment.

I continued to circulate among characters familiar with the lobbying underworld and learned from one that Grunewald had frequently been seen entering the Washington Hotel. I tried, by fabricating some pitiable emergency, to get the hotel's telephone operator to confirm Grunewald's presence, but I got nowhere. I then persuaded subcommittee investigator Martin Faye to join me at the hotel. Faye properly identified himself to the manager as a Senate investigator and introduced me as "Mr. Anderson." According to professional ethics, I should then have declared myself as a reporter for Drew Pearson, but I could not bring myself to dispel the impression that I, too, had official status, so I just glowered officiously.

The committee was looking for a Mr. Henry Grunewald, Faye said. Was he there? Did the hotel know where he was? The manager would tell us nothing and feigned offense that he should be asked to violate the confidentiality of his guest list.

Faye hesitated, pondering what he could properly do within his province. But I, with no province to ponder, began to harass the man. Would he prefer to be supoenaed? Would he like to have *all* the hotel's records seized? Did he fancy testifying in public? Was he prepared to be found in contempt of the United States Senate?

He quickly folded up and turned state's evidence. Grunewald was registered in the penthouse suite (where he fittingly enjoyed one of the very best views of Washington), but he hadn't been around lately; the hotel's records contained leads where he might be and I finally traced him to The Plains, Virginia, an aristocratic retreat of the horsy set about fifty miles from Washington. Through a telephone operator I located the manor house where he was staying, but I just missed him. He was on his way back to the capital, where he was nailed at the Washington Hotel.

Examined in closed session, Grunewald displayed the absolute loyalty to his political bedfellows that was to prevail through several investigations and numerous indictments in the years ahead. He refused to answer any question that might have led to Senator Brewster, gambling that the committee would not press the matter to a contempt citation, but he did admit to several meetings with Lieutenant Shimon and to a past association with Pan American, for whom he had repeatedly "checked" telephone wires.

Despite Senator Pepper's efforts, the committee declined to cite Grunewald or to call Brewster for questioning. The senator, under regular bombardment from Drew, put out a statement to the press which, in the tradition of political explanations, admitted the documented facts but denied their inescapable implications. He admitted requesting that Shimon be assigned to him but said it was for protection, citing anonymous threats on his person at the time of the Hughes hearings. Brewster claimed ignorance of any eavesdropping Shimon might have undertaken in protecting him. The private payments to Shimon were merely to recompense him for the extra expenses of protection. Shimon backed up Brewster, as was predictable, since Brewster's explanation exonerated Shimon as well as himself; the lieutenant said he had tapped and bugged Hughes's suite without telling Brewster, as a precaution in case designs against the senator were being hatched there.

No tribunal would even pretend to believe such an explanation except a panel of senators "investigating" another senator. The crucial importance of procedure in official investigations was again borne in on me: if Brewster was not to be forced to testify under oath, if Grunewald was not to be forced to the wall by contempt action unless he answered, the gap between what was obvious and what was proved could never be closed.

Meanwhile, Drew's success in browbeating the Justice Department into convening a grand jury was also proving illusory, for two technicalities permitted the department not to press the grand jury to act: the statute of limitations was within a few days of expiring, and the anti-wiretap law was being interpreted by the Justice Department to mean that no crime was consummated unless the eavesdropped information was *divulged* (an interpretation essential to the department to protect its own illicit wiretapping and that of police departments around the country). Since proof of divulgement could come only from Brewster or Shimon or Grunewald, and since none of these gentlemen was disposed to furnish it and thus indict himself of a crime, the matter went unresolved and the statute of limitations ran out.

But if the official probes were reluctant to draw the logical inferences, Drew was not. With his genius for reducing the most complicated machinations and motivations to a few sentences of almost Dick-and-Jane simplicity while at the same time confounding libel lawyers, he would at every pretext over the next two years present his own verdict, directed at the Pearson readers in Maine who would sit on Brewster's ultimate jury. Typical was this item from the "Washington Merry-Go-Round" of September 18, 1950:

> Senator Brewster in 1947 was chairman of the powerful Senate War Investigating Committee. He was also the bosom friend of Pan American Airways. Brewster and Pan American wanted Howard Hughes's TWA to consolidate its overseas lines with Pan Am. This Hughes refused to do. Whereupon Brewster investigated Hughes, and, during the period when he was before Brewster's Senate committee, Hughes's telephone wire and that of his attorneys were tapped, apparently under the off-stage direction of Henry Grunewald, who admits that at various times he checked telephone wires for Pan American Airways.
>
> Grunewald and others deny this. Nevertheless this is the conclusion which Senators are forced to arrive at. No wonder businessmen who come to Washington are worried about talking over telephones. They never know

when some competitor, perhaps with the cooperation of a Senate committee, is listening in. Yet this is supposed to be the capital of the U.S.A., not
Moscow.

After the effort of several years, our few sketchy items on Brewster
were to me a disappointment. One dyspeptic afternoon I wondered
aloud to Drew whether they merited the weekly dramatizations he was
scheduling as the Maine election drew near.

It was Drew's custom in those first years of our association to
greet my questionings of his grand strategies in one of two ways: he
would mumble something inaudible while ostensibly busying himself with the papers on his always cluttered desk—a signal to me to
withdraw before he began quizzing me in seriatim about the many
tasks he had assigned me on which I was as yet delinquent. Or if
the mood was on him or I had bruised a tender spot, he would
sometimes respond with excessive care, as if the time had come to
acquaint the youngster with some of the basic principles of the
business—as he did on this occasion.

"Jack, do you believe Brewster when he says he asked Shimon, the
bugger, just to act as a bodyguard, and that he never knew about the
tapping?"

"No," I conceded, "I don't."

"Of course not."

I took another tack, reminding him of the times when exposés by
the column had resulted in indictments and convictions—the war
frauds of Congressman May, the Ripps-Mitchell embezzlements in
Alabama, the Long-machine swindles in Louisiana. Didn't we detract
from those achievements by beating the drum so incessantly on
Brewster—on the basis of scraps and chaff? And I cited newsmen who
considered it unprofessional to revive and embellish old scandals unless
there were new developments that justified it.

He responded with a self-revealing monologue I presume to repro-
duce in substance because over the years I would hear its like many
times. It went like this:

"A reporter sometimes causes a conviction, but when he does it's
only a by-product; it's not our function to prove that an official is bad
enough to deserve prison—nor should we ignore him if we can't. Our
job is to advise the people as to whether he's fit for the highest responsi-

bility, and to tie a can on those who betray the people for the favors of big money.

"Most of the time, all we will ever get are *tokens* of their corruption. Once you catch one of these birds at anything, and you're sure of your facts, never worry about doing him an injustice by overplaying it. We'll never learn ten percent of the evil they do. We can't subpoena their records or threaten witnesses with jail. We have to use what's laying around in the open, or only half hidden. So we always miss the worst of it.

"Don't turn your nose up at chaff and scraps. They tell the voters exactly what they need to know about Brewster. That he's a liar. That he rigs investigations. That he uses totalitarian methods. That he manipulates millions of tax dollars into the pockets of business and then takes its favors. That he hobnobs with lobbyists for dictators and plays cards with them for high stakes—do you think he loses?

"If other journalists maintain a reticence about all this, just because it hasn't cleared the obstacles to a jury or because it was already mentioned last year, all the more reason for us to remind the public again and again until it sinks in."

During the last two years before Brewster's election day, his hoary transgressions were to be dredged up and redredged in no fewer than fifty columns. And Pearson did not restrict himself within even his own elastic definition of journalistic latitude. As 1952 approached with no opponent of stature having come forward to challenge Brewster in the June Republican primary, Drew set himself to recruiting one. The strongest possibility was Maine's popular governor, Frederick G. Payne, a moderately progressive figure. Drew began to press privately for a Payne candidacy, urging upon him and his advisers all the reasons why Brewster was overripe.

At length the governor sent word to Drew that he was prepared to make the race, but he set a condition: he must have $50,000 in out-of-state campaign funds in hand before he would announce against the darling of so many wealthy interests. That was a great deal of money for a primary campaign in a small rural state in 1952, but Drew knew where to go for it—Howard Hughes. A meeting was set up between representatives of the governor and the tycoon, with the result that Payne got the $50,000, or most of it.

With Payne in the race, Drew loaded all his press and radio artillery for the grand finale of his five-year pursuit. Our broadcasts were widely heard in the Pine Tree State and our column appeared in the only statewide Sunday paper, the Portland *Sunday Telegram,* as well as in three or four dailies, including the largest, the Portland *Evening Express,* giving us a potential audience of about half the state's voters. Not that we presumed to have influence with that many, but as Drew often observed, most elections are decided by a thin margin of 5 or 10 percent. If our barrage could change one reader in ten from Brewster to Payne, that might be enough.

"Your typical Maine voter," he would contend, "is a small farmer or artisan or shoestring entrepreneur, or he works for a two-bit company. He has the inborn hostility to big business that comes from living in a poor state that's been passed by, where little firms are shutting down all the time because they can't compete with the big boys. He thinks the moneyed interests are against him, and he's against them. All lobbyists are suspect to him. He doesn't get any subsidies and he doesn't want anyone else to. He's an independent cuss who can't abide government snooping. He's an unreconstructed Protestant who was agin Franco during the Civil War and still is. He hasn't been conditioned by big-city politics, so he's disturbed by any sign of political corruption or underhandedness with funds. This fellow was born to vote against Brewster once he knows his true record."

During the closing months of the campaign, many of our columns and broadcasts were written with that insular voter in mind. Every presumed bugbear of the down-easter was trotted out repeatedly, with Brewster's name on it—the saga of Keough's pants, the wiretapping, the bonanzas wangled for Pan Am, the association with the sinister-sounding Grunewald, the high-rolling with Franco's man, to whom Drew gave the sobriquet "Jersey Joe Clark." Sometimes the column would be given over to a grand review of Brewster's iniquities; more often, a short segment or even a one-line freshener would suffice.

The danger was overdoing it, and Drew tried to guard against this. He never boosted Payne or even mentioned him. He did not discuss the election. He avoided the use of invective. Brewster would usually be brought on stage as "amiable," "hard-working" or "frugal" before his shabby deeds were dutifully cited in an impersonal, low-key way. Drew took pains to find a pretext in the current news for alluding to Brewster. As a peg, Grunewald was a godsend; "the Dutchman" was by now caught up in innumerable scandals, was being investigated on all sides, and was continually in the news. Drew would later befriend Grunewald, and I think the origin of his kindly feelings lay in the debt he owed him for affording so many opportunities to expand on "mystery man" Grunewald's bosom friend from Maine.

Brewster was defeated by 3,000 votes out of 130,000 cast.

On the morning after the election, as Drew passed through the lobby of the Mayflower Hotel, he was ambushed by an enraged Charles Patrick Clark, who threw a roundhouse right that decked Drew. "That's for what you did to Brewster," Clark snarled and stalked off righteously while the lobby buzzed. Drew lay on the carpet, humiliated. "It hurt like hell," he later told me, "but the ringing in my ears was music."

Brewster never held public office again and lived out his twilight years as a lobbyist. Grunewald eventually was indicted for perjury and spent his last years manipulating postponements of his trial.

At long last the column ceased to be concerned with them, except for an occasional jab for old time's sake, such as: "Maine's ex-Senator, likeable Owen Brewster, has been busy buttonholing Senators to vote for a subsidy bill that could mean more money for Pan American Airways. Brewster lost his Senate seat partly because of his friendship for Pan American."

From time to time I would encounter Brewster in the anterooms of senators, waiting resignedly for ten-minute audiences with juniors he had once positioned in the committee structure and led into legislative battle, ten minutes in which to peddle the latest self-enrichment scheme of some corporation. A lucrative life, no doubt, but filled with daily reminders of fallen estate. When our eyes met, I used to wonder if he hated me, the minion of his nemesis, the accomplice in the reduction of his life to this caricature of its former promise. But he would look past me, his impassive face giving no hint of his thoughts.

In 1958, when both Brewster and Grunewald had passed to their rewards, "the Dutchman's" last mystery came to light. During Brewster's Senate heyday, Grunewald had given or loaned him $650,-000 worth of bonds of the Missouri Pacific Railroad. They were bearer bonds, as negotiable and untraceable as currency. When Brewster died, the bonds were nowhere to be found among his effects, nor did they turn up in Grunewald's. So the good widows, throwing appearances to the wind, petitioned the Missouri Pacific to restore to them the missing bonds.

There it was—the great exploitable link between the influence peddler and the corporation-serving senator that had eluded us during all the years we had made do with tokens. Oh, what uses Drew would have made of that $650,000 had he but known—what headlines, what demands for investigation, what indignant one-liners! As it was, he merely reported the matter, along with the charitable explanatory theory that perhaps Brewster had used the bonds as collateral for his political fund-raising activities. After all, the pursuit of Brewster had ended long before; the tokens had done the job.

5 · Un-American Activities

THE PARAMOUNT conflict of the era that shaped my education as a muckraker raged for seven tumultuous and ravaging years. It began, for me, in 1947 and was fought on so many fronts, smashed so many lives and careers, devoured such indigestible chunks of American history that trying to reconstruct it along coherent lines, I am hard put to it to know where to begin or how to connect the parts.

Perhaps I can best set the scene by recounting a minor but unifying event that occurred long after the seven-years war had concluded but while the mopping up was still going on. The event was a hearing of a Senate Armed Services subcommittee in 1962; the witness was Major General Edwin A. Walker. He was called to explain his public education program which used the military to inculcate in the citizenry a proper appreciation of its role in the struggle against Communism. The general would soon go on to greater glory by joining the John Birch Society and by leading paramilitary resistance to racial integration at the University of Mississippi; and on this day, he was pregnant with his newly perceived destiny.

The burden of his testimony was that a ubiquitous conspiracy was clearing the way for world Communism by systematically slandering and discrediting its effective opponents. The cast of anti-Communist victims of this "hidden policy" ran to thousands, Walker said, and he undertook to name the brightest of the fallen: General Douglas MacArthur, Defense Secretary James Forrestal, Generalissimo Chiang Kaishek, Senator Joseph McCarthy, General George Patton, Congressman J. Parnell Thomas.

Walker's litany of martyrs was standard among the "anti-Communist" right; it could have been lifted intact from the speeches of Senator Joe McCarthy or Gerald L. K. Smith a decade earlier, just as it would be reproduced a decade later in the pamphlets of the fanatical fringe, except that in the latter case the roster of unheeded prophets would be updated by the addition of Senator Thomas J. Dodd of Connecticut and Representative Michael Feighan of Ohio.

In the pantheon of the ultraright, then, authentic heroes and tragic giants are accorded equal godhood with rascals, demagogues and buffoons. For a personal reason, I have come to find this strangely reassuring. In my early years with Drew Pearson I was dismayed by his propensity for damning in the same breath a James Forrestal with a Parnell Thomas, a MacArthur with a McCarthy, as though figures so obviously disparate in ability and rectitude were joined together by a common bond so vital as to render insignificant their disharmonies. The captain of my ship was being guided by a hidden compass of his own divining, and I feared it would one day run us aground. But as the right wing claimed for its Holy of Holies one by one the figures whom Drew had early on marked down as his targets-in-chief, I came to realize that it was ratifying Drew's linkage, which I had accepted with some misgiving; clearly, there *was* a common bond.

In the field of foreign policy, Drew contended, that bond was the belief in a preventive war, preferably atomic, that would cripple world Communism before the plague overtook us. For adherents more sensitive to the requirements of public relations or less willing to face up to the gore, the preventive-war panacea took the form of a diplomacy of ultimatum and showdown, of confrontations and provocations from which Stalin and Mao would conveniently retreat. In domestic affairs, the common platform called for what, beneath the veil, amounted to the imposition of a patriotic orthodoxy sufficient for the rigors of the world struggle, to be achieved by unmasking widespread treason, making object lessons of the disloyal and the lukewarm, censoring unhelpful news, fumigating libraries, classrooms and pulpits, broadening the cloak-and-dagger function of the FBI and the CIA, and reinterpreting away whatever constitutional prohibitions might interfere.

It is an index of the initial gulf in experience that separated me from Drew that I was largely unacquainted with these underlying currents. To me, MacArthur, Forrestal and the late Patton were honored magnificoes of the war, against whom I bore only the residual hostility of the ex-GI for the higher brass. Chiang Kai-shek was to me a vaguely sympathetic figure, sinking slowly under the weight of Oriental conundrums that seemed, from my exposure to them, insoluble. J. Parnell Thomas was a clown, but no more sinister than one would expect a six-term New Jersey legislator to be. Joe McCarthy, who had not yet made his Cold War debut, was a pal of mine, irresponsible to be sure, but a fellow bachelor of vast amiability and an excellent source of inside dope on the Hill. Moreover, I was inflated with a cocky pride in America's global pre-eminence, was respectful of the leadership that had attained it and was exuberant at the prospect of reporting the international chess plays from the undoubted capital of the world.

My ardor was periodically dampened by the wet blanket of skeptical melancholy with which my mentor assessed the lions of the day and beheld the global spread of American arms and dollars.

Drew foresaw the post–World War II binge of Americanism, dollar imperialism and embezzlement. It was his view of history—reinforced by the World War I cycle that dominated his formative years—that war and its aftermath infected a democracy with totalitarian viruses and a corrupted ethos profoundly destructive to democratic ideals. A prolonged national war footing, he believed, fostered a mentality intolerant of dissent and of individual rights; it exhalted secrecy while making openness suspect; its celebrations of brutality fevered the robed and unrobed vigilante; its dislocations and frustrations opened voids that invited the repressive demagogue; its grab bag of arms contracts and economic controls stimulated a plague of fixers and wire pullers; its necessities raised to power those Drew held as least fit to govern a democracy: authoritarians developed by the hierachies of arms, acquisitiveness and industrial efficiency—namely, the generals, the Wall Street financiers, the production czars.

Wherever a self-confessed patriot raised his voice, Drew half expected to find not just an impostor but a crook; wherever imperial pomp surfaced or national secrets were guarded with excessive zeal, he divined another travesty of the democratic process in the making; and whenever generals took up the portfolios of diplomats or ex-bankers gathered to assist in the rebuilding of some unfortunate country, he sniffed about for a mouse. He was thus directed by a philosophy which led him into occasional error, but which on the whole positioned him aptly for the events of the postwar era.

He had an anticipatory eye for major disturbers of the peace. Something in the bearing of a man, in the collateral implications of his ideas, in the verbal imagery he used to project himself would sound a jangling chord that would mark him off to Drew as a coming menace. Perhaps the most elementary example of this was one that predated my relationship with Drew, though the lessons it taught me were so pivotal as to make it seem otherwise. I refer to the case of General George S. Patton.

The basic complaint Drew had against generals was that they were martial. His natural inclination was to distrust any military man above the rank of sergeant, and the higher the rank, the deeper was Drew's skepticism. He conceded that until the millennium arrived, the Army was a necessity, and that it could not be populated entirely with sergeants. But if he had to accept the existence of generals, he felt they should regard war as a catastrophe, not an opportunity, and should be modest, homely, untheatrical, subject to civil authority, and above all, unmartial. Drew's idea of a general was a George Marshall, a Dwight Eisenhower, an Omar Bradley, a Joseph Stillwell—plain fellows who could get the onerous job done without making a cult of it and without posing the historic hazards of the man on horseback.

George Patton, from the first blip he registered on Drew's radar, was the epitome of everything Drew detested in a general. Big, bluff and burly, Patton was a natural authoritarian, a curser of subordinates and maltreater of animals, an erratic prodigy. By his choice of imagery— ramrod posture, theatrical swagger, patented scowl, gory metaphors, bepistoled costume—he presented himself as the incarnation of destruction, a walking glorification of war.

A streak of mysticism reinforced his gruff certitudes. "It has been revealed to me," Patton would say when making predictions concerning battles, personal fate, even his death. He was on terms of such intimacy with the Almighty that he not only conversed with Him at length but ventured on occasion to rebuke Him. "Sir, this is Patton talking. Rain, snow and more rain, more snow—and I am beginning to wonder if *they* are in Thy headquarters. You must decide for Yourself on which side You are standing."

To Drew, Patton was all the more ominous because he was not a dismissable redneck of limited horizons. He was a military aristocrat and historian, a gifted conversationalist and writer of reports and letters, an ornament of the horsy set with a capacity for solid friendships among his peers and a knack for impressing his betters. Winston Churchill was fascinated by him. Roosevelt promised him a top command against Japan after Germany's defeat. Secretary of War Henry Stimson looked on him as a personal favorite. Eisenhower considered him to be, for certain military situations, the finest soldier America had ever produced.

In North Africa and Sicily, in the first big American operations against the Axis, Patton showed himself an inspired field commander, a genius of attack, with the electric qualities that generate popular adulation and gratify political leaders during tense times. He thus possessed a formidable range of assets that seemed destined to propel him into the field command of the grand invasion of Europe, from which could come incalculable aggrandizement.

Halfway up the escalator, in the midst of his great dash across Sicily, Patton brutalized two hospitalized soldiers who suffered from what used to be called shell shock, a malady "Old Blood and Guts" refused to recognize. He cursed, slapped and kicked the first soldier, pushing him out of the hospital tent. A second outburst was recorded by Army doctors who sent a report to Ike, written by an eyewitness, Major Charles Barton Etter:

> . . . He [Patton] came to one patient who, upon inquiry stated that he was sick with a high fever. The General dismissed him without comment. The next patient was sitting huddled up and shivering. When asked what the trouble was, the man replied, "It's my nerves," and began to sob. The General then screamed at him, "What did you say?" He replied, "It's my nerves, I can't stand the shelling any more." He was still sobbing.
>
> The General then yelled at him, "Your nerves hell, You are just a goddamn coward, you yellow son of a bitch." He then slapped the man and said, "Shut up that goddamned crying. I won't have these brave men here who have been shot seeing a yellow bastard sitting here crying." He then struck at the man again, knocking his helmet liner off and into the next tent. He then turned to the Receiving Officer and yelled, "Don't you admit this yellow bastard, there's nothing wrong with him. I won't have the hospitals cluttered up with these sons of bitches who haven't the guts to fight."
>
> He turned to the man again, who was managing to "sit at attention" though shaking all over and said, "You're going back to the front lines and you may get shot and killed, but you're going to fight. If you don't, I'll stand you up against a wall and have a firing squad kill you on purpose." In fact,

he said, reaching for his pistol, "I ought to shoot you myself, you god-damned whimpering coward." As he went out of the ward he was still yelling back at the Receiving Officer to send that yellow son of a bitch to the front lines . . .

The report described a textbook general-court-martial offense. But on General Eisenhower's orders, it was buried and "kept in the family." When war correspondents attached to Patton's forces got wind of it, Eisenhower orchestrated a classic campaign to persuade the press to let it lie buried. Reporters were told in confidence that Patton was being discreetly but gallingly disciplined by Ike, that Ike considered Patton indispensable to the war effort, that public exposure of the slapping incidents would destroy his usefulness. The reporters, eager to do their bit for the war effort, entered into a gentleman's agreement to kill the story.

So the matter rested for three months until Drew learned about the incident from an OSS official and close friend, Ernest Cuneo. Personal considerations tempted Drew to bow to the unanimous judgment of his colleagues and not print the story. A short time before, he had been publicly branded a "liar" by President Roosevelt for reporting a true but unconfirmable diplomatic story which, because it inflamed relations with the Soviets, had to be forcefully repudiated. Should the high command deny the slapping story and have the muscle to make the denial stick, Drew would find himself out on a very long limb. Touchier yet, Drew's partner on the "Washington Merry-Go-Round," co-founder Robert S. Allen, an Army officer on leave from the column, was serving on General Patton's immediate staff and was devoted to him. Allen was a combative little man of fierce loyalties who would doubtless regard Drew's breaking of the ranks as a personal treachery and an unforgivable wound to Patton. Drew's oldest and closest professional friendship was in the balance.

But to pass it by would be to betray his principles, his prejudices, and worst of all, his intuition. At stake here was not a military secret or the loss of lives, but a shabby outrage. A reporter, as he would instruct me often, is in the business of *digging up* outrages and shouting them from the rooftops, not burying them in an ecumenical silence. The very thought of reporters posing as gentlemen and entering into a pact of protective silence with the authorities went beyond the comical; to Drew Pearson, it was grotesque—the more so because it was on an issue Drew thought fundamental: the American democracy did not offer up its sons to the military caste in order to have them brutalized by their own officers, like subjects of the Prussian enemy.

To dramatize this principle in officers' clubs around the world was worth, in Drew's opinion, a dozen Pattons. Moreover, Drew was operating at cross-purposes from those reporters who united to preserve Patton for his future role. Regarding him as a general who could start a war as well as win a battle, Drew could not let pass an opportunity to slow his rise. The general could not control himself; he was subject to fits of instability, perhaps of temporary insanity; in determining Patton's future role, this fact should be weighed not just by Eisenhower and the higher-ups, but by the entire free process.

On Sunday evening, November 21, 1943, Drew broadcast to the nation the story of "the slapping incidents" with full ruffles and flourishes. A furor exploded. Eisenhower's staff rushed out a denial of essential portions, but after a hairy twenty-four hours, correspondents on the scene confirmed Drew, and the Army reversed itself. Drew kept the public uproar reverberating with additional exposés of Patton's eccentricity: while chewing out an officer, he had fired his pistol in the air for emphasis; he had shot the frightened mule of an Italian because it was blocking military traffic; another time, he had shot a polo pony for the offense of performing poorly in a match.

As a result of these disclosures, Patton was put in limbo for many months. The high command was forced to abandon plans to give him a destiny-fraught mission in Italy, designed to rescue the faltering campaign there by sending Patton on a breakout to Rome. Had he received that command and performed with his customary aplomb, his status as the greatest American combat general would have jelled and it would have become difficult indeed to deprive him of the command of American forces in the European invasion. But as it was, that command was given to Patton's subordinate, General Omar Bradley. Eisenhower astutely made use of the affair to chasten Patton, keep him submerged and eventually use him for what he was best at—as commander of the Third Army for its magnificent plunge across Europe.

Patton enthusiasts blamed Drew Pearson for prolonging the war by stunting the career of the general who became our greatest ground gainer and killer of Germans. Drew, unrepentant, waited for vindication. It came at war's end when a reinflated Patton, now the military governor of Bavaria, again grew obstreperous and insubordinate. Ordered to disarm and confine German army units in his area, Patton began to harbor the dream of amalgamating them into his Third Army

and leading a united American-German force against the "real enemy"
—the Russians. He paraded through Bavaria receiving enthusiastic
demonstrations from the subject populace; and despite orders to the
contrary, he insisted on using Nazis in his military government, com-
paring them to Republicans and Democrats back home. Just how
troublesome Patton might have become had he achieved a higher
command was illustrated when Eisenhower's deputy, General Joseph
T. McNarney, phoned Patton to relay Soviet protests about the undis-
banded German units in his sector.

"Hell," Patton exploded, "why do you care what those goddamn
Russians think? We are going to have to fight them sooner or later;
within the next generation. Why not do it now, while our Army is
intact and the damn Russians can have their hind end kicked back into
Russia in three months? We can do it ourselves easily with the help
of the German troops we have, if we just arm them and take them with
us; they hate the bastards."

"Shut up, George, you fool!" McNarney told Patton. "This line may
be tapped and you will be starting a war with those Russians with your
talking!"

But Patton refused to shut up. "I would like to get it started some
way," he said, "that is the best thing we can do now. *You* don't have
to get mixed up in it at all if you are so damn soft about it and scared
of your rank—just let me handle it down here. In ten days I can have
enough incidents happen to have us at war with those sons of bitches
and make it look like their fault. So much so that we will be completely
justified in attacking them and running them out."*

Perhaps the general's Bavarian exuberance would have been overlooked or indulged as a great hero's entitlement had not Drew previously made public spectacles of Patton's peculiarities. As it was,
SHAPE (Supreme Headquarters Allied Powers, Europe) was highly
sensitive to any signs of resurging instability in Patton and promptly
withdrew him from Bavaria and stripped him of all significant duties.

As consistent targets of the "Washington Merry-Go-Round," overweening generals held second place only to congressional guardians of
patriotic orthodoxy.

One of my earliest duties was to keep tabs on HUAC, the House
Un-American Activities Committee. Drew had been warring for years

---

*Ladislas Farago, *Patton: Ordeal and Triumph* (New York: Ivan Obolensky, 1963), p. 806.

with the committee, first with its founder, Representative Martin Dies of Texas, until Dies retired to avoid an electoral defeat, and latterly with other committee luminaries, who consequently looked on him as an agent of Moscow.

Drew was devoted, true enough, to encouraging the growth of amity between the United States and Russia as the key building block of world peace, but he was not deceived by a false amity that was merely a cover for Soviet intrigue. A year before my advent, the column had revealed the existence of a vast Russian spy ring that was infiltrating the atom-bomb programs of the United States and Canada. At first the Canadian and British governments had tried to suppress the information, but some members of their intelligence services thought it ought to be known.

"Secret revelations are stirring in Canada," the series led off. "They will make people hold their hats and run for the diplomatic storm cellars. The biggest story of espionage and intrigue is about to break. The Canadians have taken over a Russian agent, who has given the names of about 1,700 Russian agents; also has put the finger on certain officials inside the American and Canadian governments cooperating with the Soviets."

As the story developed, based on information from a defected Soviet code clerk, Igor Gouzenko, it brought a deluge of angry letters, for it destroyed the most comforting of illusions, as Pearson biographer Herman Klurfeld later observed: "The euphoria of American-Russian friendship disappeared on February 18, 1946, when Drew Pearson broke the spy story of the century. It was the first revelation of a super-espionage network in the Western Hemisphere."*

And around the time I began covering HUAC, our column made public the operation of another espionage ring—a small group of government employees that was stealing blueprints of the B-29, photostating them, and sending them by courier to New York and thence to Moscow.

Drew's posture was thus consistently and actively antitotalitarian and antisubversive; his attitude toward such questions as whether Communism was inevitably totalitarian and aggression-prone, or whether American rank-and-file Communists of yesteryear were necessarily subversive, was layered with distinctions I had not before had occasion to think through. In his view, the Communists warred against some of the

---

Behind the Lines: The World of Drew Pearson (Englewood Cliffs, N.J.: Prentice-Hall, 1968), p. 126.

right targets and had enlisted some people he admired, but its theory was checkered with error and in practice it was, like any totalitarianism, the enemy of liberal democratic values. He always hoped that the Communists would begin to evolve toward those values, and he maintained a dialogue with some of them here and abroad, conversations that one day would involve Marshal Tito and Nikita Khrushchev.

He opposed the presence of unshriven Communists in government posts and other sensitive places, but he was deeply sympathetic to those who had had a youthful flirtation with Communism, had grown away from it and were now being hounded because of it. Above all, he loathed the misuse of governmental power to arraign private citizens for what they thought, or used to think.

My preconceptions differed in degree. I regarded Communism as an across-the-board onslaught on all the basic beliefs I had been raised in, and my adult experience tended to confirm this. In my China days Chou En-lai had impressed me as an engaging and often profound figure, but I attributed that to his personal gifts, not to the dialectical baggage he lugged around with him. What I knew of Communism's slave-labor camps, mass exterminations and universal thought control struck me as the inevitable application of its credo, as sure to appear in Chou's China, if his side won out over Chiang, as it had in Stalin's Russia. As for American Communists, I was little acquainted with them or the situations that produced them. I was not a zealot, but I regarded their uprooting from government positions as a necessary function, and was not automatically suspicious of "anti-Communist" politicians.

And so I was without Drew's ingrained hostility when I first breezed into the old House Caucus Room to observe the Un-American Activities Committee in combat against its chosen foils. In the main, the prominent Communists who were paraded before the committee that year—party factotums, leaders of the Joint Anti-Fascist Refugee Committee, the "Hollywood Ten" screenwriters—were as unprepossessing as I had expected. I found it hard to whip up sympathy for them, even as underdogs, for they were insufferably self-righteous, transparent in their quest for genteel martyrdom and interminable in their spouting of the party line, with the result that many of the non-Communist movie stars who trooped to the hearings to give moral support to the screenwriters visibly wilted in their enthusiasm for confreres who, posing as champions of free expression, were so obviously the servants of propaganda.

But if these witnesses did not make plausible martyrs, neither were they respectable menaces. As the number of witnesses who would neither answer questions nor desist from harangues, thereupon to be cited for contempt, rose to twenty, then to thirty; as professional accusers were brought on to make flimsily supported charges of wholesale subversion; as a different breed of witness began to appear—quiet, ordinary citizens quaking in fear lest public exposure of some old association destroy their precarious middle-class existences—the purposes of the committee itself, which held power and bore responsibility, began to loom more alarming to me than those of the subpoenaed. Those purposes have been captured by Walter Goodman:

> The philosophy that flowered under the klieg lights of 1947 would be an inspiration for much of the committee's later work: a philosophy that held not only that communism was a subversive doctrine, not only that communists in sensitive positions were threats to the nation, but that the presence in this land of every individual communist and fellow-traveler and former communist who would not purge himself was intolerable; that the just fate of every such creature was to be exposed in his community, routed from his job, and driven into exile.*

The leader of the committee was J. Parnell Thomas. In appearance, he was improbable either as hero or villain. He was old—I thought sixty-three was old then—and fat, with a bald head and a round face that glowed perpetually in a pink flush. But as it turned out, his flat idiom and disarming corpulence concealed an unsuspected capacity to cultivate unreality, or rather, to parody reality. This was to be his passport to power and fame.

Thomas was moved principally by caricatures. Confronting a world that abounded in real Communist threats, he was obsessed with phantom, even ludicrous slapstick ones. One was his notion that the saccharine movies of that day, produced and monitored as they were by the most conformist capitalists, represented a New Deal conspiracy to Communize the free world. His approach to atomic espionage was of similar depth. He breathlessly disclosed that there were no guards patrolling the fences at the atomic installation at Oak Ridge, Tennessee, and that the yards "were being infiltrated by fellow travelers if not actual members of the communist party . . . There is nothing to prevent anyone from climbing the fence, even in daylight, and approaching within perhaps 75 yards of one of the three widely separated plants."

The Committee: The Extraordinary Career of the House Committee on Un-American Activities (New York: Farrar, Straus & Giroux, 1968), p. 225.

This fear of unguarded fences was parroted by Thomas' chief Republican sidekick on HUAC, Representative John McDowell of Pennsylvania, specialist on the Mexican wetback problem, a favorite concern of the era. With Thomas' help, McDowell was working on the exposure of a Mexican-operated "communist ring . . . sneaking in large numbers of foreign communists . . . people who come over our border to do something to our country."

The bipartisan empathy of the Thomas committee was exemplified by its ranking Democrats: Representative John Wood of Georgia advocated legislation to require that every commentator be identifiable to the public as to ethnic background and political affiliation, and whether he was reporting news or opinion. Representative John Rankin of Mississippi saw the Red Menace as merely a workaday illustration of his larger themes—the evil of Jewry and the inferiority of Negroes. In Rankin's portrayal, Communism was just another Jewish conspiracy, which used the guileless Negroes as dupes, pushing them into unwanted intimacies with whites in order to sow discord.

It is scarcely credible today that such figures could wield the power to dominate the news, eclipse careers and cause whole industries and institutions to grovel in fear. But indeed they did.

The motion picture industry was almost totally intimidated by the rising power of J. Parnell Thomas, and to appease him, instituted the blacklist that would spread to broadcasting and degrade the entertainment world for a decade to come. Under the pressure of the Thomas committee's probe into disloyalty among government employees, President Harry Truman issued a far-reaching Loyalty Order designed to circumvent legal forms in rooting out those suspected of disloyalty. Under it, grounds for dismissal were broadened to include "sympathetic association" with a "movement" or with a "group or combination of persons" considered subversive by the Attorney General. Truman's order specified the files of HUAC as a source of information on suspect employees. Meanwhile, the courts were affirming HUAC's powers and prerogatives; the Congress was close to unanimous in whooping through mounting appropriations for its probes; auxiliaries were springing up in states and localities across the country; even elements of the press, such as the Hearst chain, were bawling for federal censorship.*

Puffed up by these demonstrations of prowess, committee members

*The Hearst press waxed rhapsodic: "The need is for federal censorship of motion pictures. The Constitution permits it. The law sanctions it. The safety and welfare of America demand it!"

seemed giddy with a sense not just of power but of majesty. Representative Edward Hébert of Louisiana crowed over the committee's transcendence of judicial restraint: "Dr. Silverman, you are now before the greatest open court in this country, I believe, beyond the confines of any limited courtroom in this country." Representative McDowell proposed increasing the jail term for refusing to answer a congressman's question from one year to five years. Representative Rankin bettered him, proposing ten years in prison for teachers or users of the mail who advocated or even conveyed "the impression of sympathy with or approval of communism or communist ideology." Representative Wood opened limitless vistas by fashioning a bill that would aid private industry in uncovering and firing "communist sympathizers."

I was not to forget one heady afternoon when Chairman Thomas made a tableau of it all by suddenly ordering a lawyer accompanying one of the witnesses to take the stand himself. When the lawyer protested the violation of his right to be called only by subpoena and to be represented by counsel, Thomas' perma-flush deepened to a rich maroon and he barked out the credo of the hour: "The rights you have are the rights given you by this committee. *We* will determine what rights you have got and what rights you have not got before the committee!"

Drew's response, characteristically, was to thrust himself into the near-vacuum where opposition ought to have been. In June 1947 he appeared in federal court as a defense witness for the sixteen members of the Joint Anti-Fascist Refugee Committee at their trial on charges of contempt of Congress. Drew was sympathetic to JAFRC because of its long hostility to Dictator Franco dating from Spanish Civil War days, and he was not dissuaded by the fact that several of these defendants were undoubted Communists. His larger purposes—for he was always offensive-minded—were to attack HUAC, and by his example, to break the ice of fear that kept so many persons of influence silent. His intended argument was that the HUAC probe was unconstitutional in the first place. He offered evidence that Representative Rankin had used the committee rostrum, without rebuke, to praise the Ku Klux Klan as representative of the highest Americanism, and that the committee had steadfastly refused to probe the Klan. This disqualified it, Drew deduced, from any objective inquiry into un-Americanism and invalidated its proceedings. The court did not acknowledge Drew's jurisprudential authority, however, and would not permit him to take the stand, though it did admit to the record some of his documentation on Rankin. But the attempt to testify was widely publicized.

I began now to appreciate that Drew had the strengths of his weaknesses. One of those weaknesses was pride in his capacity to assess the character of acquaintances. He did indeed have a gift for that, but he placed an inordinate reliance upon it. Once he had made a favorable appraisal of someone's veracity, he would often accept that person's word as the basis of a news story that could not otherwise be corroborated. This journalistic sin simplified Drew's operation enormously (except on the rare occasion when a confidant proved wrong), but it was a risky business which I had come to terms with only as one excuses eccentricity in the great. This unprofessional trust in the reliability of individuals proved to be the reverse side of virtues then in short supply —a rash courage that dared to take the side of an accused friend, not knowing or fearing what might turn up in some musty dossier, a humanity that was really outraged by outrages and so could better convey it to a mass audience.

At the very pinnacle of its power to intimidate, just after information from reformed Communist Whittaker Chambers and dogged leadership from junior-committeeman Richard Nixon had given the committee its signal triumph—the Alger Hiss case—a former State Department official named Laurence Duggan committed suicide while under HUAC investigation. Drew was unashamed of his friendship with Duggan and unintimidated by the suspect circumstances surrounding his suicide. The tragedy moved Drew not to keep silent but rather to jump immediately to Duggan's defense in a column addressed to the committee in general and member Karl Mundt in particular:

> When the body of Larry Duggan crashed to the pavement from the 16th story of a New York building, you announced that Duggan was on the list of State Department suspects who had given confidential data to Whittaker Chambers. You also stated to the press, 'We will give out the other names as they jump out of windows!'
>
> ... I knew Larry Duggan intimately. He was no more a communist than you—less so, because he tried to cure the evils that cause communism. He tried to help the starving peons of Latin America. He tried to curb the Peróns who trample on people's rights.
>
> Once in 1932, Duggan attended some communist meetings in Alexandria, Va., and that may be the skeleton you now rattle in his coffin. But that was in the depth of the depression when breadlines were blocks long, when farmers in your own Northwest threatened to lynch judges, and when 20,000 veterans of World War I stormed the Capital.

Duggan was in his twenties then. And if you are going to let the distressed groping of a youngster's soul for depression's cure tarnish his reputation two decades later, then some of our greatest men might also lose their places in history.

But to those who knew him, you can never tarnish the reputation of Laurence Duggan. He was a kindly, sensitive soul, who tried to support four kids on a measly government salary because he loved his work and was passionately devoted to the good-neighbor policy.

He was the kind of man who makes this government great—the kind who slaves for it and sacrifices for it, because he believed in it—the kind of middle-of-the-roaders whom the communists consider their worst enemies.

Laurence Duggan is dead now. He cannot defend himself.

Remember, Congressman, that trial by jury and grand jury is a priceless heritage built up by our forefathers through centuries of struggle, not something to be trampled on by headline-hunting Congressmen who blast the reputations of men deemed to be innocent until they are proved guilty.

Remember also that the headline-seeking of a few Congressmen is a lot less important to this nation than our personal liberties, and that the era of terror you are promoting may do a lot more to undermine our American system than the ten-year outdated communist spies you belatedly seek to expose.

Others came forward to defend Duggan's reputation, including his State Department superiors and Attorney General Tom Clark, who bestowed upon him what was at that tortured time a prized accolade —"loyal employee." Whittaker Chambers denied ever having received information from Duggan. Nixon, who had collaborated with Mundt on the Duggan attack, slipped out the back door, talking of "misunderstanding" and "misinterpretations." Other committee members separated themselves from Mundt, and he backed off, announcing with papal summariness that Duggan was "cleared" and that his case was a "closed book."*

Heartened by this demonstration of HUAC vulnerability, we probed for a cause célèbre that would discredit it further, meanwhile chipping away via column and broadcast with the patented Pearson medley: ridicule of committee howlers, explorations into Rankin's ever fecund garden of racial obscenities, editorial defenses of the Founding Fathers

---

*Later information surfaced on Duggan that was ambiguous enough to make Nixon and Mundt regret, perhaps, their hasty apologies. Duggan appears to have maintained cordial relations with known Communist agents while not joining them, and to have rejected their urging that he pass secret information to them, though not turning them in for such overtures.

and mini-exposés of whatever we could find in the closets of committee stalwarts—e.g., that J. Parnell Thomas, who specialized in taunting radical witnesses for their inevitable use of aliases, had changed his own name from John Patrick Feeney to cover his shanty-Irish background with lace curtains; that Representative McDowell used public payroll funds to reward a nonworking GOP political angel from his Pennsylvania district; that Representative Wood kept both a personal servant and his back-home law partner on the congressional payroll and had squeezed the family of a crippled boy run over by an Army truck for a cut of the damages Congress awarded under a Wood bill; that one of the committee's chief staff members got himself deferred four times until the war's last gasp in 1945 and then, after nine months of stateside duty, was discharged upon Thomas' intervention, ahead of millions of waiting veterans.

All the while, Drew pressed us for redder meat on Thomas. What was needed was to catch the old blatherskite in some degrading act, preferably a felony, ideally a felony so sleazy that it would disgust his most refractory adherents. That Thomas was likely to have committed such acts was clear to Drew. The branch of Americanism that went in for public inquisitions into the political notions of movie actors was bound to attract the dishonest man, the cheat looking for a patriotic cover. A congressman who, able to choose from a vast array of promotional hoaxes, chose this one had doubtless been cutting corners all his life. We had but to find them.

It so happened that Thomas employed a devoted secretary named Helen Campbell, who for years had carried the burden of complicity in Thomas' practice of taking kickbacks from his congressional employees—a federal crime. She was small, gray, over sixty, but underneath her grandmotherly exterior she was a tough customer with some hard mileage behind her. Overtaken now by age, Helen Campbell had no other life outside the office, a world dominated by one man. She fell quietly in love with Thomas, notwithstanding his grossness and the forlorn prospect presented by his marital status of thirty years' standing. Just how or whether that love was consummated is a mystery I have long shrunk from contemplating, but there is no doubt that she took her role as office wife with utmost gravity.

By the summer of 1948, Thomas' Red-hunting had made him a national celebrity; perhaps dizzied by the cresting of his political fortunes, he abandoned caution and brought into his office a comely young woman. While arsenic-and-old-lace smoldered in the corner, Thomas took to tripping into the staff quarters to pay fatuous attentions to the young thing, who responded in the provocative manner of one who has glimpsed the preferability of concubinage to stenography. One fateful evening Thomas crossed the Rubicon by offering, in Miss Campbell's hearing, to drive the young woman home, since they lived "in the same direction." Miss Campbell followed the two, at a discreet distance, and observed the congressman escort her into her apartment building. The elderly secretary waited without.

At length she drove home, to agonize through the grim night of the cast-off. Grasping for a reprieve, she hit upon the saving thought that maybe Thomas had been detained by some innocent circumstance—perhaps he had made a phone call that led to another phone call, something of that sort. Early in the morning she drove past the apartment, eager to find the congressman's car gone. But it remained at the curb, in implacable accusation. Once more the old woman held logic at bay. Suppose Thomas, in a paternal gesture, had just dropped by the place to pick up the young woman and drive her to work. If so, his car radiator would still be warm. She got out of her car, and with grandmotherly dignity, advanced upon his. She paused before it, then reached out dramatically and touched the radiator.

Alas for Thomas, his radiator was cold, and in that instant his star tumbled from the heavens.

Miss Campbell embarked directly upon retribution. Over the months, she had read our blasts at Thomas; they had angered her then, but now the memory of them heartened her. Confident of an outlet, she began assembling records of various irregularities in the faithless one's accounts; for advice on how to approach us, she went to a knowledgeable Capitol Hill staffer, Howard Buckley. Along the way, she had dropped an angry hint or two of her intentions; I got wind of them and went to Buckley hoping to get the story. But displaying a fine sense of both irony and charity, Buckley explained that he wanted to help Andy Older, the unrepentant and unemployed Communist, who needed the money Drew would surely give for this story. So Buckley steered Miss Campbell to Drew through my predecessor on the staff.

Her key story was this: for years Thomas had, with her connivance, been putting no-shows on his congressional payroll and getting them to kick back their federal salaries to him. Some of these hapless accomplices were part-time menials who for the sake of small cash payments for personal or political chores lent themselves to a crime; others were relatives who derived some familial benefits from Thomas and so permitted their names to be used to defraud the government.

For several days we scurried about checking out Miss Campbell's allegations, amid the mounting air of grand expectancy that must attend the construction of a gallows. When everything had been nailed down we went to press, on August 4, 1948:

WASHINGTON—One Congressman who has sadly ignored the old adage that those who live in glass houses shouldn't throw stones is bouncing Rep. J. Parnell Thomas of New Jersey, Chairman of the UnAmerican Activities Committee.

If some of his own personal operations were scrutinized on the witness stand as carefully as he cross-examines witnesses, they would make headlines of a kind the Congressman doesn't like.

It is not, for instance, considered good "Americanism" to hire a stenographer and have her pay a "kickback." This kind of operation is also likely to get an ordinary American in income tax trouble. However, this hasn't seemed to worry the Chairman of the UnAmerican Activities Committee.

On Jan. 1, 1940, Rep. Thomas placed on his payroll Myra Midkiff as a clerk at $1,200 a year with the arrangement that she would then kick back all her salary to the Congressman. This gave Mr. Thomas a neat annual addition to his own $10,000 salary, and presumably he did not have to worry about paying income taxes in this higher bracket, because he paid Miss Midkiff's taxes for her in the much lower bracket.

The arrangement was quite simple and lasted for four years. Miss Midkiff's salary was merely deposited in the First National Bank of Allendale, N.J., to the Congressman's account. Meanwhile she never came anywhere near his office and did not work for him except addressing envelopes at home for which she got paid $2 per hundred.

This kickback plan worked so well that four years later, Miss Midkiff having got married and left his phantom employ, the Congressman decided to extend it. On Nov. 16, 1944, the House Disbursing Officer was notified to place on Thomas's payroll the name of Arnette Minor at $1,800 a year. Actually Miss Minor was a day worker who made beds and cleaned the room of Thomas's secretary, Miss Helen Campbell. Miss Minor's salary was remitted to the Congressman. She never got it.

This arrangement lasted only a month and a half, for on Jan. 1, 1945, the name of Grace Wilson appeared on the Congressman's payroll for $2,900.

Miss Wilson turned out to be Mrs. Thomas's aged aunt, and during the year 1945 she drew checks totaling $3,467.45, though she did not come near the office, in fact remained quietly in Allendale, N.J., where she was

supported by Mrs. Thomas and her sisters, Mrs. Lawrence Wellington and
Mrs. William Quaintance.

In the summer of 1946, however, the Congressman decided to let the
county support his wife's aunt, since his son had recently married and he
wanted to put his daughter-in-law on the payroll. Thereafter, his daughter-
in-law, Lillian, drew Miss Wilson's salary, and the Congressman demanded
that his wife's aunt be put on relief.

Across the void, that half-column, brief and pedestrian, still shines
for me as a classic of destructive precision. In seven short paragraphs
it exposed four inextricable crimes, minor but provable beyond the
most agile of perjuries.

But before crimes can be proved, there must be a willingness to
prosecute, not always present where the accused is a high official. In
a parody of the journalistic ethic, which holds that reporters should
detachedly report the news and shun personal meddling in the events
they write about, Drew became self-appointed avenger. He took his
information personally to the Justice Department, traced out the specific criminal offenses, pointed out where the documentary proof was
and demanded prosecution. When officials countered that they had no
witnesses, he brought in a nervous Helen Campbell. And when they
said she would have to plead guilty to participating in a conspiracy and
be indicted along with Thomas—an outcome the good woman had not
anticipated—Drew wore down her reluctance and at length she agreed.
On the night before her jury appearance, Drew sat up with her till the
wee hours, rehearsing questions and answers. By agreement, she was
not to be jailed and when the proceedings were over, Drew would make
a place for her on his payroll, which she continued to occupy for the
next fifteen years.

Meanwhile, the column kept the heat on the Justice Department
with a stream of ancillary disclosures from Miss Campbell's fertile
memory.

There is something in the nature of Homo politicus, some inherent
or induced dearth of dignity that renders him unable, upon being found
out, to go quietly. He will not, cannot rest until he has degraded into
bathos the element of tragedy that lurks in any man's ruin. Perhaps
because he has so long won out by subterfuge, he simply cannot desist
from fraudulent writhings until he has stripped himself of the last shred
of honor and inflicted upon his family the final grain of pain and
humiliation.

And so Thomas exhausted every ploy in the catalogue of evasion. He denied all charges, calling them dirty politics, as though the immutable bank records that indicted him signified some mysterious conspiracy of enemies. He stirred up American Legion posts to mount their hobbyhorses on his behalf and got congressional leaders to attempt a quashing of the case, all in vain. He obtained a postponement from the grand jury by promising to testify before it after his upcoming election, but two days after the election, which he won, he suddenly claimed his constitutional rights and refused to appear.

After his indictment, he declined to resign from the House and began a campaign to avoid trial. Five times he got trial postponements on grounds of illness, turning himself into Walter Reed Hospital every time the gavel drew nigh. On at least one occasion he was indeed sick, unless he carried deception to the extreme, for he underwent surgery. But on his sixth postponement attempt, Walter Reed refused to admit him, blocking him off at the door in a scene worthy of his committee room, and a court-appointed panel of doctors found him able to stand trial.

As the legal wheels ground on, Drew drove home some points about Americanism in an "open letter" by contrasting the conduct of Thomas the defendant with that of Thomas the chairman:

Although this column first exposed your un-American activity in taking salary kickbacks from employees, this is not written in a desire to gloat over your indictment; but rather to point out some of the great privileges of being American which all of us do not appreciate. On the basis of your previous behavior, you appear to be one who fails in that appreciation.

For instance, when you later go on trial before a jury of your peers, no inference can be drawn from the fact that last week before a grand jury you refused to testify because you might incriminate yourself.

Scores of witnesses before your own committee have been berated because they refused to testify for the same reason. But the judge, giving you the full privilege of your American citizenship, will instruct the jury to disregard your previous refusal to testify.

Furthermore, even after your indictment this week, you are presumed to be innocent until trial by jury finds you guilty. That is your privilege as an American—a privilege you have denied to many others whom you tried before the bar of Congressional public opinion. Even when you go to trial you can still refuse to testify and no inference can be drawn from that refusal. The judge will specifically instruct the jury that that is your privilege as an American.

During your trial, furthermore, the Government prosecutor cannot and will not bring up any irrelevant facts that might prejudice the jury against you. He cannot bring out the fact that you changed your name from Feeney, though you have badgered witnesses before your committee who changed their names.

. . . Unlike some of the hearings before your own committee, you will be tried strictly on the charges brought against you—namely, did you receive salary kickbacks or not?

Furthermore, it will be your privilege as an American to be represented by counsel. You can consult with him at any time you wish. He will be constantly at your side as you face the judge and jury. If you should not be able to afford counsel, the judge will appoint a lawyer to represent you at no expense to yourself. You have denied committee witnesses the right to consult with counsel as they testified, but when you go on trial, the judge will make sure that this American right is yours.

Those, Mr. Thomas, are some of the privileges of being American. They have been won by your ancestors and mine over many years of battling for the rights of man. And many millions of Americans would fight now to see that they are not torn down, would even fight to make sure that you get their full benefit—even though you denied them to others.

In the middle of the trial, after each of his kickback schemes had been proved down to the shabbiest detail, Thomas suddenly abandoned his defense, pleaded "no contest" and with a great slobbering threw himself upon the mercy of the court. He was sentenced to up to eighteen months in prison and a $10,000 fine. On the day he passed into Danbury prison, his wife declared for election to his vacated House seat, thus to perpetuate for additional weeks the daily rehashing of what must have been, even in New Jersey, a family disgrace. She was defeated.

At our 29th Street offices, the final crushing of J. Parnell Thomas brought the subdued sort of celebration befitting a profession whose triumphs entail the ruin of the adversary. The House Un-American Activities Committee was in apparent rout. Thomas was in jail, McDowell had been defeated for re-election, as had committee member Richard Vail of Illinois; Rankin at long last had been kicked off the committee and would be defeated at the polls next time out. We could not be sure of the degree of our influence on some of these reverses, though Rankin did us the honor of announcing to the press that the execrable Pearson had had nothing to do with his political demise; but the fall of Thomas, the premier offender, was our handiwork beyond doubt.

The House Un-American Activities Committee would survive for two decades, but as a spavined thing never again to regain the power or prominence it had so lately enjoyed. In terms of the larger struggle, however, the first blood would prove to have come with deceptive ease.

6 · The Pursuit of
James Forrestal

I<small>F WE MAY</small> rely upon the historical verdict that is written in monuments, no cabinet member among the giants of the 1940s inspires greater veneration today than the banker-intellectual who was Franklin D. Roosevelt's Secretary of the Navy and Harry S. Truman's Secretary of Defense, James V. Forrestal. His is the name that adorns the Defense Department's gigantic new headquarters edifice in Washington as testament that after a quarter century, he remains the highest personification of its aspirations. So is he commemorated by the majestic queen of aircraft carriers, chosen as the site of former President Gerald Ford's participation in the National Bicentennial on July 4, 1976. The popular image of Forrestal that has survived an already long filtering process reflects the monumental one—a man of vision, dynamism, high purpose, selflessness, dedication.

The living Forrestal was at the peak of his influence when I first came under Drew Pearson's wing. Drew described him at that time as the most powerful man in the Cabinet, the number-two figure of an Administration which, through the force of events, was busily recasting the shape of the world. This assessment was made in anguish, for Drew regarded the Defense Secretary as the archrepresentative of Wall

Street imperialism and of a world view that war with the Soviet Union was inevitable. During my first two years on the Pearson staff, if there was one objective that stood above all others, it was to expose Forrestal, his financial ties and militaristic inclinations. The anti-Forrestal campaign, clouded over as it would become by the tragedy in which it culminated, was unpopular in its time and still is not viewed favorably from the historical perspective, but Drew went to his grave still believing in its soundness and its necessity.

I will never forget a conversation with Drew near the end of the vendetta. On a day in March 1949, Drew signaled me into his living room and gestured toward a chair. He had a solemn hush about him, as if he were to impart something important. "Forrestal has gone off his rocker," he said. "He's mad as a hatter." There was in Drew's demeanor a bit of the dramatic, to ensure I did not miss the holocaustal potential, however hypothetical, but also a trace of that melancholy recognition of man's deceptively frail hold upon life and reality.

Drew quietly recounted a series of conversations with Attorney General Tom Clark, one of his closet confidants. Two months earlier Forrestal had called on Clark in a state of agitation over a Pearson radio attack, one of a hundred criticisms and disparagements from our camp. In this instance Drew had revived an eleven-year-old allegation that Forrestal had fled the scene when thugs robbed his wife of her jewelry in front of their New York home. The Defense Secretary asked Clark's advice as to whether he ought, at long last, to sue the infamous Pearson for libel. Clark counseled a conciliatory approach. In relating the conversation to Drew, the Attorney General emphasized Forrestal's mental state, saying at one point, "He was as nervous as a whore in church." It was an unusual characterization of the stoic Forrestal, an accomplished veteran of nine years of Washington infighting at the highest level.

And now, in their latest conversation, the Attorney General had told Drew that beginning a week earlier, Forrestal had started making mysterious phone calls to him at odd hours, saying he was worried but declining to say why. After several days of this he had opened up, accusing Clark of trying to "crucify" him. "You've got your men over here!" The startled Clark denied it, but Forrestal was adamant. One day he phoned Clark triumphantly to tell him that four of Clark's men were outside his house at that very moment, watching him. "They've tapped my wires, they've been all over the house. They're trying to get something on me." Again, Clark was unable to dissuade him.

Drew then told me of similar accounts he'd been getting from other sources. For months Secretary Forrestal had been complaining to intimates of being "followed by Jews" or "Zionist agents." And in the latest development, Drew had received a puzzling phone call from a close friend of Forrestal's, Ferdinand Eberstadt of Wall Street. Without giving a reason, Eberstadt made a "special request" that Drew suspend any further criticism of Forrestal for the time being. Drew assented.

"Forrestal has cracked—wide open," Drew concluded softly, matter-of-factly, his tone giving no hint of what sentiment he felt at this alarming turn in so long a road.

It was a road Drew had been pursuing years before I got pulled along. Before turning me loose in the Pentagon two years earlier, he had given me a word of caution: "Don't be fooled over there by that cabal of captivated reporters and paid press agents that pays court to Forrestal."

The "cabal" turned out to be a circle of the nation's most prestigious journalists—Arthur Krock and Hansen Baldwin of the New York *Times*, Lyle Wilson of UP, top syndicated columnists like the Alsop brothers and Marquis Childs, the amalgam at *Time* and *Newsweek*, and many others. If they did not pay court to Forrestal, they did see him as the paragon among the American proconsuls of the postwar world. His complex make-up gave off a contrapuntal music that intrigued and revived literary imaginations grown stale on coverage of one-dimensional politicians.

In their accounts Secretary Forrestal came through as a practical philosopher who combined a powerful mind with intellectual humility, whose brusque exterior belied a kindly inner warmth, whose upward surge to the heights of wealth and power had occurred despite an unexampled selflessness. He was said to possess a crisp power of decision untainted by ruthlessness, an appreciation for the complexity of any situation but yet a capacity for firm, clear judgment, a mastery of the bureaucratic process that was still free from petty maneuvering and political machination. I suspected there were improbabilities scattered among these paeans, but certainly the bare bones of his record left me with a favorable inclination.

An outsider of modest Irish-Catholic origins, he had while still a young man conquered the WASP citadel of high finance. Gifted with a drive and endurance phenomenal even among budding tycoons and with a flair for bringing off financial coups, the "boy wonder of Wall Street" became in his early thirties a power at the great investment banking house of Dillon, Read & Co. and was president of the firm at forty-six.

Two years later, in 1940, he abandoned his penthouse roost atop the glass canyons of finance, where he would earn $1 million in good years, to enter public life as one of President Franklin D. Roosevelt's anonymous aides. Soon he became Undersecretary of the Navy and then, in 1944, the Secretary. In these posts he was, more than any other, the driving force behind the incomparable feat of production and mobilization which created the vast fleets that won the war and now ruled the oceans of the world. So great was his stature within the rivalrous military that when President Harry Truman pushed through unification of the armed forces after the war, Forrestal, though he had opposed unification, was the inevitable choice as the first Secretary of Defense, head of our combined forces.

I could not help being impressed by such credentials and tried to regard Forrestal with a neutrality equidistant from my colleagues' lionization and my boss's disdain. The great man seemed to grasp this and made himself accessible, perhaps seeing in me a hope of getting Pearson off his back.

In his office he kept a printed motto on display: "We will never have universal peace until the strongest army and the strongest navy are in the hands of the most powerful nation."

On my guard, I thought I sensed a sudden convolution about a third of the way through that homily. What began as a pacific aspiration gracefully elided into a challenge to a perpetual arms race, in pursuit of a Pax Romana. Or was it just unexceptionable Pentagon boiler plate?

The man behind the motto was similarly sinuous. Face to face, he was impressive, even magnetic, but it was part of his magnetism that he gave off discordant vibes. Of medium physical proportions and wiry build, he seemed through some knack of carriage to be larger and more powerful than he was. He had an arresting face, on which a detached intellectuality seemed at odds with a wariness of eye, the flattened nose broken in boxing, the pencil-line mouth, with their combined intimation of the physical—what Jonathan Daniels described as features that "the movies dramatically give to the better gangsters."

Smoking his pipe reflectively, in easy command of an awesome array of strategic concept and tactical detail, he effected a calm mastery. But I felt a tenseness in him, sometimes a sense of beleaguerment as though he were at war with ubiquitous forces. At fifty-six, he displayed an athletic conditioning that was almost ostentatious but, coming and going, he would have a book tucked under his arm, often a heavy tome of Greek dramas or German philosophy.

Those of us covering Forrestal quickly learned that he was the all-time champion in the realm of what is now called the "workaholic." He actually worked the fourteen-hour day that many boast of but only the rarity can sustain, and he worked it seven days a week, decade in and decade out. Forrestal would be at his office on Christmas Day, coiled in impatience because his usual working partners were unavailable. So far as his time was concerned, he did nothing gratuitously; all was programed to advance his objectives so that even his apparent diversions, like his athletics and reading, were relentlessly targeted toward increasing his efficiency and proficiency.

He was resolutely unwilling to make minimal concessions to life's normal demands, even from family, with the result that he and his wife, Josephine, had lived essentially separate lives throughout most of their marriage. As a younger man he was said to have reserved an hour on Friday evenings for his two children, but now that they were grown, he was happily free of even that token interruption.

My initial impressions were jumbled: a formidable public servant of Draconian crochets but of great capacity, enormous expertise and obvious dedication to large purposes. Drew listened to my recitals, his ear cocked for the sinister nugget, his head shaking off the favorable estimate, like an uncle trying to weather an impatience he knew must be suffered from the invincible gullibility of the young.

"Jack," he would say, "Forrestal is the most dangerous man in America. Sure he's able. Of course he's dedicated. But to what? He's a man who lives only for himself. He has broken his word, turned his back on his friends. He is driven by one ambition; he has always craved to be top man—first of Wall Street and now of the United States. Any principles he has are the kind that will cause another world war—unless he's stopped first."

I began to inquire quietly into the reasons behind Drew's antipathy and found they had been accumulating for twenty years. To begin with, Drew held Forrestal accountable for the record of Dillon, Read & Co. during the period he had been a dominant force there. It was a record which sinned flagrantly against Drew's brightest passions and darkest prejudices—his lifelong crusade to free Latin America from U.S. exploitation, his championship of a homeland for the world's displaced Jews, his loathing of Big Oil and his fundamental distrust of the German nation, under whatever regime.

In the 1920s Dillon, Read & Co. had loaned $20 million to Bolivia, which was used to finance an aggressive war against Paraguay; it loaned hundreds of millions to the German cartels of the Ruhr during the pre-Hitler period, reviving industries which were to form the backbone of Hitler's war machine. When Forrestal, as the strong man of the Truman Cabinet, pushed for yet another restoration of the Ruhr industries and planned a lend-lease program of arms to "friendly" Latin American military regimes, Drew foresaw a magnification of the follies and tragedies of the past.

At Dillon, Read & Co., Forrestal had been banker to Big Oil and had helped underwrite its expansion into the Arab countries; and when, during World War II, our Navy grossly overpaid the Arabian-American Oil Company for petroleum, or when Forrestal vehemently opposed the partition of Palestine and persuaded President Truman to reverse his initial support for a new Jewish state, Drew saw the hated hand of the international oil puppeteers at work. There were respectable national-interest arguments to be made for the Dillon, Read loans and the Forrestal public policies, but they ran afoul both of Drew's idealism and his demonology.

But how, then, could Drew explain the admiration of Forrestal among so many observers within the internationalist, moderate-to-liberal spectrum? That he brushed aside. Forrestal had to make many surface accommodations, he argued, to survive and prosper in the Roosevelt-Truman regimes. But by a dozen litmus-test standards that Drew applied, Forrestal was a Trojan Horse of the Right lodged inside the highest counsels of a professedly liberal Democratic Administration.

His push for universal military training for every American male, his fight to perpetuate military control over atomic energy development, his preference for increased arms spending over economic improvements, his imputation of disloyalty to those who had advocated swift postwar demobilization were only the most visible parts of the pattern. By many accounts in Drew's bulging Forrestal file, the Secretary was as obsessed as the House Un-American Activities Committee with the domestic Communist threat. He had turned his office suite into a center for the preparation of dossiers on individuals and journals that had opposed American entry into World War I and World War II and that might be troublesome in the future, and he was an avid, ex-officio prober into suspected Communist influence in universities, the movies, the media and labor unions, as well as government agencies.

He dabbled in authoritarian schemes for the purification of national thought. For example, he proposed that a domestic version of the U.S. Information Agency be set up to ensure that the American people were exposed to the right kind of news and ideology, and to safeguard them against the wrong kind, he advocated a program of voluntary censorship by patriotic publishers, along with legislation that would merge all broadcast and cable facilities into one corporation operating under limited government control.

And he was a pioneer in promoting the kind of secret government with which the following generation was to become familiar. He consistently appealed for expansion of our counterintelligence and counterinsurgency activities, and proposed a super agency that would overarch the likes of the FBI and the CIA and be able to fight the Communists at their own game, abroad or at home. In the absence of such an agency, he intervened personally, raising huge funds from private donors for various works which ranged from the buying off of railroad strikers in France to the buying up of politicians in Italy.

Among Pearson's confidants were numerous high officials who came into contact with Forrestal (Cabinet members such as Harold Ickes, Oscar Chapman, Tom Clark, Louis Johnson; ambassadors like Joseph Davies and James Bruce) and who gave Drew closed-door glimpses of the Defense Secretary. The composite picture they etched was of a man who believed that a third world war was inevitable; who was convinced as early as 1943 that Russia was the ultimate enemy; who had maneuvered Truman into a tough anti-Russian stance at the outset of his presidency in 1945; who lived in a continuous state of crisis and seemed to have psychic need of it; who saw himself as indispensable to the successful prosecution of the Cold War and brooded continually that he had not been aggressive enough in alerting the Cabinet and the nation to the Red Danger.

At Cabinet meetings he talked of American-Russian relations in terms of "showdown" and "forcing the issue." He was contemptuous of his Cabinet colleagues, and of the President himself, for backing down and showing weakness to Stalin. He was haunted by what the Washington *Post* would later call "an obsession that the Cold War was the prelude to a shooting war. This obsession became an *idée fixe* as time went on." Drew did not award Forrestal the prophet's mantle for this; instead he feared that the premature and overstrident Cold Warrior had already brought about self-fulfilling prophecies of tragedy and would bring about more.

Even Forrestal's choice of witticisms placed him, in Drew's eyes, in the political camp of the reactionaries. A few months after the GOP congressional landslide of 1946—which buried scores of Northern liberal Democrats, left the ranks of conservative Southern Democrats unscathed and thus placed Congress under lopsided Republican-Dixiecrat control—the Secretary wrote to a business associate expressing pleasure at the result: "The overturn of last autumn was in many respects a healthy thing . . . Congressman John Rankin of Mississippi made the remark that the Democrats were not defeated last November but were de-loused."

Drew was as anxious as Forrestal for a de-lousing of the Democratic Party, but there was a polar difference between their respective slates of nominees for that honor, a mirror of the larger differences that made their conflict irresolvable.

The upcoming year of 1948 was a presidential-election year, the most vulnerable time for a Cabinet officer, and Drew was determined that whoever won the election, Forrestal should depart the Pentagon. I was not asked specifically to bring in stories critical of Forrestal, merely to give play to my investigative bent. In the protected corridors of the Pentagon, this was not an easy assignment, for among the military, the cult of secrecy was far more developed than on my congressional training ground, and to Pentagon people, in their thousands of look-alike cubicles, a Pearson legman seemed even more loathsome than on Capitol Hill.

But circumstance came to my aid. The armed services—Army, Air Force, Navy, Marines—were at that moment in history undergoing three simultaneous traumas: (1) they were suffering the horrors of a postwar shrinkage which in two years had caused military appropriations to shrivel from $43 billion to $12 billion; (2) they were being merged under the 1947 Unification Act, a threat to the status of each; and (3) revolutionary changes in weapons technology were bursting upon the scene with unforeseeable impacts on the future of warfare. A cruel uncertainty thus clouded the air for the military careerists; the allocation of funds, missions and future growth were all in jeopardy, and each branch felt itself in a struggle not just for status but for survival.

For the brash reporter, this produced a favorable climate for inducing leaks of classified information that would aid or embarrass this or that branch in the mortal competition. Instead of being scorned, as I had at first feared, I was soon in unseemly alliance with generals, admirals, assistant secretaries, yes, even secretaries (whose names I cannot in honor divulge even after the passage of three decades). Thanks to their whisperings, I began to bring to Drew one scoop after another: the top-secret Navy arguments for displacing the Air Force as the prime deliverer of atomic payloads in the next war; the suppressed report on the Bikini atomic weapons tests showing unexpected vulnerabilities of naval vessels to distant atomic explosions; the blow-by-blow on the Air Force's campaign to win congressional backing for a seventy-group air armada instead of the forty-eight groups backed by Truman and Forrestal; indications of shocking unpreparedness on the industrial front; various fiascoes under the unification process which were undermining the promised efficiencies and economies.

Drew was eager for such stories and would rush them into print despite the personal hazards of trafficking in classified material. There were two reasons for this, beyond their news significance. First, Drew at all times felt it a service to the Republic to dethrone brass hats from their white horses. Second, at this particular time, any exposé that revealed the leaking of secrets, feuding, insubordination or maladministration within the armed forces splattered the gleaming escutcheon of the vaunted Secretary in charge.

My stories were only part of a mix, the hard-news component which was fed into a calibrated onslaught that on an average of once a week hammered away unremittingly in print and on the air, striking and restriking over and over all the anti-Forrestal chords. I cite below a sampling that is representative, though chosen from the capsule items which were alternated with column-length treatments.

June 27, 1947—Senator Claude Pepper of Florida tells close friends that the Congressional battle over President Truman's veto of the Taft-Hartley Bill marks the beginning of a "permanent cleavage" between liberals and conservatives in both political parties . . . the two cabinet members who fought hardest against any veto were Secretary of the Navy Forrestal and Secretary of Commerce Harriman. Both Wall Street bankers, both wanted Truman to sign the bill.

November 13, 1947—Republicans who will have to pass upon the qualifications of James Forrestal for the all-important job of Secretary of National Defense have been checking into his background and have stumbled onto some highly interesting facts. Back in the first years of the Roosevelt Administration, Forrestal was exposed by the Senate Banking Committee probe for having got around a $840,000 income-tax payment by setting up a personal holding corporation. This Senate Banking probe also exposed

Forrestal's banking firm—Dillon, Read & Co.—as one of the worst high-binders on Wall Street when it came to floating bad loans to Germany and Latin America. As a result of this investigation, Roosevelt set up the Securities and Exchange Commission. Now, however, Republicans point out that the head of a Wall Street house with one of the worst records of all has become head of the combined Army and Navy.

January 27, 1948—It was the pumping of American money into Europe and Latin America by American bankers that heightened and prolonged the boom days which followed World War I. And it was the sudden drying up of that credit that accelerated the bust . . . The big German steel plants, which Hitler later turned into the most efficient war machine in Europe, all were built up by millions of American investors—the chief money-raiser for Germany being the same man who now heads our National Defense Department—James Forrestal.

February 29, 1948—Secretary of Defense Forrestal, bitter opponent of Palestine partition, invited top Washington newsmen to a hush-hush dinner the other night to assure them he isn't going to resign as a result of Palestine. Forrestal also assured them that he has great sympathy for the Jews and understands their position . . .

March 12, 1948—Forrestal has appointed as his deputy on atomic matters, Donald F. Carpenter, President of the Remington Arms Company, a duPont subsidiary . . . Back in 1928, Secretary Forrestal's Wall Street banking firm loaned $20,000,000 to Bolivia with which to buy arms for the purpose of waging war against Paraguay. This money was used, among other things, to hire Capt. Ernst Roehm as military adviser to the Bolivian Government, and it was in Bolivia that Roehm first developed his idea of storm troopers. Later he organized the same thing for Hitler.

Immediately after Forrestal loaned this money to Bolivia, Remington Arms Company, which Donald Carpenter heads, stepped in to profit by it. Remington got a juicy contract for 7.65 mm. and 9 mm. cartridges and the files of the Senate Munitions investigation contain revealing testimony on this sale. So Forrestal, the man who made the munitions loan which helped foment war in Latin America, now hires as his deputy the head of the company which profited from that loan by selling arms to Latin America.

May 4, 1948—Hard working Senator Donnell of Missouri begins important hearings today on the most powerful lobby Washington has seen in a long time—tidelands oil.

There is one phase of the tidelands oil pressure group that bears especial attention. It is the fact that exactly the same gang which overcharged the U.S. Navy for Arabian oil, which finagled lush loans from the U.S. Treasury for King Ibn Saud of Arabia, and which lobbied to kill the partition of

Palestine, is now pulling wires to turn the rich tidelands oil reserve over to the coastal states—with considerable benefit to the oil companies . . . It's significant that the Wall Street firm of James V. Forrestal, now the most potent man in the cabinet, once handled the finances of Arab-American oil interests. Forrestal is the man who persuaded Truman to kill the partition of Palestine, thus leaving the United Nations and the Near East with about the worst international mess since the war ended.

December 15, 1948—Practically all Latin America is watching the State Department to see what we do about recognizing the new Army dictatorship in Venezuela . . . the State Department's trigger-recognition of Latin dictators has brought forth a rash of military revolts, the latest being the Nicaraguan-inspired march against the peaceful government of Costa Rica . . .

Secretary of Defense Forrestal still favors his plan of sending more arms to Latin America under a new lend-lease agreement, despite the fact that new arms to Latin American generals are like a toy train to a small boy at Christmastime. They can't wait to use them—usually against their own President.

General Somoza, the Nicaraguan who has now inspired the fracas in Costa Rica, was trained by the U.S. Marines, later seized the Presidency of Nicaragua. President Trujillo, worst dictator in all Latin America, was also trained by the U.S. Marines. Unfortunately, under the Forrestal-Marine Corps program, we train men to shoot and give them the weapons to shoot with. But we don't give them any ideas or ideals as to what they should shoot for.

Week in and week out the cannonading continued; a year of it passed, a year and a half, and still no surcease. By the fall of 1948 it seemed to me that it had long since passed the bounds of effectiveness, not to speak of propriety. But like other noted propagandists, Drew believed in the necessity of overkill. Public forgetfulness was to him the bane of democracy; repetition was its cure.

His goal was to make Forrestal's little-known attitudes common parlance among the professional gripers of the key power blocs within the Democratic Party—the Jews, Labor, the blacks, the liberals—so that during the election campaign they'd be putting the screws on embattled Harry Truman to dump Forrestal after November. Drew turned up the decibels on the Ruhr, Palestine, Taft-Hartley and the rest.

Meanwhile Forrestal was positioning himself for the growing likelihood that Truman would be replaced in the White House by Governor

Thomas E. Dewey of New York. After Dewey's nomination by the assembled Republicans, Forrestal began making secret visits to him; he would deplore the condition of our national security under Truman, trot out his bold remedies and discreetly advertise his availability for service in a Dewey Cabinet. It wasn't necessary to remind Dewey that Roosevelt and Truman had developed a tradition of placing Republicans in high defense and foreign policy posts—Henry Stimson, Frank Knox, Allen Dulles, Warren Austin, Robert Lovett. The question was implied: Why not continue this patriotic bipartisanship under Republicans, via a Wall Street Democrat popular with Congress? The idea took hold; a go-between with Dewey assured Forrestal in mid-October: "I am informed Dewey would be delighted to have you as his Secretary of Defense . . ."

So as not to hamper his transition to a Republican Administration, Forrestal dissociated himself from the Truman campaign. He declined to raise money for the hard-up Truman, saying it would be inappropriate for a Secretary of Defense to embroil himself in partisan politics. This was an unkind cut from the Administration's resident financier, to whom the Democrats had for many years entrusted the letting of vast government contracts. Moreover, Forrestal negotiated most delicately the matter of his personal campaign contribution. He instructed a servitor, one Walter Dunnington, to contribute $2,500 to the Truman campaign under Dunnington's name, out of a secret fund Forrestal maintained for gifts and transactions he wanted to remain unconnected with. In the unlikely event that Truman won, Forrestal would reveal himself as the true contributor; if Truman lost, there would be no way for Dewey to find out about Forrestal's lapse.

None of this was at first known to Drew, but he devoutly suspected all of it. Scornful of the view that Forrestal was above political double-dealing and long a despairing student of the interparty traffic by which the Wall Street crowd manipulated the policy-making machinery whether under a Hoover or a Truman, Drew buttonholed his every source for signs of any slithering by Forrestal toward Dewey.

He had developed the chief fund raiser for Truman as an underground confidant, former Assistant Secretary of War Louis Johnson, latterly a Washington lawyer for corporate interests. The common bond between these unlikely bedfellows was that Johnson sought Forrestal's ouster too, in order to fill the vacancy himself. From Johnson, Drew learned of Forrestal's refusal to raise campaign money. Normally our column would have applauded a Defense czar who declined to use his clout for partisan shakedowns, but in Forrestal's case it was portrayed as hypocritical treachery:

> Forrestal was one of those who first urged Truman to run, told him it would be a walk-away, gave the White House to understand he would raise a large campaign fund. But when the showdown came, Forrestal maintained a holier-than-thou attitude toward the campaign, was the only man who asked for his $100 back from a Truman-Barkley dinner after it was called off.

From another source, who must still remain anonymous, confirmation of Forrestal's courting of Dewey finally came into our hands. On September 3, 1948, the column revealed that Forrestal had been meeting secretly with Dewey, and continued: "It's an open secret that Forrestal would like to hold on to his job regardless of the outcome of the November election. Governor Dewey did not commit himself." Forrestal was to deny this report repeatedly, but Dewey would confirm it years later.*

Drew had at last caught Forrestal in an irretrievable embarrassment, and he took every occasion to remind the nation of it. Henceforth the Secretary was presented as a faithless opportunist, a "Cabinet Judas" and "Dewey's friend." This was calculated to serve in either of two eventualities. If Dewey won, a Forrestal appointment would appear tainted, a reward for treachery that would put a needless smudge on the image of the new President. If Truman won, he was unlikely to forgive, nor be allowed to by his loyalists, the personal and political disloyalty we had exposed and raised to a public drama.

This proved to be a sound estimate in the long run, but for months following Truman's upset victory it seemed in doubt. Harry Truman had an unpredictable streak of magnanimity in him. He could be reliably petty and vindictive in the best presidential tradition, but one could never be sure just when a rash of nobility would break out. When Forrestal launched a campaign to retain his post in the new Administration, Truman seemed to succumb to a sudden attack of statesmanship. Though he had assured his outriders that he would remove Forrestal, he delayed doing so, month after month, until Forrestal's cause seemed to be daily reviving, aided by boosts from his press admirers and other persons of influence who regarded his continuance as vital to the national security.

*In a letter dated June 25, 1959, to Forrestal biographer Arnold A. Rogow. See his *James Forrestal: A Study of Personality, Politics and Policy* (New York: Macmillan, 1963), p. 276.

Louis Johnson watched incredulously as the mists of creeping ingratitude rose about him. Had he not wrought a financial miracle for Truman? Had he not kept the campaign train on the rails, the gospel on the airwaves? But despite this, despite the semiassurances, the command of our forces on land, sea and air seemed inexplicably to be slipping from his grasp. He kept in daily but covert contact with Drew, exchanging rumors and plotting the good cause. In mid-January, with only a week to go till the inauguration, "Louie" called with alarming tidings. Truman had just told him that he wanted to get rid of Forrestal, oh how he wanted to, but that the "son of a bitch" came in and "took advantage of me and put me on the spot."

This rattled Drew almost as much as Johnson, for it portended backsliding at the penultimate moment. He cast about for another stratagem, and in a war of attrition that had occasionally been marred by low blows, he now descended to poison gas. On his next national broadcast, and in the column, he revived the old jewel-robbery story which, as described earlier, had brought a shaken Forrestal to Attorney General Clark's office:

> Mrs. Forrestal, returning home at 2:10 A.M., July 2, 1937, with Richard B.W. Hall, a broker, was robbed of a sunburst with a 25-carat emerald; a platinum bracelet 2 1/2 inches wide with bands of diamonds; a platinum ring with 27-carat emerald, a platinum ring with 14-carat diamond, and other expensive jewels.
>
> The Secretary of National Defense, then an executive of Dillon, Read, investment bankers, was asleep in his home when the robbery occurred just outside his house at 27 Beckman Place. New York newspapers next day featured the fact that, after hearing the police alarm, Forrestal slipped out the back entrance, vaulted the rear fence, ran down an alley, and caught a taxi to his club where he spent the remainder of the night.
>
> New York newspapers also described how his wife went to the police station to look over the rogues' gallery and face the lineup without her husband.

It was a hit-and-run treatment of an incident that in eleven years had never been clearly confirmed, adequately denied or intelligently explained; in the absence of clarifying information, it should have been left interred.

Drew's January offensive, aided by Walter Winchell, his only peer in radio influence, enraged the President. This was a predictable hazard in a delicate calculation of risk versus gain. Truman, our sources told us, was deeply disturbed by our revelation of the Forrestal overtures to

Dewey, but the President had long bridled at Pearson's stirring up of anti-Forrestal pressures on him, which from a half-dozen directions were pushing him toward a decision he was reluctant to take. And so, to intimates he bellowed objurgations, one of which was snitched to us in sanitized form: "Pearson and Winchell are too big for their britches. We are going to have a showdown as to who is running this country —me or them—and the showdown had better come now than later."

Drew was unmoved. "You can't make a President do something he doesn't want to do by treading softly or cultivating his good will," he instructed me. "You have to hold his feet to the fire and burn him; he hates you for it, but he hates the fire more."

The overall pattern of our White House intelligence bore out Drew's sanguinity; the heat was getting uncomfortable for Truman. In late February, Drew had breakfast with Truman aide David Noyes, who tipped him that Forrestal was definitely "out" and would be gone as soon as a face-saving exit could be orchestrated. On March 1 an elated Louis Johnson met with Drew just after a luncheon with the President and reported that Truman had definitely "promised me Secretary of Defense" by not later than April 1 and had refused a Forrestal request to stay on until May 1. Two days later Truman publicly announced Forrestal's replacement by Johnson, the changing of the guard to take place at the end of March.

The long siege was over. The "most dangerous man in America" was at last to be replaced by a Pearson friend and co-intriguer, dedicated to cutting back military spending. In congratulating Johnson on his appointment, Drew told the lawyer-lobbyist that henceforth the adversary relationship that existed between our column and high officials would be in force and that "as a friend I am going to watch you more closely than if you were not a friend, and call the shots accordingly." (True to his word, Drew was later to expose Johnson's law firm for arranging prohibited sales of restricted metals to the Red Chinese.)

During Forrestal's last months in the Pentagon, as it had closed in upon him that he was likely to be ousted, a marked deterioration in the man had become visible to intimates—loss of weight, a sudden aging, moods of apparent depression. He had frequently alluded to the suicide of Jan Masaryk, and had at times seemed preoccupied with the physical and mental stability of various of his colleagues. For many months he had been wont to imply that he was the victim of various "plots" and "conspiracies."

Speculation grew within the Cabinet that he might be suffering from physical and nervous exhaustion. Or worse. Sometimes his eyes bulged in a way that reminded one colleague of his own insane daughter. Sometimes his mind wandered erratically, but soon it would clear again. A month before he left office he "gave the impression of taking dope" to Louis Johnson, who was then meeting daily with him in the transition process. Forrestal had a direct telephone in his office to the Alsop brothers, Johnson would later tell Drew, "and in the middle of conversations would pick up the phone, call the Alsops and tell them what was going on. Sometimes he even told them things that had never happened."

As early as January 1949, Tom Clark revealed Forrestal's agitated state to Drew. But apparently none of his Cabinet colleagues or the admirals or generals or politicians or press intimates who had frequent opportunity to glimpse the approaching tragedy made a definitive move to protect Forrestal, or more important, to protect the national interest from Forrestal.

The actual leaving of office brought his condition to a head. At the conclusion of the ceremonies Forrestal was found sitting behind his desk in a rigid posture with his hat on, holding a ceremonial bowl and repeating the words "You are a loyal fellow."

An alarmed associate drove him home, where he began to search the closets for hidden "Communists" and "White House people." The first thought of his colleagues was to hide him in a place where he could be examined in secret; requisitioning an Air Force Constellation, they hustled him off that very day to the vacation home of Averell Harriman in Hobe Sound, Florida. Several days later it was announced that he had been admitted to Bethesda Naval Hospital for treatment of exhaustion from overwork. He was at first placed in a closely supervised ward on the ground floor, but in the interest of concealment, and over the objections of his "physician," Dr. George Raines, a decision was made to move him up to the sixteenth floor, to quarters never intended for mental patients. There, a rotation of Marine guards blocked observance by the outside world, and Forrestal's true condition remained concealed behind a smoke screen of press handouts about "exhaustion."*

Within five or six days, we had pieced together the following facts:

On his arrival at Hobe Sound, a haggard, ashen-faced Forrestal had greeted Undersecretary of State Robert Lovett by saying, "Bob, they're

---

*For a valuable account of the advance indications of Forrestal's condition, and of the nonmedical considerations that influenced treatment, see Rogow, *op. cit.*

after me." He was convinced that the Communists were planning an imminent invasion of the United States, that they had infiltrated the White House and the Defense establishment and that he, like Masaryk, was their number-one target for liquidation. Lovett and his companions shared a twenty-four-hour-a-day watch on Forrestal, even following him to the bathroom. They flew in two psychiatrists, Captain George Raines of Bethesda Naval Hospital and Dr. William Menninger of the Menninger Foundation at Topeka, Kansas. While at Hobe Sound, Forrestal made three suicide attempts, by drug overdose, by hanging and by slashing his wrists. On the night of April 1, the sound of a fire-engine siren prompted him to rush out of the house in his pajamas screaming, "The Russians are attacking!"

With hospitalization unavoidable, Bethesda was chosen rather than an avowedly mental institution where admittance would complicate the public relations plan. On April 2 Forrestal was secretly flown to Washington by the Air Force. En route he demanded that before he got off the plane the airport must be cleared of "all Air Force men and Jews." During the drive from the airport to the hospital, he tried repeatedly to hurl himself from the automobile.

We had assembled most of this by April 9, a week after Forrestal's entry into Bethesda Naval Hospital. We knew that the "Forrestal cabal" of reporters, as Drew called them, knew more than we did, and had known it earlier; columnist Marquis Childs, for instance, had entreated mutual friends who knew the facts: "Don't tell Drew."

But for all the insider knowledge, none of it had surfaced. Day after day the muted official announcements lied to the public, and the "prestige" press, which knew the truth, carried the lies without refutation. In truth, Forrestal was suffering from a severe psychosis. His insanity was brought on by a complex of causes that prominently included despair over his dismissal and six years of increasing torment over what he saw as an inadequate facing up to the Red menace. The Washington *Post* published stories of nervous exhaustion from overwork, which was soon rendered to the shorthand "job fatigue"; the New York *Times* called it "operational fatigue." "Rest" was universally prescribed as the course of treatment. Forrestal's psychiatrist was disguised as his "physician." All sides reported that the outlook for recovery was excellent. Soon, they said, Forrestal would be off on a round-the-world inspection trip for President Truman.

At our 29th Street offices, frustration was building to the point of explosion. For days Drew had grumbled about an "iron curtain of secrecy." And now he called me into council—or what passed for a council under his authoritarian regime—over whether we should be the ones to rend that curtain.

The purpose of the secrecy, he began, had nothing to do with protecting Forrestal's health. The news could have no effect on that, for Forrestal was not allowed to read newspapers or listen to the radio or have any communication from the outside that was not strictly controlled. No, the purpose was to protect the investment that others had made in Forrestal's reputation, in his policies, in the mystique of military infallibility and establishment competence, Drew said. If it got out that their linchpin, the Secretary of Defense, was now a madman, might it not encourage a critical review of the Forrestal policies? Might it not bring about a re-examination of the hazards of having atomic bombs as the centerpiece of our foreign and military policies?

He expressed a restrained sympathy with the motives of those who might be trying to safeguard Forrestal's future from the stigma of mental instability, and of those who feared that revelation would inevitably give the Russians a propaganda feast. But it was true that a madman had presided over the Pentagon, and the nation, Drew firmly believed, was strong and stable enough to be told the truth. Essential questions would not be answered, or even asked, unless the public knew the truth: How long had Forrestal been demented? What orders, policies or security breaches might be attributable to his condition? Why was his malady not detected or acted upon until he had disintegrated into a raving lunatic? Which colleagues were responsible for concealing so obvious a danger to the national security, and what were their motives? To what extent had Forrestal's medical treatment been compromised by being subordinated to considerations of public relations?

Drew did not want to be the one to break the taboo, for it would be attributed to personal malice; the backlash would be thunderous. He disclaimed, in a leap of rationalization, any personal animus toward Forrestal and reminded us, rightly, that our pursuit of him had ended on the day his dismissal from office was assured. But the story had to be told. He proposed to do it on his broadcast the following night. Like most of Drew's policy conferences, this one had, I think, been convened to marshal support for a decision already made; but in any event, I did not dissent from his view.

Executives of the ABC radio network were waiting for Drew with their censor's scissors. The control room had orders to cut him off the air if he mentioned the word "insanity," nor could he make the charge that the Secretary had been unbalanced while in office and that high officials knew it—to Drew the most important point. Drew partially outmaneuvered the control room by leaving his text and beginning to ad-lib, then sneaking in phrases like "temporary insanity" and "out of his mind." Before he was through he had managed to recount the "Russians are attacking" incident at Hobe Sound and to raise the question as to whether Forrestal's recent decisions and policies should be reviewed. And what could not be gotten on the air was revealed in the column.

But instead of following our lead, the media in general ignored or challenged our reporting, thus muting its effect; the questions were to remain unanswered. News coverage was reviewed many years later by Forrestal biographer Arnold Rogow, who found that:

> . . . those who discounted Pearson's reporting—and with few exceptions almost all newspapers, newsmagazines, reporters and columnists refused to publish "sensational" accounts of Forrestal's illness—could believe either that Forrestal was suffering from no more than "fatigue" and "exhaustion," or that he had experienced something that was identical with, or similar to, a "nervous breakdown." The government officials and newspapermen who were familiar with the details of the case were unable, or unwilling, to provide the public with an accurate report . . . despite the fact that he was suffering from a severe psychosis, the public was repeatedly assured by government spokesmen and the news media that Forrestal was not seriously ill and that his complete recovery was probable, even certain.*

Six weeks passed, and the "quick recovery" had not occurred. On May 21 Forrestal spent an apparently satisfactory day in his sixteenth-floor suite. His wife and a son were in Paris; his doctor had been away for two days attending a medical convention. Forrestal chatted pleasantly with three visitors, ate a large steak for lunch with seeming relish and stayed up far into the night reading one of his prized Greek volumes. At 1:45 A.M. the hospital corpsman who stood guard outside his door looked in and suggested a sedative. Forrestal declined, saying he preferred to read for a while longer. When he heard the corpsman's footsteps recede down the hall as he went to a nearby room to report,

*Ibid., p. 14.

Forrestal placed his book on the night table, opened to a page of Sophocles' "Chorus from *Ajax*" on which appeared these lines:

> When Reason's day
> Sets rayless—joyless—quenched in cold decay,
> better to die, and sleep
> The never-waking sleep, than linger on,
> And dare to live, when the soul's life is gone . . .

He got up, slipped out the door and quickly crossed the hall into a darkened "diet kitchen," a room where windows were not guarded with the steel screen that protected the windows of his own room. A few seconds later he leaped out into the night.

Had I not, from the first bulletin, been struck by the specter of our possible share in the Forrestal suicide, the near-universal reaction would have brought it home. Forrestal was the first American of exalted rank to take his own life; the national shock was deep and the arraignment of guilt was quick and, alas, one-dimensional. I have saved the clippings.

Hansen Baldwin of the New York *Times:*

> Drew Pearson and some others maligned and traduced and attacked Forrestal in various commentaries . . . for which the radio and press must bear the burden of shame . . . The dirty infighting of politics and the corrosive personal abuse of gossips and keyhole commentators had their share to do with the final act of the Forrestal tragedy.

Westbrook Pegler of Hearst Publications:

> For months, Drew Pearson and Walter Winchell hounded Jim Forrestal with dirty aspersions and insinuations, until, at last, exhausted and his nerves unstrung, one of the finest servants that the Republic ever had died of suicide.

Arthur Krock of the New York *Times:*

> What part in bringing the tragic climax was played by those who, in the press and on the air, steadily aspersed Forrestal's official record, his courage, his character and his motives while he was Secretary of Defense and followed him to the sickroom with every fragment of gossip that could nullify the treatment his doctors hoped would restore him?

It was almost unanimous. *Time* said we had "overstepped the bounds of accuracy and decency"; the New York *Herald Tribune* spoke of "juvenile savagery"; our own Washington outlet, the *Post,* condemned our "below-the-belt blows." The Hartford *Courant* said: "Americans are sick at the stomach over the cur-pack that long yelped at the heels of this man."

Drew's response, both to the suicide and the avalanche of outrage that followed, offered me only partial guidance at the time, for I had not been tempered in the fires that had raged about his life nor was I sustained by his particular certitudes. In most respects, he was a titan of enduring charity and gentleness; where his causes and the resultant conflicts were concerned, he was girdled with an implacability that could not be pierced by sentiment nor softened by tragedy.

Hours after Forrestal's death, Drew entered a last assessment in his diary:

May 22: Jim Forrestal died at 2 A.M. by jumping out of the Naval Hospital window. . . .

I think that Forrestal really died because he had no spiritual reserves. He had spent all his life thinking only about himself, trying to fulfill his great ambition to be President of the United States. When that ambition became out of his reach, he had nothing to fall back on. He had no church; he had deserted it. He had no wife. They had both deserted each other. She was in Paris at the time of his death—though it was well-known that he had been seriously ill for weeks. But most important of all, he had no spiritual resources. . . .

But James Forrestal's passion was public approval. It was his lifeblood. He craved it almost as a dope addict craves morphine. Toward the end he would break down and cry pitifully, like a child, when criticized too much. He had worked hard—too much in fact—for his country. He was loyal and patriotic. Few men were more devoted to their country, but he seriously hurt the country that he loved by taking his own life. All his policies now are under closer suspicion than before. . . .

Forrestal not only had no spiritual resources, but also he had no calluses. He was unique in this respect. He was acutely sensitive. He had traveled not on the hard political path of the politician, but on the protected, cloistered avenue of the Wall Street bankers. All his life he had been surrounded by public relations men. He did not know what the lash of criticism meant. He did not understand the give-and-take of the political arena. Even in the executive branch of government, he surrounded himself with public relations men, invited newsmen to dinner, lunch, and breakfast, made a fetish of courting their favor. History unfortunately will decree that Forrestal's great reputation was synthetic. It was built on the most unstable foundation of all—the handouts of paid press agents.

If Forrestal had been true to his friends, if he had made one sacrifice for a friend, if he had even gone to bat for Tom Corcoran who put him in the White House, if he had spent more time with his wife instead of courting his mistress, he would not have been so alone this morning when he went to the diet pantry of the Naval Hospital and jumped to his death.*

Drew's public response to accusations that he was responsible for Forrestal's suicide was of a piece: "If the Navy had taken proper precautions instead of minimizing the facts, Jim Forrestal would be alive today."

Drew traced the long chain of negligence that led to the moment when a suicidal psychotic, at the most dangerous stage of his illness, was left unwatched, abandoned by his doctor, up on the sixteenth floor, with access to an unshielded window.

> In the end, it may be found that Mr. Forrestal's friends had more to do with his death than his critics. For those close to him now admit privately that he had been sick for some time, suffered embarrassing lapses too painful to be mentioned here . . .
>
> Yet during most of the last winter, when Jim Forrestal was under heavy responsibilities and definitely not a well man, the little coterie of newspapermen who now insinuate Jim was killed by his critics, encouraged him to stay on. This got to be almost an obsession, both on their part and on his, until Mr. Truman's final request for his resignation undoubtedly worsened the illness.

Drew's defense-offense concluded by raising the key question and giving his answer: "Are public officials to be immune from criticism or investigation for fear of impairing their health? . . . Then the government by checks and balances created by the Founding Fathers is thrown out of gear."

This was all true, but it was not the whole truth. Certainly many factors besides criticism had entered into the suicide. Certainly the patient's keepers were guilty of negligence, the more shameful because it was spawned in an atmosphere that put public relations first. Certainly blame fell upon those newsmen and aides who had flattered and exhorted a failing Forrestal to battle for his secretaryship and who concealed to themselves the evidence of their eyes and ears that his

---

Drew Pearson Diaries 1949–1959, Tyler Abell, ed. (New York: Holt, Rinehart & Winston, 1974), pp. 50–51.

mind was faltering. Certainly there was simplism and even deceit in the charge of Arthur Krock and others that Drew had followed Forrestal into his sickroom and nullified his doctor's treatment, for reporters knew, though their readers probably did not, that nothing Drew said or wrote could reach the attention of Forrestal in his sickroom. And certainly Drew was right in insisting that the free press would castrate itself and nullify its mission if it withheld the accusing fact or the critical judgment for fear of harming an official's health.

But yet our hand was surely in this tragedy. To argue, as Drew did, that it was dismissal from office and the thwarting of ambitions, not the press attacks, that drove Forrestal over the edge was to gloss over the reality that the press onslaught helped cause the dismissal and explode the ambitions.

But it was not that, even, which put us in the wrong. A commentator has the right, even the duty, to campaign for the sacking of an official whose philosophy or conduct he opposes. It was our means that were open to question. The Forrestal suicide brought to the surface differences of method and proportion between me and my mentor that had been building up during the first two years of my apprenticeship.

The once-a-week assault, based only occasionally on fresh, hard news and usually consisting of rehashes of old complaints, crossed the line that separates propaganda from advocacy, let alone reporting. The constant use of scare symbols by which Forrestal, after nine years of public life, was still pictured always as a "Wall Streeter" or a business accomplice of oil barons and Arab sheiks, was wall-poster stuff that to me demeaned the legitimate issues we raised. The repeated draping of Hitler around Forrestal's neck, because Hitler had appropriated the benefits of Dillon, Read loans made to German industry in the pre-Hitler era, was historical shorthand that went beyond the license permitted even to advocates. The overconfident use of the simplistic historical parallel—for instance, our column's regular insistence that Forrestal's policy of rebuilding the German economy could set the stage for a third German-instigated world war—was so divergent from Drew's characteristic optimism about human regeneration, and from his professorial awareness that yesterday's enemy is tomorrow's ally, that it seemed to me to carry shorthand into the realm of demagoguery.

I was slow to acknowledge my differences with Drew over questions of journalistic ethics and propriety. I was mightily impressed by Drew's ethics on the grand scale, his foul-weather championship of the rights of the weak, his discriminating delineation of the elements of social justice. And in most matters in dispute between Drew and the tone setters of our profession, I sided enthusiastically with Drew, for the latter were oriented toward justifications for *not* publishing.

But there was also a cleavage between us. I tended to look on journalism as a craft to be learned, a discipline whose rules circumscribed and shaped one's approach to public disputes, a vocation to excel in; Drew, however, for all the art, fire and ingenuity he brought to journalism, saw it as essentially a tool for the advancement of larger causes. His columns and broadcasts were to him weapons in a just war, with truth as their only acknowledged restriction—and truth was often a subjective matter. I would raise misgivings with him about a particular tactic, but I was too much bound to him, too largely in agreement with him, to let these misgivings become a cause of personal division between us. I contented myself with making mental lists of abuses to be shunned in the remote future when I would be on my own: no Ahab-like pursuit of adversaries; no rehashes of old charges unless justified by a fresh discovery or a special circumstance; no prejudicial symbols or tendentious parallels to bolster up a story that couldn't stand on its own; no ideological excursions or propaganda; no behind-the-scenes machinations with the political rivals of one's target. Just the spare, hard exposé.

Such exercises were invariably followed by doubts. Without the passion, the partisanship, the war-to-the-death zealotry, would there be the crusading spirit that makes the great muckraker? Drew did not believe reporters could conquer the unscrupulous by encapsulating themselves within the canons of good taste, by furnishing meticulous information and then standing aloof. He believed that to get the job done he must intrude during all phases of the battle; not only would he expose the abuse, he would hound the tribunal until it investigated, invite its members to dinner, instruct the witnesses in their testimony. He would intimidate, if he could, the propounders of the opposition, propagandize the galleries, help draft the remedial legislation, and write the popular history of the affair, to be reissued whenever a like crusade was in the offing.

Thus had he pursued Forrestal, with an excess that trespassed beyond our province and our code, I thought. But confrontations lay ahead of us that for a long time to come would seem to give Drew the better of the argument.

7 · MacArthur: The Last Hero

THE PASSING of James Forrestal left but one "militarist" titan among the foes I had taken on unwittingly when I signed with Drew Pearson. This last, however, was the great avatar of the breed—General of the Army Douglas MacArthur.

No one remotely comparable to MacArthur exists today. Out of two world wars he had emerged a hero of almost supernatural proportions by virtue of a dramatic flair and an appalling physical courage in the first instance, and in the second, a strategic genius and the projection of an eerily majestic presence. It is a verified fact that amid the most sweltering of jungle exertions MacArthur did not sweat. As Commander for the Allied Powers in Japan, he reigned in patriarchal absolutism over 80 million Japanese; his troops called him the White Mikado, and he was in truth an imperial personage to whom the Emperor of Japan was but a deputy. It was perhaps inevitable that so grand a figure would look upon Presidents and department secretaries, not to speak of Joint Chiefs he had once commanded, with a disdain that, while benevolent, was disdain nonetheless.

On a wall of his personal headquarters in Tokyo's Dai-Ichi Building, General MacArthur flaunted a framed credo attributed to Lucius

Aemilius Paulus, a Roman general during the interminable wars over Macedonia. Its theme was disparagement of civilian control of the military, and it fueled a long-held suspicion of Drew's that MacArthur would one day try to set up shop for himself. It read in part:

> Commanders should be counselled chiefly by persons of known talent . . . who are present at the scene of action, who see the country, who see the enemy . . . and who, like people embarked in the same ship, are sharers of the danger. *If, therefore, anyone thinks himself qualified to give advice respecting the war which I am to conduct . . . let him come with me into Macedonia . . . Rest assured that we shall pay no attention to any counsels but such as shall be framed within our camp.* [Emphasis added.]

In December 1949 I came into possession of the text of a top-secret cable from MacArthur to the Joint Chiefs, a cable which heralded the historic conflict soon to erupt between MacArthur and his nominal superiors remote from Macedonia. It dealt with a MacArthur plan to join forces with Chiang Kai-shek on Formosa in a common defense against Communist China. I brought the text to Drew, who perceived in it not only an important news story but the flowering of deep suspicions about MacArthur that had been festering since the 1920s. For the first time I became acquainted with the gamier details of the acrimony between MacArthur and Pearson, which I pause to recount in brief.

From the time MacArthur first came into prominence as the youngest American general of World War I, and then the youngest commandant of West Point, and then the youngest Army Chief of Staff, he displayed certain peculiarities that tended to raise the hair on the back of Drew's neck: an unfailing theatricality; a tendency to portray his life as a series of triumphal processions; and a rhetoric with a martial ring that, for instance, identified pacificism with Communism. Here was a hero in unheroic times, unhappily hemmed in by the humdrum of peace and the flummery of civilian politics, a general looking for a star of destiny; worse, a general who had the Roman profile, the messianic urge, the oratorical artillery, the mastery of imagery, the brains and the guile to create a great deal of mischief should a fortuitous conjunction of events arise.

If Drew had one emotional spring that ran deeper than his fear of military men of destiny, it was his sympathy for the downtrodden and the derelict. He never forgave Chief of Staff MacArthur for the gung-ho manner in which he had carried out President Hoover's order to break up the ramshackle Washington encampment of down-and-out veterans who were demonstrating for a speed-up of their promised World War I bonuses. To the end of MacArthur's life, Pearson would periodically lampoon him for changing into his dress uniform and personally leading the assault on the tattered vets, and for prancing about before the news cameras like Napoleon on the field of Austerlitz, and for his overblown post-mortems on the great victory. But for his action, MacArthur had proclaimed, "I believe the institutions of our government would have been severely threatened . . . I have entered villages in wartime which have been in the grip of the enemy for three years and I know what their gratitude means. But never have I seen, even in those days, such expressions of gratitude as from the crowds today."

Drew periodically pricked MacArthur with ridicule in the years that followed, much of it told to Drew by MacArthur's ex-wife, Louise Cromwell, the most offensive item alleging that MacArthur's promotion to major general had come through the political intervention of her father, Edward T. Stotesbury, a J. P. Morgan partner. In 1934 the tormented MacArthur descended from Olympus and entered the pit with the muckrakers, slapping Pearson and Robert S. Allen with a $1,750,000 libel suit. MacArthur contended that the column had portrayed him as, among other caricatures, "dictatorial, insubordinate, arbitrary, harsh, disloyal, mutinous and disrespectful of his superiors"; in later years Drew would point to this complaint as a classic demonstration of his prescience, but at the time he was hard pressed to prove his case. Had the litigation been successful, or even partially successful, it would have wiped out the two partners, financially and professionally.

Drew suffered a jolting reverse when Louise Cromwell refused to testify in court and corroborate the jibes she had so gaily told him over cocktails. And so he determined to meet MacArthur's attack with guerrilla tactics. He had heard that MacArthur, then fifty-four years old and unattached, had set up in an exclusive Washington hotel a Eurasian girl of uncommon beauty whom he had imported from the Philippines with promises of undying love. In the fullness of time, the general's ardor had dampened and he was now trying to pack his mistress back to Manila or to Shanghai, where she had once danced in a chorus line.

The deportation had little appeal for the lady; she demurred, and there followed those mundanities that apparently attend the paling of covert love affairs even among the world's immortals. MacArthur cut off her allowance, sent her some one-way train and boat tickets and included a collection of help-wanted ads clipped from the newspapers. The girl checked out of her hotel, with her wardrobe of tea gowns and exotic lingerie, and disappeared. So stood the blighted affair when Drew got wind of it.

He made a frantic search, located the girl, offered her his protection and aid, hid her from Army sleuths now in hot pursuit and inveigled her into handing over a packet of love letters written to her by MacArthur with his customary grandiloquence. Pearson laid the letters before MacArthur's representatives and dictated harsh surrender terms, which the crestfallen general immediately accepted. MacArthur was to call off his suit in perpetuity, pay off the $16,000 in legal expenses thus far incurred by the defense and ante up another $15,000 (which MacArthur produced in cash) for the rehabilitation of the estranged one, who must accept this payment as restitution in full for her grievances. In return, Pearson would turn over to MacArthur the original letters while keeping copies under a formal pledge not to publish them during MacArthur's lifetime.

All promises were kept. The dancer from Shanghai was taken to the Middle West by Drew's brother, Leon, and established as the proprietress of a successful beauty parlor.

A year later, upon the expiration of his term as Chief of Staff, MacArthur abandoned spiteful Washington and returned to the scene of his early years, the Philippines, there to be appointed field marshal and charged with building up an indigenous army that would be able to defend the island by 1946—the year of promised Philippine independence. Now fifty-five, he intended this as the final scene of his career; instead it was to be a new beginning, for in the skies of the Southern Cross he found his long-sought star.

For a dozen years and more, Douglas MacArthur was largely beyond Drew Pearson's ploys and barbs, separated by nine thousand miles and elevated by one of the great apotheoses of American history. For many in the West and the East, his image became the one later rhapsodized on the floor of the United States Senate by Democratic Senator Thomas Dodd of Connecticut:

> To millions of people at home and around the globe, Douglas MacArthur has seemed a symbol and almost a personification of America in its finest

aspects. Outwardly there was the unforgettable surface picture, the striking countenance, the confident stride, the legendary hat and glasses and corn-cob pipe, the resonant, authoritative voice, the grand phrase, the dramatic gesture, and behind this surface picture were all the attributes of excellence, the supreme competence, the serene confidence, the intellectual power, the noble purpose, the complete commitment to the vision of an America that was unconquerable in the service of a just cause . . .

It was a much aggrandized MacArthur, then, whom we faced in December 1949 when I appeared in Drew's den with the Supreme Commander's cable to the Joint Chiefs. In it the general sought authorization to reverse President Truman's policy of no further aid to Chiang Kai-shek and to use U.S. troops and naval forces to defend Formosa, Nationalist China's last refuge, against the mass invasion from the mainland that U.S. intelligence thought was imminent. I told Drew that MacArthur's position had considerable support among the Joint Chiefs and some of the service secretaries, but that Secretary of State Dean Acheson was adamantly against it and the word was that Truman might decide either way.

The way to abort a bold venture bound to end up a catastrophe, Drew believed, was to publish the plan before it became a *fait accompli;* we rushed the gist of the MacArthur cable into print on December 22 under the lead: "Most important backstage debate over U.S. foreign policy now involves Formosa. General MacArthur has sent a triple-urgent cable urging that Formosa be occupied by U.S. troops . . ."

The public disclosure of this top-level dispute caused a quiet ferment in official Washington that took about three weeks to reach the general press. In the meantime Drew and I added more yeast. Our combined sources enabled us to piece together and publish, on January 1, 1950, the highlights of a White House meeting at which the MacArthur proposal was presented sympathetically to President Truman by General Omar Bradley, Chairman of the Joint Chiefs of Staff, but trenchantly opposed by Acheson. Truman seemed, from his comments, to waver back and forth as the argument unfolded; at the end he sought to compromise the issue by sending more weapons and instructors to Chiang, but no fleet and no troops.

We followed up with a story that MacArthur was "stirring up a furor" in Congress over Formosa by presenting his case to visiting delegations of congressmen. We revealed that after the State Department refused transportation to Formosa for two senators who wished to confer with Chiang, MacArthur had the senators flown to Chiang in one of his planes.

On this modest foundation Drew portrayed an insubordinate MacArthur "trying to dictate U.S. foreign policy in the Far East" and risking our involvement in a senseless war with Communist China. By now, other press organs were following up our leads and expanding on them. President Truman was thus compelled to spike a growing controversy and did so with a firm-sounding announcement that "the United States Government will provide no military aid to the Chinese forces on Formosa."

Five months later came the event that was to again move MacArthur to the center of the world stage. I learned of it at the Pentagon on a June morning when a key source told me that in a few hours, President Truman would announce that he was ordering American intervention to stop the overnight North Korean invasion of South Korea. A newsman does not often get advance notice of a war; Drew was unreachable, in the air en route to Chicago, and so I put out a war announcement in his name over ABC Radio. We arranged to get a message to Drew, on his landing, that he must not speak to a soul until he had phoned me in Washington. He complied in the nick of time, and when he turned to face a surrounding crowd of newsmen he was able to reaffirm his scoop that we were again at war.

When Truman ordered MacArthur to undertake South Korea's defense, the President partially succumbed to the MacArthur view on Formosa when he decided to station the Seventh Fleet between Formosa and China to shield it from invasion by the Chinese Reds. This, we thought, was a grave mistake. It brought us into an uncomfortable embrace with Chiang, whose only chance to regain the mainland was to involve us in a war with Red China.

Chiang immediately tried to pull up the covers. Magnanimously forgiving the United States for past shortcomings in his behalf, he declared that "no difficulties . . . will arise if United States relationships are placed in the hands of Douglas MacArthur." And the Generalissimo offered 33,000 Nationalist troops to help MacArthur's outnumbered, makeshift forces then being pushed back to the Pusan perimeter at the southern tip of Korea. Acceptance might have goaded the Communist Chinese to enter the Korean conflict, and Chiang would have had his mainland war. The President opted to keep the Chinese out of Korea and declined Chiang's nettly offer.

But one month later MacArthur flew to Formosa's capital, Taipei;

after two days of conferences at the summit, Chiang announced that "the foundation for Sino-American military cooperation has been laid" and added a peroration about "final victory in our struggle against Communism." While consternation percolated in foreign capitals and in segments of the American press, MacArthur kept an ominous silence on the substance of his talks with Chiang, as befitted confidences between potentates. Truman dispatched Averell Harriman to Tokyo to impress upon the general that United States policy was simply to neutralize Formosa, to keep it out of the Korean War, not bring it in as a combatant. But shortly after the Harriman briefings, on August 27, MacArthur sent out to the American press the advance text of his message to a forthcoming convention of the Veterans of Foreign Wars in which he declared that Formosa was "ideally located to accomplish offensive strategy." President Truman, his bluff called publicly, ordered the statement withdrawn. MacArthur complied.

It was Drew's belief that the put-down of MacArthur was an essential step toward asserting presidential control over the headstrong general and that our exposés of the previous nine months had influenced it. Truman tended to be deferential toward MacArthur, Drew said; but the shining of a spotlight on MacArthur's disagreements with his Commander in Chief had heightened Truman's sensitivity. Thus the rather delphic VFW statement became an intolerable affront to the feisty Truman.

The month of September 1950 brought the first of the great turn-arounds that characterized the early phase of the Korean War. General MacArthur's brilliant, last-ditch defense of the Pusan perimeter evolved into a counterattack which, first, threw back the North Koreans, and then, after the Inchon landing behind North Korean lines, a MacArthur masterstroke, routed them altogether, touching off opportunities and dangers of vast import.

As MacArthur's United Nations forces punched toward the border which divided the two Koreas at the 38th parallel, it devolved upon President Truman to clearly define the ultimate goal of his "police" action: was it the mere repelling of aggression, as initially conceived, or had MacArthur's successes now raised his sights to the total conquest of North Korea? In Peking, Chou En-lai issued repeated public and private warnings that Red China would not permit the occupation of its neighbor, North Korea, and would enter the war if MacArthur crossed the 38th parallel. The United States, acting through Indian and other intermediaries, gave Peking assurances that whatever was decided about North Korea, no designs were harbored against Communist China. Washington tended to disregard Chou's warnings as bluffs, Peking to discount Truman's assurances as tricks.

For two weeks and more, the President had it within his power to command events. By setting the 38th parallel as the limit of our advance, he could end the war, and end it on a note of substantial victory, with all its initial goals met: South Korea preserved, aggression repelled, collective security vindicated, general war averted. But Truman hesitated, assailed by doubts. Should he settle for substantial victory when the total victory heralded by MacArthur and his encircling legions shone so iridescently on the near horizon? Should he leave North Korea intact, in a position to rebuild its armies and, someday, to renew its attack? Should he, with congressional elections only six weeks off, hand the opposition an issue by preventing MacArthur from delivering the final blow? Day after day passed without decision as the President grappled with that most delicate of determinations, upon which all conquerors are finally judged—when to stop.

We of the Pearson foreign office were for stopping at the 38th (I thought I saw a disturbingly earnest ring in the warnings of my old-time Peking counselor now come to such immense powers). During the hiatus of indecision we tried, in our journalist's presumption, to influence the decision by hoisting a number of alarms based on classified information. We disclosed the contents of a cable from Premier Nehru to President Truman informing him that Indian negotiations with Red China to block their entry into the war had been aborted by MacArthur's talk of using Formosa as a base for American bombers. We revealed ominous Pentagon intelligence reports that the decimated North Korean army ranks were being mysteriously filled up and that the source had to be Red China. We published a confidential warning to the White House from its United Nations Ambassador Warren Austin that most of our UN allies were getting intelligence which made them apprehensive about the consequences of crossing the 38th parallel. We declassified another Nehru dispatch, and a U.S. intelligence report as well, both advising that major trouble was brewing between Peking and Moscow. Drew used this to press his pet theory that a conciliatory U.S. policy toward Red China not only would avert a disastrous war but would hasten the conversion of Mao Tse-tung into another Tito. And using as backup the more supportive of the scenarios being studied by the Joint Chiefs of Staff, Drew issued a barrage of dire predictions such as these:

The Joint Chiefs of Staff are now among the eagerest people in Washington to avoid any conflict which would cause Chinese troops to be sent into Korea. If Chinese troops stay out of Korea, there seems to be a pretty good chance the war will be over early this winter. But if the Chinese pour their vast hordes into Korea, the war could last almost indefinitely.

And:

It is foolhardy to get embroiled with Asia's limitless pool of manpower. For the more Orientals killed in battle, the more men rise up to take their place. This kind of war could absorb all our energies for decades.

By late September an impatient MacArthur was poised at the 38th parallel, cabling assurances to Washington of a complete victory that needed only to be picked up. At length, the President emerged from his deliberations, and in his jaunty way, stepped firmly onto one of history's great banana peels. His decision was to cross the parallel and strike deep to the north, as MacArthur wished, a policy that was in the following week successfully promoted among our wary but semidependent UN allies. On October 7 MacArthur swept into North Korea.

The lack of impact of all our columns was for me a deflating experience. Where was the gratification in being able to alarm 60 million if there was no heeding? Drew was less subdued; in his hard-learned wisdom of the ways and rhythms of exerting pressure, he had confidence, like the Chinese interrogator, in the cumulative effect of interminable drops of water. His question was not "Will there be an effect?" but "Will it come in time?"

Throughout October the policy of advance toward the China border prospered. The rout of North Korean forces was all but consummated. The Yalu River, boundary between North Korea and Red China, loomed ahead. Red China had not intervened, and hard-nosed realists congratulated themselves on not falling for the bluffs of the Communists and the caterwauling of sob sisters like Pearson. But to the perceptive, Chinese "volunteers" began to appear in Korea like the cubs before the mother grizzly bear.

So rapid and heady was the tide of conquest, meanwhile, that a week or two after the crossing of the North Korean border, the new controversy was over the question "Should we cross the Chinese border?" The echo of MacArthur in the Senate and House chambers became increasingly clamorous against the official policy of respecting that border.

Republican Senator William Knowland of California proposed that we cross the Yalu and annex a piecemeal buffer area of Chinese soil for the protection of a unified, anti-Communist Korea. Our old friend Republican Senator Owen Brewster of Maine was demanding that we end the "coddling" of the Chinese Communists by allowing MacArthur to cross the Chinese border as he saw fit and by placing in his all-wise hands the decision as to the use of the atomic bomb.

In mid-October, President Truman flew to Wake Island in the Pacific for a half-day meeting with the supreme commander. It was widely leaked that Truman's basic purposes were to disabuse MacArthur of any thought of collaboration with Chiang Kai-shek and to place explicit curbs on MacArthur's advance to the Yalu so as not to provoke the Chinese to intervention. What in fact transpired at Wake Island was submerged under a bland official communiqué and a news photo of a smiling Truman pinning a medal on a gracious MacArthur. The penetration of secret meetings was our traditional forte, and we pressed our every White House, State Department and Pentagon source for any scraps we could get. But the scraps were meager, and they contained no evidence that curbs had been placed on MacArthur's push northward.

Five days after the Wake Island meeting, on October 20, 1950, MacArthur's forces captured Pyongyang, the North Korean capital. He was now only a few miles below the Chinese border and was advancing toward the great network of hydroelectric dams which was on the North Korean side of the Yalu but which provided Manchuria with most of its power. U.S. Army intelligence, meanwhile, detected the massing of hundreds of thousands of Chinese Communist troops along the Manchurian side of the Yalu. Ten days passed without any unit-sized crossing into North Korea and without any reassuring statement to Peking from either Tokyo or Washington. On the eleventh day, October 31, the first Chinese regiment was identified in combat against United Nations troops. On November 1 the first Russian MIG fighters were sighted in action over North Korea.

At 1313 29th Street, this seemed the last possible opportunity for stopping the MacArthur advance before the police action blew up into a major war. Surely the fall of Pyongyang and the possession of five sixths of North Korean soil presented President Truman and General MacArthur with both the symbol and reality of a splendid victory. To insist upon gaining the last mile and rounding up the final North Korean regiment, in the face of the new Chinese and Russian presences, seemed folly that bordered on fanaticism. And so Drew abandoned the last shred of journalistic caution.

From my Pentagon informants I had obtained information about two secret Administration efforts to defuse the border confrontation, efforts which MacArthur was impatiently thwarting. The first was a Joint Chiefs order to MacArthur to use only South Korean troops in occupying the forty-mile belt at the top of North Korea along the Siberian and Manchurian borders. The second was a State Department warning/suggestion, transmitted to MacArthur by General Omar Bradley, that Red China might go to war to protect the hydroelectric projects and that MacArthur ought not enter the area of the dams and should issue a public declaration saying so. MacArthur got around the first restriction by reporting to the Joint Chiefs that the South Korean troops in the forty-mile zone had run into trouble and needed rescuing by U.S. troops; the Joint Chiefs reluctantly acceded, and overnight, a scattering of U.S. troops appeared in the sensitive forty-mile zone. As for the State Department message, the general curtly rejected it, wiring back: DO NOT CONCUR.

The question of publishing this classified material was the thornier because it dealt with military operations still in progress, but hoping it might precipitate a tighter Washington rein on MacArthur, Drew published the ominous news on November 8, with follow-up details added as the month progressed. He concluded:

> What happened was that MacArthur would cable the Joint Chiefs of Staff, demanding that he be allowed to override Washington instructions. Couched in MacArthur's vigorous, sizzling language, his messages usually predicted dire consequences if his ideas were not followed. So, after some sputtering among the Joint Chiefs of Staff, General Bradley usually concluded that the commander in the field should be permitted to make the final decision.
>
> "General MacArthur knows the situation better than we do over here," kindly General Bradley would tell the President. And Truman, not the forceful military strategist Roosevelt was, invariably gave his O.K.

In the first week of November, two U.S. battalions were surprised and torn to pieces by Chinese troops, but MacArthur remained magnificently composed, serene in his special insight into the Oriental mind; it was a matter of bluffing, a matter of facing them down. He continued his advance and was confirmed in his judgment when Chinese combat flurries ceased in mid-November and their regiments melted away before him. To Drew it was the silence before the avalanche, the very last chance to avoid full-scale war. On November 20 we dropped into the "Washington Merry-Go-Round" pipeline a speculative warning that while the Chinese might be backing off, they might also be "sucking our troops into a trap." That column appeared on November 24, and as I was reading it, word came in on our office news ticker that General MacArthur had launched what he called his "end-the-war offensive."

Three days later the trap snapped shut. Rising from the snow-drifted valley of the Yalu, surging outward across a desolate, subzero mountainscape, a massive Chinese onslaught roared down the Korean peninsula for 120 miles, sweeping before it MacArthur's stunned, misaligned armies. When its fury was spent, all North Korea had been reclaimed under the Red flag, and MacArthur was again dug in deep in the south. This time he was confronted not by a thin Korean line that could be turned and enveloped but by infinite layers of Chinese, who measure their wars in decades.

The combined miscalculations of the President and the general had resulted in a debacle so inextricable, a prospect so gloom-laden as to spoil the I-told-you-so's that console the spurned pundit in moments of general calamity. Drew conveyed to us a picture that held little but woe for the causes in which we were enlisted. An America conditioned to victories and happy endings had, against all his warnings, blundered into a stalemated war from which there was no satisfactory exit. At best, the nation would tolerate the stalemate, which would be long, bloody, costly and was bound to end ingloriously in a semidefeat—an embittering wound that would demoralize the national psyche, undo the Democrats, discredit the saner sort of public figure and everywhere inflate firebrands and know-nothings. At worst, the nation would refuse to tolerate stalemate, and thrashing about, muddle into a larger, longer, bloodier bog on mainland Asia, in Russia's backyard, that could mindlessly evolve into a world war fought with atomic weapons.

Nor could Drew permit himself, at this long last, to savor MacArthur's apparent humiliation. Too long had Drew exhorted in vain against the Hero of Bataan to discount his capacity for emerging from any reverse unscathed. He was, in fact, the more dangerous in defeat, Drew insisted, for in disengaging himself from it, he would subtly shift the blame to those above him, so that, to the extent he succeeded, he would undermine the civil government.

MacArthur proved equal, alas more than equal, to Drew's apprehensions. In the midst of headlong retreat he lofted by communiqué, interview and leak a series of contentions and controversies; these statements either vindicated his Yalu generalship or obscured it behind inflammatory issues: he had neither been taken by surprise nor been defeated by the Chinese; his advance to the Yalu had been a calculated risk that foresaw the possibility of the Chinese onslaught; his only surprise had been the refusal by Washington to permit him to bomb the Chinese staging bases and rail lines in Manchuria, by which he could have stopped that invasion in its tracks; when a "million Chinese" flooded down from "privileged sanctuaries" upon his gallant few he had responded, as planned, with a "brilliantly executed planned strategic withdrawal" that had thwarted the enemy's objectives; despite political shackles that imposed on him "disadvantages unparalleled in the history of warfare," there had been no rout, except in the imagination of biased, sensation-seeking commentators. The pro-MacArthur press thundered out its champion's implied challenge to national policy: would our politicians, influenced by counsels of fear and by unworthy allies who demanded restrictions on MacArthur while trading with the enemy for profit, continue to deny him permission to win the victory within his grasp? It was a superb show. Any general can be a hero in victory; only MacArthur could project himself as the hero of catastrophes.

Though he had not set foot in the United States for fourteen years, MacArthur commanded a looming presence here, a presence that was intimidating to policy-making Washington; a presence that, if vaguely chilling in the more self-consciously reflective circles across the land, was deeply inspirational in vast hinterlands of space and spirit. Nature aided by art and circumstance had invested Douglas MacArthur with a unique gift for passive incitement. His public statements were crafted to skirt overt insubordination yet permit insurrectionary inferences to be snapped up by a great following that swelled with empathetic frustration. Something overarching in his total appeal spanned the chasms that distinguished him from most of his followers. Though he was far removed from demagoguery—too austere and aloof to indulge its grossnesses—he was the rallying point for demagogues, the graven image before which bowed impostors as diverse as Gerald L. K. Smith, Harold Stassen and Joseph McCarthy. Though he was a complex thinker who tinkered with humanitarian, internationalist, even pacifist, notions which ought to have scandalized the more stridently orthodox, he was seen by millions of fundamentalists as a mountain peak silhouetted against the lightning, the last bearer of the true flame.

For whatever reasons, such was his appeal that as his armies fled one of history's more humiliating ambushes, the congressional Republicans voted a resolution of impeachment, not of MacArthur, but of Secretary of State Dean Acheson for allegedly hindering him; congressional Democrats prudently declined to notice his disarray; various senators demanded that powers constitutionally reserved to the President be transferred to the general; the Veterans of Foreign Wars, the Am Vets and the Navy League joined the furor that the Administration give MacArthur what he wanted; and in Montana a draft board refused to call up any more inductees until the use of the A-bomb against China was placed at MacArthur's discretion.

At this juncture MacArthur cabled to the Joint Chiefs a secret win-the-war plan which showed that neither the rigors of defeat nor the advent of his seventy-first year had diminished his panache. He asked for unrestricted air strikes against China to destroy its military installations, industrial sites and transportation facilities; a blockade of China's coast; naval shelling of its coastal cities; a second front on the Chinese mainland, to be opened by Chiang's Chinese Nationalist troops transported by our Navy and supported by our Air Force. The overthrow of Communism in China was thus to be added to the unification of Korea as a war goal. If, for political reasons beyond his ken, these measures could not be taken, he offered an alternative that would at least salvage Korea: he proposed that the Chinese forces in Korea be sealed off from Manchuria, their source of supply and re-enforcement, by laying a radioactive belt composed of nuclear wastes across the top of North Korea. When the cordoned-off Chinese armies ran out of supplies, he would destroy them via new Inchons, in the grand MacArthur style.

Several weeks would pass before the Pearson ship was able to ferret out and piece together the complete plan (except for the radioactive belt, which we never penetrated), but from the day of the Yalu reverse, Drew had assumed that MacArthur was urging upon Washington a glorious, I-shall-return comeback. MacArthur had been a consistent champion of the sweeping strategies required for total victory and had never pretended to believe that the concept of limited war was other than a contradiction in terms, a perversion of military logic, a betrayal of the troops in the field.

It was clear from reports of MacArthur's discussions with congressional pilgrims to Tokyo that he regarded the defeat of Chiang as a watershed calamity that could have been avoided by greater American involvement and better military tactics by Chiang. The general would later repeat these views in public:

> It is my own personal opinion that the greatest mistake we made in a hundred years in the Pacific was in allowing the Communists to grow to power in China. I think, at one stroke, we undid everything, starting from John Hay, through Taft, Leonard Wood, Woodrow Wilson, Henry Stimson, and all those great architects of our Pacific policy. I believe it was fundamental, and I believe we will pay for it, for a century.

It was becoming increasingly clear that MacArthur regarded the Korean War as an opportunity to correct this fundamental mistake and to redeem the hundred years of punishment.

The question mark was Harry Truman. We knew he was disposed to accept the counsel of his most trusted advisers—Acheson, Marshall, Harriman, Bradley—that Russia, not China, was our main antagonist; that Europe, not Asia, was the decisive theater, for which we must conserve our resources; that our policy was the containment of Red expansion through means short of all-out war, not the escalation of hostilities inherent in the bombardment and invasion of China and the reintroduction there of Chiang; and that, therefore, the most logical policy was to stay out of the Chinese civil war, accept a military stalemate in Korea and try for a negotiated settlement that abandoned the goal of a unified Korea and sought only the preservation of an independent South Korea—the goal we had entered Korea with, had once achieved, but had discarded in the post-Inchon exuberance.

Truman the Commander in Chief agreed, but Truman the politician-in-trouble was trying to keep a foot in both camps and his equilibrium was shaky. One day he would proclaim his aims in the approved language of containment and limited war. The next day he would deny that any difference existed between him and MacArthur on Korean policy, or he would threaten to bomb Manchurian bases as soon as he could get the United Nations to brand China an aggressor nation, or he would announce, or at least appear to announce, that he was considering the use of the A-bomb against Chinese forces and might leave the decision in MacArthur's hands. So concerned was the President to avoid a break with the general, and the horrendous domestic explosion it would set off, that he practiced an unwonted delicacy when speaking of him even to his intimates. He warned his men to avoid criticism of MacArthur, and he mollified him with messages of personal praise and with assurances from the Joint Chiefs that his four-point plan to roll up China was receiving the most serious consideration.

To us, the Korean crisis reduced itself to two components: a charismatic, always decisive general boldly in pursuit of the wrong policy, and a pedestrian, sometimes indecisive President who haltingly supported the right one. From late November on, our daily mission was to do whatever we, as scribes, could do to cut MacArthur down to life-size and to stir up the vain, bellicose side of Truman's nature to the end that he would boil over, and in Lyndon Johnson's phrase, "lift up the cow's tail and look the situation straight in the face."

With respect to MacArthur, we needed only to follow our traditional methodology. Behind the Yalu rout, as with any such debacle, there were bound to be what in hindsight would shine as inexcusable blunders, preposterous predictions and face-saving lies. We had but to find them and document them. Once MacArthur was shown culpable as a commander, he ought to be vulnerable as a demigod.

It was left to me as Drew's Pentagon man to dig out the details. By this point, after three years of covering the Pentagon, I had developed a number of highly placed sources. Some were old collaborators, dating back to the postwar peak of interservice rivalry. Others, whose assistance had in the past been perfunctory, could now be approached on grounds that MacArthur's mastery of public relations, if not counteracted, would enable him to overturn *their* global policies. Others could on occasion be reached by the plea that the time comes when the public has a right to know the undisguised truth about claimed victories, glossed-over defeats and threatening calamities. All knew by now that I could be trusted to conceal their identity in any circumstance.

I worked by padding ceaselessly from one to the other, each day trying to widen the previous day's rapport by an inch. One source would speak only on a theoretical or high-policy plane of the possible differences between MacArthur and the Joint Chiefs over strategy and global priority. A second would show me, if I asked the right questions, documents in which those theoretical differences took on the flesh of dispute over combat decisions between Washington and Tokyo. A third gave me access to daily intelligence digests, including some from MacArthur's headquarters which contradicted his public communiqués. A fourth would let me watch, on occasion, a new-fangled

Pentagon screen on which was flashed the secret dialogue between the Joint Chiefs and the supreme commander.

A dozen times during the tumultuous month of December 1950, our columns and broadcasts featured authoritative, exclusive exposés, based on secret assessments by the Joint Chiefs, smuggled reports of White House briefings, and classified cables sent to MacArthur or received from him. Some representative fragments follow:

On MacArthur's tailoring of intelligence reports to suit his predilections:

> MacArthur refused to believe reports of Red intervention. And, for about 10 days, MacArthur's assurance to Washington that there was no real Chinese intervention led to a false understanding of the entire Korean picture . . .
>
> On October 30, MacArthur's spokesman for the first time admitted the presence of Chinese troops in heavy strength. Actually, they had been in North Korea for about 10 days, and Washington now interprets MacArthur's sudden statement that three Chinese divisions had invaded North Korea with Soviet tanks, self-propelled guns, bazookas and minesweepers as propaganda to cover up a bad military blunder. Actually the Chinese troops did not have this heavy Soviet equipment. (December 1, 1950)

On MacArthur's claim he had not been routed:

> President Truman, as host, opened the [Anglo-American] conference by proposing to Prime Minister Attlee that General Omar Bradley give all present an up-to-the-minute briefing . . . Bradley then disclosed calmly and solemnly that the United Nations forces in Korea had suffered a complete collapse. He described this as the greatest military disaster in the history of the United States . . . American casualties in the preceding four or five days, Bradley said, had exceeded anything that the Allied Forces had suffered in a comparable period of World War II or World War I. (December 8)

On MacArthur's rejection of Allied intelligence:

> French Ambassador Henri Bonnet, acting on instructions from his government, warned U.S. officials against this advance before it started. Specifically, he warned that there were 700 miles of Chinese border toward which MacArthur was headed, along which the Chinese were concentrated. The British also warned against advancing into this area, and these warnings were relayed to MacArthur by Washington. (December 12)

On MacArthur's claim that his retreat from the Yalu was a "brilliantly executed planned strategic withdrawal":

> Worried Pentagon strategists will only talk about it privately, but one of the most serious military errors of any recent war was responsible for trapping the First Marine Division and the two Seventh Infantry regiments which made their painful, gallant fight out of Hogaru. One tragic fact is that they never would have been trapped but for three unforgivable military errors.
>
> The first error was lack of liaison between Lt. General Walton Waller, Commander of the 8th Army, and Major General Edward Almond, Commander of the 10th Army. For some strange reason known only to MacArthur, these two generals had no battle communication with each other, but had to talk to each other by way of Tokyo some 700 miles away. Second, both generals had their men racing for the Manchurian border to see which could get there first. Reassured by MacArthur's intelligence that they had nothing to fear from the Chinese, the troops fanned out, instead of driving forward in a strong, compact spearhead. Furthermore, the 10th Corps under General Almond went racing off toward the north, instead of sticking close to the 8th Army. The Joint Chiefs of Staff cabled a reminder to MacArthur that General Almond had no battle communication with General Waller. MacArthur sent back a curt reply that he knew what he was doing.
>
> Result was that the Chinese wisely hit at the vacuum between the 8th Army and the 10th Corps. They also hit between the advancing units of the two armies which were fanned out, not expecting resistance. (December 12)

On MacArthur's claim that his 150,000 troops were opposed by a million Chinese:

> MacArthur's public statements in Tokyo are frequently at complete variance with the confidential reports cabled back by his intelligence . . . For instance, MacArthur estimated publicly . . . on December 4 . . . more than one million Chinese in Korea or on the border, while on December 15 he announced that "a bottomless well of Chinese Communist manpower continues to flow into Korea."
>
> However, this is not what his intelligence Chief was cabling the Joint Chiefs of Staff. On December 6, just two days after MacArthur had announced his million-man Chinese Army estimate, General Willoughby identified six Chinese armies on our Eighth Army's front . . .
>
> If all these six Chinese armies were of full strength with no casualties— which is doubtful—the total Chinese force which sent the U.N. Eighth

Army on a 120 mile retreat in less than two weeks was only 96,000 men. Yet, the U.N. Eighth Army had more than 100,000 front line combat troops; not counting engineers and reserve troops behind the lines.

[Willoughby] now estimates that the total Chinese strength in Korea facing not only the Eighth Army but previously facing the Tenth Corps around the Hungnam Beachhead is 285,000, plus 150,000 North Koreans. The size of the U.N. forces is a military secret. But it can be stated that they are somewhat more than the Chinese strength.

It is supposed to require a manpower supremacy of 3 to 1 to launch a successful offense. Furthermore it is an indisputable fact that we have complete control of the air while the Chinese have almost no artillery except that captured from us . . . (December 30)

As our missives rained down day after day, raising a discordant clangor amid the symphony of MacArthur acclaim, two sorts of reaction immediately surfaced. First, elements of the press at large picked up or expanded on our stories, and developed new ones of like vein, encouraging a more even-handed climate of debate. Second, a backlash of protest struck us. Each day brought accusatory letters by the mail sack. The great man himself twice condescended to denounce stories of ours—the one that revealed how Washington had warned MacArthur about Chinese intervention, placing a prohibition against the use of American troops near the Yalu, and the one that revealed how the Joint Chiefs had warned him, just before the deluge, against splitting his forces. (Both stories would be vindicated in testimony by Generals Bradley and Collins at the Senate inquiry in May 1951.) Taking a different tack, several senators joined in demanding that we be investigated and prosecuted for printing stories that were too authentic, having been spirited from classified information. The Justice Department and the Army announced that probes of us were under way. Because of this, a crisis that threatened the continuance of our network radio show developed while rising rumbles of protest reverberated through the ranks of our newspaper-publisher clients—matters to be treated in the following chapter.

In the meantime, we confronted what we saw as the Truman half of the problem—his vacillation toward MacArthur's insubordination. Our approach here would be guided by amateur psychology, a form of quackery in which Drew delighted. During the years of his contentions with the President, he had learned to despair of either converting or intimidating him; however, he *could* infuriate him, as was shown by numerous Truman tirades against Drew, public and private, and he could provoke Truman into petty reversals calculated to confound us, such as retaining someone we had revealed was to be fired, or promoting someone we had said *ought* to be fired. The capacity to elicit even a contrary reaction from a President was not to be dismissed, and in this case seemed to offer peculiar possibilities.

The President's vulnerable spot, Drew believed, was his compulsive self-portrayal as a combative man of iron will and resolute decision. In many respects a solid, down-to-earth character, Truman sometimes showed the insecurity of an assertive but limited man engulfed by unlimited responsibilities. In self-defense, Drew felt, he paraded as the take-charge boss who never shrank from deciding the tough ones, who never lost a moment's sleep, even over dropping the atom bombs; he was the self-consciously salty fellow who took no guff, told 'em off and gave 'em hell. In reality, Drew contended, Truman was often indecisive and could be led around by the nose, as he had been by MacArthur. But he could not bear to be *seen* as such, and that was our key. Ever since the outcome of the first Formosa flap, Drew believed that a continuing portrayal of a weak President being gulled, ignored and even intimidated by a strong general, especially if this portrayal was joined in by other journalists, would raise Truman's sensitivity to MacArthur's challenges and at some point, in conjunction with events, provoke him to confound his belittlers by making a demonstration of who was the boss. Looking back, I have no explanation for our effrontery except to say that I was young and bumptious, and Drew was as vain about his influence, even influence in reverse, as Harry Truman was about stopping the buck.

A typical column in this campaign would begin by saying that though Truman denied its existence in hopes it would go away, "all groups agree that the political and military tug-of-war between Tokyo and Washington probably has been the most spectacular and difficult ever to exist between any President and a commander in the field." We would report that Truman's failure to bring MacArthur to heel was demoralizing the State Department, or frustrating the Joint Chiefs to the extent that General Bradley was talking to friends of quitting, or creating havoc with the attempt to launch the North Atlantic Treaty Organization. "MacArthur to the British, is an advance warning of what could happen in any allied war. An American general, they fear, would dominate a weak White House and likewise the fate of Britain."

Drew would occasionally inflict little historical essays on readers about how FDR dominated his generals, and how Lincoln fired his, one after the other, till he got what he wanted, in contrast to the current spectacle of "a brilliant, strong-minded general who knew exactly what he wanted and a President not versed in military strategy who, as a former National Guard artillery captain, was dazzled by braid and brass."

Drew assumed this sort of thing was making Truman boil, the more so because the nation's most prominent cartoonist, the widely syndicated Herblock, was regularly caricaturing Truman as a little man marching in one direction on a treadmill on wheels, while a larger-than-life MacArthur casually pulled him along behind him in the opposite direction. But editorials and cartoons, Drew knew, could get you only so far. What was needed was an investigative coup, an inside story that could dramatize a waffling Truman being taken into camp by MacArthur.

The most likely prospect for such a story lay in the true account of what had happened during the only personal encounter Truman and MacArthur had ever had—at the Wake Island Conference. I resumed my efforts to crack that story in early January, hopeful of a breakthrough now that the solid MacArthur-Washington front of October was starting to crumble.

For three months the principal details of that conference had remained locked in all the secrecy that the necessities of war and the taboos of patriotism can impose. But I discovered that the Truman party at Wake Island, true to the tenets of White House honor, had hidden a stenographer, Miss Vernice Anderson, behind a door left ajar so that some sort of transcript could be made of the full-dress conference. Knowing that a transcript existed and that some copies had been made (and numbered so that their whereabouts could be traced at all times), I was in a position to press our sources effectively for it; by late January a colonel in a Pentagon cubbyhole showed me a copy.

With a start, I saw that the account was not just a summary or a paraphrase, but a verbatim copy of what was said—the direct quotes of Truman, MacArthur, Frank Pace, Omar Bradley, Admiral Arthur Radford, Averell Harriman, Philip Jessup, and the other generals and diplomats of the President's party. As I gulped down the paragraphs, my assimilation was distracted by the intruding worm of self-aggrandizement; here was the stuff of which Pulitzer prizes are made.

The transcript provided little corroboration of the inspired rumors that Truman had staged this conference to humble MacArthur and reduce him to strict conformance with Washington policy before the big push north (a version Truman stoutly maintained unto his grave). On the contrary, it revealed a convocation of the nation's civil, military and diplomatic leaders dominated, indeed captivated, by Douglas MacArthur.

If the overseers from Washington had come steeled to face down an intransigent, anachronistic war dog, proposing risk-fraught ventures and demanding more divisions and wider latitude, they were wondrously disarmed. The old master of the high-level conference,* his mythic glory even brighter in the refulgence of Pusan and Inchon, had descended upon Wake Island as the captain of a war already won, the surmounter of crises averted the day before yesterday, the architect of a peace and reconstruction for which the blueprints were in hand.

He began by hailing them: "No commander in the history of war has ever had more complete and adequate support from all agencies in Washington than I have."

He set the tone by magnanimously assessing the shattered remnant of his enemy: "There is little resistance left in South Korea—only about 15,000 men—and those we do not destroy, the winter will.

"In North Korea, unfortunately, they are pursuing a forlorn hope. They have about 100,000 men who were trained as replacements. They are poorly trained, led and equipped, but they are obstinate and it goes against my grain to have to destroy them. They are only fighting to save face. Orientals prefer to die rather than lose face."

A merciful, quick encirclement below the Yalu would end it; then an immediate evacuation of American troops and a restoration of local self-rule: "We should turn Korea over to the Koreans as quickly as we can."

To delighted diplomats, the Restorer of Japan outlined plans for civil, not military, agencies to take over aid and reconstruction programs, with the Army humbly helping when requested, all at a cost only one-third of what had been anticipated in Washington. "Military occupations are always failures. I want to withdraw all our troops as soon as possible." (The transcript here indicated the President nodding in agreement.) For the politicians and generals, MacArthur was laden with unhoped-for boons: he planned to have the Eighth Army back in Japan "by Christmas," and soon after, he would begin turning over his

---

*For example, at Pearl Harbor, in 1944, a virtuoso presentation by MacArthur persuaded President Roosevelt to junk the Navy's plan for winning the Pacific war and to adopt MacArthur's. In Tokyo, two months before the Wake Island Conference, MacArthur had turned around the U.S. military high command on the question of Inchon.

divisions to "Omar" to rescue the lagging build-up of NATO in Europe.

Amid such felicities, the Supreme Commander deftly eluded the fundamental question: possible Chinese intervention. "Had they interfered in the first or second months it would have been decisive. We are no longer fearful of their intervention. We no longer stand hat in hand . . . Only fifty to sixty thousand could be gotten across the Yalu River. They have no air force. Now that we have bases for our Air Force in Korea, if the Chinese tried to get down to Pyongyang there would be the greatest slaughter."

With affairs so obviously well in hand, the discussion soon relaxed into trivialities. When a diplomat suggested the use of sound trucks for selling democracy to Koreans, the President asserted his hegemony. "I believe in sound trucks," he said. "I won two elections with them." (The transcript indicated laughter at this point.)

On such jovial notes the Wake Island Conference ended without curbs being placed on the advance to the Yalu, or any challenge being voiced to the MacArthur policies.* His objective attained, even to the exemption of South Korea from UN-supervised elections that might endanger his deputy, President Syngman Rhee, the alert MacArthur did not wait around for the coming of second thoughts. When the President invited him to lunch, the general looked at his watch, and as gracefully as it is possible to trample on protocol, declined, saying he had to get back to Tokyo before dark. In a twinkle, the legend was gone from among them, but the euphoric spell he cast lingered, as it would for several weeks. As the presidential party headed for lunch, Truman declared, "This has been the best conference I have ever attended."

I hurried to Drew with the extensive notes I had copied from the Wake Island transcript, suffering the proud apprehension of one who has pulled out a very fat plum but who fears he won't be allowed to eat it. Could we, already under mounting fire for revealing wartime secrets, publish the contents of a grand council of war, at a crisis point in that war? Drew scanned the dialogue in great drafts with a deepening frown and then addressed the conundrum of the press's right to inform versus the government's need for secrecy. After wrestling with

*A private meeting between Truman and MacArthur preceded the general conference, for which there is no record. It is possible that Truman laid down the law to MacArthur at that meeting, as Truman subsequently insisted, but highly unlikely, judging not only from the contrary tenor of the general conference that followed immediately but from the history of subsequent events.

himself for three or four seconds, he came down, as he invariably did, on the side of our scoop. The really sensitive aspects of the conference, he judged, had by now been overtaken by events; we were not likely to get another such opportunity to expose MacArthur's epic misjudgment of events to the public, and Truman's gullibility in swallowing it.

We discussed the wisdom of using our exclusive information as bait to draw participants at Wake, and other officials, into interviews that would update matters and make even more news that we could run in a series of columns, but we decided that to let the White House know what we had would invite a move either to suppress it or to upstage our exclusive revelation by making selective leaks from the transcript to sympathetic outlets. And so we compacted the bulk of our Wake Island story into one column,* which paraphrased the most damaging quotes to confuse the search for our source, and concluded on a note of appraisal: "Highlight of the Wake Island meeting was the brilliant exposition of one man. MacArthur completely dominated the conversation and virtually no effort was made to challenge his opinions. Perhaps also this was the most tragic part of the conference."

Our final stratagem was based on two judgments: that MacArthur would prove too proud to suffer in silence the existing military stalemate on South Korean soil and would find ways to speak out against it, which he had lately been forbidden to do; and that Truman, who among his circle of intimates was a habitual curser and blusterer, was bound to be threatening mayhem to MacArthur for not quietly toeing the mark. Why not dig up some anti-MacArthur tough talk from Truman about what he was going to do to MacArthur next time, and taunt Truman with it when each "next time" came and went unrequited? Might it not escalate the frustration building up in Truman's boiler?

We combed every likely source, but could unearth no contemporary example of anti-MacArthur bombast, an indication of the unaccustomed caution with which the President now regarded the general. We had to go back to the flap over MacArthur's VFW statement on Formosa, in the early months of the Korean War, to dredge up two examples. The best one—a Truman statement that he was considering firing MacArthur for his insubordinate remarks—we couldn't use, for

---

*From the viewpoint of professional acclaim, this proved a mistake. Three months after we published the heart of the transcript, the New York *Times* got hold of it and came forward with an ambitious series based on the transcript but padded with interviews and learned speculations. For this the *Times*, which didn't need it, got the Pulitzer Prize I had vainly glimpsed.

it was made to an audience of one, and though it had probably been repeated to others, we couldn't take the chance of exposing to Truman a Pearson source within his bosom. At about the same time, Truman had told a group of congressional friends that MacArthur knew better than to send out a statement that contradicted his policy and that "the next son of a bitch who shoots off his mouth over foreign policy without official clearance will find himself out of a job."

Whenever MacArthur lamented Washington policy, we would re-float this bit of bravado and cite the series of futile gag orders the President had issued for MacArthur's benefit. And the lamentations from Tokyo recurred with increasing frequency as the prospect of military deadlock deepened. MacArthur knew the hazard of his course as only a past master of the military bureaucracy could. He had obviously resolved to take a great gamble. Unwilling at the zenith of his fabulous career to acquiesce in what he regarded as a pusillanimous defeat and an epochal appeasement of Communism that would set in train an irreversible erosion of our national spirit and of our posture in Asia, which he saw as the key to the world struggle, he determined to rally the "patriotic opposition" and force upon the unsteady Truman a change of policy—or go down in the attempt.

With increasing vehemence he publicly attacked the "extraordinary inhibitions" that were handcuffing his forces, avowed that an "undeclared war" with China already existed, prophesied a stalemate in that war under present hobbles while insisting his forces could beat the Communists if "the politicians removed the curbs"; offered his "profound thanks" to American Legion spokesmen for urging Truman to authorize him to bomb the Manchurian bases. Through it all ran the theme he increasingly juxtaposed to Administration attempts to sell a limited war and a compromise peace: "In war, there is no substitute for victory . . . war's very object is victory, not prolonged indecision."

In late March 1951, in the midst of State Department efforts to get truce talks going, MacArthur, in his capacity as commander of all the United Nations military forces in Korea, addressed a semiultimatum to Peking in the guise of an offer to undertake personal peace negotiations with his Chinese counterpart. It contained a scathing assessment of China's incapacity to sustain a modern war, made a guarded threat to enlarge the war in area and weaponery, and insisted on the unification of all Korea as the basis of peace—a Truman goal of happier days but one from which the Administration was now tiptoeing away.

On the heels of that shocking usurpation a message was read to the assembled House of Representatives from MacArthur to the Republican leader of that body, Joe Martin, which reintoned the litany of forbidden causes for which MacArthur contended: the use of Chiang Kai-shek's armies to open a second front, the rejection of the Administration's Europe-first strategy, the recognition of the Korean War as "the key to the world's situation," and the repudiation of the limited-war–compromise peace doctrine to which MacArthur again appended the catch phrase that had now become his anthem: "In war, there is no substitute for victory."

At which point, on April 11, Truman finally boiled over and fired MacArthur, setting off a daily heightening typhoon of national emotion that found visible expression in the fervent crowds which in all the great cities of the land flooded out in record-breaking numbers to hail the returned hero-martyr.

The day after the dismissal, according to our sources, Truman asked his Cabinet members for their comments. Secretary of State Dean Acheson led off. The dramatic firing reminded him, he said, of an Army couple who had reared a stunningly beautiful daughter at a succession of military bases. She was constantly surrounded by the troops, who courted her assiduously. One day the husband was greeted at the door by a distraught wife who announced that their daughter was pregnant. Acheson said the husband reached for his handkerchief, wiped his brow and said, "Thank goodness that's over."

Drew regarded the midnight dismissal as no less than a hair's-breath deliverance from World War III. He counted on the institutional defenses of the Republic to at length contain the "temporary" public uproar. The important thing was that the incendiary had been removed from where the powder kegs were kept and that the more cautious elements of both parties would now control the levers and somehow muddle through without Armageddon. Drew would uphold Truman's side in the struggle for public opinion that was to rage for months, but in his heart he believed that Truman had made a sorry hash of things that would disable the liberal cause for years to come.

MacArthur, to his undoubted dismay, faded away almost as quietly as his oratory had prophesied. Though the American public cheered him in unprecedented millions as a symbol, it would not follow his prescriptions. The seeds of uncertainty about his judgment, of fear of his adventurism, had been planted. He was not even a factor in the presidential contest of the following year in which, though Truman was repudiated, both parties turned to standard-bearers who shared Truman's limited-war, Europe-first policy of containment and who based their appeal on their capacity to *end* the war, not *win* it.

In retrospect, I do not know if all our schemes and strategems affected the outcome one whit. Drew believed they did. He was sure the then small liberal media presence had been a major factor in deflating MacArthur and that our columns and broadcasts had often been its cutting edge. As one who always saw current dramas as related parts of decadal struggles, Drew contended that the "near escape from MacArthurism" could not be separated from our campaign against Forrestal.

"Suppose," he would argue, "we had not made Forrestal too controversial for reappointment. Suppose he had stayed in power a year longer. The onset of the Korean War would have made him a hero, for he had been the great exponent of the Communist menace, the champion of a continued military build-up. Korea would have vindicated him, superficially, and his influence within the Cabinet would have again been paramount. Remember that Forrestal agreed with MacArthur about Red China and the need for a showdown with Communism before it was too late. Supposing Forrestal had been running the Pentagon, instead of George Marshall, when MacArthur's demands for escalation came. Instead of being cautioned against landing Chiang and shelling Shanghai, Truman would have been under redoubled pressure to do it. We broke that up before it could happen."

Drew was not alone in this expansive estimate. At the height of our exposés of MacArthur's Yalu misadventures, Senator Joseph McCarthy took the Senate floor to charge that Drew Pearson, in collaboration with international Communism, had caused the death of Secretary Forrestal and now planned the destruction of General MacArthur. Before he sat down, McCarthy had touched off two criminal investigations into our activities.

It was the opening gun of the major phase of a struggle for personal survival.

8 · Joe McCarthy: The Falling-Out

As MID-CENTURY arrived in America, the more apoplectic wing of anti-Communism stewed in an impotence unwarranted by events. Surely the period was spawning grievances enough for a rousing crusade: Red spy cases galore—Alger Hiss, Judith Coplon, Klaus Fuchs, the Rosenbergs, the Canadian ring; terrifying Soviet progress in nuclear bombs sped along by the theft of Anglo-American secrets; the eerie disappearance of China into the Communist maw, a fourth of the human race in one swallow; the gradual coming to light of past laxity by the Roosevelt-Truman regime regarding Communist infiltrators, laxity which had maddeningly escaped the law of political retribution.

Such were the possibilities of the hour that Homer Capehart could incite the Senate galleries to unruly demonstration with but a short blast from his bassoon: "How much more are we going to have to take? Fuchs and Acheson and Hiss and hydrogen bombs threatening outside and New Dealism eating away at the vitals of the nation. In the name of Heaven, is this the best America can do?"

But frustration welled up only to be aimlessly dissipated, left unfocused by an ineffectual, undirected anti-Communism shorn of its heroes and prophets. Martin Dies languished in political exile, J. Parnell Thomas was in prison, John Rankin lacked geographical spread, Richard Nixon hovered in calculating detachment, torn between the opportunities and liabilities of the cause. Then, in early 1950, a brash newcomer, unschooled in the formulations of Red-baiting but gifted with a raw genius for commanding attention, breezed into the void. He picked up the mantle and put it on. At donning, it looked a touch incongruous, but after minor alterations it fit so snugly that thereafter the cause would bear his name.

The good ladies of the Ohio County Republican Women's Club could not have suspected, as they assembled in Wheeling, West Virginia, on February 9, 1950, that they were providing the stage for a historic event. Their featured speaker, furnished from Washington by the Republican National Committee, was, to be sure, a bona-fide United States senator who looked encouragingly hearty as he back-slapped local notables on the dais, but still, he was an unknown, the sort assigned to third-echelon towns during the fortnight of "Lincoln Day" speeches that each year purpled the February air. His name was Joseph Raymond McCarthy, young, rumpled, handsome in a bull-necked, black-jowled, unchiseled way. As a speaker he was unpolished, with an Irish baritone that under stress soared up into a whine, but he was not without an arresting quality. He plowed into his text with earnest ferocity, replete with arm waving, scowling and stalking. With the help of Alger Hiss and atheistic World Communism, he soon gave his sponsors comforting assurance of a gratifying evening. Amid the histrionics, the line that was to launch the cataclysm padded in on cat's paws, so softly that there was later an unresolved dispute as to the exact words uttered, but here is the wording of the advance text Senator McCarthy had handed to the local press and which was transmitted on the AP wire: "While I cannot take the time to name all the men in the State Department *who have been named as members of the Communist Party and members of a spy ring,* I have here in my hand a list of 205 that were known to the Secretary of State as being members of the Communist Party and who, nevertheless, *are still working and shaping policy in the State Department."* (Emphasis added.)

What we do not know about heroes is whether the secret of their prowess lies in a truly intuitive audacity or in a mere foolhardiness that is oblivious to obstacles and that conquers or fails according to luck and the quality of the adversary. McCarthy's accusatory technique represented a quantum jump beyond the relative caution of Congressmen

Thomas, Rankin and the other fathers. He found their epithets off target, their alarums lackluster, and their bogies superannuated. The mass of people weren't going to get really whipped up about "fellow travelers" and "Communist *sympathizers,*" especially if they were only actors or writers or professors, particularly if all they had done was join clubs or sign petitions. Even government clerks who joined clubs and signed petitions pale as menaces when it turns out that it all happened ten years before.

And so his 205 (or 57, as he later claimed to have said) were not merely cited, as if from archives; they were drummed across the stage in the figurative flesh. He had the living list, he said, had it in his right hand even as he spoke, and would wave it aloft. Why, he would have called the ugly roll then and there were it not that the roll was long and his plane was taking off in twenty minutes. Nor were McCarthy's subversives *unimportant* people; they were spies and sitting top officials, "members of a spy ring," "members of the Communist Party," "card-carrying Communists," "men in the State Department" who were "shaping policy."

To fully credit the boldness of McCarthy's debut, one must consider that he had no proper list at all of spies or Communist Party members and possessed only a rudimentary knowledge of the subversive lore compiled by his congressional forebears. A lesser impresario, pressed as he was by reporters along the route to bring out for inspection the two-headed men he was advertising, would have toned down his claims or at least retreated into unavailability. But McCarthy, with the higher instinct that senses the boundless sweep of currents taken at the flood, merely turned up the steam in his calliope. On his second night out, in Salt Lake City, he issued a challenge over the radio to Secretary of State Dean Acheson:

"Last night I discussed Communists in the State Department. I stated that I had the names of 57 card-carrying members of the Communist Party . . . Now I want to tell the Secretary this: If he wants to call me tonight at the Utah Hotel, I will be glad to give him the names of those 57 card-carrying Communists . . ." And on his third day, from Reno, Nevada, he accelerated again by releasing an open telegram to President Truman. "I have in my possession the names of 57 Communists who are in the State Department at present," he said, and he challenged Truman to simply ask his underlings for the same official data that he had and cleanse his house.

As abbreviated word of McCarthy's sallies traveled eastward via the news ticker, millions who had all along known in their bones that the government was swimming with Reds fixed upon McCarthy as their awaited champion. But sophisticates on diverse sides of the issue scorned his simplisms. Ring-wise defenders of the State Department were delighted with a foe so green at the game as not to know that there was no longer a single "card-carrying Communist" anywhere, for the party had abolished its cards three years before; the department confidently demanded of McCarthy his list of names. Democratic senators, in consultation with the White House, prepared to convene an investigation that would make an object lesson of this reckless lout and thus bury the nagging "soft on Communism" issue, which in abler hands could prove troublesome for Democratic incumbents. The soberer sort of Republican congressman feared exactly this. Senator Taft quietly bemoaned "a perfectly reckless performance." Richard Nixon cautioned McCarthy on his innovations and urged him to return to the old tactics. Lay off the card-carrying Communist stuff, Nixon warned, because it couldn't be proved; concentrate on persons with "communist-front affiliations—which could be proved."* And anti-Communism's intellectuals, oft-shamed in the past by their movement's penchant for rococo leaders, despaired that, as Eugene Lyons put it in the *New Leader,* "the luck of the Communists held good."

Thus it was that Senator McCarthy returned to Washington a magnet for mixed attentions. With matchless bravado, he reserved time on the Senate floor for an address which he promised would lay bare the sordid, treasonous mess. For years the Communists-in-government issue had smoldered desultorily; in a week McCarthy had inflamed it to the level of a national confrontation.

Joe McCarthy and I were on close terms for a senator and a muckraker. We had arrived in Washington, in our unequal estates, at about the same time. From the day I first began making the rounds of Capitol Hill as a Drew Pearson legman, McCarthy's door was a hospitable oasis in what often seemed a desert of hostility. He knew how to make a footsore reporter feel esteemed. Sometimes when we were talking alone in his office, his secretary would interrupt to say that such-and-such Cabinet member was on the phone, and Joe, in a violated tone, would

---

*Earl Mazo and Stephen Hess, *Richard Nixon: A Political Portrait* (New York: Harper & Row, 1968), pp. 140–41; p. 144.

protest, "I can't take any calls. I'm talking to *Jack*. Tell him I've gone to China."

In the back of my mind I knew McCarthy must have his motives. Drew had already published a couple of small reproofs and had handed him a bouquet or two, as was Drew's wont during the period of sizing up a formidable newcomer. McCarthy had deduced, no doubt, that if Pearson was indeed the malevolent force conjured up by the elders of the Republican cloakroom, it would be the part of wisdom to propitiate him, or better still to turn him into an ally. With his gift for straightforward deviousness, McCarthy made himself available to us as a source, a purveyor of inside information about his colleagues and their secret conclaves. At my prompting he would phone fellow senators to ask what had transpired this morning behind closed doors or what strategy was planned for the morrow. While I listened in on an extension he would pump even a Robert Taft or a William Knowland with the handwritten questions I passed him. This blot upon senatorial honor was for a reporter a professional coup of high rank and I rejoiced in it, prying out of McCarthy every last morsel of confidential information.

He displayed in all this a recklessness that was, to its beneficiary, irresistibly appealing; had it not been for the hours I would put in conducting unfruitful interviews with uncooperative senators in order to cover McCarthy's tracks, he would have been exposed as a traitor to the Club and appropriately exiled; as it was, he was never identified.

Beyond his value as an intelligence bonanza, McCarthy seemed to me a figure of considerable human interest. For a member of "the world's most exclusive club" in the status-conscious 1940s, he was refreshingly unpretentious. Teetering back behind the great block of his government-issue senator's desk, he would hold rump court in his shirt sleeves and not infrequently in his undershirt. He was comfortably old-shoe. The traditional outlets for foppery—clothes, accessories, dinner menus, wine lists—tempted him not a bit. Until his marriage some years later brought a sartorial shake-up, he was chronically rumpled and scuffed. "If his tie ever matched his socks it was by accident," Roy Cohn assures us. His dish for all occasions was steak ("cremated") and he was well content with almost any drink put before him.

As each day wore on, he would collect an odd aggregate of people that filled up his office, overflowed into his anteroom and moved on with him when he took off. In the egalitarian atmosphere he encouraged, the most obscure addition to his entourage would, within five or ten minutes, begin to call him "Joe" and to proffer advice on matters of state, which Joe would entertain gravely, as though coming from Foster Dulles himself. More than a good listener, he was a good laugher at jokes, an unceremonious drinker, quick to take out a bottle but under control, a harum-scarum gambler who bluffed convincingly, bet boldly, but who at length ceased to pay attention and began to lose. He was said to have a yen for pretty girls that was commensurate with his vigor and his opportunities as a young bachelor senator. Above all, he was affable, a quality especially appreciated by one of his most prominent backers, Joseph P. Kennedy, the sire. McCarthy was an occasional visitor to Hyannis Port, and the ambassador once recalled that no injury or indignity suffered while horsing around with the Kennedy clan ever soured his nature. "He went out on my boat . . . and he almost drowned swimming behind it but he never complained . . . He was always pleasant; he was never a crab."*

McCarthy drew some sort of psychic comfort from the clatter and confusion with which he surrounded his affairs, but at times I noticed in him an inner mechanism that detachedly went on clicking and calculating amid the camaraderie of impromptu card games and movable mob scenes. At such times I would be reminded that an obscure outsider does not, at the age of thirty-eight, get elected to the United States Senate from a politically sophisticated state unless he possesses a singular upward drive. When I later began to look into McCarthy's past, I found that a compulsive will to achieve throbbed and swelled visibly at every phase of his life: the fourteen-year-old school dropout building up a poultry flock of twelve thousand birds in five years of lone labor; the grocery-store manager of nineteen who, deciding he must go to college, chewed through four years of high school in nine months; the Marquette University student, initially rough and awkward in social intercourse, gladhanding his way to the presidency of the class; the young circuit court judge making a statewide name for himself by handling three times as many cases as some of his colleagues; the Marine desk officer in the Pacific who, for the faraway Wisconsin newspapers, managed to project his uneventful days in a backwater of the war as an ongoing drama of heroic derring-do. Looking out from behind his cheerful disorganization was an inner eye that was never off the ball.

From time to time he asked me out on a double date, but I always begged off on some pretext or other out of recognition that the restric-

*From an interview in the New York *Post* (January 9, 1961).

tions imposed on me by a thin purse and a no-nonsense religion would likely render me rather disenchanting as a boon companion to Joe McCarthy. Our relationship flourished nonetheless. I became a familiar in the inner sanctum of his office; at my wedding in 1949 he was a prominent and engaging ornament.

If McCarthy the man was something of a riddle, McCarthy the politician was an unformed entity, an unguided missile apt to veer off in any trajectory. He shed, without pause, his first political skin—that of a New Deal Democrat—when he realized that in his part of the world opportunity lay with the Republicans. As a convert to the Wisconsin GOP, he slipped back and forth between the "reform" and "old guard" elements, and between progressivism and reaction. In his only venture into national politics—the Wisconsin presidential primary of 1948—he successfully spearheaded the bid of liberal Minnesota Governor Harold Stassen against the faraway hero of the right, General MacArthur, whom McCarthy semirespectfully portrayed as too old, too out of touch, and too often married.

Even Drew's favorite index of measurement—position vis-à-vis the "special interests"—was confounded by McCarthy's inconsistency. My efforts to nudge Drew into running little puffs about Joe in honor of his heroic services to us as often as not backfired when his affinity for real estate promoters and commodity traffickers registered on Drew's graphs, causing him instead to run little knuckle-rappers; but when the same McCarthy would, with fearless truculence, maul insurance moguls, bankers or military brass hats who had run afoul of one or another of McCarthy's pet projects, Drew would perk up, acknowledge an untapped potential in the man and allow a modest accolade.

In the field of anti-Communist politics, McCarthy had been a particular enigma. At the time he won his political spurs, Communists had an unusual impact at the polls in Wisconsin because they dominated much of the state's labor movement. In his threshold campaign, against the celebrated Senator Robert M. La Follette, Jr., whose family was a Wisconsin institution, McCarthy stood to gain from old Communist antipathy to La Follette, so he sent cooing signals to the local comrades, such as "Stalin's proposal for world disarmament is a great thing and he must be given credit for being sincere about it." When reporters chided him, he replied, "Communists have the same right to vote as anyone else, don't they?"

McCarthy won the primary by an eyelash margin, which was attributed to labor votes switched by the Communists. In the general-election campaign, however, McCarthy saw he would not again corral the leftists when the *Daily Worker* endorsed his opponent, a liberal college professor named Howard McMurray. Nor would McCarthy need Communist support, for Democrats were a bedraggled minority in the Wisconsin of those days, and a national Republican landslide was in the wind. Always one to wrest advantage from disadvantage, McCarthy began to belabor McMurray as "the Communist candidate" and "nothing more than a megaphone being used by the Communist-controlled CIO Political Action Committee." This occasional tactic probably added to the McCarthy landslide victory—620,430 to 378,-772.

The pre-1950 McCarthy, then, was neither a Red-courter nor a Red-baiter; he was a facile politician circling a volatile voting bloc, though grosser than some in his opportunism. If he could get the Communist vote by veiled gesture, fine; if not, he would make whatever capital he could out of its opposition.

In later years McCarthy would date the birth of his obsession with Communist subversion from a conversation with Navy Secretary Forrestal shortly after his election to the Senate in 1946. But three years were to pass after that Damascus before the scales fell from his eyes; as he later told Roy Cohn, it was late 1949 before he began to warm to the subject.

In the weeks before his debut at Wheeling, McCarthy was, I knew, canvassing friends for advice as to how, in the time remaining to him before his re-election campaign in 1952, he could beef up and solidify his thin, unfocused image. As part of this survey, he met with three advisers in early January 1950 at Washington's swank Colony Restaurant: the liberal lawyer William A. Roberts, who was a close friend and legal adviser to Drew; Father Edmund Walsh, Dean of Georgetown University's Foreign Service School; and Professor Claude Krauss, a political-science teacher at Georgetown. McCarthy came to the table buoyant with a likely scheme: that he plump for a radical increase in government pensions for all the elderly, thereby becoming Mr. Senior Citizen. But he was dissuaded by his counselors on the ground of extravagant cost. Attorney Roberts suggested that McCarthy become Champion of the St. Lawrence Seaway, but McCarthy demurred—too bland, too tedious, too lacking in sex appeal. It remained for Father Walsh, a thirty-year veteran of the international anti-Communist wars, to save the evening by suggesting that McCarthy seize upon the issue of Communist infiltration of our government. The bulb installed by

Forrestal blinked on. It is humbling to speculate that had our friend Roberts and the others been receptive to the senator's proposal for a grandiose old folks' dole, Joe McCarthy might well have gone forth, in all his aggressiveness, to win for himself a pedestal in the pantheon of fighting liberals.

Directly upon his return from Wheeling and points west, McCarthy phoned me in a mood both expansive and agitated. He had "hit the jackpot," he said, and had gotten hold of "one hell of an issue." But he needed all the help he could get in building up his files on Communist infiltrators. "You guys must have leads that would help me," he said.

He was aware that spy stories, like organized-crime stories and Ku Klux Klan stories, were a speciality of ours. He recalled that the column had first made public the existence of the Russian atomic spy ring in Canada, and the Communist operation near Washington that was smuggling blueprints of the B-29 bomber to Moscow. And I had told McCarthy of how Drew had information that Alger Hiss was a Communist a year or two before he was publicly named, but unable to substantiate it, had quietly passed it on to the government. It sure would be helpful, McCarthy was saying, if we could pass on something like that to him.

I cautioned him that any unpublished allegations we were sitting on would be only tips that we had been unable to nail down, otherwise we'd already have gone to press. That was fine, he said, acknowledging the difficulty in distinguishing the dupe and the dabbler from the committed Bolshevik and intimating that he had investigative resources beyond a reporter's. I took this to mean that he was getting some help, probably bootlegged, from the FBI or one of the other intelligence outfits. I said I'd see what I could find out and get back to him.

As I recall, the decision to help McCarthy was almost automatic. I'm sure I underwent none of the soul-searching that subsequent events would suggest was appropriate. For one thing, I owed him; for another, he might be able to flesh out some of our inconclusive material, and if so, I would no doubt get the scoop. Nor did I regard cooperation with him, or with his avowed mission, as repugnant. The McCarthy I knew was quite a different animal from the ogrish caricature that later became obligatory. As to the mission, I had encountered enough evidence of bureaucratic laxity in the security field to believe that there might well remain a serious infiltration of subversives in government.

I went to our offices, sifted through our files and pulled out what I thought was the most promising—that of a presidential aide named David Demarest Lloyd. It seemed the most promising not so much because of any blatancy in Lloyd's record as because of his position at the right hand of the President. Our information on Lloyd demonstrates the conundrums inherent in the game of identifying subversives. It now seems a tedious lot of hocus-pocus to most people, but perhaps I should elaborate on the considerations that tugged at me that evening as an introduction to the temper of the times and to the nature of the ambiguities that made McCarthyism possible and probably inevitable.

What we knew was not at all lethal until joined to what could be speculated from it. We knew that shortly after Lloyd's arrival in Washington from Harvard Law School, he had joined at least two Communist fronts—the National Lawyers Guild and the Washington Book Store Cooperative. His wife was also a front-joiner. His great-aunt, Mrs. Caroline Lloyd Strobel, was an avowed Communist who had been a financial angel and co-owner of the *Daily Worker*. While Lloyd was not responsible for his elderly relative, and maybe not even for his wife, it was a constantly recurring fact that Communists came from families with Communist backgrounds.

We knew that after working in a number of government agencies between 1935 and 1946, David Lloyd applied for a State Department post in 1946; he did not receive a security clearance and did not get the job. Two years later he turned up on the payroll of the Democratic National Committee, became a speech writer for Truman in the 1948 re-election campaign, and after the great victory he was moved over to the White House staff. We knew, or at least we had received information we were not in a position to confirm, that in early 1950 the Loyalty Review Board had raised a challenge to Lloyd which was still unresolved, and that the White House staff had confiscated the offending files and was applying political pressure to have the challenge dropped.

Beyond this gruel of fact and tip, there was a pattern to Lloyd's career which, while innocent enough to the average observer, was fraught with suspicion for the subversion buff. It was a mark of the Communist infiltrator that he had entered the government in one of a very few hospitable places, and that thereafter he moved frequently from agency to agency in accord with the party's priority of the moment. The target agencies of these migrations within the government made up a discernible pattern: in the 1930s, agencies concerned with reform and recovery; in the World War II period, agencies concerned with war production and military intelligence operations; and from the latter part of the war on, agencies designed to distribute the billions in rehabilitation aid and shape the postwar world order.

Viewed from that prospective, Lloyd's progress through government had an ominous look to it, for it was a migration along a familiar route, from one identifiable infiltration center to another. He had entered the federal government through the Resettlement Administration, the domain of Communists Nathan Gregory Silvermaster, Lee Pressman and William Ludwig Ullman; there, within the broader confines of the Department of Agriculture, were gathered a platoon of key Communist agents who would soon move to other departments—Harold Ware, Victor Perlo, Alger Hiss, John Abt, Nathan Witt, Henry H. Collins, Jr., Bela Gold, Henry Julian Wadleigh, Harold Glasser, Charles Kramer and Margaret Bennett Porter.

From Agriculture, Lloyd had gone to the small staff of the Senate Committee on Civil Liberties, later to be exposed by its chairman, Senator La Follette, as a nest of Communists who had fooled him— a nest that included fellow graduates of the Agriculture Department, John Abt and Charles Kramer, as well as Allan Rosenberg and Charles Flato. During the war Lloyd, along with old shopmates Perlo and Kramer, went to the Office of Price Administration.

Next for Lloyd was the Foreign Economic Administration, *né* the Board of Economic Warfare, run by subsequently named Communists who were old colleagues of his, Lauchlin Currie and Allan Rosenberg and the venerable Silvermaster, and staffed by others regarded as security risks—Michael Greenberg, soon to go to the White House under Currie, Frank Coe, Mary and Philip Keeney, and Irving Kaplan. Lloyd's subsequent bid to enter the State Department, which as we have seen foundered during the security investigation, came at a time of heavy Communist infiltration of that department; had Lloyd made it, he would have been back in the departmental company of Hiss, Wadleigh, Collins, Glasser, Keeney and others.

All this was, of course, merely informed speculation. All that I could prove beyond doubt was that Lloyd had joined two Communist fronts, a common occurrence in the 1930s. As for the matters of suspicious association, every infiltrated place Lloyd had been, except perhaps for the La Follette committee staff, was populated by an incomparably larger body of loyal Americans. Lloyd's career moves, which so followed the pattern of Communist migration, also followed the pattern of patriotic, ambitious government activists who wanted to be where the main focus of government activity was. According to our information, Lloyd had told security investigators that like thousands of naïve front-joiners, he had dropped out of them when he belatedly recognized their Stalinist warp; and he had pointed to his role in helping draft the anti-Communist charter of the Americans for Democratic Action as proof-positive of where his true sympathies lay. A score of distinguished Americans vouched for his character and loyalty.

Such claims were difficult to evaluate. They might be entirely genuine, and indeed they were convincing enough to Drew to banish the Lloyd file to inactive status. On the other hand, it was the policy of the Communists that once a member showed promise as a high-level infiltrator, he was pulled out of visible party activity and buried deep underground; in the same vein, the joining of a professedly anti-Communist organization could be merely an evasive tactic. And party discipline aside, there were the ambivalences of the fellow traveler to contend with, the enthusiast who had played around with the party when it seemed the wave of the future, who had meanwhile developed a promising career in democratic-capitalist government, and who now threaded his way between the demands of present ambition and former allegiance.

Lloyd's appointment to the White House indicated that he must have passed a rigorous security probe. But had he? He had welded his relationship with the President and the top White House staff from a position at the Democratic National Committee, where the security question did not arise; he came into the White House already an insider, as one who had proved himself to the most influential people there, people with the power to disregard or browbeat the security pests.

The you-can-call-it-either-way aspect of our Lloyd file illustrated the hazards of subversive evaluation. The same man's dossier contained entries that could damn as well as exculpate, patterns of involvement as well as patterns of disengagement. If loyal Americans were not to be ruined and disloyal ones perpetuated in high office, all depended on the depth of information and on the breadth of the analyst. I put my emphasis on the depth of information; Drew, on the breadth of analysis.

To Drew, this was a job for the anonymous, disinterested expert analysts within the bureaucracy; their clearance of Lloyd for so sensitive and politically explosive a place as the White House was convincing. I was not so easily persuaded. Let the reporter use Congress to prod the bureaucracy and vice versa, I felt, and in the process, get an inside track on the results. And so, without consulting Drew, I took the contents of our Lloyd file to Joe McCarthy.

The McCarthy outer office gave off its familiar air of strenuous disorganization, now supercharged with a current of excitement. Someone whispered to me that Joe was preparing an epic indictment for the Senate floor; someone else portentously waved me into the inner office. McCarthy loomed above his folder-piled desk in rolled-up shirt sleeves. In the week since we last met, he had become a storm center of national controversy, but notoriety seemed to ride easily on his beefy shoulders. All smiles, he reached out for my folder with one of the huge mitts that had made him boxing champ at Marquette. He scanned it. "This is terrific," he said.

"If you have access to the government's security data," I said, "the key things to find out are these—did the State Department withhold clearance of Lloyd four years ago, and is the Loyalty Review Board divided on him now, and if so, why?"

"We'll get right on it," he replied, and he thanked me profusely.

I attempted to pry, saying something to the effect that he had bitten off quite a carcass in the past week and did he think he could chew it. He rolled his eyes heavenward and opened his hands as if to say it was all in the lap of the gods.

"Between us," he admitted, "I've got mostly old congressional-committee stuff. It's still good. The longer they've been dragging their feet in getting rid of traitors exposed years ago, the more of a scandal it is. But what I need is fresh stuff. Something sensational. And it's starting to come in. Maybe your man Lloyd will be it."

A phone call came in, and he apologized for taking it. "It's Dick Nixon, I've been twisting his arm to give me the current Un-American Activities Committee files." I stood up to leave but he waved me down. For ten minutes he worked on Congressman Nixon. Repeatedly McCarthy pressed the theme that he was on the spot, the *cause* was on the spot, and he needed all the help he could get. As nearly as I could judge from the McCarthy end of the conversation, Nixon became a backroom collaborator.

The calls were pouring in from people whose names I recognized as belonging to anti-Communist afficionados. I left him so that he could get on with his business. But I felt a twinge of apprehension in the pit of my stomach. His performance seemed that of a man who was just putting together the evidence after he had already returned the indictment. On the other hand, it would be like Joe, in exhorting for help, to exaggerate his need, like a prudent general pleading for more divisions when he already had more than he needed.

Back at our office I found Drew putting the finishing touches on a withering blast against McCarthy. In the main, said Drew's copy, McCarthy's charges were old canards first launched three years before by another man from Wisconsin, Representative Bartel Jonkman, and discredited at the time.

> When the Senator from Wisconsin finally was pinned down, he could produce not 57, but only four names of State Department officials who he claimed were Communists.
>
> A careful scrutiny of these names is important. Of the four accused by McCarthy, one, Dr. Harlow Shapley, at no time worked for the State Department. Two, Gustavo Duran and Mrs. Mary Jane Keeney, resigned four years ago; the fourth, John Service, was reinstated after a prolonged and careful investigation and after virtual apologies to him for ever questioning his loyalty.

I protested the assault on McCarthy, seeking a "stay" on two grounds—prudence and self-interest. First, I argued, we should not dash into a major controversy on the basis of glib rationales based on overnight research. I admitted that technically, Drew was on unassailable ground given away by McCarthy when he advertised his targets as current, card-carrying Communists in the State Department. To debunk this shotgun indictment, it need only be shown that a target had no card and was not in the State Department, or not currently in the State Department.

But should we rush out a quick exoneration merely because McCarthy had misphrased his indictment? I had checked out the four names, too, in the half-blind way open to a reporter in that twilight zone in which you saw only parts of the whole, and what I found seemed troublesome.

Dr. Harlow Shapley of Harvard was neither a State Department employee nor a "card-carrying Communist" but he *was* serving on a United Nations Commission for which he was paid on a per diem basis by the State Department, and he was an indubitable fellow traveler who had joined more than twenty Communist fronts (or at least eight if one disregarded the classifications of legislative committees and relied only upon the Attorney General's list) and he had remained active in fourteen even after the Cold War began in earnest in 1946. Shapley was a big mover behind the 1949 Stalinist rally at Madison Square Garden known as the Waldorf Peace Conference. This permitted McCarthy to say that even as the State Department was describing the Waldorf Peace Conference as a "sounding board for Communist propaganda," it maintained on its payroll the conference's chief organizer.

John Stewart Service had been "cleared," all right, as Drew said, but he was cleared despite the uncontested fact that in 1945 he had been caught slipping classified documents about our Far Eastern policy to a known Communist, Philip Jaffe, editor of the party-line *Amerasia* magazine, and had been spared prosecution not because of innocence but because the FBI had compromised the government's case by an illegal wiretap.

Gustavo Duran had, as Drew said, resigned from the State Department in 1946, but did that make him a dead issue? He was currently the head of a department of the UN Secretariat, and his resignation from the State Department had come only after persistent charges over a three-year period from U.S. military intelligence that he had functioned in Spain as a member of the Soviet secret police. If military intelligence was right, did not the State Department's nonprejudicial separation of Duran deserve examination rather than a perfunctory endorsement from our column?

The forced resignation of Mary Jane Keeney from the State Department in 1946 seemed to support Drew's view of a State Department that was vigorously cracking down on subversives four years before McCarthy appeared with his moldering files. But a closer look at the Keeney case was less reassuring. Keeney had been permitted to "resign" after four months in the State Department when an FBI report depicted her as having been a courier for the Communists during her years in the Foreign Economic Administration. Spared the notoriety of a security firing, she quickly reappeared, along with Duran and three dozen other loyalty-security refugees from U.S. agencies, on the central staff of the United Nations, then a significant factor in the implementation of U.S. foreign policy as well as a key intelligence-gathering outpost. There she and her peer group were permitted to burrow in for several years, unhampered by their past records. In 1949 UN Secretary General Trygve Lie, disturbed over the apparent infiltration of his Secretariat by Communists who were former employees of the United States government, pressed the dormant State Department for aid in identifying known American subversives in his ranks. The department agreed to check names submitted by Lie against its existing security data and to designate which of these Americans were "Communist or under Communist discipline," but it performed in lethargic fashion, taking an average of fifteen months per case to check existing files and make an adverse identification. At this snail's pace, Mary Jane Keeney would eventually be caught up with and dismissed, along with thirty-five other Americans in the UN Secretariat.

Whatever reassurance was derivable from the State Department's ouster of Mrs. Keeney was thus overshadowed by its incredible laxity in permitting the UN Secretariat to become, and to remain for several years, a center of American subversives.*

My point to Drew, in short, was that though McCarthy was stumbling around, he seemed to have stumbled onto something worth investigating. But Drew was adamant; no stranger to the uses of exaggeration, he judged that McCarthy had purposefully hyped his charges to stir a public uproar that responsible statements could not have kindled; therefore, he deserved to be shot down on his own terms without benefit of any doubt.

There was in Drew's eyes and voice a grim hardness, intended not to be mistaken, which was not typical but became typical where McCarthy was concerned. "The loyalty business is a bog," he said. "A selective mind can twist a file to read either way. Only people of the highest personal integrity, the broadest sophistication, belong in it. Allow a corner-cutting politician like your friend McCarthy, whose motives are promotional and partisan, to rummage around in this field and before he's through no one's reputation will be safe, the whole political process will be poisoned. McCarthy disqualified himself the first time he opened his mouth. Yet, he gained an instant following. Unless he's cut down *now*, he will become a walking national disaster."

"He is our best source on the Hill," I remonstrated.

Drew replied, "He may be a good source, Jack, but he's a bad man."

I made a last stab. Could we not reserve judgment, briefly, until McCarthy had made his presentation to the Senate?

We could not. In this sort of contest, said Drew, the initial impact was three quarters of the game. He was concerned that many newspapers were featuring McCarthy's accusations just as he made them

---

*Mary Jane Keeney later took the Fifth Amendment, as did twenty-five other American employees of the UN Secretariat, in refusing to answer questions of the Senate Internal Security Subcommittee about Communist activities.

without an organized effort to ascertain their truth; if McCarthy's version gained an immediate credence out in the country, the task of rebuttal would be complicated beyond measure.

I had been overruled but not persuaded. To debunk McCarthy's errors was one thing—that was a newsman's job. But to leave undebunked the State Department's errors? To adopt the Administration's defensive line?

I was uncomfortably off balance, deprived of my usual certitude. My judgment was skewed, I acknowledged, by a self-serving reluctance to alienate a source and by sheepishness over our ill repayment of so many favors. But I felt that Drew's judgment was also skewed by his sense of protectiveness toward the liberal-left. Half immobilized, I looked to McCarthy's upcoming Senate speech as a gauge of measurement.

The Joe McCarthy who rose on the red-carpeted Senate floor in the late afternoon of February 20, 1950, was a more prudent man than the barnstormer who only eleven days earlier had kicked off his Lincoln Day tour to fame. In the interim he had gained a rough mastery of the nuts and bolts of his subject, and having already succeeded in attracting the national spotlight, he deigned to move more carefully in its beam. In place of the generalized broadsides of Wheeling, Salt Lake City and Reno he now proceeded to inundate the Senate with specifics by reading highlights from 81 individual security cases (76 as it turned out, for, awash in files and harassed by more than a hundred interruptions from colleagues, he occasionally lost his way). Gone were such gaffes as "card-carrying Communist," replaced by the more deliverable "loyalty risk." No longer did he contend that all his targets were State Department policy shapers. The harsh absolutes of the banquet circuit were softened by occasional acknowledgments of the difficulty of ascertaining guilt.

"It is possible that some of these persons will get a clean bill of health."

Unabashed by his fortnight of accusation, he said that his purpose was not to pronounce a verdict but rather to show that there was enough evidence of subversive infiltration to warrant a formal Senate investigation of it, and of the security breakdowns that permitted it. In order to protect those who might be proved innocent, he would designate his cases by number instead of name.

But though McCarthy wore regulation gloves and bowed formally toward the Marquis of Queensberry, he was not above using the thumb and the head-butt and slipping in an occasional rabbit punch in the clinches, where his moves could not be seen clearly. "If we can get rid of these big three [numbers 1, 2 and 81] we will have done something to break the back of the espionage ring in the State Department."

He had carved out a considerable area where he could not be seen. By not naming names, he not only protected the innocent but deprived would-be debunkers of the means to challenge him, an advantage he compounded by implying to the Senate that his information had been smuggled to him by members of a loyal underground he would not name for fear of reprisals against them.

Early in his recital he took up what I recognized as the Lloyd case I had brought him. With tightening apprehension I heard him declaiming as conclusive what I had vouchsafed to him only as grounds for suspicion: "Case Number 9" and his wife had been members of Communist front organizations . . . a relative had a financial interest in the *Daily Worker* . . . he had failed to get clearance from a loyalty board when he sought a job in the State Department in 1946. No mention was made of the countervailing facts: that only two fronts were involved; that he claimed to have left them upon realizing their nature; that there were anti-Communist associations, too; that the *Daily Worker* "relative" was rather remote, a great-aunt; that "number nine" had later obtained clearance. I waited expectantly for reassuring clues that McCarthy had come up with information beyond ours that justified the worst interpretation. But there was only an oratorical flourish: "And where do Senators think that man is today? He is now a speech writer in the White House!"

And Joe went on to Number 10.

I stared down from the Senate press gallery on a gyrating prestidigitator in full flower, putting down one folder with a grim finality, hoisting another portentously, holding at bay a querulous, confused multitude with sunbursts of awesome reverberation but untested substance. The burn of shame singed through me. Gone up in smoke was my arrogant assumption that I could play along in the wake of, and even bend to my uses, what now stood revealed as an elemental force which expropriated what it might and raged where it would. Hours passed and still the torrent flowed. I could see that I had given McCarthy the main news dish of his smörgåsbord, and could visualize tomorrow's headlines: "McCarthy Presents Data on 81 as Security Risks; Truman Speech Writer Implicated." And David Lloyd's identity could not long be concealed behind a number; there were too few White House speech writers.

So it was to be; in a day or two Lloyd was known to the better-informed newsmen as Number 9; within a week he came forward to acknowledge himself as the target and to defend himself along the lines previewed in our file. That this defense was valid would be demonstrated by the continuing confidence displayed by his patron and by the default of his accuser. President Truman not only kept Lloyd on but promoted him to the post of Administrative Assistant, thereby challenging McCarthy and making Lloyd an even fatter target. But McCarthy quietly threw in the towel on Lloyd, and except for a perfunctory protest when Truman promoted him, never publicly spoke of him again, even in his years of unbridled power. At my instigation, then, Lloyd had been done an injustice that was saved from being grievous only by Truman's steadfastness.

In retrospect, my chagrin seems tinged with absurdity. Having sat at Joe's side while he conned trusting colleagues of his own party in order to provide news items for the column of their ancient enemy, I should not have needed this proof of his tendency toward roguery, but now, having been hit over the head with it, I never again allowed my self-interest to veil his ugly propensities. I kept my new antipathy to myself, for a newshound does not foreclose his access to a newsmaker. But beneath the surface, my attitude would hereafter be faithful to that ideal of fell pursuit that should obtain between the press and the politician.

To growing numbers, it was of no account that McCarthy had awkwardly shifted from 205 to 57 to 81, or that he couldn't find Case Number 37, or that in the midst of declaiming the sordid facts of Case Number 77, he stopped, a bit confused, and admitted he seemed to have covered this matter earlier under a different number. "I can't keep all the details in my head. There are too many of these slimy creatures," Joe would explain, and millions empathized. Americans who had always been leery of Communist Russia were unconvinced by the excuses of their betters about Russia's having been our ally in the war; all along, they had understood all they needed to know about Stalin's crimes and about Russia's alliance with Adolf Hitler until Hitler attacked. Nor were they impressed by such arguments as that this particular security risk was *no longer* in the government or that another had not been in the State Department at all, only the Commerce Department. What millions wanted to know, it soon became clear, was why these "slimy creatures" had *ever* been in *any* department and who was responsible for it.

From what they garnered from the news media of McCarthy's lone stand before an inhospitable Senate, he had deluged it with data of the most alarming nature, and they expected a serious investigation of it. Senators, too, from the moment they saw McCarthy's folder-piled desk and grasped the extent of his presentation, knew that a formal investigation would be required, and two days later they voted to set one up under the chairmanship of a senior autocrat, Senator Millard E. Tydings of Maryland. But most senators, and especially the Democrats, continued to misread the portents, assuming that the upstart would quickly be dispatched. "Let me have McCarthy for three days in public hearings," crowed Chairman Tydings, "and he will never show his face in the Senate again."

Unlike the cocksure establishmentarians who dismissed McCarthy, and the liberals who refused to acknowledge any valid basis for the pent-up public frustration that was now welling up in his support, Drew Pearson saw from the start the appeal of "McCarthyism," in part because Drew recognized that grave offense had indeed been given the public and must be acknowledged forthrightly before demagogic exploitation of it could be confronted effectively. In one column, after ticking off a list of security lapses in the mid-forties, he wrote:

> While the American people have every reason to be sore, the time for them to have been sore was three and four years ago. Today the secrets are stolen . . . If Senator McCarthy had begun making his charges in 1946 when first elected to the Senate, not only would he have been entirely justified, but he might have stopped the leaking of some secrets. All he had to do between 1945 and 1947 was to have read this column.

Then his countertheme:

> But likewise the present administration of the State Department has done the greatest personnel house-cleaning of all time. It was the Acheson regime which fired the 90 homosexuals, the Acheson regime which ousted a long list of bad security risks. And though Acheson personally pulled a boner in indicating his continued personal loyalty for Alger Hiss, the real fact is that the men under him have orders to do a thorough, vigorous job on loyalty checks.

To complete his initial fix on the overnight apparition McCarthy presented, Drew needed an illustration for his intuitive judgment that, beyond coming along at the wrong time, McCarthy was the wrong man, a sleight-of-hand artist rather than a scrupulous sentinel. I kept mum about one such incident—the Lloyd matter—but I helped him establish another.

In his Senate appearance McCarthy had for the first time put all his models in the show window, albeit under shrouds. Now knowing the approximate dimensions of his information, and alerted by my recollection of his urgent efforts to pry loose from the House of Representatives any old documentation that would bail him out, we quickly located the main source of his "81 cases," a classified report of the House Appropriations Committee. This showed he had misled the Senate in contending that his information was smuggled to him by undercover patriots within the State Department. On the day after the Senate speech, Drew put this in the pipeline:

> Senator McCarthy is way off base . . . The alleged Communists which he claims are sheltered in the State Department just aren't. McCarthy picked the names from an old subversive list examined by the 80th Congress three years ago, and most of the men on his list were either ousted or, after thorough examination, found to be O.K.

In the opening phase of his crusade, Joe McCarthy did not display the zealot's enmity toward detractors. Publicly he thumped his critics tit for tat, for tactical reasons, but privately he seemed free of resentment. Certainly he gave no sign that he held our columns against me. In part this reflected the ring philosophy he had adopted on the Marquette University boxing squad—that of a roundhouse slugger who knew his wild swings left him vulnerable but who was willing to soak up punishment in order to land blows. And in part it was due, I think, to the native tolerance nurtured by his brand of realism-cynicism: he saw reporters, like politicians, as role players, trying to make out, who must stoop to occasional perfidies in the plying of their trade; one does not take umbrage at a process. And in my case there were the further considerations that I was only a junior partner, that Drew set the column's policy and that I might yet be useful as a countervailing weight. He continued to welcome me to his office with almost the old jocularity, though there was now in our relationship an imperceptible distance, the shadow that looms between old associates whom circumstance seems likely to change into adversaries.

From day to day I could see the new cause tightening its grip on him, as though the compulsive upward thrusting that had so long driven him forward willy-nilly had at last found its true focus. Self-mockery came to him less easily now, the slight palsied shaking of his head seemed more frequent, more pronounced. One day while we were walking down one of the long, echoing corridors in the Old Senate Office Building he began to pour out with rising vehemence a string of names of people he said were Communists who were betraying the nation. At length I said, "Slow down, Joe. Remember me? I was there at the start, when you were beating the bushes for names to bail you out. Save it for the Senate floor."

There was a time when he would have winked appreciatively at this, just as he loved to repeat a greeting given him by Senator John Bricker: "Joe, you're a real son of a bitch, but sometimes its useful to have sons of bitches around to do the dirty work." But not this time. "No, no, no," he said insistently, as though putting behind him the accommodations of the futile past, "this is the real thing, Jack. This is the real thing."

For a less assured chairman than Millard Tydings it might have taken months to prepare for the opening of public hearings on so vast and intricate an agenda as McCarthy had laid on the committee in his "81 cases" speech. Tydings took only two weeks, and the reason for such haste was soon revealed.

What McCarthy had sought was an investigation that would throw the power and resources of the United States Senate into proving his case, into exhuming several years of curious performance by the State Department security apparatus, using his leads for starters. "I intend to submit to the committee information bearing upon the disloyalty, the bad security risks in the State Department. Then it is up to the committee to investigate those particular cases . . . I do not have the investigative staff, I do not have access to the [State Department] files, to make any complete investigation and make any formal charges. All I intend to do, Mr. Chairman, is to submit the evidence I have gathered."

What McCarthy got was an investigation of McCarthy, of his veracity and reliability; his was to be the burden of proof. Chairman Tydings, pointing his finger at McCarthy, set the tone as soon as the gavel fell: "You are in the position of being the man who occasioned this hearing, and so far as I am concerned, in this committee you are going to get one of the most complete investigations ever given in the history of the Republic . . ."

The sagacious chairman of a controversial hearing that is loaded with a potential for running amok—facing as he does the sensationalists of the press, surrounded as he is with balky senatorial individualists— almost invariably has a predetermined end in view and seeks to impose upon the proceedings a grand design and a procedural format that will hew relentlessly to that end. Tydings came to the hearing room obviously determined that McCarthy should never be allowed to get off the ground. There was logic in this; Tydings, who in his twenty-four years in the Senate had survived even the machinations of Roosevelt, was not a fool. It was essential to the governing establishment—and as Tydings saw it, to the good cause—that McCarthy come up dry *every* time. Such was the volatility of the subject matter that if McCarthy was shown to be wrong 90 percent of the time, if only 8 of his 81 cases came up a gusher, the government would have not a victory but a profound scandal on its hands. If McCarthy even *seemed* to be making headway, if in the opening days he was allowed to get some of his straw men set up and reported on seriously in the media, the hearing could begin to skew off, take on its own directional momentum, pushed hither and yon by the weight of each day's unscheduled events, and end up no man knew where.

In so combustible a situation, Tydings deemed that the option of allowing McCarthy "enough rope" was not open. Senate tradition calls for the protagonist of a Senate hearing to lead off with a prepared statement which lays out his case in an orderly manner, before he is questioned on it. A deeper tradition demands that when the witness is a fellow senator, even one accused of a high crime, he be heard not only with deferential respect but with elaborate courtesy.

But almost as soon as McCarthy began to read his compendious statement, he was challenged by Tydings and the other two Democrats who made up the committee majority, Brien McMahon of Connecticut and Theodore Francis Green of Rhode Island. McCarthy was challenged so violently and constantly that it took him two days to present his evidence on the first of the scores of cases in his prepared indictment. Bourke Hickenlooper, the Iowa Republican, protested; he could be dismissed as a predictable McCarthy ally. But the other Republican on the committee, the prestigious and moderate Henry Cabot Lodge, Jr., was a pig of a different bristle, whom the majority needed if its indictment was to carry certainty in the land. And at length Senator Lodge, too, objected to the gang-up.

Senator Owen Brewster, not a committee member but a McCarthy ally, and as we have seen, a grizzled political infighter, was quick to exploit the situation. "Whitewash!" he cried, and he submitted some meticulous calculations: in McCarthy's first 250 minutes on the stand he had been allowed only 17 minutes and 30 seconds of uninterrupted testimony—only 7 percent of the time. "On at least thirteen occasions," Brewster reported, "Senator McCarthy was forced to plead that he be allowed to answer the question of one Democratic member before being required to answer the question of another Democratic member who had interrupted or heckled him."

McCarthy bore it all with a mien of earnest dismay, but I sensed that he was eating it up, knowing as he did that in political brawling nothing is better than to be the victim of an outrage.

The bolder the strategy, the greater the risk. Tydings' unbridled offensive against McCarthy had one desired effect: McCarthy's side was getting out only in confused and contested dribbles. But it robbed the committee of that veneer of objectivity that was required if there was to be a general acceptance of its verdict. It also changed the imagery. Up to now, McCarthy had borne the onus that attaches to the scold who accuses all and sundry of unspeakable crimes; henceforth it would be possible to cast him as the lone tribune who was being ambushed by politicians with something to hide.

To solidify the David vs. Goliath pose, McCarthy needed to strike but one resounding blow. He decided he had the means to do just that, and with his talent for news management, he began the build-up toward a winner-take-all confrontation. His opening flourish was to tell newsmen that he would soon name "the top espionage agent in the United States," the "boss of Alger Hiss" in the espionage ring in the State Department. For the next few days he let the "Who is Mr. X?" speculation heighten and spread across the nation's newspapers and airwaves.

Joe and I were still on reasonably cordial terms, though events had forewarned each of us to hold the other at arm's length. Like other reporters covering McCarthy, I tried each day to pry out the secret; one day when he was ready he told me, though not for attribution. "The top Russian spy" was Professor Owen Lattimore, director of the Walter Hines Page School of International Relations at Johns Hopkins University. In deadpan seriousness, Joe told me a Gothic tale about Communist spies who had been landed on the Atlantic coast by an enemy submarine and who had hastened to Lattimore for their orders.

I took this unlikely story to Drew. It happened that he knew Lattimore personally. He was not a State Department official but rather the reigning Asian-affairs scholar, an authority whom the department frequently called in for consultation, the author of "influential" books said to be relied on by government officials. In Drew's judgment, Lattimore was not disloyal, though he held a world view that was often compatible with the Communist line. More to the point, Drew could not, in the wildest leap of imagination, picture the Lattimore he knew as a spy to whom submarine-borne agents reported for assignments. If the Russians had indeed snared an advisory giant like Lattimore—who had been called in to counsel President Truman on the Asian settlement just before Truman left for Potsdam, who set the tone of American scholarship on Asia, who controlled the leading reviews of books on Asian politics—it would have been an absurd miscasting to waste and risk him as a mere spy. The prospect excited Drew. If McCarthy was building his house of cards around Lattimore, could it not be toppled at one stroke? He began to prepare the demolition.

Meanwhile McCarthy continued the tantalizing build-up. Any day now, he kept assuring, he would name the name. The Tydings committee, aware that its open partisan disarray diminished public confidence, had become more orderly and shifted into "executive session," where McCarthy was now being heard in secret. I had cultivated an informant within the committee staff, who reported to me on McCarthy's testimony. Behind the closed doors McCarthy named Lattimore as his Mr. X, named him with a finality that was awesome in its bridge-burning: ". . . definitely an espionage agent . . . one of the top espionage agents . . . the top Russian spy . . . the key man in a Russian espionage ring." Propelled by the gambler's bravura, he raised his bid even higher: "I am willing to stand or fall on this one. If I am shown to be wrong on this, I think the subcommittee would be justified in not taking my other cases too seriously."

With the hearings in secret session, McCarthy used three alternate forums to wage his end of the publicity war with a hostile committee —the leak, the press conference and the Senate speech. When and how would he "go public" on Lattimore? I learned that a Senate speech on Lattimore was in preparation.

On March 25, a Saturday, Drew weighed all the information I had brought him, along with his own. He saw the opportunity to strike a crippling blow at McCarthy, and he saw, too, the risk of self-destruction. The senator's extraordinary show of certainty might well mean that he had the goods on Lattimore. Would he so expose himself if he did not? But Drew leaned to another explanation: that McCarthy was caught up in the demagogue's compulsion toward escalation. Was it not his tendency to upgrade fellow travelers into Communists, and pro-Communists into spies? And there was something almost pathological in McCarthy that pushed him to extravagant risks.

Since the moment I had first given him the name, Drew had been collecting information for the defense. Lattimore himself was unreachable, on a United Nations mission in Kabul, Afghanistan, but Drew was in contact with Mrs. Lattimore and had come up with an exculpatory tale almost as bizarre as Joe's submarine adventure. Years before, Lattimore had befriended a group of Mongol refugees from the Communist regime in Outer Mongolia and had at length brought them to Johns Hopkins. The most important of these anti-Communist Mongols was a picturesque old fellow called the "Living Buddha," a high panjandrum of the Lama Buddhist Church. They were an esoteric business, these Mongols. Lattimore's sponsorship of them might have had any of a number of motives, but Drew liked the feel of it. It fit the picture he had formed of Lattimore as a visionary, independent scholar who veered to the left but was under no one's discipline.

Drew's conclusion was that we had McCarthy exposed in a mammoth error and must move immediately to impale him on it. On the following night, Sunday, March 26, he opened his national broadcast as follows: "I am now going to reveal the name of the man whom Senator McCarthy has designated the top Communist agent in the United States. Senator McCarthy had said that he would rest his entire charge of State Department communism on this case. The man is Owen Lattimore of Johns Hopkins University."

Drew went on to rebut the charge against Lattimore, trotting out Mongols, Living Buddha and all, in a challenge to McCarthy to honor his "stand or fall" pledge by either proving that Lattimore was "the top Russian spy" or withdrawing from the field.

The next day the press swooped down upon Johns Hopkins and invaded the meditations of the Mongols, who, forewarned by Drew, rose to the occasion by staging a press conference in which they rang all the right chimes. The Living Buddha, resplendent in a dark-red robe with brocaded vest of gold and scarlet, told how he was saying "furious prayers" for Mr. Lattimore, who had been his protector since his flight from the Communists in 1931. Two lesser Mongols flanked the Living Buddha like archdeacons and told of their former lives, one as bodyguard, the other as secretary, to "Prince Teh, who is still holding out, with an army of five to ten thousand, against Communist domination in western Mongolia."

McCarthy, unhorsed by Drew's sneak attack and perhaps mystified by his exotic props, failed to show at that afternoon's session of the Tydings committee; instead, he promised a Senate speech on Lattimore. When he gave it three days later, he backed off but did not bow out: "I fear that in the case of Lattimore I may have perhaps placed too much stress on the question of whether he is a paid espionage agent."

In his embarrassment, McCarthy found escape in Lenin's dictum that two steps backward can be one step forward. Even as he closed down one failed drama, he announced the coming of a new and more fascinating one: he would in due time produce before the Tydings committee a mystery witness who would confirm that Lattimore had been a "high up" Communist Party member for many years.

Every forced retraction, every contrived escape from a tight corner, however successful, depletes the limited store of trust accorded the public man, but not in an immediately measurable way. A new build-up of anticipation commenced. Who was the mystery witness? What would he say?

I learned the identity of the witness almost as soon as McCarthy transmitted it to the Tydings committee: Dr. Louis Budenz, recanted Communist leader, long-time editor of the *Daily Worker*, rehabilitated Catholic, professor of economics at Fordham and lecturer at Notre Dame, and the key witness for the United States in several trials of Communists.

Budenz could discuss the Communist conspiracy with authority. If some of it was now to rub off on McCarthy, there was no telling where this would all end. Drew called Lattimore's lawyers, Abe Fortas and Morris Ernst, and warned them to get ready to discredit, or at least refute, Budenz. Then he went to see J. Edgar Hoover, hoping Hoover would tell him what Budenz was likely to say, on the basis of three thousand hours of interviews he had given the FBI. Hoover was cooperative; though the two distrusted each other, they had been scratching each other's back for two decades. Budenz, Hoover predicted, would testify that members of the Communist Party had told him that they had "used" Lattimore; Hoover doubted that Lattimore was a party member but regarded him as a "poor security risk," easily manipulated by various Communists he had associated with.

The appearance of Dr. Budenz, on April 20, 1950, was the dramatic high of the Tydings hearings. McCarthy's visage that day was drained, white and intense, his preoccupied demeanor in marked contrast to the usual burly show of locker-room bonhomie, a measure of the crisis point at which his cause stood and of the physical toll these daily high-stakes confrontations were beginning to exact.

Drew had been depressed by Hoover's estimate of what Budenz would say, and the event was worse than the prediction. Lattimore, though not a spy, was a concealed Communist, Budenz swore, assigned by the party the task of using his great influence to discredit the Chinese Nationalists and promote the Chinese Communists. In his capacity as editor of the party's organ, Budenz had to be kept informed about underground Communists so that the *Daily Worker* would treat them with whatever nuance the situation required. On several occasions, he testified, three different leaders of the party—Earl Browder, Frederick Vanderbilt Field and Jack Stachel—had told him to consider Lattimore as an important concealed comrade, and to treat his activities as under Communist discipline.

The difficulty inherent in the true identification of subversives was manifest here. Both sides had to depend on evidence that would carry little weight in normal judicial proceedings. Budenz had never met Lattimore; he spoke not from personal observation of him but from what he remembered of what others had told him five, six, seven and thirteen years before—conversations he had never thought important enough to reveal until McCarthy's charge against Lattimore. How much should be allowed to hang on what, in other circumstances, would be treated as hearsay? On the other hand, the Communists Browder and Field, who were brought on to deny Budenz's testimony, and who did so, were the least credible of witnesses.

In such circumstances, Budenz's reputation for veracity loomed as decisive. Challenged often in the past, he had a record, wrote Arthur Krock of the New York *Times,* of being "sustained by subsequent events." He had exposed Gerhart Eisler as the leading Communist operative in the United States at a time when Eisler was generally unsuspected; he was the key witness in the successful New York prosecution of the eleven Communist leaders; he had fingered Alger Hiss in 1948, when Hiss was still riding high; he had exposed Sam Carr, subsequently convicted of assisting the Communist spy ring in Canada; the United States government had again and again vouched for his veracity, and it now began to dissociate itself from Lattimore and to fudge on previous intimations of confidence in him.

From the ashes of his "top Russian spy" fiasco, McCarthy rose higher than ever on the wings of Budenz's credibility. A rejuvenated McCarthy, cocky and truculent, appeared before the American Society of Newspaper Editors, an audience of discerning skeptics from all corners of the nation, and won a tumultous ovation. "I knew it would be thus—that vilification, smear and falsehoods would follow, peddled by the Reds, their minions, and the egg-sucking phony liberals who litter Washington with their persons and clutter American thinking with their simple-minded arguments."

Drew believed that Budenz had lied to bail out McCarthy and save the cause. If Lattimore had performed the vital role in the fall of China attributed to him by Budenz, what possible explanation was there for the failure of Budenz to have heretofore mentioned Lattimore to the FBI or in his voluminous writings about the Communist conspiracy, even when he was writing about Lattimore's old stomping ground, the Institute of Pacific Relations? Budenz's answer—that Lattimore was only one of hundreds whom he had to indict in an orderly way, or in response to the pressing event of the moment—did not satisfy.

The muckraker cannot be fastidious about the source of an incriminating document; it is the *authenticity* of the document that counts. Even so, the source of our disparagement of Professor Budenz still, after the passage of almost thirty years, gives off a stink most foul. Budenz had testified for the government in a deportation action against a Communist, in camera. In doing so, he was examined on his past by Harry Sacher, a busy lawyer for Communists, and was of course confronted with all the embarrassments his ex-comrades could dig up on him. The transcript was ordered sealed by the judge, but a copy was given, under seal, to Sacher on his plea that he needed it to prepare an appeal from the verdict, an appeal that was never filed. Sacher now slipped the sealed transcript to the Lattimore camp, which slipped it to the Tydings committee staff, which slipped it to me.

The transcript revealed a more colorful past than was hinted at by the austere comportment of the present Fordham professor. During those halcyon yesterdays before his conversion, when Budenz the Communist was plotting murder attempts on Trotsky and stage-managing a plague of labor disruptions for which he was arrested twenty-one times and acquitted twenty-one times, and even before he formally joined the party, the good doctor was sampling the one compensatory amenity which Communist discipline, that harsh mistress, permitted her disciples—sexual philandering. While married to one woman, Budenz had lived with a second for several years. A third female showed up with him on various hotel registrations in Connecticut, Pennsylvania and New York. In the wake of all this there were three illegitimate children, a trail of forged hotel registrations and a divorce on grounds of desertion. After Budenz reconverted to Catholicism and conventionality, he tried, naturally enough, to put the most decorous face possible on things for the sake of all concerned. He faked a marriage date in his self-penned *Who's Who* biography; stumbled lamely, in the timeless manner of errant husbands who are ambushed, through interrogatories about his incontinent past; and even took the Fifth Amendment about some of his trysts. It was a document filled with the small personal confessions which our adversary system wrenches from witnesses to large conspiracies, yet it raised valid questions about a credibility that had assumed crucial proportions.

There were to be four columns on Budenz. In his best shoe-dropping manner, Drew led off with praise of Budenz's services to society; it was not until the third column that he got down to the nitty-gritty, reproducing the gamier portions of Sacher's sealed cross-examination with this introduction and summary:

> It is an accepted rule of American courts that if a man has lied once or his background is unstable, his testimony cannot be relied on—Budenz was married to two women at the same time . . . Three children were born out of wedlock . . . He also had relations with a third woman. Apologists for Budenz minimize this on the ground that Budenz has now reformed. Nevertheless, untruthful statements made regarding his past and refusal to answer questions have a bearing on Budenz's credibility . . . All in all, Budenz refused to answer 23 questions on the ground of self-incrimination.

The lofty authority of the accusing professor was diminished by this demonstration that like other mortals and indeed with more alacrity than most, he took off his pants one leg at a time.

Dr. Lattimore revived and for a time prospered, to the corresponding discomfort of McCarthy. The darker charges against him were never proved, but it *was* shown that he had dallied longer and more deliberately with the party liners than he had admitted on the stand, and he was to have his ups and downs for years to come: cleared and praised by the Tydings committee; lionized by liberal circles; condemned by the McCarran committee as "a conscious, articulate instrument of the Communist conspiracy"; indicted for perjury allegedly committed while defending himself before the McCarran committee; freed of all charges when the main count was thrown out of court on constitutional grounds and the prosecution eventually dropped the case.

By the time of our Budenz columns, almost three months had passed since Joe McCarthy's opening salvo at Wheeling. This was not a long time as against the five years his race would run toward climax, but more than long enough for a forward observer, even one who felt ties to both sides and skepticism toward the claims of each, as I did, to decide whether McCarthy presented just a story, to be pursued with bloodless efficiency, or a cataclysm, to be fought with passionate commitment.

For me, up to now, it had been a story. McCarthy's errors and abuses were obvious to me, having myself uncovered some of them, but so were the deceits and cover-up tactics of the Administration and the Tydings committee. I informed Drew, without result, that the Tydings committee was refusing to pursue at least a dozen lines of inquiry suggested by McCarthy that seemed valid to me, and I brought Drew a story (which he published) indicating that some agency of the Administration was tapping McCarthy's phone and giving the results to his senatorial opponents. I was thus observing the "plague on both houses" attitude that well serves the reporter's work and his emotions.

But I had come to feel that it was a snare to excuse McCarthy because of his opponents, or to judge him as against political norms. He had climbed up on a unique pedestal as Grand Accuser of the most odious, emotion-kindling and mysterious of crimes—disloyalty—and he must be judged by the most stringent standard. After writing off his early gaffes to inexperience, one at length had to make a judgment about his basic character. Did he have the capacity to be scrupulous and discriminating? Had he shown sufficient signs, as his friends claimed, of being chastened and disciplined by the terrible responsibility he had seized? Or was there a basic defect in his character, a blind spot in his vision, that shaded off toward opportunism and recklessness, toward the habitual cheap shot, toward an instinctive hyping of charges rather than a judicious narrowing? Was he capable of a disciplined surgical strike against a precise target, or was he an incorrigible looser of poison gas that would float far and wide?

By the third month of his campaign, I could see that he was a poison-gas man. Despite the warnings drummed into him by the band of earnest anti-Communists who now advised him, despite the moderating caveats they pressed on him during rehearsals, as soon as he got out of the paddock he would jump the fence into the green pasture of demagoguery.

An incurable vein of recklessness showed in his acts. Grandly did he fling away his senatorial immunity: "I will not say anything on the Senate floor which I will not say off the floor. On the day I take advantage of the security we have on the Senate floor, I will resign from the Senate." Ignominiously did he snatch it back, refusing, despite raucous heckling, to repeat the specifics of his Senate charges in public.

Drew, who operated without immunity, was in a good position to rowel McCarthy on this, and frequently did so; when the senator defended his welshing on the ground that he could not afford the cost of defending himself against a barrage of Communist-inspired suits, Drew made the grandstand offer, and kept repeating it, to pay McCarthy's legal expenses if he would keep his pledged word. "Hiding behind senatorial immunity" quickly became one of the standard anti-McCarthy reproaches. This self-inflicted wound raised a basic question: If, to make a momentary hit, McCarthy would make *himself* hostage to inevitable humiliation later, what would he do to others?

Akin to this recklessness was an apparently ungovernable impulse toward the cheap shot. Four and a half years later he would betray himself into the hands of the Army's chief counsel, Joseph Welch, because he could not resist a warned-against swipe at unknown young Fred Fisher; it was a weakness he showed from the beginning. In the course of his self-defining presentation before the Tydings committee, he interjected that Mrs. Dean Acheson, the wife of the Secretary of State, had been a member of a Communist front. He had no case to present against her, but some aide had spotted her name on an old list and McCarthy could not resist the commotion-lure of spewing it out. It turned out that Mrs. Acheson had once upon a time contributed $2 to some rump organization of women shoppers protesting high prices in the local grocery stores; later this organization merged into a larger one that still later turned up on a HUAC list of Communist fronts. That, at so pivotal a moment, McCarthy should demean the gravity of his cause by indulging such a high-risk, hit-and-run whim showed a lack of discrimination that seemed irremedial.

By now I had gained access to the secret congressional report that McCarthy had used as the basis for most of his February 20 speech on the "81 cases." In that speech he had said, "I am not giving my evaluation of the evidence. I want it understood. If the Senators will listen, they will note that what I am doing is to recite the facts, which the State Department's own security agency dug up . . ."

But as I compared what McCarthy said on the floor that night with what "the State Department's own security agency" had said, I found that McCarthy had exaggerated their findings in at least 38 cases. He could seldom resist promoting a "fellow traveler" to a "Communist" or an *alleged* pro-Communist" to a "pro-Communist." It was not so much the individual increments that struck me as the compulsive pattern of doctoring.

From the beginning Drew had insisted that McCarthy's direction and goal could be read from his character. He was not by nature a patient investigator trying to unearth facts or a careful jurist trying to weigh them, nor was he a man to be attracted by so undramatic a goal as the reopening of a few score security investigations of yesteryear. He was the kind of political animal whose inclination and talent lay in the way of marshaling semi-facts and exploiting half-truths for maximum uproar. As such, he aimed at discrediting an Administration, a foreign policy establishment, a political party, not on the lackluster grounds of mistaken judgment or laxity or ineptitude, but on the megaton charges of betrayal at the top, of Cabinet-level conspiracy, of pervasive disloyalty.

At the time Drew made that judgment I thought it premature, and said so. Now, sifting through months of personal recollection and public utterance, I could see from the evidence that Drew was right. I thought back to that corridor conversation with Joe before the Tydings inquiry began, when he spewed out the names of a string of high officials he said had sold out the country. In that torrent were the names of Dean Acheson and General George C. Marshall. The conversation was informal, the indictment was imprecise, and I attributed it to a letting off of steam.

But now, in rechecking his public statements, I saw that this theme of betrayal at the highest level emerged and re-emerged, beginning with the very first broadside at Wheeling, when he added to the charge of massive infiltration the graver charge that the infiltrators *were known to the Secretary of State* as being members of the Communist Party and who, nonetheless, were still working and shaping policy in the State Department." In subsequent forays, McCarthy drew back from the charge of treason at the top, but he would circle it inferentially, and on occasion, as if breaking free of irksome constraint, plunge toward it, as when he called the Secretary of State "the mind and voice" of Lattimore, who was "the top Russian spy" and the "boss" of Alger Hiss.

All the while, the elevated figure of George Catlett Marshall glowed for McCarthy like the flame for the moth. Four world leaders— Churchill, Roosevelt, Truman and Eisenhower—had ranked Marshall as the greatest American of his epoch. Richard Rovere captured the essence of a widespread estimate of the soldier-statesman in a memorable passage:

> He was, above all, a man of vast and palpable dignity. The dignity was in his bearing and in his entire mien, in his aloofness from controversy, in the silence with which he had borne disappointment and defeat and sorrow, with which he was well acquainted. He was the very image of the strong, noble, gentle Southern man of arms who could be no more dishonored by enemies and critics, if he had any, than the great progenitor of the tradition, Marshall's fellow Virginian, Robert E. Lee.*

From corridor aspersions, McCarthy quickly progressed to public denunciations of Marshall. In his speech before the American Society of Newspaper Editors at the height of the Lattimore-Budenz confrontation, he departed from his anti-spy histrionics to assault Marshall, then in retirement, as "completely unfitted" and "pathetic," and said his assumption of diplomatic posts was "little short of a crime."

That Joe McCarthy, in the face of all the cautions that reason shouted, should raise his sights from the nonentities of the old lists such as Haldore Hanson and Esther Brunauer to General Marshall was to me an earnest of his intent, or rather of his instinct, to pull down the pillars, as Drew had prophesied.

As of that moment, in May of 1950, McCarthy had not yet called Marshall a traitor, had not yet cried "treason in the White House," had not yet charged the Democratic Party with "twenty years of treason," had not yet tied all his accusations together in his blanket indictment of June 14, 1951:

> How can we account for our present situation unless we believe that men high in this Government are concerting to deliver us to disaster? This must be the product of a great conspiracy, a conspiracy on a scale so immense

---

*Senator Joe McCarthy (New York: Harcourt, Brace, 1959), p. 172.

as to dwarf any previous such venture in the history of man. A conspiracy of infamy so black that, when it is finally exposed, its principals shall forever deserve the maledictions of all honest men . . .

But he had already revealed the pattern of false accusation that would ineluctably produce all this. I put aside the sentimental recollections of happier days when Joe and I were helping each other upward, and the various calculations that had for three months made me reluctant to join Drew wholeheartedly in all-out attack.

I had often tried to put myself in the shoes of a victim suddenly descended upon by the "Washington Merry-Go-Round." From observation and post-mortem inquiry I had learned the basic patterns of response. Typically, the target, after a panicky round of consultations with Washington folklorists and survivors of past Pearson raids, would emerge with two uppermost questions: Was Pearson merely reporting, impersonally, a juicy story that happened to come his way? Or was this a prelude to one of his major campaigns? If the former, the course was to lie low; a few columns can easily be swallowed up in the vast output of the press, and are soon forgotten. If the latter, one must arm for a long and miserable siege.

By the fourth month of what Joe McCarthy called his "fight for America," he could no longer doubt that Drew was out for his hide. Up to that time Joe had suffered in good humor, if I could judge from his continued accessibility, the several hurts we had done him. While he must have been resentful, he outwardly accepted it as within the permitted range of reportorial mischief. He retained half a hope that I could contain Drew within that range. I had not told him that I was now at one with Drew, for I was practicing that deceit which the investigative reporter proclaims, and even believes, to be a professional virtue. But by the end of June 1950, more than forty daily columns, and a like percentage of weekly broadcasts, had been devoted in whole or in part to discrediting McCarthy's charges, and more significantly, to disparaging his pre-crusade record in Washington and Wisconsin.

We had retrieved and set rolling again four old Wisconsin embarrassments: that as a state judge, McCarthy had made his court a haven for out-of-jurisdiction "quickie" divorces for clients of his campaign contributors; that he had violated a provision of the Wisconsin constitution by running for the Senate without resigning from the bench, which had prompted the Board of Bar Commissioners to recommend his disbarment; that in his first Senate primary race, in 1944, he had spuriously attributed $18,000 in campaign contributions to his father, brother and brother-in-law, a threadbare trio which, we showed, did not earn $5,000 among them that year; and that in 1943 he had failed to disclose $42,000 in taxable income to the State of Wisconsin, his defense being that while a Marine overseas he was not a taxable citizen of Wisconsin, a plea made the more dubious by his retention, throughout his military service, of his state judgeship.*

McCarthy, at length, concluded that his investment in us of time, hospitality and hope was a washout and that Drew had crossed the line of incorrigibility. One day he approached me after one of his hallway press conferences, and in a tone of dispassionate practicality, said what I recall as this:

"Jack, I'm going to have to go after your boss. I mean, no holds barred. I figure I've already lost his supporters; by going after him, I can pick up his enemies."

I conveyed—lamely, I fear—my regrets that circumstances had made us opponents, and in a last friendly gesture, cautioned him for his own good not to make things nastier than they had to be. "I'm going to break Drew," he retorted. "I'm going to put him out of business."

"Joe, long after you're out of the Senate, we'll still be around," I replied.

Thereafter our meetings were by chance and painful, at least for me, as he pushed his advantages of status and turf, and his posture of wounded sensibility.

"I hear you've been sneaking around Wisconsin posing as an old friend of mine," he challenged me in one hallway encounter, a charge that was all too true.

"I thought I was an *old* friend of yours," I parried.

Again, I was waiting for an elevator in the Senate Office Building one afternoon when McCarthy strode up brusquely and pressed the button three times, a signal to the distant operator that a senator was waiting and to come immediately. When the elevator door opened, McCarthy jumped in and said, "You wait for the next elevator, Jack. I don't want you stinking up this one."

---

*On the tax charge, McCarthy eventually had to make a compromise back payment; the Wisconsin Supreme Court declared him in violation of the state constitution and the ethics of the American Bar Association but did not do anything about it; the other charges did not lend themselves to official action.

The door closed instantly, leaving me tongue-tied, to his great grinning delight.

Months passed without the onslaught on Drew that McCarthy had threatened. With uncharacteristic caution he dallied, seeming to alternate between savoring the gratifications of bloodying his detractor and agonizing over the consequences. A minority among his advisers pressed him not to return Pearson's attacks because it would only heighten the level of hostility. To do so, they argued, would magnify Pearson's vindictiveness and eliminate the few restraints on his venality. They would call the roll of past victims, illustrating by the sour fate of this one and that one how McCarthy risked never again knowing a moment's surcease from the peck-peck-pecking of the Vulture, until death or ruin. According to a later McCarthy speech, one senator warned him: "Don't do it, McCarthy. It will be like standing in the mouth of the Cloaca Maxima and trying to stop the flow. You will be inundated by slime, and he will go every day polluting the airwaves."

But though McCarthy would temporarily be sobered by such visions, his true communion was with the troop of Pearson-haters who had flocked to him as their latest and all-time most promising vehicle for at last settling accounts with the ancient enemy. To the huzzahs of these companions, McCarthy would rehearse the retaliations upon Pearson soon to come; enough reports got back to us to make us suspect that McCarthy planned it that way, for he believed in psychological warfare.

The senator kept on display in his bedroom, for exhibition to select visitors, a baseball bat with the name "Drew Pearson" graven on it in earnest of its intended use. One night a friend of Drew's, Assistant Attorney General Joe Keenan, by chance fell in with McCarthy and his entourage during a drinking bout in celebration of the senator's latest triumph. The next day Keenan reported to Drew. It seems that McCarthy and his group were regaling themselves over the various advantages of "bumping Pearson off" as compared with "a little permanent mutilation." McCarthy favored the gentler course.

"I'd be a hero with many senators if I could pull some of Pearson's teeth, break his insteps—permanently—or break fifteen ribs." I remember Drew's efforts, in relating the story to me, to mimic McCarthy's soaring, nasal delivery and to mime the ecstatic effect on Joe's outriders. As for the "fifteen" ribs, Drew attributed that to McCarthy's weakness for exaggeration.

The mayhem theme reappeared a few weeks later when Drew, at a Gridiron Club dinner, was approached by McCarthy himself. With his beamiest smile, Joe offered his hand and said, "Someday I'm going to break your leg, Drew, but for the time being I just wanted to say hello."

More weeks passed without incident. One day the Justice Department phoned our offices to check out an anonymous report that Drew had been beaten up.

"Not yet," Drew replied. Was this more of McCarthy's psychological warfare?

We narrowed our interpretations to two: (1) McCarthy was deliberately giving Drew food for thought, as does the enforcer of the Mob who tries to scare his subject into submission before pursuing the messier, riskier course of violence; (2) the opposite, that the skein of threats and symbols represented the progressive enlargement of a McCarthy compulsion.

The long wait was not without its impact on our councils. Some of Drew's advisers, like their counterparts in the other camp, entreated with him to lower the acrimony to a prudent level. Themselves anti-McCarthy, their urgings were entirely concerned with Drew's welfare. He was already too overextended in powerful enemies, they argued, to add a blood-war with a tiger like McCarthy, backed as he was by a large and impassioned cross section of the public, the clergy and the press.

In truth, Drew was particularly vulnerable to a McCarthy-type attack. To millions, Pearson the archcontroversialist was mysterious, sinister, disreputable and radical, a brittle image to have in parlous times. And there was many a stray fact that played into McCarthy's hand. Out of his long-time zeal for the anti-Franco cause, Drew had volunteered as a defense witness for the leaders of the Joint Anti-Fascist Refugee Committee, many of whom were sent to prison for contempt of Congress after refusing to answer questions about their Communist involvement. As we have seen, one Pearson staff member, Andy Older, was a bona-fide Communist during the years he worked for Drew, and Drew's belated firing of him could be derided as mere window dressing. Another assistant, Dave Karr, who had recently left Pearson's employ, had in his background a string of innocent but exploitable associations. Among the myriad sources Drew had cultivated in the past and had defended under fire were several whose names now figured prominently in charges of conspiracy to betray the nation, for instance, Owen Lattimore, Laurence Duggan and Harry Dexter White. Adolf A. Berle,

Jr., a former Assistant Secretary of State, had told HUAC that confidential material handled by Alger Hiss had consistently been leaked to the Pearson column. In another age, all this would have been but testimony to the vaunted ubiquity of Pearson's sources; now it had an ominous ring.

Add to the mix Drew's apparent specialization in hounding anti-Communist toilers like Martin Dies, J. Parnell Thomas, James Forrestal, Douglas MacArthur and now McCarthy, and there were more than enough ingredients for a classic McCarthy drama.

Typical of the advice from concerned friends was that of Ernest Cuneo—a former geography student of Drew's at Columbia University who had been an aide to Fiorello La Guardia, a speech writer and brain truster for FDR and was now lawyer-writer-adviser to Walter Winchell. From an entry in Drew's diary:

> Cuneo thinks that I am nuts to go after McCarthy, claims the tide is in the opposite direction and that the entire country is determined to clean out the Communists. I agree except I think that the Communists have been pretty well cleared out. Now it has got to a point where anyone who was sympathetic to Russia during the war is in danger of being called a Communist.*

Drew heard out the counsels of his friends, and of his peers, that he soften up on McCarthy, but it was never in the cards that he would heed them. It was not that he did not know well the world of prudent compromise. Operating as he must through newspapers and radio stations owned by others, dependent as he was on many lines of access to news, confronted daily with the inconvenient shortcomings of the discoverable fact as a revealer of the obvious truth, he was no virgin to accommodation. He had made a hundred deals, with others and with himself. He had swapped silence on one story to gain access to another, had excused in allies what he pilloried in foes, had cut corners to get there first, had traded small pieces of formal integrity in order to stretch the fabric of fact to fit the pattern of intuition, had on occasion crossed the line into vindictiveness so as to keep the felled foe from getting up. He lived with the small compromises exacted by networks and newspaper chains; he had bowed many times to the peering executive in the control room who with a wave of the hand could switch him off the

Pearson Diaries (April 11, 1950), p. 118.

air in mid-broadcast; he knew what it was to roll over and wait to fight another day.

Well, then, McCarthy was not demanding much—not Drew's support, or even his neutrality, just moderation in attack. Why not bend a little now?

Because when Drew Pearson made a deal, even with himself, he had in mind to trade up; when he husbanded his strength, it was to use it on a greater field; when he waited to fight another day it was because there was time and because he knew he would come back to claim that day, knew the moment would come when the peering executive was lolling in the control room or when a favorable news break would enable him to revive the killed story.

"Responsible" journalists condemned him for his overstatements and excesses and for the true stories that never should have been told, but what harried *his* conscience was the bomb that did not go off, the harsh truths still left untold, the battles not yet joined. What plagued him in the dark of night was: would he live long enough, grow strong enough, to be able to print what he knew about, for instance, the cardinals of the Church or the barons of the press? Alone among the great journalistic controversialists of the day, he did not trade a veto over his copy to corporation libel lawyers in return for their assumption of his financial liability in case of suit. Because he was willing to pay the price, in a dozen coins, he would, soon or late, have his say.

At the center of his concept of integrity was the idea that though his situation permitted him, required him, to deceive others, his raison d'être crumbled the moment he deceived himself. McCarthyism was to him the ultimate windmill, the clear and present danger. You could not trade up on McCarthy, nor wait for a convenient year to charge. For the sake of fighting just such a battle, he had long justified the smaller ones not yet fought, the petty scandals exploited to build readership, the hundred personal tragedies he had wrought over comparative small change. And so there was no truce with McCarthy.

In the second week of December 1950, word reached us that McCarthy's patience had expired and that he was about to make a massive indictment of Drew as a Communist agent, and was to do it on the Senate floor, where he was immune from earthly restraints. During the previous month, in the senatorial elections, McCarthy's stature had swelled immeasurably with the victory of his friends, and more to the point, the defeat of his enemies, notably Millard Tydings and Majority Leader Scott Lucas, the most prominent symbols of Senate opposition to him, which now collapsed abjectly. Drew needed a defender on the floor to neutralize the predictable flood of adverse news coverage. After considering who among senators owing him favors would be most appropriate for the task, he called Senator Lyndon Johnson of Texas, whom Drew had championed in early Texas campaigns and who had once, perhaps fulsomely, credited Drew with his election to the Senate. Johnson turned him down.

On the night before the scheduled speech, Drew received a last token of his intent from McCarthy, a graphic illustration of Whittaker Chambers' general observation that McCarthy was a "heavy-handed slugger who telegraphs his fouls in advance."

It was Drew's birthday. His wife, Luvie, thought to celebrate by bringing him to a "quiet little party" given in honor of Republican Senator Joseph Duff of Pennsylvania, at Washington's exclusive Sulgrave Club. Drew has described the evening:

> It was one of those supper-dance parties where people dance between courses. Joe McCarthy was sitting at the other end of the table next to my wife. He told her he was going to make a speech attacking me the next day which would cause a divorce in the family. During an intermission he came down to my end of the table and told me the same thing, that he was going to put me out of business with a speech on the Senate floor and that there would be nothing left of me professionally or otherwise when he had finished. I listened for some time. Then I said: "Joe, have you paid your income taxes yet?"
>
> He got very sore and challenged me to come outside. [Congressman] Charlie Bennett . . . held on to me. Bill McCracken came by and restrained McCarthy. Nothing happened. I spent the rest of the evening dancing with Mrs. McCracken, who was indignant over the incident, having listened to a good part of it.
>
> As the party broke up I went downstairs to check out my overcoat. McCarthy came up halfway behind me and pinned my arms down on each side. He claimed afterward I had my hand in my side pocket getting a gun. Actually I had a hole in my pants pocket which my wife had forgotten to mend so I was keeping change in the coat pocket. He proceeded to kick me in the groin with his knee. Richard Nixon came up and pulled us apart. As he did so McCarthy took a swing at my left ear which landed but not with any damaging effect. Nixon had some pacifying words to say that we shouldn't embarrass our hostess. I picked up my coat and left, keeping a wary eye to my rear. . . .*

---

*Pilat, *op. cit.*, p. 27.

The accounts of the other two witnesses differed in emphasis: McCarthy, magnanimous amid the backslaps of his colleagues, described it as less violent; Nixon, the peacemaker, as more: "If I hadn't pulled McCarthy away, he might have killed Pearson."

The reactions that filtered back were not warming to a fifty-four-year-old self-perceived Quaker pacifist bushwhacked by a former heavyweight boxer a dozen years his junior. Much of the Washington cocktail circuit was a-chuckle over the congratulations given McCarthy by Senator Arthur Watkins, the dour Utah Republican, who said he had heard two differing versions as to where Pearson was hit and was hoping both were accurate. A similar response would develop some time later when Drew was again floored by a surprise haymaker, this time from Franco's Washington lobbyist, Charles Patrick Clark (see Chapter 4). When Clark was convicted of assault and given a token fine of $25, he found his next day's mail filled with small checks mounting up to more than $400, accompanied by messages of the "Hit him again for me" genre; the congressional joke of that hour was that a license to slug Pearson could be had for only $25—the best bargain in town.

9 · The Coalition of the Aggrieved

LATE IN THE afternoon of December 15, 1950, the three-bell alarm clamored urgently throughout the Senate side of the Capitol, summoning senators to the floor. Into the historic old Supreme Court chamber, crowded with antique desks, they shuffled; this was a temporary gathering place while their own great oval chamber was undergoing repairs. After answering to their names, a few barged off again with the harried looks of men too busy to bother with parliamentary interruptions. But many of the senators lingered on, held by the promise of fireworks to come. For Joe McCarthy, after postponing his Pearson speech for a day to take advantage of the Sulgrave-incident publicity, had spread the word that he would today "tie a rocket to the tail" of their common plague.

The senator, unsuitably sporty in a maroon tie, a nervous grin upon his darkly foreboding face, seemed ill at ease. Usually he appeared to enjoy these ex parte jousts and to savor the air of anticipation among senators and newsmen as he lined up his documents and readied the unveiling of yet a new Catiline. But on this occasion the grin was thin, the twitch of his huge head more pronounced, the short, muscular arms pumping restlessly. He had directed his aides to hand out copies of the speech the moment he gained the floor, and they had started the distribution process, with a synchronized movement upon the press stall at the rear of the chamber. But then he had been interrupted by a quorum call before he could begin his speech and the anticipation mounted.

When he at length began, it was clear from the outset that this was not to be an anticlimax. For more than an hour the senator flogged Drew with the gravest charges ever made by a high official against an American newsman. To begin with, Pearson was "the voice of international Communism" and "a Moscow-directed character assassin." On top of that—like the candidate in Alben Barkley's story who, in addition to being bald, hunchbacked, stuttering and shy, was also crosseyed —Drew was "diabolical," "fiendishly clever," "a fake," "an unprincipled liar," "the owner of a twisted perverted mentality" and "a prostitute of journalism."

As I watched from the press section I felt that Joe McCarthy was crossing a divide in this speech. Up to now, his offenses tended toward exaggeration, distortion, irresponsibility, overspontaneity; he would upgrade a misdemeanor into a felony, or twist a half-truth into a half-lie, or run with information he had not bothered to verify but at least divined might be true, or squeeze out of a tight corner with outrageous bombast that had the one defense of not being calculated. But in this speech he entered the realm of pure, deliberate fabrication, inventing an elaborate conspiracy he knew, and had to know, was made out of whole cloth.

"It appears that Pearson never actually signed up as a member of the Communist Party and never paid dues," McCarthy began—but, you see, that was only part of Pearson's satanic cleverness. He was under the discipline of Moscow—that was the important thing; his supervisor from the Kremlin was David Karr, who had only posed as his aide; Pearson's assigned task was "to lead the character assassination of any man who was a threat to international Communism"; the Kremlin picked Pearson's targets for him and informed Karr, "who carries instructions and orders to Pearson."

The senator, warming up to his subject, traced the results of this grisly alliance: "One of Pearson's extremely important tasks was the destruction in the eyes of the American people of Chiang Kai-shek . . . He [Pearson] and the Communist Party murdered James Forrestal in just as cold blood as though they had machine-gunned him." Pearson was now "undertaking to destroy General of the Army Douglas MacArthur" and, of course, McCarthy himself.

McCarthy was not one to merely view with alarm; he went beyond a legion of Pearson-hating predecessors by sounding a call to action.

If the loyal American newspaper editors and publishers and radio-station owners refuse to buy this disguised, sugar-coated voice of Russia, the mockingbirds who have followed the Pearson line will disappear from the scene like the chaff before the wind. The American people can do much to accomplish this result. They can notify their newspapers that they do not want this Moscow-directed character assassin being brought into their homes to poison the well of information at which their children drink. They can notify the Adam Hat Company by actions what they think of their sponsoring this man. It should be remembered that anyone who buys an Adam hat, any store that stocks an Adam hat, is unknowingly and innocently contributing at least something to the cause of international Communism by keeping this Communist spokesman on the air.

It was dusk by the time McCarthy finished. The press stall cleared out, and I started for the corridor. At the entrance I encountered Joe swinging through the doorway with a buoyant stride, as though he had just accomplished the Lord's work. He saw me and stopped: "I wasn't talking about you, Jack," he said. I fumbled for something appropriate to say and again came up dry. "I see you're wearing a red tie, Joe," I mumbled. "Maybe you ought to investigate yourself."

He moved on with the lofty resignation of one whose gallantry is uncomprehended. As he passed out into the December night, he put on a gray fedora which I recognized—an Adam hat, size 7-⅜, presented to him a year before by Drew Pearson.

During his campaign to destroy Pearson, McCarthy rose to a new plateau of ferocity and perserverance. In its opening phase, he made seven Senate speeches in seven weeks, loosing an accelerating barrage of epithets, accusations both criminal and moral, demands for official prosecution, exhortations to citizen vigilanteeism, that in its range, venom and gravity was unprecedented, even for McCarthy.

The gravamen of his indictment, always, was that Pearson's columns and broadcasts were Communist-directed. "Everything they touch is smeared with filth . . . The blackness of their lies is mixed with the blood shed by American boys, who are the real victims of the Communist conspiracy . . . bought and paid for by the Adam Hat Company." Drew was variously described as the "grease monkey of the Communist conspiracy," "the Communist Party smear artist," a skunk whose smell

McCarthy was willing to bear in order to protect the hen house, a degenerate blackmailer who used threats to suppress evidence of his personal perversions.

This latter flourish was McCarthy's approach to a long-held fantasy of Pearson-haters. In 1915 a teen-age Drew Pearson, working on a Chautauqua tent crew, had been arrested in Reidsville, North Carolina, around three o'clock in the morning, along with a young black co-worker, for cavorting around naked near the railroad yards. They were promptly acquitted when they explained that they were merely taking a sponge bath to wash away the grime of the all-night labor of taking down the great tent.

That was all there was to it. But over the decades, successive waves of hopeful investigators would make the pilgrimage to Reidsville only to learn from the presiding judge, the newspaper editor, the local lawyers, and later, their descendants, that there was nothing sinister involved, no charge of moral turpitude, no suggestion of homosexual hijinks, and that in honor of the incident, the Reidsville Chamber of Commerce had staged a gala dinner for Pearson after he became famous.

When McCarthy's investigator, Morris A. Bealle, rendered his un-satisfying report, the senator abandoned plans for a frontal attack (unlike Senator Thomas Dodd two decades later, who went ahead anyway) but Joe couldn't bear to surrender the thing altogether. Hence the never-quite-explained adjectives "degenerate" and "perverted" that crept into his denunciations. And hence the following flight of pure fancy from his Senate speech of January 5, 1951:

> The other day he [Pearson] sent a man to me to ask me not to use certain photostats which somehow he found I had in my files. He explained why he did not want them used . . . If I do not use these photostats, it is only because I refuse to sink to his level in exposing to the American people exactly what type of man this individual is . . . I tell him here and now that if he sends another man to my office, either with threats or promises in regard to the use of these photostats, then on the next day these photostats will all be presented to this Senate.

Drew promptly denied the incident and challenged McCarthy to release the dread photostats, but the senator's innate sense of propriety prevented him from doing so. The "photostats" disappeared forever into the void where dwelt McCarthy's cases against David Lloyd, the

Mongolian "agents," the "big three" of the State Department espionage ring and other abandoned enthusiasms.

But some charges did not disappear so conveniently. Just when Joe seemed to have exhausted his material, Drew placed live ammunition in his hands, knowingly but, in Drew's scales, unavoidably. It so happened that McCarthy's offensive coincided with General MacArthur's retreat from the Yalu, and with my acquisition of the dispatches which revealed the blunders that brought on the debacle and punctured the exaggerations of Chinese strength by which the general was trying to publicly absolve himself of blame as he privately pressed Washington for the green light on massive retaliation against mainland China. To affront the taut public mood by publishing top-secret decoded military dispatches that bespattered the national hero even as he was rallying his routed armies against the yellow hordes that threatened to hurl us into the Sea of Japan was, among other risks, to play into McCarthy's hands in the most obvious way. But there was no help for it, given Drew's priorities, and he went to press promptly with each revelation.

With live meat to devour, McCarthy was something to behold. Who could doubt now, he would thunder, that the "diabolically clever" Pearson was in league with "a spy handing out military secrets . . ." that Pearson was "guilty of high treason . . ." that his continuance on the air and in print (thanks to Adam Hats and your local editor) "endangered the lives of millions of young Americans and the very life of this nation."

Taking a leaf from Drew's manual, McCarthy demanded investigation and prosecution of the Kremlin accomplice, and appointed himself to ride public herd on the process lest it meander inconclusively in the bureaucratic labyrinth and die out. Designating Army Secretary Frank Pace as personally responsible for the initial probe, McCarthy propounded a detailed questionnaire on Pearson's access to military secrets for Pace to answer publicly; demanded and received progress reports and issued his own; enlisted fellow senators to join him in his demands for action; alerted the press to the progress of the case as it passed from agency to agency, lauded FBI agents for their energetic pursuit; warned political higher-ups that he had sources of information within the Justice Department and that they had better keep their tainted hands off the case. In due course he announced:

> The investigation is to all intents and purposes completed. While they
> have not been able to spot the spy in the Pentagon, they have produced

enough evidence to make a clear-cut case of violation of the espionage laws by Mr. Pearson.

Whatever McCarthy said about Drew on the Senate floor could be quoted anywhere with the same immunity from legal retaliation that McCarthy enjoyed. The charges, epithets and exhortations to boycott were processed into a many-sided effort to put Drew "out of business." Three of the speeches, studded with appeals to patriotic editors to drop Pearson, were combined into a pamphet and mailed at taxpayers' expense to 1,900 newspaper editors and to other VIP mailing lists. Congressional anti-Pearsonites used their free printing and mailing privileges to further circulate the McCarthy attacks; one mailing, for example, under Senator Owen Brewster's frank, was 75,000 copies.

Our fears that McCarthy would catalyze a general rising of enemies were quickly realized. Other senators, including William Jenner of Indiana, Arthur Watkins of Utah and Harry Cain of Washington, joined McCarthy in his denunciations. Columnists and commentators in the McCarthy camp—Westbrook Pegler, Fulton Lewis, Jr., George Sokolsky and numerous imitators of lesser stature—kept the McCarthy attacks rolling. Copies of his speeches were put in the hands of newspaper-syndicate salesmen for discreet use in persuading editors to drop Pearson in favor of rival columnists.

Ten days after McCarthy's call for a "patriotic boycott," Adam Hats, Inc., withdrew as Drew's radio sponsor. For a time, Drew would keep the program on the network through a series of short-term arrangements, but McCarthy was assiduous in keeping the threat of boycott hanging over the negotiating table and Drew never again obtained a permanent sponsor. He was finished as a network commentator; McCarthy's first offensive had wiped out half our fire power.

The shock raised an instant question: How secure was the other half? Losing the world's most widely read newspaper column was a complicated affair, dependent on the individual decisions of hundreds of publishers. We were in fact deeply entrenched in newspapers whereas in broadcasting we had only *thought* we were, and wars of attrition were supposed to be *our* forte. Yet the great majority of our publishers were hostile to Drew's politics and journalistic style, and tolerated the column only because of its appeal to a large segment of readers. How long would that merely pragmatic tolerance hold up under a militant onslaught?

As the months passed we were slowly losing, a trend that our pro-liberal stance would worsen as the bitter 1952 political campaign approached. Drew usually kept the statistics of our decline close to his vest, but once, in as low a mood as I had ever seen him, he told me that in the mail on his desk were a dozen cancellation notices from publishers and that twenty more were threatening to cancel.

The blood drawn by the continuing attacks of the McCarthy alliance encouraged in litigious hearts the notion that, at long last, the monster was wounded and ready to be taken. For twenty years Drew had painstakingly promoted an aura of legal invincibility in order to discourage libel suits. Would-be plaintiffs were often intimidated by the discouraging precedents: Pearson had fought every libel suit tooth and claw and had never lost one; equally foreboding, he was known to keep up an unremitting pursuit of former courtroom antagonists. But hope bubbled up now. Two lawsuits in particular, each with the potential for destroying Drew financially and professionally, were being pressed by the comrades of the right.

Both involved incidents going back a couple of years. Drew had accused California Attorney General Fred Napoleon Howser of consorting with mobsters and of taking a bribe from gambling interests, exposés which drove Howser from office when he sought re-election; and in a marvelously gratifying coup against an old foe, Drew had claimed the famous right-wing "radio priest" from Royal Oak, Michigan, Father Charles Coughlin, had paid $68,000 to one Bernard Gariepy to pacify him after alienating the affections of his wife. In each case the targets had been reluctant to challenge Drew in court but had at length done so. In Howser's case, lawyers for McCarthy's radio champion, Fulton Lewis, Jr.,—Roger Robb and Herbert Bingham—had encouraged Howser to sue Drew for $350,000 and were representing him on a contingency basis—that is, for free unless they won, in which case they would get a share of the winnings. Mrs. Gariepy, suing for $225,000, had been similarly egged on by Catholic clergymen and high laymen who regarded Drew's occasional roustings of prominent churchmen—a no-no in that cloistered period—as attacks on the Church itself.

When Drew had first run the Howser and the Coughlin-Gariepy stories in 1949, he felt fully able to prove them, but since then witnesses had re-defected to the other side, court documents had mysteriously disappeared, his own public image had become more sinister, and it was now touch-and-go as to what a jury would decide, with the early omens rather disconcerting. And so, as Drew defended his front against McCarthy, he found himself besieged on either flank by court actions of a potentially terminal character.

But it was the simultaneous caving in of the rear—the Truman Administration—that most exposed the lonely extremity of our situation. Drew had expected help from the White House, for by his reasoning the victims and likely victims of McCarthy should, according to the Churchillian formula, bury their differences and join forces for the duration. In that spirit Drew had called off his deepest personal vendetta, one of almost two decades, against Senator Millard Tydings, who in the 1930s had hounded Drew's reformist father out of office as governor of the Virgin Islands. Drew had stifled the temptation to enjoy Tydings' pummeling by McCarthy and had even tried to help save his old enemy, though to do so stuck in his craw. But Harry Truman, who had authority over the agencies McCarthy was daily summoning against Drew, was unwilling to rise to a similar expediency. Underestimating McCarthy as a danger and scorning Pearson as an ally, he settled back to enjoy their dismemberment of each other as though he were an unaffected spectator.

The President had his reasons and they went far beyond our baiting of him over General MacArthur. For years we had been romping through his Internal Revenue Service, which, demoralized by over-political appointments, had been taking dives left and right on the cases of wealthy tax cheats.

Closer to the bone, Drew had infuriated Truman by his persistent nibbling at the raffish types with whom the President liked to relax at day's end, such as Harry Vaughan, the old National Guard buddy and former Kansas City tea salesman whom Truman had made his military aide, with the rank of major general. We faithfully chronicled a series of Vaughan misadventures, including his bringing into the White House family a Kansas City ex-bootlegger named John Maragon who gave gaudy gifts—costly perfumes, fancy refrigerators, furs—to General Vaughan to pass out among Truman intimates while he used the White House as a base for influencing government contract awards, for which Maragon took a 5 percent fee. Our exposés of Vaughan and Maragon, and the congressional and Justice Department probes they touched off, gave rise to such anti-Truman campaign slogans as "five percenters," "mink coats" and "deep freezes." Drew was scrupulous to distinguish the essential integrity and historic achievements of the Truman presidency from its gamy pratfalls in the lesser arenas, but the

Republicans, naturally enough, were not; our exposés furnished the scaffolding used by GOP orators to paint the Truman regime as corrupt. The President's antagonism toward Drew was thus deepened by a rankling sense of having been given a bum rap. When Senator Clinton Anderson tried to heal the breach by telling Truman how helpful Pearson had been to him during the 1948 campaign and on basic issues, Harry would have none of it, saying, "He's a blank page in my book, and always will be."

The President was not one to repress resentments. When Drew was named by the Norwegian parliament in February 1949 as one of the twenty nominees for the Nobel Peace Prize, Truman snorted at a press conference that Pearson "must have nominated himself." Gael Sullivan, a friend of Drew's, told him that when he was brought to the President after being named Assistant Postmaster General, Truman told him, "There are just two things I want you to do. Never talk to Drew Pearson and stay away from Tom Corcoran."

For a time Truman restricted his public invective, in the tradition of other Presidents, to calling Drew a "liar," but not for long. Defending General Vaughan in a speech, he blurted out, "No SOB like Pearson is going to prevail on me to discharge anyone by some smart-aleck statement over the air."

This was a "first" in presidential profanity before a microphone and it set off a public uproar; Drew kept it rolling by ostentatiously giving out awards to other "Servants of Brotherhood." After the Forrestal suicide two months later, Truman saw a chance to recoup; one of our White House sources quoted him as telling his inner circle: "That son of a bitch Pearson got the best of me on the SOB thing but I'm going to get the best of him on the Forrestal suicide. I'm going to rub it in until the public never forgets." We knew that the White House helped to stimulate the wave of public and press attacks on Drew that followed, but I've always doubted that any stimulation was necessary.

There was an authentic ring, then, in the report that Harry Vaughan delightedly rushed to Truman the text of McCarthy's first Senate attack on Drew, and that after browsing through it approvingly (it contained some of Truman's own quotes on Drew), the President said, "I hope they both kill each other off." And it was a reaction Truman would cling to. Years later, in his pugnacious dotage, when interviewer Merle Miller raised the subject of McCarthy, Truman snorted, "The only good thing McCarthy ever did was to knock down Drew Pearson."

The most important effect of Truman's hostility at this critical juncture was this: in the year following McCarthy's cluster of demands for official action against us by the Defense Department and the Justice Department, we were caught up in eight different government investigations. It became routine for the investigative arms of the government to launch a probe after each of our stories that featured inside information, in order to uncover and punish our sources and to determine if we had violated the law and could be prosecuted.

We knew the bare outlines of what was happening; each time investigators from the Pentagon or the FBI would begin a new round of questioning people, some friend along the interview route was bound to clue us in. And at one point in the spring of 1951, the FBI confirmed to Drew that, on impetus from above, it had undertaken five different investigations since the first of the year.

The atmosphere of government snooping we now lived in made our own snooping more and more complicated. One day, for example, a call came to our office from a State Department informant who had just returned from Cairo and had some information for us regarding Guy Burgess and Donald Maclean, two missing officials of the British Foreign Office who had defected to the Soviet Union. It was arranged that Fred Blumenthal of our staff would visit the caller in two hours. About an hour later the informant called again to say that during his interview with Fred he had neglected to give him some notes he had. This was surpassing strange, for Fred had not yet called on him.

Fred and I rushed over to the diplomat's office. He described the meeting he had just held with a person representing himself as Fred Blumenthal, presumably an intelligence agent acting on the basis of a tapped phone conversation. We concluded that since the government can't prosecute on the basis of information obtained by an illegal wiretap, it had rushed over an impersonator to get admissible proof of the transfer of classified information. Fortunately a certain awkwardness in the impersonator's performance aroused suspicion, and our source did not pass him anything incriminating. But if this sort of thing kept up, all but the most foolhardy of our sources would soon flee from us.

For a period of months in 1951 I was under continual surveillance by the FBI. I did not know the extent of the surveillance until many years later,* but I sometimes saw signs of it. (One of the agents

---

*In 1977, to be exact, when, through a lawsuit against government officials, I obtained parts of the FBI files compiled on me over a thirty-year period.

following me noted in his first written report on my activities that Anderson was "surveillance conscious" and made his moves "deliberately.") The perceived necessity for eluding pursuers and the fear of tapped telephones turned every meeting with an important source into a time-consuming game of evasive tactics; at times I began to wonder how much longer I could continue to function as a reporter.

The situation was not without its lighter moments, however. One day a conclave of intelligence brass was convened at the Pentagon to work out a plan for tracing and stopping the leaks to our column. One of the brainstormers, a general, happened to be a key source of mine, and after the meeting, he phoned to brief me on it. The most popular proposal of the day, he said, was to station intelligence men at every entrance to the Pentagon building so as to spot me whenever and wherever I arrived and initiate an elaborate surveillance scheme. The plan disturbed my source, for it had the potential of being effective. And so he intervened. "Has anyone here counted all the entrances to the Pentagon?" he asked. "Has anyone figured out the number of shifts and the total manpower this will take? Or how we'll look if this ever gets out?" A less ambitious plan was adopted which, forewarned of, I was able to neutralize.

Periodically, throughout the early 1950s, reports surfaced in the press, and tips came to us from friends within the government, that Drew was about to be indicted, presumably along with his staff accomplices. On February 11, 1951, the New York *Times* revealed that the Army had completed its investigation of us in what was being dubbed "the military secrets case," and had turned over its findings to the Justice Department for action. Later on, Clayton Fritchey, the press officer at the Pentagon and an old friend of Drew's, cautioned him that President Truman was determined to get him prosecuted for revealing excerpts that I had obtained from a White House conversation on Korea between the President and the Joint Chiefs. Fritchey quoted Truman: "I'm going to have this man jailed for treason!"

Still later, Drew got three reports in one fortnight that he was about to be indicted by the Justice Department for what was called "causing secret information to be passed without authority." One of the predictions came privately from me, the other two were published in the columns of Walter Winchell and Marquis Childs. Within days, about a dozen papers canceled the column. What would happen, we wondered, when the prediction became reality?

It was not a good thing to have Truman so exercised, but I felt some security in the thought that he was a mercurial and busy man, and that between him and us were calming layers of due process and bureaucratic objectivity. That notion had been nurtured by an incident of two years earlier.

It was the time of the SOB contretemps. The column was in the depths of White House disfavor over our revelations about Harry Vaughan and John Maragon, which would in the end lead to dismissal and jail for Maragon, and for General Vaughan, the humiliation of being linked to the Tanforan Race Track scandal.* One day my key source at the Pentagon told me that FBI agents had been there asking catch-all, fishing-expedition questions about me. He showed me the Pentagon file that had been started on me; it included excerpts from an FBI file, complete with the file number. I was not then inured to being the object of criminal investigations and a slow burn smoldered as I headed for the office, a burn Drew ignited by judging that the White House was trying to discredit me because of the Vaughan-Maragon business.

The next morning I stormed into the office of J. Edgar Hoover's deputy, Stan Tracy. "I've committed no crime," I declaimed. "I've applied for no government post. What right do you people have to be investigating me?" Then I answered my own question. "We both know you are investigating me because I work for a controversial columnist. Will you show me your authorization to investigate a newspaperman just because he is controversial?" At first Tracy said that I was wrong, that there was no investigation of me and never had been one.

I quote from Tracy's memo to Hoover on our conversation, a more bland version than my own memory of the incident.

> Anderson said he checked carefully and had confirmed that the FBI was investigating him and that the following questions were being asked:
>
> 1. Is there any evidence that John Northam Anderson tried to evade the draft?
>
> 2. Is there any evidence that John Northam Anderson passed out any unauthorized information while in the Army during the war; further, did he give out any classified information to any unauthorized persons?"
>
> [I hasten to interject that the FBI eventually concluded that the answer to all three questions was "no" and closed the inquiry.]

---

*During the postwar housing shortage, rationed lumber, supposedly destined for veterans' housing, was diverted to Tanforan for the repair of stables; after Drew set a fire under the case, which Vaughan was trying to damp down, several track officials went to jail.

Anderson stated that the questions were in writing and that he had proof of the investigation.

Drew Pearson had been advised and wanted to call Mr. Hoover immediately. Anderson asked him to do absolutely nothing and he would ask the question at the FBI and advise Pearson the answer.

Anderson was asked if he was positive the investigating Agents were from FBI and he was positive they were.

Anderson stated that he had always had the utmost confidence in the FBI and the only thing he could think of that might have caused any inquiries would be his recent membership in the White House Correspondents' Association, although he had not applied for a White House pass. He stated that he hoped that if an investigation was being made that it was the result of a formal request because he would not like to have his confidence in the FBI shaken.

I remember citing the FBI file number and Tracy saying, "This is over my head. I can't discuss it further."

That afternoon Hoover called Drew. The Director did not leave for prying posterity a memo of that conversation, so I here rely on Drew's account. "There is nothing to this," Hoover said. "The White House ordered it; you know how Harry is. We have to follow orders and make inquiries. But I assure you there is nothing for your young man to worry about. We're not after you."

In retrospect, Hoover's assurance that it was only the White House, not the FBI, and therefore nothing to be concerned about, provides an interesting view of the Director's perspective on the world. But at the time, though not assuaged, I was relieved, and it puffed the vanity to be wrongly pursued from on high so long as one was not caught.

In 1951, as the investigations proliferated, Hoover continued to project a benign face toward us, but the comfort we derived from this was illusory. What we did not know then, and what I found out decades later from FBI documents, was that, all along, the Director was keeping a close and unfriendly eye on us. Memos were routed to him on everything pertaining to us, however trivial: gossip picked up about us, comments of our relatives overheard by FBI informants, rumors of dissension in our staff, our routine requests of the FBI for information and interviews, as well as reports of massive field investigations into where we got hold of classified documents.

On these memos to Hoover there was a place for his comments. As long as the documents crossing his desk dealt with mere questions of national security, his notations, if any, reflected a detached professional

equanimity. But the day came, on April 30, 1951, when he found
before him a report that I had called the Bureau to ask why an FBI
agent was chauffeuring Joe McCarthy's vacationing girl friend, Jean
Kerr, around Hawaii. At this, Hoover was stirred to append this notice
to the Bureau high command of a break in relations between the
United States and the Pearson "gang": "This fellow Anderson and his
ilk have minds that are lower than the regurgitated filth of vultures."
Hereinafter, the "young man" of happier days was to be known as "a
flea ridden dog," and the Bureau was instructed to treat any person in
any way associated with me as "infected."

A malconvergence of events thus left us teetering on the edge of
whatever it is that can destroy a prominent journalist overnight, even
in a free society—the edge of too much notoriety, or too much con-
troversiality or too lessened credibility which, once crossed over, permits of no return to the tolerable graces of public opinion. We were
at the mercy not so much of particular enemies as of random events
—a decidedly tighter bind. A blow from any of several quarters could
now push us over: a guilty verdict in a libel trial, a federal indictment
for "espionage," a reportorial gaffe on our part, a jelling of anti-Pearson
congressional sentiment into a public investigation, a major cancellation by a publishing chain or a prestige paper that could incite a
stampede.

Drew's reaction came through on two levels. On the action level, he
pranced boldly on the high wire, forbidding the slightest retreat on
"sensitive" stories. On the reflective level, he wavered between frustration, attempted humor, self-pity and near-despair.

> Sometimes I think that this administration is so dumb it is not worth
> saving. The tragic thing is that the Republicans at the moment are worse.
> And if the things Truman stands for fall, the whole liberal era in this
> country collapses. I sometimes wonder why I should be trying to help out
> a Defense Department and a White House which three times has de-
> manded of the Attorney General that I be prosecuted for publishing one
> of MacArthur's intelligence reports which showed up MacArthur in his
> true light even as early as last December.*

In his office he would grouse about the strange bedfellows in league
against him: Catholic priests in Brooklyn collecting anti-Pearson peti-

---

*Pearson Diaries (May 23, 1951), p. 163.

tions, an editorial attack in *Pravda,* a tip that General Vaughan in the White House was slipping information from Drew's FBI file to his newspaper and libel-suit opponents.

"When you get caught between the Catholics and the Communists, you're finished," he gloomed one morning, apparently resigned to his fate, at last. But by noon he was trying, in the column, to draw advantage from the diversity of his detractors.

> I have now been called a "communist" by Senator McCarthy, a war-monger by the editor of *Pravda,* and an S.O.B. by President Truman. With my profession, of course, you can't help being called names. But I have one complaint. Why can't the name-callers be a little more original?

He was especially disappointed by the general failure of the press to rally to his support, in its own self-interest, and when the St. Louis *Star-Times* did, he sent out to all his papers a reproduction of its editorial which closed:

> If Joseph McCarthy can silence a critic named Drew Pearson, simply by smearing him with the brush of Communist association, he can silence any other critic.

Oliver Pilat, then a reporter for the New York *Post,* later recalled that Drew was not as alone as he felt:

> . . . Pearson . . . was by no means alone in fighting McCarthy, but he occupied the most isolated spot in Washington. To many observers it seemed that if he faltered and fell, an antidemocratic tide would sweep across the country.*

Up to this point in my apprenticeship, I had paid primary notice to the aggressive, Barnumesque side of Drew Pearson, the spirit and method of attack that always propelled him to the cutting edge of controversy. But now that it was we who were under siege, I began to appreciate how intricate and well fortified his lines of *defense* were.

Part of his defensive depth was the natural harvest of the thousands of altruistic seeds he had sown over the years. A man who is, over a generation, regularly honored as "Father of the Year" or "Big Brother

*Pilat, *op. cit.,* p. 30.

of the Year" or "Pet Owner of the Year" cannot be transformed overnight into a traitorous monster.

And part of it lay in the abiding soundness of a key standard by which he gauged his approach to any political movement or foreign regime: Did it expand or repress human freedom? To him a police state was a police state; he had not fallen into the trap of excusing the Communists while condemning the Fascists. His news beats about Communist espionage, his campaign that stimulated millions of letters from Italian-Americans to relatives in Italy urging them to vote against Communism and for democracy in their pivotal election of 1948, his public identification with the Friendship Train and the "tide of toys" and their massive distributions of food and gifts aimed at strengthening our ties with the still-free peoples of Western Europe, even his recurring Rube Goldberg schemes for penetrating the Iron Curtain with the democratic message by such stunts as the floating of thousands of message-filled balloons on the easterly winds—all had helped to build a public perception of him that was not easy to deface for those who would now paint him a Kremlin agent.

Nor did the "Communist" charge have credence in insider Washington. Cabinet members, diplomats, congressmen, military officers, press moguls who had for years been inveigled by Drew into dinners or meetings where they had to hear out yet another Pearson scheme for "taking the propaganda initiative against the Communists" might have their own reasons for wanting Pearson out of the way but they could not credit McCarthy's, so the senator's drive suffered from a lack of high-level contagion.

Though Drew had tangled with Francis Cardinal Spellman and feuded with Father Coughlin, he had too often taken up the cause of oppressed Catholics to be a credible object for any wide-based Catholic boycott. His personal intervention had prompted Marshal Tito to free Archbishop Stepinac from prison; Drew was a champion of the cause of Joseph Cardinal Mindszenty; and as the final credential, Pearson had had the good fortune to be attacked by Protestants on the ground that the food distributions of his Friendship trains favored Catholics. And so his fears of hierarchical ostracism proved to be phantoms.

Drew's use of journalism for the waging of politics stripped him of the immunities generally accorded "responsible" reporters, but it also won him the kind of allies that thumbsucking detachment cannot claim.

Lyndon Johnson, that exquisite measurer of the appropriate favor, did not march into the breach for Drew against McCarthy, but he did sit up nights calling the publishers of Texas newspapers to urge them not to drop the Pearson column. Attorney General J. Howard McGrath, like his predecessor Tom Clark, continued to swap advice and confidences with Drew even as the Justice Department was probing him. Chief Justice Fred Vinson, a key confidant of Truman's and a figure of wide influence, kept coming to the Pearsons' for dinner throughout the hostilities, symbolizing in his genial presence the hopeful promise of a bridge over troubled water. Even J. Edgar Hoover continued to evince a surface cordiality; when an investigation came up dry he would tell Drew so through his deputy Lou Nichols, a gesture that boosted our morale more than one might think—for it meant that in the Director's cunning appraisal, Pearson had a fighting chance of surviving relatively intact and of being around to do mutually profitable business with for the next twenty years, as during the previous twenty.

More direct help came from the soulmates of not-forgotten barricades. At the Pentagon, Clayton Fritchey helped to confound the investigators loosed on us by his chiefs. Senator Estes Kefauver, whose investigations were at the moment riding a crest higher than McCarthy's, stood up for us at our moment of need; he publicly lauded Drew as being in large part responsible for launching the Crime Investigating Committee, first by dramatizing the organized-crime issue through exposés I had written, then by helping Kefauver to manipulate through the restive Senate the resolution establishing the committee. Other friends who were scattered through the Senate—J. William Fulbright, Clinton Anderson, Wayne Morse, Brien McMahon, Charles Tobey, Blair Moody, Warren Magnuson, William Benton, Tom Hennings—helped to blunt moves against Drew and cooperated with his anti-McCarthy responses. Immediately after McCarthy's opening blast at Drew, Senator Anderson, a giant of credibility among his colleagues, demolished beyond serious revival the heart of McCarthy's case—that ex-aide Dave Karr was a Communist who passed Kremlin orders to Pearson—by entering in rebuttal the findings of McCarthy's own bible, the Republican House Appropriations Subcommittee Investigations of 1947–48:

> I was a member of a select committee of the House of Representatives, chosen from the members of the Appropriations Committee, to pass upon a great many cases certified by the Dies Committee . . .
> Among those were certain charges against David Karr. The charges were

examined as carefully as possible by the committee. They were examined in great detail by me. So far as I could find, and so far as any other member of the committee was concerned, no member of the committee found anything in the charges which would in any way justify the assertion that David Karr was connected with any Communist front organization, or was himself in any way a Communist.

I began to appreciate that at the core, Drew's defenses were strong because he had lived his life as though in preparation for the contest now upon him. His incessant journeys across the continent during decades when travel was hard, and the spiritual wear he had long endured as perpetual host to visiting press firemen, now firmed up his line. Editors in remote provinces on the verge of canceling the column in order to appease local boycotters held off as they thought about the day Drew Pearson himself had turned up in their bucolic newsroom to talk shop, or the night during that visit to Washington when the rascal had invited them to his house, where they dined with national celebrities. And they would remember how, during every brouhaha over the years, he had always sent them a letter explaining his side of it, and how, every six months or so, another letter would come in reminding them of all the newsbeats the column had scored lately. To hundreds of local newspaper baronets who held a piece of his fate, Drew Pearson was not just a by-line; he had made himself an acquaintance, a long-time presence, and it was harder to cancel a presence. In the end, most of them never did.

For the same reason—the relentlessly vigilant life—he did not lose either of the two libel trials that menaced his future as 1951 opened, just as he had not lost in any of the scores of trials that preceded them. The Howser jury ended an awful silence by ruling in favor of Drew on the best of grounds, that he had told the truth—a finishing blow for Howser. The Gariepy-Coughlin suit was thrown out of court by the judge at the critical juncture; eventually reinstated, it was tried before a jury three years later and again dismissed, this time for good, because of a hung jury, hung 11 to 1 in Drew's favor.

These courtroom victories were in part the fruits of a Draconian career-long regimen that few could or would endure. Drew had learned to live in perpetual anticipation of a court summons, and that anticipation shaped his daily life. In preparing for trials, he would often do the on-the-scene detective work himself because he had found that his celebrity status encouraged more cooperation from prospective witnesses and officials possessing inside information than would be accorded a hired detective. During the months before a high-stakes trial, he was continually leaving Washington late at night for Detroit or Cleveland or the West Coast to seek out the witness or the document that would turn another tide. In time, he moved a libel lawyer right into our offices on a permanent basis, the meticulous John Donovan, whose malleable expertise enlarged rather than restricted Drew's destructive range.

It was Drew's rule to contest every suit and to attend every session of every trial, wherever held, despite the cost in time and amenities. He had once been sued, for the same column, in seventy different jurisdictions by Congressman Martin Sweeney of Ohio, whom Drew had called "the mouthpiece of Father Coughlin" and whose legal costs were being borne by Coughlin devotees. Drew contested the congressman everywhere, but the Honorable Sweeney kept retrying the same suit in different jurisdictions, in an obvious attempt to break Drew financially and immobilize him physically. After thirty-five successive defeats for Sweeney, Drew was still an implacable presence in remote courtrooms, ready for number 36. Sweeney and his backers dropped out —thereafter to serve as living trophies of Pearson's tenacity.

He ran such marathons, and went to bed each night under the overhanging cloud that one loss amid a hundred victories could bankrupt him, as the routine price of carrying the banner. And from this routine he gained an intimate knowledge of what it took to avoid defeat —in the shadings of the written word, in witness-stand demeanor, in the knowledge of those collateral weaknesses in a plaintiff that would reduce him to a vulnerable adversary. He developed a sure instinct as to the maximum that could be gotten away with on offense, and the minimum he must produce on defense. In an era far removed from the protections today given reporters in libel suits, friends and enemies of the seemingly reckless Pearson were alike mystified by his unbroken string of court victories, which sometimes even to me seemed fortuitous deliverances. But they were the end products of a discipline and a craftsmanship that seldom broke the breathless stride of our hyperbolic prose.*

It was likewise defensive ringmanship that thwarted, one by one, the

---

*There was one exception that proved the rule. Drew eventually lost one case, to Norman Littell, but in an amount, $40,000, and at a time, 1953, that were not crucial; to pay Littell, Drew mortgaged his Potomac farm.

official investigations into our various publications of so-called military secrets and "sensitive" stories. When I brought Drew such finds as the MacArthur cables to the Joint Chiefs and the Wake Island Conference transcript, I did so with two fears. One—that in his exposed position he would be afraid to publish and my enterprise would go for naught; two—that when he did decide to publish, as he almost always did, it would turn out to be one outrage too many, the proverbial straw that would cave us in. I came to learn, however, that there was more than heedless courage and combative élan behind each decision to further tempt an already uncoiling fate. Before he would print the unprintable, he would have us contrive lines of defense, comprised in part of observing protocols, in part of luring high officials into advance collaboration and in part of measuring to a fine calibration whether or not a forbidden story about war strategy or peace moves was inherently unprosecutable, in that a trial would force admissions and revelations that the government could not tolerate.

Our story on the true strength of the Chinese forces at the Yalu is a case in point. Senator McCarthy promptly charged that to get such information, we had procured the decoding of a classified document—a criminal offense—and that by publishing it we had allowed the Communists to break our secret code—another criminal offense. Had we been guilty, we would surely have been in desperate trouble, especially since McCarthy was conducting a shadow prosecution on the Senate floor. But we were not guilty. In obtaining the contents of the cable, I had done so in a way that avoided the "procurement of decoding" charge, and before publishing it, we had gotten a Pentagon official to tell us how to go about paraphrasing the actual words of the cable and protecting its date and number so as to eliminate the possibility of code breaking. McCarthy, by the way, revealed, in his careless haste, both the date and the number in his Senate attack on Drew.

So, too, with McCarthy's charge that a story of ours about atomic-energy developments had broken the security laws. Drew had gotten an AEC spokesman to listen over the phone to a reading of our proposed column; not only did the gentleman thus protect us from error and give a form of imprimatur to our publication, but he also told us that some ingredients of our story had already been published in bits and pieces in esoteric journals, so that we were surrounded with defensive bulwarks. Similarly, our publishing of sensitive portions of White House conversations between the military and civilian chiefs was on occasion sanitized in advance by no less a personage than General

Omar Bradley, the Army Chief of Staff. Drew would phone him, say he was about to go to press and prevail on him to listen to our proposed text so as to correct misinterpretations and warn us of unmentionables. Bradley cooperated, in part to make sure that the inevitable was at least accurate, in part because he was contesting with MacArthur for public opinion, and in time two more investigations ran aground on his cooperation, for the government could not very well expose the complicity of its Army high command in order to nab a newspaperman.

We held another high card. So far as I know, neither the FBI nor any of the armed forces intelligence units ever conclusively identified a source of secret information passed to us. In all departments which held a continuing interest for us, we maintained many contacts, most of them routine, and we surrounded our key source with a bewildering array of people who had access to classified information and with whom we made it a point to keep up relations, however cursory. Any of these could be guilty and all would be interviewed and watched during periods of investigation, but only a confession by us or by our actual informant could end the search. We were always able to instill in a source the confidence that we would never under any circumstance betray him and that as long as we both sat tight and avoided traps, he was in the clear. Encapsulated in this confidence, our informants rode out each squall. Only one source, because of his own carelessness, was fired after he aroused the suspicion of Pentagon snoops who wired his office with eavesdropping equipment.

The character of Harry Truman played its part in our escapes. Whatever scruple or wrinkle it was that kept him from winking at our incursions merely because we were the enemy of his enemy also kept him from rigging the prosecuting process against us. He would launch probes with the eagerness of the combative man but he did not pursue them with the follow-up of the vindictive man. His lieutenants at Justice, and at the Pentagon, knew that once his dander was down he went by the book and would take no for an answer.

For a variety of reasons, then, all the probes of us, initiated with such bombast about high treason, came to dead ends, and each report of indictment proved premature. Even our great defeat at McCarthy's hands—the loss of our network broadcast—was resisted in a way that salvaged much. Drew was not too vain to hang on by his fingernails through a succession of temporary sponsors, changed time slots, short-term contracts and slashes in pay, and thus he dragged out his departure from network radio for more than two years. When the end could no longer be held off he set up a syndicated weekly broadcast and peddled it station by station; hundreds of local stations picked it up immediately. True enough, they did not have the instantaneous hitting power of the Sunday-night ABC show, but Drew was content to pop up here and there on the dial at odd hours, unexpected and ubiquitous.

10 · The Maximum Effort

THERE WAS a big difference between the way Drew Pearson chose his enemies and the way he fought them. The first decision was made on the lofty plane of high politics and represented Drew's values; the second, on the amoral level of pragmatics, and exemplified his determination not only to fight the good fight but to try to win it. His first principle of warfare against a maximum opponent, as we have seen, went something like this: It is not enough to challenge him on his strong front (oh, part of the battle must be waged on his own ground, on the theory that the foe must be engaged everywhere and must be repulsed everywhere), but the main hope of inflicting crippling damage lies in skulking around to the rear or the flanks in search of a soft spot. Once the ideological battle lines are drawn, it is impossible to convince, say, 30 million true believers that on the Big Issue, their hero is all wrong, but half of them can be disaffected, and all the right side energized, by the demonstration that he is corrupt.

Thus, though our columns and broadcasts dutifully and interminably pushed up the hill the heavy load of argument that McCarthy's spies were phantoms and his pinks were superannuated, and the even heavier load that Acheson & Company had been vigilant watchdogs and that our foreign policy needed their undistracted attention and morale, our main hope was to bag McCarthy for some offense remote from the charged contentions about Communism. In prospecting for McCarthy's soft underbelly, I sat cheek by jowl with Drew, not only because it would fall to me to do most of the investigating but because I knew Joe from close observation over a three-year period.

The character profile we drew up of McCarthy suggested various soft spots. As he was a compulsive exaggerator, he was likely to have gilded his past in ways that might embarrass him now. As he was a carefree spender, a habitual gambler, an impulsive plunger on market tips, his finances had their desperate hours, indicating scrutiny of the sources of the eleventh-hour loans that bailed him out. A confirmed penchant for corner-cutting cast suspicion on his tax returns and on his steward-ship of the $10 and $1,000 contributions that were pouring in upon him from earnest citizens anxious to help him finance his anti-Communist probes. Laxness as administrator and a good-natured overtolerance as boss made him liable for the inevitable escapades of an overweening and underdisciplined staff.

In a juggernaut like McCarthy these vulnerabilities offered scant encouragement. As convictable offenses go, the raw material here was marginal. He was the kind of senator who took dubious favors but not outright bribes, whose ill-gotten gains were accumulated in small, de-fendable increments rather than in one spectacular raid. His breaches tended toward the ethical, the civil, rather than the criminal. We saw no opening for the kind of one-punch knockout that had felled J. Parnell Thomas, and resigned to another campaign of trench warfare, we systematically beat the bushes along the routes we had marked off.

There was at the outset one consideration of great promise. McCarthy was by nature erratic, unruly and contumacious, traits that did not seem to reduce his effectiveness while he kept in constant motion as accuser at large but which showed him off poorly when pinned down on defense. He did not roll well with hostile questions. When challenged by another senator on the incompatibility of what he said today with what he said yesterday, he was not up to the Senate standard for facile glibness. He would heavy-footedly ignore the ques-tion, then he would begin muttering spooky hints that secrets impor-tant to national survival prevented him from clearing it all up. If the challenge continued, he would lash out wildly against the good faith of his questioner. Drew saw this ungovernability under pressure as McCarthy's Achilles heel.

"He would be a total catastrophe as a defendant," Drew assured me with a bright gleam, "the kind who is brought into court to pay a five-dollar fine for committing a nuisance and winds up in jail for slugging the judge."

As we saw it, then, we were taking part in two overlapping processes —the day-to-day skirmishing to refute and disparage McCarthy, thus to keep public opinion from jelling in his favor, and the long-term thrust-and-maneuver to set turning the wheels and shafts of official investigation that would pin him down and on which, in all his brash recalcitrance, he would likely impale himself. In the first effort we marched in the ranks of a platoon, or at least a squad. Of the second effort, we were the spearhead for years.

This account concentrates on *our* activities, in collaboration with our Senate allies, for it is only a personal recollection, not a general history of the McCarthy era. If it were a general history it would recount the blows struck by others, among them the newsmen—Walter Lippmann, Joseph and Stewart Alsop, Marquis Childs, Doris Fleeson, Martin Agronsky, Elmer Davis, Edward R. Murrow, Quincy Howe, Edward P. Morgan—and the news organizations—the Milwaukee *Journal,* the Madison *Capital Times,* the New York *Times,* the New York *Herald Tribune,* the Washington *Post, Time,* the *New Republic,* the *Nation,* the *Progressive.*

An example of the day-by-day denigration approach was our effort to impugn McCarthy's basic honesty by showing him as a chronic liar about a subject that, unlike the Communist conspiracy, was something on home ground to most American households of that era—the simple facts of a wartime service record.

The broad outline of McCarthy's record—the humble enlistment as private, the rise to captain in the field, long celebrated in Wisconsin and lately in the nation—was impressive and seemed authentic: the photographs of "Tail Gunner Joe," seated behind his rear cockpit machine gun, grinning gamely from under his paraphernalia of flying goggles and cartridge belts; the stoic performance of duty despite a burned, shrapnel-riddled leg; the Distinguished Flying Cross with four air medals; and finally, the letter of commendation from the highest auspice, the great Nimitz. Yet if our assessment of McCarthy held water, he would turn out to be the hoaxer.

I set out, first, to dig up and assemble all that he had claimed or implied about his record, in old political speeches, in interviews, press handouts, radio broadcasts and campaign pamphlets, even in the sparse biographical résumés he had drawn up over the years for routine purposes. All this I checked out against less subjective chronicles—the recollections of the scattered eyewitnesses I could locate, the sometimes conflicting facts in the back-issue morgues of rural Wisconsin newspapers, the official Marine Corps histories of the units McCarthy served in, and ultimately, his individual Marine Corps "jacket," to which I wangled illicit access.

Joe McCarthy could have avoided service in the war; as a state circuit judge, he was draft-exempt. But seven months after Pearl Harbor he began turning up in Wisconsin newspaper offices to modestly announce his decision to enlist, dropping along the way such inspirational homilies as "We can't win the war by letting our neighbors do the fighting" and "I'm more interested in a gun than a commission." According to the local news stories of July 1942, he told the papers three things: he was giving up his judgeship; he was joining up "for the duration"; he was enlisting "as a buck private" or—and here surfaced his unappreciated gift for subtlety—"anything else they want me to be."

As it turned out, all three portions of his announcement were leavened with blarney. He did not give up his judgeship. On the contrary, with his sound agrarian instinct to hold fast to what was his, he went to great lengths to avoid giving it up, persuading the other judges on his circuit to take over his share of the caseload so it would not be seen necessary to replace him. Thus, he held his judgeship in absentia, and it was waiting for him intact when he decided he had soldiered long enough. He did not serve "for the duration." He quit the Marines at the height of the Pacific war, coming home on extended leave in the summer of 1944 and filing for discharge in October 1944 in order to campaign for the political plums that were now open to military heroes, the more open while the other heroes were still away at war. Nor did he enlist as a private; his initial approach to the Marine Corps, I found, was to request a commission, which was immediately granted. That commission as first lieutenant was figuratively in his pocket when he made the rounds of Wisconsin newspaper offices posing as an aspiring candidate for buck private. In fact, he was sworn in to the Marines as a first lieutenant and was wearing his officer's uniform before he ever left Wisconsin to report for duty. I came upon an item in an old Milwaukee *Journal,* a touching tableau of Judge McCarthy's last day on the bench, disposing of one final case while wearing the Marine green and silver bars of a first lieutenant. Yet he clung tenaciously to his up-from-the-ranks epic. In 1944 the returned hero stated in a press release that he had "enlisted as a buck private in the Marine Corps. He was sent to an officers' training school, where he earned a second lieutenant's commission." And in the *Congressional Directory* of 1947, the new senator made this entry: "In June of 1942 applied for enlistment in Marine Corps as buck private and was later commissioned." Not bad. It is a tribute to his political sagacity that he would alter the facts so as to be known as a worthy kind rather than an accredited gentleman.

In the spring of 1943 Lieutenant McCarthy reached the Pacific. In due course the Wisconsin newspapers began to record the dire consequences for the Japanese. He was a one-man band, variously described as intelligence officer, tail gunner and aerial photographer. One story, an Associated Press dispatch, credited McCarthy with having fired more rounds of ammunition in one day—4,700—than any other soldier in the war. Another one heralded him and his squadron establishing the record for the number of missions flown in one day. The Wisconsin *State Journal* carried an account by McCarthy which, in a self-deprecating, somebody's-got-to-do-it way, described how, distressed by our inadequate high-level photography of gun positions, he volunteered for a hazardous mission over "the Jap strong points" and brought back better pictures. On November 15, 1943, the Appleton *Post Crescent* announced that their hometown hero "was wounded in one of the actions."

After McCarthy returned to the home hustings, more touches were modestly added to the portrait, a graceful admission of gallantry here, a lament there for comrades who fell beside him, a not-quite-disguised limp over yonder. In the wake of his personal appearances, two war-wound stories spread (years later I encountered them frequently in Wisconsin)—one, that he had been wounded by exploding shrapnel; the other, that he had hurt his leg when a Marine bomber, coming in for a landing, ground-looped and burned. In a speech in Badger Village, Wisconsin, he had revealed that "I carry ten pounds of shrapnel in this leg," a part of the legend that was soon retired, perhaps when McCarthy learned that his claim was a biological impossibility.

A later version was, "I had a leg badly smashed up, burned and broken. In fact, I got a citation from Nimitz based on that. Now, I don't claim that I'm a hero, you understand. I think there's nothing wonderful about being injured."

For a flier, the prerequisite for hero status was accumulating "missions," and the Tail Gunner Joe saga was fueled by steadily accelerating totals. I came across one of his campaign leaflets of 1944 which said that McCarthy "participated in 14 dive-bombing missions over Japanese positions." By 1951 he recalled a larger number: "I was on 30 dive-bombing missions, plus liaison missions." I noted a similar progression in other McCarthy accounts. In his biographical entry in the 1948 *Congressional Directory,* he wrote: "Had 17 official missions in the South Pacific." Later, in applying for a medal, he claimed participation in "32 air missions." But whatever the version, there were more than enough missions to sustain the legend.

No strain of the heroic was absent from the McCarthy odyssey. In an ABC radio broadcast after he became a senator, he told a national audience of how, after smiting the Jap by day, he would at night struggle with the greater burden of writing to the mothers and wives of his fallen comrades. He recalled "the rough days when we lost a number of our pilots and gunners" such as the time of "our first dive and torpedo bombing attack upon the Jap airfields at Rabaul. My task at night was to write home to the young wives, to the young mothers, with the hope that we might be able to make the blow fall less heavily." On the night of the first Rabaul raid "a great number of letters had to be written . . . in my dugout."

Such was the record I assembled in early 1951, and which I now sought to demolish. On the face of it, the only obvious soft spots were the discrepancies: Was he an intelligence officer or a rear gunner or a photographer? Was he wounded by shrapnel or by a crash? Were there fourteen dive-bombing missions or thirty? But as to the essential validity of McCarthy's account, the official citation of Admiral Nimitz seemed to leave no doubt.

> For meritorious and efficient performance of duty as an observer and rear gunner of a dive bomber attached to a Marine scout bombing squadron operating in the Solomon Islands area from September 1 to December 31, 1943. He participated in a large number of combat missions, and in addition to his regular duties, acted as aerial photographer. He obtained excellent photographs of enemy gun positions, despite intense anti-aircraft fire, thereby gaining valuable information which contributed materially to the success of subsequent strikes in the area. Although suffering from a severe leg injury, he refused to be hospitalized and continued to carry out his duties as an intelligence officer in a highly efficient manner. His courageous devotion to duty was in keeping with the highest traditions of the naval service.

Yet even the Nimitz citation ingeniously straddled that question of discrepancies by its generality, by the absence of hard facts about when, where and how many. More suspect still, the same note of vagueness permeated the supporting document on which the Nimitz citation was based—a recommendation, passed upward through channels, from McCarthy's immediate superior, Major E. E. Munn. For example: "On 22 June 1943, Captain McCarthy suffered a broken and burned foot and leg. He, however, refused to be hospitalized and continued doing an excellent job as intelligence officer, working on crutches."

But how and where and under what circumstances did this citation-winning wound take place? One specific in Munn's account, the date, provided the means for reconstructing the event with the help of naval shipping records, the official Marine Corps account of McCarthy's unit, and the eyewitnesses they led me to. The date of McCarthy's injury turned out to be some ten weeks before his unit first saw action against the enemy. On June 22, 1943, McCarthy and members of his squadron were crossing the equator aboard the Navy's seaplane tender *Chandeleur,* en route from Pearl Harbor to the island of Espíritu Santo. The war zone was hundreds of miles away. McCarthy was listed as an "officer passenger." Years later, shipmates still remembered his injury because of the bizarre circumstances attending it.

In honor of the equator-crossing, there was a "shellback" ceremony for the hazing of first-timers. McCarthy, always a lion for horseplay, was memorable in his shaved, stained head, clad in pajamas and bare feet. Toward the end of his initiation, recalled one participant, McCarthy "was going down a ladder with a bucket fastened to his foot when he slipped . . . he fell backward injuring his foot. I watched them put a cast on his foot."

McCarthy's assignment was that of an intelligence officer, handling the paperwork for a squadron of pilots, his main task being to debrief returning fliers on what they had done or seen. It was the kind of plodding desk work necessary for the waging of modern wars, but it offered thin opportunity for heroics. For the Outagamie County dramatist, however, it served well enough. By going along on occasional flights as an observer, by getting his picture taken in combat gear, and by exploiting the native genius for embroidery and news management that would one day convulse a nation, he easily floated the image of Tail Gunner Joe.

The official Marine Corps history helped in the dismantling of that image. The islands McCarthy served on were not the hurricane centers of the war portrayed in his clippings. Each had been taken from the Japanese and "pacified" months before he arrived. The total fatalities suffered by his unit were five officers and two enlisted men—not in a single raid on Rabaul ("a great number of letters had to be written"), not in the year McCarthy was with Squadron 235, but in the entire war. Nor did McCarthy have to "struggle" over letters "in my dugout." He was always housed aboveground, so safe from enemy action that he sought to bring attention to his tent and the adjacent vehicles by plastering them with large placards proclaiming in bold letters: McCARTHY FOR U.S. SENATOR.

The official accounts were helpful to me both in what they said and on what they kept silent. For instance, their failure to substantiate the feats of McCarthy and his squadron which I had read about in Wisconsin newspapers raised a red flag. Eventually the accounts of Marines who served with McCarthy revealed that they were spoofs. The 4,700 rounds of ammunition were fired by McCarthy as a lark, at foliage, causing his fellows to put up a huge sign: SAVE OUR COCONUT TREES. SEND McCARTHY BACK TO WISCONSIN.

The record-breaking number of missions for a single day was also a stunt gotten up to relieve the boredom of "milk run" bombings of abandoned Japanese airfields to keep them unusable. It was on safe missions such as these that desk officers like McCarthy were permitted to go along and sit in the gunner's seat.

Our debunking of the McCarthy military saga was carried on through a flurry of network broadcasts in June and July 1951 and in the column. The impact must have been disturbing to the McCarthy forces, for their trusty spokesman, Republican Senator Harry Cain of Washington, took the Senate floor, the Nimitz citation in hand, to protest the misuse of the national airwaves to poison the minds of 20 or 30 million listeners at a clip with calumnies that were difficult for the maligned hero to defend against. Who did the nation want to believe? Admiral Nimitz and Major Munn or the well-known liar, Pearson?

Other reporters were on the trail of the elusive tail gunner. I remember a highly effective series in the New York *Post* by Oliver Pilat and William Shannon, published a month or two after Drew's radio series, which expanded on our findings. Among other things, Pilat and Shannon got McCarthy to extend his area of vulnerability by telling them, in extricating himself from the shrapnel-wound hoax, that he had been wounded "in a plane crash on a runway at Guadalcanal."

Both sides to the dispute were handicapped by the lack of conclusive proof, and a race was on between them to get it. McCarthy held the advantage in that only the Navy and its Marine Corps, to which he had become a valuable property, had the kind of exact records that could prove him an impostor, and they were sitting tight on those records, in accordance with the law. They had spoken through the Nimitz citation and that was their official word. But there were questions that a mere citation could not indefinitely quiet. If McCarthy was wounded, then of course he had a Purple Heart. Where was it? If he had been a hotshot gunner, how many Jap planes and installations was he credited with destroying? If he had flown all those dangerous missions, where was his Distinguished Flying Cross? Where were his Air Medals?

With the quiet pride of the bona-fide hero, McCarthy scorned to be drawn into vulgar discussions of the specifics of his exploits, and while he played Gary Cooper playing Sergeant York, both sides scrambled undignifiedly in a behind-the-scenes plunge toward vindication. I knew that the answers to those questions were lying snug in McCarthy's Marine Corps service record, and I was putting the squeeze on my Leatherneck sources to pry a look at it. Concurrently McCarthy was putting his squeeze on the military politicians to, for God's sake, get up those medals that would snuff out the skeptics.

McCarthy won the first lap. In November 1952, during the interregnum between the thrown-out Democrats and the incoming Republicans, the Navy came through with the Distinguished Flying Cross and four Air Medals. It was a grand coup and I had to tip my schemer's cap to him. McCarthy moved from platform to platform amid the reinvigorated strains of the "Marine Corps Hymn" while we besmirchers and mud-spatterers were consigned to the scorn of all right-thinking Americans.

But not for long. A few weeks after the bestowing of medals, I finally got an hour alone with McCarthy's "jacket." The contents were all we had hoped for, vindicating our past stories and giving us new ones. McCarthy had requested a Purple Heart and been refused because he had never been wounded, his only injury having been the foot-in-the-bucket affair. His official job was at a desk, throughout his tour. There were no Japanese planes shot down or installations shot up by the Terror of the Skies. The dive-bombing missions he had claimed ("I was on 30 dive-bombing missions") were unrecorded; instead, the file noted that he had gone along as an observer on some extracurricular convoy cover duty. His initial application for the Distinguished Flying Cross in 1944—for which the flying of twenty missions automatically qualified—was rejected because the record did not support his "statement as an officer and a gentleman" that he had flown thirty-two air missions. His successful application later was pushed through on the higher-up level and was approved by an Assistant Secretary of the Navy whose civilian job was with the Chicago *Tribune*'s law firm.

In response to our charges of hoax, no official explanation for the flip-flop, no validating details about newly discovered missions, was forthcoming from the Navy, leaving us in possession of the field. When Marine Corps security officers launched a probe of our ability to obtain and publish details from McCarthy's service record—a confidential file —they did us a favor, for it was an official admission that we had indeed gotten hold of the record and that what we had printed was the real thing.

On our second track, progress came harder. Drew had long been trying to provoke official probes of McCarthy into his finances and other traditional areas of criminal investigation. Such an investigation —with power to subpoena records and put witnesses under oath—was essential if several inquiries we had begun were to be carried through to a conclusion and to a publicly accepted verdict.

It was our faith that once an official probe got started, however feeble, however hobbled and diluted by politics, it slowly took on a life of its own. Once it was under way, we were confident we could get inside of it. Official investigators probing stories we had started would inevitably come to us for our initial cache of information; we would develop a cooperative relationship with them, and the exchange of information would continue, or the time would come when the investigation required defense from its enemies outside, or from superiors inside, and there would be need for well-placed leaks to blast away obstructions. That, anyway, was our scenario.

Drew intrigued persistently but vainly for an Internal Revenue probe that would flesh out our stories of McCarthy tax-finagling. A forgery prosecution would do nicely; when a presumed FBI document McCarthy was using to clinch his charges against State Department employee Edward Posniak turned out to be a fake, I went to Attorney General J. Howard McGrath to open up a probe into McCarthy's possible complicity. "We don't want to make a martyr out of McCarthy," was McGrath's answer. Nor would the armed forces heed our advice to lay off us for a while and begin probing *McCarthy's* purloining of government secrets.

The Truman Administration was reluctant to proceed legally against McCarthy because it would look like political retaliation, and when the Eisenhower regime came in, it would not pursue McCarthy because he was a prime GOP asset and because to move against him would detonate an intraparty civil war.

The United States Senate, cowed though it was by McCarthy after 1950, offered greater hope in that it was a decentralized, multi-celled body of great diversity, possessed of a dozen investigative units, each accountable to itself. We had a number of covert allies there, and to them we shuttled with our investigatory produce.

From the first months of McCarthy's crusade, our columns and broadcasts accused him, with slowly accumulating detail, of three distinct lines of shady financial conduct that could not, we hoped, be explained away by patriotic flummery.

We charged that he had misused his office to act as an errand boy for the Pepsi-Cola Company (at a time when government allocations of scarce sugar could make or break a bottler); that he had introduced legislation tailored to Pepsi's needs while accepting various favors from company figures; that when a Wisconsin bank put the pressure on him for a long-overdue debt, the sugar lobby bailed Joe out, in the person of Russell Arundel, Washington sugar lobbyist and owner of Pepsi-Cola bottling plants, who co-signed a $20,000 note for McCarthy.

We made various charges of income-tax finagling, pointing out, for example, that "eight of McCarthy's past twelve income tax returns have been found in error. In each case the error was in McCarthy's favor."

We periodically called attention to marvels in McCarthy's personal finances and mysteries in the sources of his income. For example, upon his election to the U.S. Senate he owed $170,000 to the Appleton State Bank but wiped that debt out after a few years in the Senate on an annual salary of $12,500. Indeed, his bank account was continually being refurbished from unknown sources; in four years as a senator he had deposited $19,000 in cash and $40,000 in checks—all from unidentified sources, while his assistant, Ray Kiermas, was depositing another $29,000 in cash.

And we exposed a classic conflict-of-interest relationship between McCarthy and the Lustron Corporation, a government-bankrolled builder of prefabricated houses. Before he took up anti-Communism,

McCarthy's major field in the Senate was housing, a key domestic concern in that postwar period of acute shortages. As a housing legislator, McCarthy's main thrust was against government-sponsored public housing and for government loans to commercial-housing developers. The most conspicuous of these was Lustron, which proposed to mass-produce prefabricated aluminum houses and had obtained a $37.5 million government loan to do so. As acting chairman of the Senate-House Joint Housing Committee, McCarthy crisscrossed the country whooping it up for prefabricated houses. One day, during the time of our friendship, he asked me to give him a critique of a booklet he was working up and hoped to sell about prefabricated homes; later he presented me with a different version, and I learned that several hands had been at work on the copy—Senate aides, agency employees and a writer hired by Lustron. Soon thereafter McCarthy made his literary debut as the author of a pamphlet called "A Dollar's Worth of Housing for Every Dollar Spent." Several months later, in my capacity as an investigator of McCarthy, I disinterred the matter, and the result was the following story, which, launched in our column on April 19, 1950, was to have a long run:

By 1948 Lustron, fast running out of the $37.5 million in government funds, was starting to slide down the path to bankruptcy and default. It was also trying to ward off two congressional investigations of its activities, one by the Joint Housing Committee, of which McCarthy was the Senate boss, another by the Senate Investigating Committee, of which he was a member. As an investigator and overseer of Lustron, McCarthy was obligated to shun any personal involvement with the company. Yet he would go to the race track with Lustron President Carl Strandlund, and when McCarthy's horse lost, the broke senator would write checks which the accommodating Strandlund honored with ready cash. As the relationship ripened, McCarthy approached Strandlund with the proposal that Lustron pay him a $10,000 fee for a favorable housing pamphlet.

I got the McCarthy-Strandlund connection into the public record by happenstance. I learned one morning that Strandlund was appearing at a hearing where Senator William Fulbright would preside. I caught up with Fulbright in the corridor as he was heading toward the hearing room. Breathlessly I related what I knew about McCarthy's cozy relationship with the housing tycoon, including the race-track reports. The scholarly Fulbright, whom McCarthy deprecatingly called "Senator Halfbright," strode into the room, slumped behind the rostrum and peered at Strandlund's prepared text through Ben Franklin glasses resting on the end of his nose. He frowned as Strandlund read his testimony; then, in his nasal drawl, Fulbright began asking questions that staggered the man from Lustron. Before Strandund left the hearing room, he had confirmed under oath that he had torn up McCarthy's race-track checks.

McCarthy kept the committee he controlled off Lustron's back, but the Senate Investigating Committee proceeded. One week after it opened its probe of Lustron, that company gave McCarthy its check for $10,000. This represented $1.43 per word for the neophyte author, which, as we were fond of pointing out, was a world's record, 43 cents higher than the previous record for literary heavyweights set by Winston Churchill when he sold his war memoirs. McCarthy, though he later claimed to have divided up the $10,000 among the actual writers, pocketed it and duly entered it on his income-tax return. Lustron President Carl Strandlund considered it a good deal for his corporation, later declaring he had "purchased the name" of Senator McCarthy. "McCarthy named the price," Strandlund said, "but the price was worth it."

Our prospects for a full-fledged investigation narrowed down to one —the Senate Committee on Rules and Administration. One of its standard tasks was to inquire into irregularities in the elections of its members, and in that capacity, one of its subcommittees had routinely probed the notorious Maryland Senate campaign of 1950, in which the four-term dreadnaught Millard Tydings had been torpedoed by an elegant and euphonic cipher, John Marshall Butler. The Butler campaign had been quarterbacked by Joe McCarthy, and its symbol was a composite photograph, distributed in the hundreds of thousands, that had been faked to make Tydings appear in a cooperative pose with Earl Browder, head of the Communist Party, U.S.A. The subcommittee was critical of McCarthy's tactics in Maryland but was too timid to recommend action against him. But committees that are trying to get rid of hot potatoes invariably, in their embarrassment, create an opening for further mischief; the subcommittee covered its retreat by saying to its parent Rules and Administration Committee, in effect, "Here is what we found out, perhaps you would like to do something about it."

It was only an exculpatory gesture, but Drew saw it as a springboard, and he exhorted Senate friends to take up the subcommittee's suggestion, pressing upon them the potential of our own published and unpublished investigations of McCarthy which, for want of subpoena power, lay inviting but unconsummated. Two members of the Rules Committee were particularly thick with Drew: William Benton of Connecticut, a fiesty millionaire gadfly, and Thomas Hennings of Missouri, a flawed but masterful Senate heavyweight.

Benton seemed to Drew ideally cast as the bell ringer summoning the Senate to its duty. He was venturesome; he was a propagandist, trained in the school of Madison Avenue advertising; he had behind him several successful careers, in business, education and government; and he had courage, both the natural kind and the kind that is nourished by constant success and by the awareness that one has the wealth and career options to see him through adversity. Hennings, a deep-voiced, border-state Democrat with black hair parted in the middle and a foot in both the liberal and conservative camps of his party, was an astute and popular member of the Senate establishment, ideally equipped to shepherd an investigation through its back rooms.

I cannot, at this remove, claim baldly that Drew caused Benton's decision to demand a broad probe of McCarthy, with a view to his being expelled from the Senate. I do know that Drew tried to cause it and that we provided most of the effective investigative material used in the indictment of McCarthy which Benton presented to the Senate in support of his expulsion resolution. Benton's proposed bill of particulars, as he first discussed it with Drew, centered on a series of McCarthy lies on the Senate floor by which he had committed the offense of misleading his colleagues. Drew thought this approach a bit quaint. Mendacity, deceit and exaggeration are integral and traditional components of a senator's armaments and prerogatives; they are even protected by the Constitution. Benton agreed to broaden his indictment to include the financial irregularities we had been trumpeting and welcomed our help in preparing the specifications.

Most members of the Committee on Rules and Administration were aghast at Benton's proposal to embroil them in a brawl with McCarthy. The fine hand of Tom Hennings steered the committee as it backed into an investigation by stages, the first step being to authorize a preliminary staff inquiry into Benton's charges. To some anti-McCarthyites, this seemed an uninspiring gesture, but Drew was satisfied; he saw the staff inquiry as a beachhead that could steadily be widened.

So it turned out. At the outset, the chairman of the subcommittee to which the Benton resolution was referred, Iowa Democrat Guy

Gillette, said he had "no plans for hearings or any other action"; a New York *Times* headline summarized the reactions of other subcommittee members: DEAD END AWAITS DRIVE ON MCCARTHY.

But our ally Tom Hennings was one of the five subcommittee members; imperceptibly he nudged the thing along, and the inner momentum of fact-gathering asserted itself, and lo, an official investigation of Joe McCarthy's finances slowly groped to its feet, a spavined one, to be sure, but an investigation.

McCarthy was as contumacious of the "Gillette Committee" as we had prophesied, refusing to appear before it and abusing its members in public letters to Chairman Gillette:

> Frankly, Guy, I have not and do not intend to even read, much less answer, Benton's smear attack. I am sure you realize that the Benton type of material can be found in the *Daily Worker* almost any day of the week and will continue to flow from the mouths and pens of the camp followers as long as I continue my fight against the Communists in government.

And again:

> As I have previously stated, you and every member of your subcommittee who is responsible for spending vast amounts of money to hire investigators, pay their traveling expenses, etc. . . . is just as dishonest as though he or she picked the pockets of the taxpayers and turned the loot over to the Democratic National Committee.

What we had not fully anticipated was that the fear of McCarthy was stronger in the Senate than the inner pulls of its tradition and the automation of the machinery erected on that tradition. The Senate is a collection of inordinate egos and aggressive capacities that is held together as a cohesive institution by a web of rules, protocols and courtesies which protects the sensitivity and turf of each ego and distributes its powers and prerogatives on the least divisive and most impersonal basis that can be devised—seniority. It is an institution that in normal times eviscerates the abrasive member through ostracism and crushes the rebellious one through arraignment and humiliation. When McCarthy refused to appear, when he called the subcommittee's ranking Republican, Senator Robert Hendrickson of New Jersey, "a living miracle, born without brains and guts," when he patronized Gillette and accused Hennings of harboring Communist sympathizers in his law firm, he invited swift destruction. But the Senate's egos are political egos, which is to say that they are cowardly in all that affects the next election; and so the senators chafed silently under McCarthy's abrasions and tolerated his refusal to submit.

Hennings could do no more than to sustain the subcommittee in half-life and wait for the Senate to recover its native bile. We tried to hurry the process of shame-building, sometimes by indicting the subcommittee's timidity, sometimes by republishing our store of McCarthy stories, now fleshed out from our collaborations with the subcommittee staff, to show the public what was being sat on.

For instance, we reported that $10,000 contributed to Senator McCarthy by Mrs. Alvin Bentley and her congressman husband "to fight Communism" had been unilaterally treated by McCarthy as a personal loan and used to speculate on soybean futures. When Mrs. Bentley disappeared while subcommittee investigators were searching for her, we revealed that she had high-tailed it to the Bahamas under an assumed name, in the company of McCarthy helper Harvey Matusow, where she was out of subpoena reach.

And we reported on McCarthy's use of dummy stand-ins to conceal his financial activities. These dummies included his brother William and his sister-in-law Julia. In our column of October 20, 1952, we traced the outline of one intrafamily transaction:

> On August 26, 1948 . . . a commodity credit account was opened with Dan F. Rice and Company, Chicago grain traders, in the name of William P. McCarthy. Though in his brother's name, the $10,000 used to open the account actually came from Ray Kiermas (McCarthy's aide) to the extent of $6,223.72, while the balance was supplied by a draft on the Appleton State Bank which suddenly seems to have lost its records and cannot now identify the source of this money.
>
> Three years later, on March 8, 1951, the account with D. F. Rice was closed out, a check for $7,159 going to William P. McCarthy. This check was cashed, and the cash was deposited ten days later back with the same D. F. Rice Co.
>
> This time, however, the trading account was in the name of Julia Connelly, the maiden name of William McCarthy's wife.
>
> In 1951, the date when the commodity account was closed out and then re-established under Julia Connelly's name, it so happened that the Senator from Wisconsin was beginning to come under the scrutiny of his fellow senators for extracurricular conduct.

Little wonder, went our inevitable refrain, that this senator, who set himself up in judgment over his fellow-men, refused to testify about his own affairs.

There was one bizarre event that is worth recording. I had been dividing my energies between two main investigations: I had followed McCarthy's trail all the way to the catwalks and crossroads of his native Wisconsin, and I had pursued the bosses of organized crime into the back alleys and night clubs of New York City. In the Big Apple, I asked questions about Frank Costello, the kingpin of the underworld, a dapper mobster who was always manicured, pressed and pomaded, and who wore expensive suits adorned with an immaculate white breast-pocket handkerchief bearing his name emblazoned in red. He was concerned about his image and sent a public relations man to intercept me and educate me on his finer qualities.

The next day Costello's man telephoned me from Miami and announced that he had an important matter to discuss with me; he asked whether I would see him if he caught the next available plane to Washington. A meeting was arranged in a dark corner of a Washington bistro, and the underworld messenger appeared mysteriously a few hours later. He was aware, he told me, that I had been investigating one of Costello's minor political contacts. Would I be willing to drop the investigation in return for evidence that the mob had contributed heavily to Senator McCarthy's past campaigns? It was true that I had been investigating Costello's ally, but I had uncovered nothing of consequence. Since I would be giving up nothing, I agreed to the deal. Costello's man gave me elaborate directions where to find Milwaukee's rackets boss; I was assured he would give me the evidence linking McCarthy to the underworld.

I flew to Milwaukee and followed the directions, which led me unerringly to the crime lord's lair. He did not seem surprised to see me; indeed, I had the impression he was expecting me. Yet he denied any knowledge of the arrangements that had brought me to him, and with a shrug of his shoulders, disclaimed possessing any evidence of underworld contributions to McCarthy. The episode left me quite bewildered. It seemed unlikely that Costello's man would go to such lengths just to send me on a wild-goose chase; I suspected that something had gone sour after I was already on my way to Milwaukee. But I never heard anything more of the incriminating evidence, if it ever existed, against McCarthy.

In early 1952, with the subcommittee investigation becalmed, I rushed to conclusion a book I had been writing off and on for more than a year, with the collaboration of Wisconsin reporter Ronald W. May. It was called *McCarthy: The Man, the Senator, the "Ism,"* and was aimed at providing the scattered anti-McCarthy movement with a complete arsenal under one cover. The scheme of the book was to bring together all the verifiable offenses in the McCarthy record in chronological order: the early promise, the ruthless ambition, the switched allegiances, the trampled friends, the "quickie divorces," the tax scams, the faked war record, the conflicts of interest, the shady backers, the false charges, the corrupt pattern. The format was brief chapters, of which there were fifty-five. I had hoped to bring out the book on the heels of the Senate investigation, thus to have some of our most damaging accusations supported by official findings, but the foundering of that probe caused us to rush publication as a part of the effort to keep it alive.

For a while our literary venture seemed doomed. Publisher after publisher rejected it, rejections the more dampening to the ego of a fledgling author because McCarthy was so obviously a timely subject; no book on him had yet appeared though he had been the most controversial figure in the land for more than two years. Drew salved my spirits, blaming the fear of the big publishers to tangle with a McCarthy who was on the rise and who had been not unsuccessful at organizing reprisals.

Finally we got an acceptance from a little-known house, Beacon Press of Boston. The caution with which even these doughty souls approached our opus was advertised in a rather embarrassing "Announcement" on the jacket of each book:

> This book has been rigorously checked for factual accuracy. If, in spite of these precautions, substantive errors in statements of fact slip by, then Beacon in co-operation with the authors, upon the receipt of documentation, will promptly issue a supplement for all copies of the book printed. These will be distributed free of charge. Take this coupon to your bookseller or mail to the Editors of the Beacon Press, 25 Beacon St., Boston 8, Mass. Please print name and address below, and enclose self-addressed envelope.

Beacon Press was enterprising but small, lacking the promotional and distributive resources of the great houses; our book's chance of getting any attention was dependent on the major reviews, if indeed there were to be any. We awaited their appearance with not a little anxiety, feeling, as authors tend to do, that something more than a book's success was riding on them. They began to appear:

> The first full-length book on McCarthy . . . with many details which are known to few . . . the authors provide, for the first time, an understanding of the compulsions that move this strange man . . .—*Saturday Review*

> This is the first book to attempt to tell the story of McCarthyism in a detailed, accurate manner . . . an amazingly successful book and just about as valuable as any that is likely to be published in this era of decision . . . It is clear that any later and more definitive account will owe a tremendous debt to this pioneer work.—*New York Herald Tribune Book Review*

> By what appears to be a vast amount of legwork with many persons . . . they have filled out the picture. There are still too many people who close their eyes to the problem of McCarthy and McCarthyism . . . This book will help to make it plainer.—*New York Times Book Review*

> Two newsmen . . . have done a devastating piece of work . . . They have taken most of the major McCarthy lies—lies in fact and lies in implications—and have given the painstaking, space-consuming, point by point explanation of what was the truth in the matter. They have taken the major episodes in the McCarthy story . . . and have demonstrated in each case the same pattern of deliberate deceit fattening on its own virulence . . . Those who fancy themselves experts on McCarthy are in for a surprise . . . Anderson and May have dug up much more documentation on each incident than was generally known to exist . . .—Washington *Post*

The reviews hurried the book to the best-seller lists, and I think it is fair to say that it became the basic factual reference for the journalistic counteroffensive against McCarthyism, adding its mite to the slow-building public pressure on the Senate and the Executive to curb McCarthy.*

But if our side was registering victories in "the battle for men's minds," they were the nonmeasurable kind whose effect had to be taken on faith; it was McCarthy who continued to nail up the visible scalps. Instead of McCarthy being on the defensive, it was the investigating committee that trembled behind sandbags, while its captains,

---

*Almost twenty years later, when Fred J. Cook published his exhaustive history, entitled *The Nightmare Decade* (Random House, 1971), containing 33 pages of credits, the Anderson-May book, written on the run before the McCarthy era was half over, was still the most referenced volume.

one by one, defected. Nine times the Gillette committee politely requested McCarthy to appear before it to respond to its staff's findings; nine times he refused. He did appear once, but only to present charges of his own against his accuser, Benton, "the mental midget from Connecticut," to which the committee gravely agreed to give equal scrutiny. Intermittently, McCarthy raked the membership with disdainful grapeshot, giving each of his appointed judges food for late-night self-examination: were they really all that interested in McCarthy, so interested that they were willing to risk waging their next election campaign against a barrage of McCarthy charges that they were chore boys for the Kremlin? Almost without exception, they were not. Margaret Chase Smith, the distinguished Republican senator from Maine, against whom McCarthy was planning to run a primary opponent, left the committee, making room for a McCarthy stalwart, Herman Welker of Idaho. When the opportune time for folding up the committee arrived, Welker resigned too. Then Chairman Gillette resigned, ending a year of feeble futility. Then Mike Monroney of Oklahoma resigned, on grounds that his absence on a European tour of indeterminable length would keep him from being a productive member. Hennings of Missouri, now the chairman, who had been linked to the Communists by McCarthy and who had in his closet the skeleton of alcoholism waiting for McCarthy to rattle, found the mounting pressure too great, and ending a years-long perch atop the wagon, fell off with a terrible thud.

The fifth and last member, Robert Hendrickson of New Jersey, the committee's senior Republican, submitted to McCarthy's demand that he, too, resign, and the end was in sight. But then McCarthy wrapped a congratulatory arm around him in the Senate cloakroom and chortled in his ear, "You are doing the right thing by resigning, Bob. It's the only thing to do with your prejudice." Hendrickson glimpsed the depth of his own ignominy and withdrew his resignation, but he lingered on a shell-shocked case, his ear ever cocked for New Jersey rumblings from pro-McCarthy Republicans, and little could be expected from him. When, in November, Benton himself was beaten for re-election, with McCarthy assisting, and the Republicans won enough seats nationwide to take over the Senate from the Democrats, the situation seemed in irretrievable shambles.

Drew believed that no situation is entirely hopeless. In the eight weeks of life left to the expiring Democratic Senate, a way must be found to revive if not the subcommittee, then enough of its members to file a final report. We knew what the report would say if the committee remnant could muster the resolve to pass it, for we had seen a working draft; at the heart of it were the stories we had been pounding away at in the column, verified and refined.

To Drew, the adoption of such a report assumed monumental importance. Both of his preassumptions about the probe had proved true: the staff investigation of McCarthy's finances, hobbled though it was by the clay feet of the senators, had yielded many a discrediting nugget; and McCarthy's response to the Gillette committee—the agent of the Senate—had been one of concealment and contempt, a calculated rebellion which the Senate in its normal tenor would not brook. If the probe now petered out without a conclusion, all this—the offenses and the rebellion—could be washed away, but if the subcommittee remnant filed a report that even remotely reflected the facts in its files, that report would have a continuing life, would become official truth that must, at the least, gain a seeping recognition, would suspend above the Senate a living, unredressed provocation that must be brought to a reckoning if the institution was to remain what it had been.

Senator Carl Hayden of Arizona, chairman of the parent Rules and Administration Committee, provided the technical possibility for resurrecting the Gillette unit by appointing himself to it, thus giving it a quorum for the transaction of business. But Hendrickson, the indispensable Republican, dallied in New Jersey, under pressure from national and local GOP leaders to let the Democratic assault on McCarthy die; and Hennings, who alone was equipped—by virtue of a powerful, persuasive personality and an intricate mastery of the eighteen-month investigation—to keep Hendrickson in line through cozening, cajoling and bargaining, was nowhere to be found.

As in other cases when there was a key vote to be taken and some salvageable Solons to be firmed up, Drew enthusiastically donned his lobbyist's hat. Each day he would confer with one or another senator, and he assigned to me about two dozen senators to lobby. I disliked this role that was so unseemly for a reporter, and he would spur me on each night by reporting items that demonstrated progress in the campaign: Senator Hayden was sacrificing his vacation and was flying back from Arizona to try to get the old Gillette unit on its feet; Senator Irving Ives, the New York Republican, had promised Drew to ride herd on his friend Hendrickson; so had Senator Charles Tobey, the New Hampshire Republican; so had Senator Fulbright, the Arkansas Democrat; as for Hennings, the resource-laden Benton was assisting Drew in a discreet search.

Hennings' trail had grown cold in Lincoln, Nebraska, according to his wife, Elizabeth, with whom Drew kept in close touch. In mid-November, Benton called Drew to say that he had located Hennings in New York; after working his way across Manhattan from bar to bar, Hennings had collapsed in a room at the Plaza Hotel. Drew called Elizabeth Hennings with the news and rearranged his schedule in order to fly to New York and take the gifted prodigal into custody. But just before he left, Elizabeth Hennings called to say that Tom had just arrived home, in a dreadful heap, and would be bedridden for days to come.

There was a considerable amount of whistling past the graveyard in a column Drew published on November 17, 1952:

> Though Senator Welker of Idaho and Gillette of Iowa have been induced to resign from the committee, another Republican, Senator Bob Hendrickson, despite considerable pressure, has stuck to his. guns.
>
> Senator Mike Monroney of Oklahoma, a Democratic committee member, left for Europe without even telling colleagues, but Senator Tom Hennings of Missouri, chairman of the probe, and Hendrickson seemed determined to go through with it.

For six weeks, while the sands ran out on the Eighty-second Congress, Chairman Hennings remained in the throes of an epic bender. Again and again he failed to show up for meetings arranged by Hayden at which the few unresolved sections of the report were to be agreed upon. Christmas came and went and suddenly there were only a few days left before the expiration of Democratic control of the committees.

Through it all, Drew had kept abreast of Hennings' situation through Mrs. Hennings. How could he exert just enough pressure on his volatile friend without overdoing it and blowing the game altogether? He had helped to orchestrate a surveillance-and-encouragement operation manned by mutual friends. When its successes, heralded to me by Drew, proved illusory, Drew had shifted to hardball, warning Hennings that where momentous matters hung in the balance, a friend's patience was not inexhaustible and that Hennings' protectors in the press would not forever keep silent about a vice that resulted in such chronic neglect of duty. On the day after Christmas, Drew set aside his usual nocturnal working schedule and took up position at the senator's house.

It was Hennings' inclination in this period to rouse himself in the late December afternoons, as darkness was falling outside, dress fastidiously in one of those funereal, near-black ensembles he affected in winter (he was partial to all white in summer) and quietly tiptoe down the stairway with a view to slipping out for a night's tour of his haunts. One can imagine his distress, of a dusk, when he reached the bottom of the stairs to find the abstemious Pearson camped in his foyer, warm with solicitous inquiries about his health, bright with wholesome suggestions for the evening—dinner together, a movie or perhaps a long-overdue chat, and then early to bed. Hennings, a renowned master of extrication, would be half launched on an ingenious improvisation on how he'd just love to but couldn't possibly tonight, all the while edging toward the door, when wife Elizabeth would sweep in from the wings to complete the capture.

By December 28 Hennings had rallied, under this species of house arrest, and had begun to function with his customary effectiveness. The report on McCarthy was soon trimmed by a process of compromise to the point where Hendrickson agreed to it in principle. But now Hendrickson began to waver again. On December 31 McCarthy flew up to Hendrickson's New Jersey home for half a day of reasoning together; Hayden and Hennings, in hourly contact with Hendrickson by phone, could sense him slipping away from them. But he promised to return to Washington in the morning. Hayden, his authority to expire in forty-eight hours, ordered the Government Printing Office to print up the report as an official document, ready for distribution, relying on Hennings to come up with the signature from Hendrickson that would validate it.

Hennings had sensed something other than weakening resolve during his phone talks with Hendrickson on the day of McCarthy's visit: Hendrickson was drinking. The following day, using all his fabled guile and charm, Hennings enticed the beleaguered Hendrickson to escape with him from the tension-laden Hill for a relaxing lunch in a quiet restaurant, and perhaps a drink or two. Hendrickson suspected nothing —Tom Hennings was hardly a man to suggest a drink under false pretenses. A few hours and many drinks later, Hendrickson's courage was at high tide. His doubts about signing the report had been assuaged and Hennings—who, in an historic feat of self-control, had remained sober—pulled the McCarthy report out of his overcoat pocket and got Hendrickson's signature on it.

The report, though it suffered from the timidity of political compromise and the anemia characteristic of senators' investigations of a colleague, bestowed credence on matters "Washington Merry-Go-Round" readers were long familiar with but which up to now had been only allegations: McCarthy's ties to Pepsi-Cola and to the real estate lobby; the financing of his plunges on the securities market; his pocketing of the $10,000 from Lustron; his income-tax eccentricities; the suspect manner in which he had handled the $10,000 from the Bentleys and other funds donated to him to finance the fight against Communism.

Of equal importance, the report spelled out McCarthy's many obstructions of the subcommittee investigation and made out a case of contempt of the Senate:

> For reasons known only to Senator McCarthy, he chose . . . to charge that the allegations were a smear and that the subcommittee was dishonest and was doing the work of Communists . . .
>
> The record leaves the inescapable conclusion that Senator McCarthy deliberately set out to thwart any investigation of him by obscuring the real issue and the responsibility of the subcommittee . . .
>
> The issue raised is one for the entire Senate . . . a matter that transcends partisan politics and goes to the very core of the Senate Body's authority, integrity and the respect by which it is held by the people of this country.

The eleventh-hour nature of the report, and the uninspiring history of the subcommittee, caused it to come out not as a clarion call but as the last gasp of a lame duck. It did not have the immediate effect we had hoped for. But it was a report the Senate could not forever ignore.

By the advent of 1953 we had used up almost our entire bag of tricks against McCarthy, without marked effect. We could comfort ourselves that all the body blows we had landed were bound to take their toll in the late rounds, but, Lord, three years had passed since Wheeling and he was still coming on stronger.

He had formal power now. As chairman of the Government Operations Committee he had a broad mandate to investigate government agencies. And he had informal powers over his colleagues in the new

Republican Congress and the new Republican Administration, powers rooted in both affinity and intimidation. As he had profited from Truman's hip-shooting opposition during his rise as an outsider, so now, during his consolidation as an insider, he profited from Eisenhower's calculating cooperation. Half of his party believed he was dead right and the other half, with a few exceptions, judged that to row with him would rend the party in two at the very moment of its entry, after twenty years a-wandering, into the promised land. And so when McCarthy constituted himself ambassador plenipotentiary, elbowed Eisenhower's pencil-pushers aside and negotiated an agreement with Greek shipowners not to carry trade between our allies and Communist countries, the Administration swallowed its pride and praised him. "I'm not going to get down in the gutter with that guy," Ike privately told his men, and when "that guy" came athwart Ike's new department heads, gunning for security risks, they got in the habit of backing off. McCarthy was now able not just to make accusations but to issue subpoenas and to record a series of visible successes in terms of job dismissals, high-level backdowns and Administration-wide adoption of his ideas on security safeguards; consequently, both his popularity with the public and his capacity to terrorize the elitists took quantum jumps.

As we reviewed our game plan amid the ruins, we noted one item in our original list of McCarthy weak spots to which we had given only sporadic pursuit: his incapacity as an administrator, his inability to run a tight ship.

Up to January 1953, these weaknesses had had scant occasion to flower; as a junior member of the minority party, from a relatively sparse state, he had a small staff, and that staff had limited access to public attention. Even so, we had kept up a watch of sorts and had on occasion hung a small mouse under McCarthy's eye: one of his men had been arrested during a homosexual encounter and McCarthy had been slow to purge him, though he had made great sport of the State Department over its ninety or so homosexual "security risks"; a second McCarthy staffer, Don Surine, had been discharged from the FBI for an excess of zeal in fraternizing with a buxom Baltimore prostitute he was assigned to investigate; a third investigator, Daniel Buckley, had a record of mental illness and was drawing 30 percent disability for that reason from the U.S. Air Force.

Our running of such items, in addition to pointing up the burlesque of McCarthy as security monitor, had the purpose of encouraging informers to approach us with personnel tidbits. We now upgraded this operation, for Chairman McCarthy was putting together a large staff, and his underlings, by virtue of their new status and importance, were coming out of the shadows and onto the public stage.

Our interest centered on two McCarthy appointees who bore certifiable earmarks of future trouble for their boss. One was Roy Cohn, the new chief counsel, an unphotogenic young man whose natural cockiness was inflated into a gross arrogance by the helium of McCarthy's power—an infallible forerunner of political catastrophe. The other was a handsome, dreamy-eyed investigator, Gerard David Schine, a millionaire's son, an heir to great hotels and theaters, a night club habitué and escort of such Hollywood starlets as Piper Laurie. In one respect Cohn and Schine were more like children of the 1970s than of the 1950s and were therefore targets for the denigration that pursues cultural pioneers: both were only twenty-six years old and neither had served in the armed forces, though the country was in its third year of war in Korea. This pacific strain in their otherwise pugnacious anti-Communism piqued our interest.

Cohn, we found, had arranged for himself a safe and politic berth in that draftproof haven for young celebrities—the inactive reserves—but Schine's continued presence on the night club scene was due to a suspect series of draft deferments—educational, occupational, physical, mental—which pretty well exhausted the known excuses for escaping service. The story was detailed in his draft record, which was slipped to me.

Our first column on the noncombatant side of Cohn and Schine, which featured a play-by-play account of Schine's retreat from the draft —Harvard; draft-exempt status as a customs clerk; draft-exempt employment as a vice president under his father; a slipped disc; a schizoid personality—was sent out on July 14, 1953, for publication on July 17. We knew from the start that we had hold of one of those issues that tweaks a chord of envious resentment in almost every household. And so did McCarthy, who well understood the grass-roots sentiment that if the average nonpolitical lad was draftable to fight in Korea, so should be the elite young superpatriots who were daily tooting the horn of Armageddon. On July 15 the Bell-McClure Syndicate, distributor of our column, received protests from McCarthy's office about the as yet unpublished story, and a demand that it be recalled. As Drew dominated the Bell-McClure Syndicate, the protests got short shrift, so on that same day the McCarthy camp took two immediate countersteps: the senator called in General Miles Reber, the Army's chief of legislative liaison with Congress, and told him that he would like a direct commission arranged immediately for Schine; and after an hour or two had passed for paper shuffling, Schine called the Army to ask if he could come right over "to hold up my hand."

But despite all this harried countermarching aimed at having Schine resplendent in uniform by the time the "Washington Merry-Go-Round" hit the streets two days hence, the Army could not immediately adapt to making an instant lieutenant out of one so often excused as a private; Schine's commission was referred to three branches of the Army most likely to be receptive, but all three demurred.

We kept up the heat on Schine's California draft board, touching up the issue in columns in July and August and making ourselves generally obnoxious to the board with our prying questions; in the aftermath Schine was reclassified 1-A and a couple of months later was called up for service. McCarthy ought to have been relieved to have had thus dispelled the overhanging taint that his patriotic front was a haven for draft dodgers, but instead he was rankled; months later he would erupt at a Senate hearing with a charge that Schine had been unfairly sacrificed by the draft board to stop Drew Pearson's "screaming."

If McCarthy was rankled over Schine's capture, Cohn was inconsolable. Word reached us that the young chief counsel had refused to take "no" on the commission, had gone to the Navy and the Air Force to seek commissions for Schine without success, and then had called on the Secretary of the Army to discuss (a) investigation of the Army's security failings by the McCarthy committee and (b) special treatment for Schine. We also heard that headstrong Roy was exerting daily pressure on a reluctant but accommodating McCarthy to do something for Dave. We sensed a chasm opening up before McCarthy, and kept close watch on the Army's newest conscript.

When Schine did not show up at Fort Dix to get his haircut and broom but instead was seen at his old New York haunts, we checked into the reasons why and found that McCarthy had asked the Army to station Schine in New York and assign him the task of analyzing West Point textbooks for left-wing bias, and that when the Army could not quite swallow the vision of Private Schine as its grand censor, McCarthy bargained downward, asking that Schine be assigned to his committee for two weeks on "temporary duty." This request the Army granted. We reported on November 22 the latest detours in the journey of G. David Schine to boot camp.

At length the recruit arrived at Fort Dix, but from the first reveille, Cohn made clear to the Army his intention to mother Schine through basic training. A Fort Dix contact called me to a late-night meeting in a residential neighborhood adjoining the base and told me a story of preferential treatment given Schine that was unprecedented in his Army experience, a story of petty favors touched off by calls from Roy Cohn and sometimes requiring approval from the Pentagon itself. With half the story in hand, I was able to pry the other half from my Pentagon sources.

Two or three times a week, week after week, Roy Cohn was on the phone about special privileges for Dave—to the commander of Fort Dix, General Cornelius Ryan; to the Secretary of the Army, Robert Stevens, and his aides; to the Army's general counsel, John G. Adams. When Adams suggested to Cohn that to single out Schine for special treatment would not be in the national interest, Cohn snarled, according to Adams' memo of the conversation, "If the national interest was what the Army wanted, he'd give it a little and then proceeded to outline how he would expose the Army in its worst light and show the country how shabbily it is being run."

Under Cohn's ardency, the Army, which thus far had acted rather well, began to yield as General Ryan would pass the buck to Secretary Stevens as to whether this or that regulation should be waived for Schine. How far down into absurdity the Army of the United States had permitted itself to be dragged by McCarthy and Cohn could be seen when the Secretary of the Army deliberated gravely on a complaint from General Ryan that Private Schine was getting too many late nights out, and emerged with the Solomon-like decision that Schine would lose his nightly liberty but retain his weekend passes.

We were secretly delighted, for the Pentagon was magnifying Cohn's importunings into an Administration-wide scandal which could be blown up into a national rhubarb. For several weeks we bided our time, collecting the petty details that mounted up into a pattern of favoritism: Schine excused from KP duty; let off guard duty; fraternizing with officers; permitted leave on weekends denied to other boots; given passes each night while his buddies swabbed the floors and suffered the age-old privations of privates. On December 22 we ran the story. McCarthy promptly denied any improper pressure, calling Pearson a liar.

The bomb simply would not go off. In six months we had written about Schine's favors five times, apparently without building up that snowball of public resentment that can start landslides. The press at large had not picked up on the story and sent its hotshots swooping in to flush out more galling details. Nor had we been successful in getting friendly senators to attack McCarthy on this issue, thus to make it a legitimate story for that dominant element of the press which in those days would not move on an abuse until some kind of official notice had been taken of it.

Was the subject matter too trivial? After half a year spent intermittently on such minutiae as what hour in the A.M. Private Schine got back to camp, I sometimes thought it was. Drew was adamant that it was not. He was convinced that at last McCarthy had been caught in the one offense that is indefensible in a society that runs on egalitarian rhetoric—the use of political pull to excuse a millionaire's boy from peeling the potatoes that other mothers' sons had to peel. We prepared yet another column.

If the press did not see the potential in this, McCarthy, the Army and the Administration did. McCarthy had made it a point, when Cohn wasn't around, to tell Secretary Stevens and John Adams that he was sorry that Roy had gone overboard on Schine but that he just couldn't bear to cross him on it. The Army was getting complaints, presumably from our readers, and with the self-protective caution of any great bureaucracy, had stiffened up to Cohn and had quietly started a routine Inspector General type inquiry into the complaints, word of which reached the New York *Times* readers on January 30, 1954. And with McCarthy and Cohn daily ripping into alleged security lapses in the Eisenhower Administration Army—a "spy ring" at Fort Monmouth, the promotion to major of a known Communist dentist—the Administration's political heads, at a January strategy session in the Attorney General's office, set John Adams to compiling a list of all the interventions on Schine's behalf by the McCarthy camp.

But the moves of the Army and the Administration, we suspected (rightly, as events were to show), were aimed not at confrontation with McCarthy but at cutting a quiet deal with him: the Army would drop the Schine matter if McCarthy would stop roughing up generals and Cabinet officers. To throw as much sand as we could in the wheels of amity we published, on February 15, our most attention-grabbing charge to date—that Cohn had threatened to have Secretary Stevens fired if he did not show more sensitivity toward Schine (who had by now been transferred to the Provost Marshal's School at Camp Gordon):

As of today, the dream boy [Schine] is taking the eight weeks basic training given to all military policemen. Right now he's learning to direct traffic.

This menial work, however, has brought a howl of protest from his pal and partner, Mr. Cohn, who wants his friend to go direct into criminal investigation, not horse around with basic police training and traffic problems. Mr. Cohn is so upset about this that he has been telephoning the office of the Secretary of the Army Stevens demanding that Gerard David be spared this basic training.

If Gerard is not spared, Roy warns, he is going to see to it that the Secretary of the Army is fired.

To stimulate the kind of pressure on the Army that would cause it to lose control of the Schine matter, we told the Pentagon that we had more details than we did have; we advised reporters that the Army possessed records which would substantiate all our charges; and on March 5 we sent out a story claiming that the Army had transcripts of all Cohn's telephone interventions in Schine's behalf. Suddenly, press interest in this story that had smoldered for eight months boiled over, and overnight the word was all over Washington that the Army was selectively leaking the Cohn transcripts to the press. In a few days those transcripts, which backed up everything we had printed, and much more, were public property.

As the fifth year of the McCarthy phenomenon opened, in February 1954, he was still rising, and at an accelerating pace. The past year or more had bred the usual crop of howlers and fiascoes, but he seemed to feed on error as though he had rendered inoperative the defense of proving him wrong.

In a national broadcast he had faked a nonexistent quotation, which he placed in a book by General Walter Bedell Smith, to make Adlai Stevenson responsible for forcing Communists into the postliberation Italian government. In the same speech he had doctored his own prepared text in order to twist a quote by Arthur Schlesinger, Jr., into an unqualified endorsement of letting Communists teach in college. He had attributed to the Truman era a scheme to obtain passports for Communists that actually took place in the Administration of Calvin Coolidge. He had staged a Strangelovian investigation of the Voice of America, seeking to prove that American scientists had tried to sabotage a new transmitter by erecting it in Seattle, Washington, instead of Southern California, because it was easier for the Russians to jam broadcasts from Seattle.

He had been forced to sack his new executive director, J. B. Matthews, because of the untimely publication of a Matthews article in the *American Mercury,* which led off, in a most impolitic vein: "The largest single group supporting the Communist apparatus in the United States today is composed of Protestant clergymen." He had for weeks staged hearings on the infiltration of the Fort Monmouth, New Jersey, radar labs, hyped by twice-a-day press conferences in which he promised to produce proof of ongoing espionage, but he had no proof and was unable to refute the conclusion of Army intelligence that it was "unable to find anything relating to espionage." Heedless of the power of symbolism, other than his own, he had allowed Cohn and Schine to get him tagged as a "book burner" over their antic attempts to purge "subversive" books from the overseas libraries of our International Information Administration.

And Joe's old trouble of mistaken identity had cropped up again; as he had before indicted the wrong Anna Rosenberg, so now he indicted the wrong Annie Lee Moss, a Pentagon clerk, on the basis of an informant who had never seen the person but who remembered the name from old party dues lists.*

But why should Joe McCarthy pay heed to the toothless wailings of his critics in the face of so many current demonstrations of his triumph? In January 1954, the public opinion polls had shown him at his highest point of public esteem: for every citizen who disapproved of him after four contentious years, two approved of him; feared till now because he led a potent minority, now he had the majority. On February 2, 1954, despite all the sins and errors laid on his investigations, the U.S. Senate awarded him $214,000 for yet a new round of investigations, and by a vote of 85 to 1, with only Fulbright dissenting. For the past year the entire federal bureaucracy had been sifted and resifted by security investigations according to the formula he had demanded, and the Administration was about to announce that in one year it had fired 2,429 "security risks." (He would protest one statistic—that only 29 had been classified as security risks because of disloyalty, whereupon the Administration would amend its statistics to show 422 firings of "subversives.") To be sure, the new Administration was often slow on the

---

*Fourteen years later Roy Cohn, in his book, *McCarthy,* claimed that in 1958 some FBI documents surfaced which showed that an Annie Lee Moss was a party member in the 1940s. But this was not in dispute. There were two or three Annie Lee Mosses and Cohn does not show he had hold of the right one. More to the point, he and McCarthy were unable, at the time they were challenged and the controversy raged, to clearly identify the woman they had dragged forth for public accusation as the right Annie Lee Moss, or to discredit her denials under oath of any Communist associations.

draw, but it had consistently shaped up when McCarthy pressed: Drew Pearson was out with a list of ten Ike "appeasements" of McCarthy, updating a trend Richard Rovere had noted a year earlier: "Four times in these ten days, McCarthy . . . has let his views on State Department issues be known, and four times the State Department has made McCarthy's views American policy within a matter of hours."*

And so he could take a week off from pummeling the Army and do a little political speechmaking. Lincoln Day time had come again and McCarthy, the premier attraction, had consented to a tour of eight speeches, kicking off, as before, in West Virginia. It was a kind of sentimental journey on which he could measure, by the adulation of the thronging crowds and the size of the headlines that followed him, the long, long distance he had come from rude, beleaguered beginnings.

It was past time, he had decided, to take off the gloves with the Democrats. Grown weary of dispatching them one by one he would now confront them wholesale. He had a refrain, a motif, for this tour ("Twenty years of treason"), and lest there be any misunderstanding that he was just talking about a few leaders he cleared it away in his opening broadside: "The hard fact is that those who wear the label, 'Democrat,' wear it with the stain of an historic betrayal." This coming November, he suggested, was the time for Americans to settle accounts with the congressional Democrats.

Thus refreshed, he returned to the committee-room wars under a full head of steam to interrogate, behind closed doors, General Ralph Zwicker on the momentous question: Who promoted the Communist dentist Irving Peress to major? When General Zwicker demurred to confess error regarding Peress, McCarthy denounced him as "not fit to wear that uniform" and promised to work him over again in public. The abuse of a general caused a reaction that abuse of diplomats and professors had not stirred. Secretary of the Army Stevens ordered Zwicker and other officers not to appear before McCarthy, and a confrontation loomed. But after a few days of being reasoned with by Administration realists and Senate Republicans, Stevens met with McCarthy on February 24, and quickly outbargained, agreed to produce his officers for testimony, after all. It was of course everywhere interpreted as a monumental capitulation to McCarthy by the Army and the Administration, a view McCarthy confirmed by his scornful

* *The New Yorker* (February 27, 1953).

observation that Stevens could not have surrendered "more abjectly if he had got down on his knees."

For many, McCarthy now seemed darkly invincible. Richard Rovere, one of his most persevering critics, wrote: "If the prevailing view here is sound, the country has in McCarthy no ordinary demagogue but a political figure of the first rank, a man cast in a large, unique mold, quite possibly an authentic genius, and, at the very least, the most daring and original innovator since Franklin D. Roosevelt."*

But though Joe McCarthy hurtled through the roiled waters like a great whale, awing the watchful multitude with his spouting of geysers, overturning the fragile boats of his pursuers with random swipes of the tail, and raising panic aboard whenever he turned and hove up for a head-on, red-eyed charge, he already bore deep in his vitals the mortal impress of a dozen harpoons.

The lost skirmishes, it turned out, were not lost after all. Each deceit rebutted over the years, each accusation contested, each financial oddity exposed, each prober's question asked and evaded, each act of resistance that provoked an excessive response—all claimed their attrition, all added their trickle to a current that welled up beneath the surface until suddenly the latest accretion turned the tide.

On March 12 the story we had been nursing along for eight months —on the petty favors wangled for Schine by McCarthy and Cohn— came to fruition with the public release of the Army's transcripts of the McCarthy-Cohn interventions. It "shocked the nation as had nothing else in the whole long record of McCarthy investigations," records Fred J. Cook in *The Nightmare Decade*. And so it did, but only because the public had decided at last that it was ready to be shocked.

A universal cry went up for a Senate investigation, the métier McCarthy had caused the public to grow accustomed to. The battle was over then, really, though the drama had to be played out for many months. Drew's theory of McCarthy as defendant would now have its test, and the scaffolds he had designed and helped erect—the Schine hearings and the Gillette investigation—would prove their utility.

McCarthy was at the top of his form for the Army-McCarthy hearings; he reran all his best moves of half a decade, loosed the identical specters and anathemas, introduced into evidence, with undiminished panache, the cropped picture and the bogus letter, but all the contor-

Ibid. (March 13, 1954).

tions which had before borne him upward when practiced on the run in the half-light now, in the dock under the steady klieg bulbs, merely whipped the maelstrom that sucked him down. It was inevitable that when he began to give off the red stain of vulnerability, his long-abused, long-dishonored colleagues would be emboldened to attack; inevitable that the stalled Senate machine for grinding down abrasive rebels, which had run off the road under Tydings and sputtered feebly under Gillette, would now begin to hum again its inexorable hum; inevitable that when the Schine-Stevens business proved a bit flimsy for a hanging, the earlier scaffold—the tissue of McCarthy's financial irregularities and his contumacious refusal to explain them to the Gillette committee, all officially established in the Hennings-Hendrickson report—would be pressed into service.

A committee under Republican Senator Arthur Watkins of Utah, an early applauder of McCarthy, was formed to consider whether he should be censured. The straight-laced Watkins, who represented my native state and belonged to my local church, disliked our column and our politics but collaborated with me on this McCarthy investigation. And so the column's long labor of discovery and maneuver was marshaled and brought to bear at a critical moment.

The Watkins committee recommended condemnation on the following proposition:

> It is our opinion that *the failure of Senator McCarthy to explain to the Senate* these matters: (1) whether funds collected to fight Communism were diverted to other purposes inuring to his personal advantage; (2) whether certain of his official activities (Pepsi-Cola, Lustron) were motivated by self-interest; and (3) whether certain of his activities in senatorial campaigns involved violations of the law; was conduct contumacious toward the Senate and injurious to its effectiveness, dignity, responsibilities, processes and prestige.

The committee also condemned the senator for his bully-ragging of General Zwicker, but that plank was deleted on the Senate floor, and in substitution, another "slugging the judge" plank was added to cover McCarthy's abuse of the Watkins committee during *its* deliberations.

On December 2, 1954, the Senate voted to condemn McCarthy by 67 to 22. Even in his extremity, McCarthy commanded half of the Senate Republicans; 22 voted with him, 22 against.

Whatever hard quality it is that enables a Napoleon or a Lenin or a Hitler to sneer at repudiation, in his heart of hearts, and recommence to scheme for power, McCarthy did not have it. His external position was still strong. The Senate vote did not strip him of any of a senator's formal powers. His term had four years to run. After the Schine hearings, after the fickle goddess of publicity had done its worst, he still held the support of 36 percent of the American people, a hard-core following capable of vast retributions. At least half of his party clung to him, as the Senate vote showed. And events were ahead—the Sputnik demonstration of Russian missile superiority, the Communist takeover of Cuba—that offered ample springboards.

But the repudiation of his colleagues had crushed him *internally*. He accepted the defeat. Despite efforts of his circle to rouse him, he permitted himself to become an off-stage figure. A witness told me of a Republican political rally in Wisconsin at which McCarthy was asked to leave his place on the dais so as not to embarrass—of all people—Vice President Richard Nixon. The old tiger left in a docile manner; the curious witness followed him outside the building and found him sitting on a curbstone weeping. He sank into alcoholism and in two years was dead of cirrhosis of the liver.

A little while before he died he called Drew, and they exchanged their first words since the Sulgrave incident. He wanted Drew to know he was inserting into the *Congressional Record* a "Merry-Go-Round" column about the Israeli situation.

"I haven't always agreed with your column," he said, "but in this case I'm sure it's completely accurate. I'm telling you in advance what I've done so you won't faint." Drew almost did.

11 · Eisenhower: To Penetrate a Myth

THE "Merry-Go-Round's" relationship with Dwight D. Eisenhower started off in the clouds but lost altitude rapidly after he became President—as it had with Harry Truman—an alienation I thenceforth knew must ever be the rule between muckrakers and Presidents.

In the beginning Drew was impressed with Ike. His open face, the blue eyes as clear and guileless as the sky above his native Kansas, compelled trust and confidence. There was an all-American quality about him. Perhaps it was his easiness of manner, his engaging sincerity, the way his whole personality smiled every time his face lit up in a grin. He had a gift, too, for expressing himself movingly and for reducing great issues to simple moral principles. On the surface there was nothing suave or subtle about him, none of those sophisticated mannerisms which Americans are inclined to distrust.

The movers and shakers saw in this folksy, relaxed war hero of uncertain but assuredly benign ideology a father figure for the American people and a vehicle for their own political agendas. After one visit with the general, Drew was moved to write in his diary: "In many respects Eisenhower reminds me of F.D.R.—the same contagious charm, the same ability to talk and the same tendency toward pleasant-sounding generalities. Whenever I talked to Roosevelt, I felt sort of lifted up during the conversation, but when I left I always wondered what it was that he had said that was of any importance. The talk with Eisenhower this time was a little bit more specific . . ."*

The initial associations between Eisenhower and Pearson during the immediate postwar years were most agreeable. In 1947 the Army and Navy Union shared its annual awards between Eisenhower, Omar Bradley and Pearson (who was included in this company by virtue of his being the Honorary Inspector General). In 1948 Eisenhower presented Drew with the "Father of the Year" award, and as newsreel cameras rolled, Drew responded, "In the words of the Kaw tribe in your state of Kansas, I hope you become 'little White Father in Big White House.' " Drew saw Candidate Ike as the way out of a Democratic presidential defeat and for a time touted him for the Democratic nomination.

Four years later, though committed to Estes Kefauver for President, Drew promoted Eisenhower for the Republican nomination over Senator Robert Taft, exercising the liberal Democrat's prerogative to help Republicans harken to their better instincts.

In early 1952 he visited Ike at SHAPE in Paris and spelled out for him how the Taft forces were "stealing" all the Southern delegates. This was news to the general, apparently, and he wanted to hear all about it. Several months later in Chicago, the delegate-stealing charge was the successful rallying point of the Ike forces at the Republican convention. I've often wondered if Ike's convention managers, surprised at the speed and decisiveness with which Ike grasped their advice to exploit this fateful issue, realized that their champion had been first tutored on it by the reviled Pearson.

As Republican candidate and then Republican President, conciliatory toward McCarthy, surrounded by plutocrats, his Administration staffed by the accomplices of plutocrats, Ike's attraction quickly paled for Drew, who found a ready excuse for his own self-deception about Ike in a conversation with Speaker of the House Sam Rayburn. "When Grant got into the White House," Rayburn told Drew, "they ruined him. Some of us tried to tell Ike he should run as a Democrat, in which case he would have had men around him to tell him how to run things. But the people around him now don't want him to know."

The column's basic view of the Eisenhower presidency jelled early;

Pearson Diaries (April 15, 1952), p. 209.

a President of prudence on matters of war and peace but who, unschooled in government and politics, of narrow intellectual horizons, of reduced vigor in his illness-flawed sixties, had turned the daily operation of his presidency over to Republican party pros—which in Drew's judgment meant rule of, by and for the monied interests.

Time and again in the early Eisenhower years, Drew fought Eisenhower appointments to the great procurement and regulatory posts, by column, broadcast and lobbying visits to Capitol Hill, appointments of men whose past records suggested to Drew either a proclivity for feathering their own nests or an incorrupt self-identification with the business interests they were charged with restraining for the public good: Harold Talbot to be Secretary of the Air Force; Lewis Strauss to be Chairman of the Atomic Energy Commission; Jerome Kuykendall to be Chairman of the Federal Power Commission; George McConnaughey, Richard Mack and James Doerfer to the Federal Communications Commission. In years to come, as shall be seen, each of these Eisenhower appointees would be exposed in improprieties, or would fail of confirmation for higher office, or would be forced to resign under a cloud. But at the outset, Drew's opposition uniformly failed.

Year after year passed, and we made scant headway peddling our view of Ike to the American people. He floated placidly above such squalls as mere reporters could stir, secure in the esteem of a large majority despite a listless Administration and a holiday-oriented regimen. Alone among the popularly chosen Presidents of the Republic— except for the incomparable FDR—he still held majority support as his second term waned, a feat that seems the more impressive today after the passage of another generation of Presidents of short welcome.

In part, this was due to the conjuncture of an extraordinarily appealing personality with a particular need by the public for patriarchal reassurance after two decades of domestic and international turmoil. In part it was due to Ike's unfathomable genius for avoiding the big mistake that has entrapped every other President of the postwar era, and for projecting a steady, competent, sincere, at-ease-with-power, above-petty-politics image.

There was a perversity to the Eisenhower popularity—at least to those who, like Drew, did not acknowledge that benign neglect must have its season and that from time to time the majority craves a respite from the progressive agenda—a perversity that would have challenged the validity of democracy itself had it not been explainable in the "protection" Ike was given by the big-circulation newspapers.

Certainly the Eisenhower Administration deserved more press-ragging than it was getting. It presided over three economic recessions, a spectacular loss of space-technology supremacy to the Russians, the Communist takeover of neighboring Cuba, the staffing of the great departments and regulatory commissions with business puppets, a general atmosphere of aimless national drift, a do-nothing posture toward the heightening demands of blacks for basic rights that was backing up pressures which must sooner or later explode. Yet Ike was relatively immune from the press scourging that had illuminated every mishap of his Democratic predecessors.

Our columns were censored, and even killed, as never before, and equally distressing to us, the pro-Eisenhower press—and that was about 80 percent of all the press—no longer swooped down on our little White House exposés and kept them reverberating until they became stuck in the public mind. For a time it seemed that Ike's imagery could not be penetrated even by our patented stories of first-family cupidity and perk-grabbing that in times past could keep the White House in hot water for days. Eleanor Roosevelt's acceptance of an aquamarine from the President of Brazil, or Bess Truman's semi-inadvertent acceptance of a deep freeze from a lobbyist, even a gift to Harry Truman of a twelve-pound ham, were automatic *causes célèbres*, but when Drew made bold to tweak Mamie Eisenhower for latching on to a diamond necklace from King Ibn Saud and a gold mesh bag from Emperor Haile Selassie "so heavy she could hardly carry it around," the stories died the quick death of press neglect. Similarly, our Harry Vaughan type dramas about Mamie's brother, Colonel Gordon Moore —for instance, that he had accepted the gift-loan of a prized Irish stallion from oilman Clint Murchison, or had helped wangle a government franchise for an air carrier he had lately been associated with— failed to strike sparks.

Cupidity stories about Ike himself fared no better: his lobbying for himself (as a five-star general) of a unique tax loophole by which his million-dollar income from the book *Crusade in Europe* was taxed as capital gains at a fraction of the rate assessed other authors; his settling in (as President) in a $200,000, eighteen-room, seven-bathroom "cottage" in the Georgia foothills convenient to the Augusta Golf Course, donated by his big-business friends; his acceptance from other friends of an incredible list of gifts, which we tediously catalogued (twenty-five head of cattle, a tractor, an instant forest of forty-eight tall Norway spruce trees and four hundred nut trees, two thousand bulbs, $1,000 worth of shrubs, a pony, a sorrel mare, a black Arabian filly, antique furniture, a General Electric kitchen, a $3,000 putting green, a corn planter, a disk harrow, a side-delivery rake)—the list went on and on as we made new discoveries, and eventually totaled more than $500,000 worth of inputs from big-business well-wishers.

Our reports on this freeloading, instead of inspiring the big-circulation press to raucous fishing expeditions and caustic ridicule, were generally treated as tasteless acts of *lèse-majesté*. Inevitably, the once friendly relationship with Ike disintegrated, reaching its nadir when Eisenhower uncorked an anguished attack following one of our accounts of his gift-taking: "Pearson's yen for lying about somebody brings stupidity to the fore in concocting his lies!" And again in refusing to answer questions about one of our columns: "I don't read any newspaper I consider irresponsible, and I consider any newspaper that carries Pearson's column to be irresponsible."

From the earliest days of the Eisenhower Administration, the sea change in editorial policy in most of the press as to what was fair game and what was *verboten* in writing about the White House caused Drew a good deal of melancholy reflection that went deeper than mere frustration over stories not "picked up on."

"When I think of how I hurt Harry Truman with piddling stories about hams and refrigerators, I feel ashamed," he said more than once. He would mull over anecdotes of Truman's personal straightness—as when he had ordered his ambassador to Switzerland to refuse a Swiss gift of three magnificent watches for himself, Bess and Margaret. Out of such maunderings came the determination to accomplish two things: to make amends to Truman and to find a way, a vehicle, for penetrating the protective press blanket around the Eisenhower White House.

The opportunity to do Truman a service came early. We learned in March of 1953 that Senator McCarthy was planning an attack on the ex-President. With some hesitancy, considering the years of epithets and conspiracies between them, Drew put through a call to Independence, Missouri, to alert Truman. Drew identified himself to the person who answered the phone and waited, wondering whether Truman would even take his call, and if he did, whether it would only be to give him a tongue-lashing such as he had administered during their last interview seven years before.

Truman came to the phone immediately, saying "Hello, Drew" before Drew could make his salutation, in that long-familiar voice that brought back a passed era. Drew has left an account of the conversation:

> I told him that McCarthy was investigating a report that he had taken about $10,000 worth of steel filing cabinets when he left the White House.
>
> "That," replied Truman, "is a damned lie. It's a lie out of whole cloth. I bought those filing cabinets and have the receipts to prove it. The only thing I have are some old wooden boxes about to fall to pieces which General Services lent me for my papers until I could get them sorted out and put away in my new building.
>
> ". . . McCarthy had better get his facts straight if he's going to tangle with me or he'll get his ass in a sling."*

A rapprochement ensued; thereafter Drew visited with Truman once or twice a year. As the indecisiveness and pro–big-business orientation of the Eisenhower Administration made Drew ever more appreciative of Truman, so Drew's regular attacks on Eisenhower caused the ex-President to upgrade the Pearson style of reporting: "Somebody has to fight," Truman said to Drew in 1957. "You've been pouring it on. That's why I talk to you. You're doing such a good job of pouring it on 'em."

Ghosts from the days of their long hostility still hovered over their conversations and would occasionally intrude. When Drew would hand Truman one of his current critiques of the Republicans, he would feel constrained to say, "I know you haven't always agreed with what I write, but I know you'll agree with every word of this." Once, when Drew paid Truman a compliment, the ex-President said, "You can say that—after all I've done to you?"

The remark piqued Drew's curiosity no end; of the many things Truman might have been referring to, Drew assumed it was probably a revelation just made by the lawyer Edward Bennett Williams in a *Time* magazine interview to the effect that the Truman Justice Department had turned material over to him from its file on Drew to use against him in the Norman Littell libel suit.

The reconciliation reached a point where Truman gave Drew a statement to use in his libel trials to counteract the old Truman denunciations which legal adversaries were forever introducing as evidence of Drew's falsity. Truman walked a measured line in his statement so as not to totally repudiate former utterances, causing Drew to value it the

---

Ibid. (February 26, 1953), p. 253.

more: "In my judgment Pearson is by and large a force for good in the country. He is sincere, fearless, has the courage of his convictions, and hammers away at what he believes is right, however unpopular it may be. He takes the side of the less privileged."

But finding the story that would shatter the Eisenhower imagery was a more elusive goal. As 1958 opened—Ike's sixth year—our gospel of Republican perfidy and ineptitude had made little headway and time was running out. For more than half a decade we had dutifully mined the veins of intersection between Republican officeholders and favor-seeking businessmen, had regularly come up with mini-scandals that, in a minimizing climate, seemed too complicated, or too petty, or too far removed from Ike and his immediate circle, to qualify as real pay dirt. The net impact had perhaps been more injurious to us than to the Eisenhower Administration; we more and more cast ourselves in the position of out-of-step scolds. "Pearson can be counted on to attack the Eisenhower Administration every other day," went one quip, "sometimes with facts."

Then, one day, back at the veins of intersection, I caught a glimpse of something that looked as if it might lead us to the mother lode. It was a few documents no worse in content than hundreds I had seen over the years, except that this time the possible culprit was the most important figure in the Eisenhower Administration next to Ike himself —Governor Sherman Adams, the one-man band who had run the White House for five years. Like all discoveries, this one had its element of luck, but it was also rooted in a complicated labor of many years.

The Eisenhower regulatory commission appointees were scarcely in place when Drew began a long campaign of personal and public agitation for congressional investigations of them. This entry from Drew's diary is typical of incidents Drew would mention to me:

> . . . Talked with Senator Ed Johnson of Colorado about the FCC and about Commissioner John Doerfer. I didn't need to talk to him. He launched forth in a tirade against the Eisenhower administration as the most graft-ridden in history. He said the Harding administration had turned out to be a piker in contrast. He pointed out that commission after commission is bent on robbing the public, that the quasi-judicial process had disappeared, and that all you had to do was to know Presidential Assistant Sherman Adams to get television licenses, oil pipelines, and increased utility rates. Ed, who is the ranking Democrat on the Senate Commerce Commit-

tee, is considered quite a conservative, and I was surprised at his outburst. He said that he had voted against Doerfer and would demand a hearing . . . I suggested to Ed that John Carroll, now running for the Senate in Colorado, is an old enemy of Doerfer, and he should make up. They have been political enemies since Carroll ran against Johnson in the primaries. Johnson smiled and said he thought that could be arranged. I called John afterward in Denver and suggested he might make some overtures to Ed and I believe they are going to get together.*

Johnson's estimate of the extent of corruption in the Eisenhower Administration, discounting the conversational hyperbole, squared with what Drew had begun to say in private and, increasingly, in public.

When the Democrats regained control of Congress and its investigating committees in January 1955, Drew believed that the public interest and the partisan interest that Democrats presumably had in deriding Republicans were conjoined, and he stepped up his agitation for a major investigation of the regulatory agencies, which were by law the creatures of Congress, though dominated by Eisenhower appointees and under close White House control. On March 3, 1955, Drew went to the top—Sam Rayburn, Speaker of the House of Representatives. Both the context and the time were propitious, for Rayburn was the father of most of the regulatory commissions, and in his more sentimental moments, regarded them as his legacy to the nation; moreover, Eisenhower had just attacked Rayburn over differences on a tax measure, and the Speaker figured to be in a combative mood. Drew has left an account of Rayburn's comments, from which I quote in part:

"I was in on the borning of every one of these commissions except the Interstate Commerce Commission. I wrote the law that passed the Federal Communications Commission and the Securities and Exchange Commission, and I was in Congress when we planned the Federal Trade Commission and the Federal Power Commission. And I wrote the law for the Civil Aeronautics Board.

"The people don't know that these commissions are an arm of Congress. They do what we don't have time to do. Yet Eisenhower has taken over and even appoints his friends.

. . . "If you have a good law and appoint bad administrators, you just about kill the law. That is what Eisenhower is doing today. They haven't

Ibid. (June 21, 1954), p. 324.

amended a thing but they have appointed the worst commissioners this country has seen.

"Take this man McConnaughey [the new Chairman of the FCC]. He wasn't even honest enough to admit he worked for telephone companies. His appointment is going to cost the taxpayers millions. . . .

. . ."Eisenhower is sabotaging these commissions. . . ."*

Rayburn and Drew agreed that the "sabotage" was the work of the men around the President, Sherman Adams chief among them. Drew was elated when he left the Speaker, thinking that an investigation was at last in the works. But the Speaker's indignation waned, and seemed to disappear when his nephew (and surrogate son, for Rayburn was a bachelor), Robert T. Bartley, was appointed to the Federal Communications Commission.

Another two years passed, two years of deepening disillusion for Drew. He could understand the reluctance of Republicans to investigate Republicans and of Democrats to investigate Democrats, reprehensible though it was, but when Democrats would not investigate Republicans where the vested interests were involved, the implications were chilling—in addition to being an affront to his own presumed influence.

Then, in February 1957, Speaker Rayburn—ancient, short, squat, dour, spectacularly baldheaded—who wielded a personal authority unknown in government today, descended from his throne on the Speaker's Rostrum to the well of the House and honored his vassals with a brief speech. The administration of the regulatory laws, he said, was a mish-mash; the landmark acts of Congress, wrought with such care and pain over many decades, were not being administered as planned, and he wanted something done about it. What he wanted done was the creation of a special subcommittee of the Commerce Committee to find out why, when Congress said "A," it invariably came out of the regulatory funnel as "B." We do not know what particular crotchet moved the Speaker on that day; months later he would disown the project he had set afoot. But in the meantime, the oracle had spoken, the subcommittee was established, and I began to try to infiltrate it.

At first glance, the Special Subcommittee on Legislative Oversight seemed unpromising. It was handpicked by, and under the thumb of,

*Ibid. (March 3, 1955), pp. 342–43.

the chairman of its parent House Interstate and Foreign Commerce Committee, Oren Harris, a wily, soft-spoken Arkansan whose collusions with the regulated industries were so notorious that liberal House members refused to sanction the new oversight subcommittee until it was informally agreed that Harris would *not* be its chairman. But Harris was adept at remote control. Most of the members he picked were safe tools of the regulated industries, a built-in 7-to-4 majority on any contested issue. Its staffers, instead of aggressive professionals recruited from outside for the task, were familiar retainers chosen from the staffs of the members; one was the son of the ranking Republican member, Joseph O'Hara. The chairman, Democrat Morgan Moulder of Missouri, was an earnest but pliable fellow, his pliability enhanced as he had lately acquired a glass jaw from creeping into the beds of his secretaries; a candidate for blackmail was not the man to crack the whip on the unscrupulous lobbies of the regulated industries. The chief counsel, Professor Bernard Schwartz of New York University, not appointed until August 1957, when the staff of Humpty Dumptys was already in place, seemed hardly the white hunter that a safari through the regulatory jungle required. Studious-looking, retiring, at thirty-four the author of several heavy tomes on administrative and constitutional law, Schwartz was an academic's academic, the holder of five degrees, a doctor of laws who had never participated in a court case or a congressional hearing. To my cynical eye, Oren Harris had cleverly produced a prestige name in administrative law who had no experience whatever in government, and by his own statement, lacked even those wary instincts which gird the prudent citizen in the presence of congressmen and commissioners. "When my work with the subcommittee started, I had no idea," he wrote later on, "that there were instances of corruption and improprieties in the regulatory agencies."

Professor Schwartz planned a noncontroversial study of gaps in legislation and snarls in administrative flow charts, an inquiry the committee leaders felt would discharge the task set by Speaker Rayburn without harming a hair on anyone's head. Oren Harris was manifestly pleased by the Schwartz plan; he couldn't have charted a more felicitous course himself.

Nonetheless, I tried to ingratiate myself with the new chief counsel in order to get on a confidence-swapping basis with him. He had an inquiring mind, and I filled it with recitals of what I knew or suspected might explain regulatory decisions. For instance, there was the curious trend that had long plagued Drew: once the Eisenhower commissioners had gained control of the Federal Communications Commission, every decision it had handed down in awarding television channels, despite all the legal rigmarole of hearings, exhibits and testimony, had favored Republican over Democratic partisans where there was a contest. Not only were the television industry, the legal profession and the FCC being corrupted by such fixes, but freedom of the printed press was being bartered away by newspaper publishers who made themselves supplicants before the Eisenhower Administration in order to get in on the millions in easy money that television offered.

I pressed upon the scholarly Dr. Schwartz old "Merry-Go-Round" fragments suggesting that the White House had dictated this or that decision, and would explain the pattern of pro-industry decisions in terms of the appalling variety of freebies, honoraria and career enhancements which commissioners accepted from the litigants before them. In particular, I was diligent to acquaint Schwartz with the admittedly imprecise warnings we had received about Sherman Adams from such insiders as Senator Ed Johnson and Speaker Sam Rayburn.

Encouraged by glimmers of receptivity from behind the professor's spectacles, I urged that all I was telling him called for a more aggressive inquiry. "What good will it do," I would query tiresomely, "to investigate inadequacies in the law and bottlenecks in the administrative process if the real decisions are in the hands of White House politicians?"

I was surprised that Schwartz did not break off my accessibility; on the contrary, he began following up my leads. His open-mindedness and heedless curiosity taught me for all time the sustaining wisdom of the door-to-door salesman and the womanizer: there is no such thing as the hopeless prospect; one must always make the pitch and play the percentages. Other reporters covering the new subcommittee, notably Clark Mollenhoff of the Des Moines *Register*, came away from Schwartz with similar vibes. We began to hope that we had here not a sheep in sheep's clothing, but a live ram.

Within a few weeks of his arrival Schwartz rerouted his course of investigation. In a formidably systematic way, he cast out an information dragnet to bring in substantiation of the allegations that only yesterday had seemed so unlikely to him. Zeroing in on the "big six" —Interstate Commerce Commission, Federal Power Commission, Federal Communications Commission, Civil Aeronautics Board, Federal Trade Commission, and Securities and Exchange Commission— he requisitioned such records as seemed too harmless to his congressional overlords to deny him, such as travel vouchers and telephone logs, and then he put his whole foot in the water by requesting commission officials and industry lobbyists to voluntarily inform him of all gifts and favors that had passed from businessman to official. As he enthused over the task, he invited employees of the several commissions to come to him with any knowledge they might have of upstairs improprieties, and in an inspired impertinence, he appeared before the Federal Bar Association—which contained the private and government lawyers who practiced before the commission tribunals—and appealed to those among them whose clients might have been victimized by corrupt decisions to come to him with their reasons for thinking so.

A skunk had thus ambled into the regulatory lawn party; embarrassed committee members assured commissioners and lobbyists that they need pay no attention to the impetuous Schwartz; by all means, as dignified officials and patrons they should keep their gift lists to themselves. In order to do so unitedly and under some cover of respectability, representatives of all six commissions met in fevered conclave (these mere creatures of the Congress, as Rayburn had aptly described them) and resolved to withhold the requested information on the lofty grounds of the separation of powers that existed between sovereign branches.

Oren Harris set about putting Schwartz under wraps, gently at first, by urging his subcommittee chairman, Morgan Moulder, to give Schwartz more direction. But Harris had begun to perceive that Moulder was lacking in leadership aptitudes, for he told a New York *Post* reporter: "I've tried to help Morgan out. Then he says he'll go in and tell Schwartz what to do. The trouble with that is . . . to teach a dog tricks, you have to know more than the dog."

Although the flow of incriminating information to Schwartz was largely staunched, so pervasively shabby was the deportment of the Eisenhower commissioners that even a sample inquest revealed a shocking situation. For instance, not only were five out of seven commissioners on the FCC permitting the regulated industries to pay frequent travel and watering-hole expenses for them, they were also billing the government for the same tabs and pocketing the profit. Fifty cases of false billing by the FCC heads were quickly documented, acts which were criminal as well as tawdry—as a legal opinion of the U.S. Comptroller General certified to Schwartz. Beyond the freeloading and false billing, most commissioners—quasi-judges though they were—were on the take from their regulatees for television sets, free servicing thereof, tickets to Broadway plays, night-club tabs, recreation at industry nooks, and the like. A similar pattern extended through all the Eisenhower commissions except the Federal Trade Commission, which, not having regulatory authority over industry, was not deemed important enough in day-to-day matters to corrupt.

A gratifying case in point was our old target, Chairman John Doerfer of the Federal Communications Commission. As befitted a Chairman's post of superior responsibility, Doerfer was a *triple* biller; on at least one occasion he collected expenses for the same travel from two business hosts and then billed the government for yet a third reimbursement. Chairman Doerfer had other moneymaking variations afoot. He would pocket speaking honoraria from the regulatees and then charge the taxpayers for the attendant travel expenses. He was an insatiable moocher at the tables of those on whom he sat in judgment—traveling in their executive airplanes, letting them pay his restaurant and hotel tabs, freeloading on them, with his wife, at a Miami Beach resort, hunting in the duck blind of NBC.

Schwartz assembled a memorandum showing that specimens such as Doerfer were prevalent throughout the Eisenhower commissions and brought it to his committee superiors; he included a request that the subcommittee *command* the commissioners to produce the records previously requested and a proposal that a set of public hearings be launched, based in part on the double billing and gift-taking among the nation's regulatory czars.

Professor Schwartz expected a pat on the back and a green light, but he was rudely disabused. The token Northern Democrats on the subcommittee, Morgan Moulder, John Moss and Peter Mack, supported him, but two thirds of the members were aghast, even indignant. The first concern of the Republican members was to conceal this information and to prevent the eliciting of any more, for the sake of party and patron alike, while Southern Democrats opposed revelation on the obvious ground that the profitable ambience which united them with Republicans and business lobbies was more solid and abiding than the partisan falderal that was supposed to divide them.

"A lousy thing to do," said Representative Joseph O'Hara, the subcommittee's ranking Republican, of Schwartz's proposal to make commissioners reveal gifts received from those subject to regulatory authority. Republican Representative Robert Hale of Maine denounced Schwartz's proposed hearings and the bent of his activity. "I note that . . . Dr. Schwartz's memorandum imputes misconduct on the part of members of the FCC which might result in criminal charges or, at the least, in the removal of the officials concerned. I am shocked. I had no idea when I voted to set up this subcommittee and agreed to serve on it that we would go into this sort of thing. It's none of our business."

From on high, Speaker Rayburn, whose nephew was one of those holding out against disclosure, accused Schwartz of "fly specking" and disassociated himself from the chief counsel's proposal for hearings, saying this was not what he had in mind when he proposed the subcommittee inquiry. Oren Harris took charge of the subcommittee session long enough to have the Schwartz agenda rejected 7 to 4, and a noncontroversial one adopted in its place. The press was told bluntly that Schwartz's wings had been clipped. "We had to cut him down to size," said Republican John Heselton of Massachusetts. "He thought he was going to blow the top off this town."

Perhaps the reader notes with surprise the barefaced candor of the congressmen quoted here, their unabashed championship of the suppression of scandal, as if it were a public service. This is a reminder that all recent change has not been for the worse, that progress has been made since the day when an O'Hara, a Hale, a Heselton, a Harris was made arrogantly secure by the hierarchical congressional rules, by a passive press uncomfortable with investigative journalism, and by a more structured, controlled-from-above electoral politics in which the business lobbies cut a grander figure than today.

In the Eisenhower era, congressmen were well insulated from the world around them. They were treated with adulation; their staffs acted as buffers between them and disagreeable news. Many ordinary men among them were lulled into believing they received this treatment because they deserved it, and even those who resisted the narcotic of flattery were not entirely immune to the intoxicating atmosphere on Capitol Hill.

For the muckraker in those times, it took as much conniving as digging to get beneath the surface. So I slipped around to see Morgan Moulder, who was nominally in charge of the investigation. He was a timid lion, full of boastful bluster but betraying a nervous manner. I alternately cajoled and prodded him to do his sworn duty, and he made more than half an effort to conduct a real investigation. But Oren Harris was an accomplished lion tamer. He deprived Moulder of the two most important powers of a chairman—the power to issue subpoenas and the power to authorize expenditures—keeping a tight grip on both.

The political education of Professor Schwartz was mightily accelerated by the subcommittee's actions. He now recognized that he "was hired, to put it bluntly, as a harmless academic type who could be trusted not to upset the congressional applecart by an unduly vigorous investigation." He began to see a concerted design in all the circumstances which had inhibited his work and he took a significant step by telling me about them. That he did not have a responsible professional staff of his own choosing he now realized was no coincidence; he was surrounded by people who saw it as their main function to spy on him and report on his activities to the senior congressmen who had placed them on the subcommittee staff. He was a chief counsel who did not have a private office, a private phone or a private staff; he now realized that this was so not because of budget restrictions and space shortages, as he had been told, but in order that he might have no meetings and phone calls or undertake staff initiatives that were not monitored and reported on. He had discovered that the instructions he gave his "investigators" as to what to look for were immediately taken to the target commissioners.

His own appointment as chief counsel, he learned, had been cleared by Oren Harris with Sherman Adams' office, and not made until the White House check indicated him to be an unmenacing pedagogue, a Republican who had no fire in his belly and who didn't know the Rotunda from the cloakroom. Thus the chief prober had been okayed by the chief suspect of the probe.

Schwartz also learned some things about Harris that explained both the congressman's particular subservience to Sherman Adams and his general resistance to the probe. His aspiration of the moment was to be appointed a federal judge—a hope which was at the mercy of Adams. And Oren Harris was in the television business, or rather what a congressman conceived of as being in business: shortly after he became Commerce Committee Chairman and, ipso facto, a power for the television industry to contend with, he had acquired a 25 percent interest in KRBB-TV (a television station potentially worth millions, in the fullness of time) for the congressman's price of $500, plus a $4,500 promissory note he had never bothered to pay off. Not only had Harris a proprietary interest in the status quo; he was in no position to launch a probe of payoffs to commissioners that might encourage some kettle to start inquiring into the color of the pot.

The professor's disillusion with the ways of Congress soon extended to the federal bureaucracy. His appeal to commission employees to come forward covertly with tales of the malfeasance they were forced to wallow in got the usual jobholder response—a resounding silence from 99.9 percent. Surrounded with obstacles but determined to press on, Schwartz looked outside the government for help. Two sources responded: a few reporters and a host of private attorneys who had lost out before commission tribunals because of suspected political fixes.

Schwartz was as surprised by the rousing response of the lawyers to his call for incriminating data as he had been by the guilt-laden silence of the government employees. In trooped the aggrieved lawyers, and on occasion their clients, to tell him their theories of why commissioners had been so cold to their splendidly argued cases, theories such as the following involving one commission alone, the FCC: that Commissioner McConnaughey was so shameless a shopper for favors that he had asked CBS to hire his son and had actually placed him in a post with one television station which had an upcoming case before the FCC; that Storer Broadcasting Co. had increased its standing with Chairman Doerfer by treating him and his wife to a free vacation on the Caribbean island of Bimini; that Commissioner Mack had promised his decisive vote in a Miami television-channel-award competition, in advance of the commission proceedings, to the applicant rejected by the FCC examiner as the least qualified of four, when that applicant covertly hired a notorious fixer and Mack benefactor, the attorney Thurman Whiteside, to lobby its case.

When a group as tolerant of fraud as corporate lawyers, whose daily business it is to influence the government, becomes so disoriented as to inform on professional colleagues, it is a sure sign that corruption has become so chaotically pervasive as to confound the need for rationality and to thus induce despair.

If he was to develop such leads and not have them suppressed by the subcommittee majority, Schwartz realized more and more that his greatest ally, and his only weapon against his collusive bosses, was the press. I had done my best to persuade him of this from the start, and as events relentlessly confirmed me, had been allowed to worm my way into the interstices of Schwartz's small operation, as had my industrious rival Clark Mollenhoff. Schwartz had one able, vigorous investigator, Baron Shacklette, and I developed a close working relationship with him (close enough to cause us both considerable embarrassment later on). Out of this alliance between press and staff grew that uprising most perverse to the congressional elder, the "runaway investigation."

A key example of how the alliance worked, both to develop information and force its public airing, was the case of Commissioner Mack. Within the Pearson organization the name of Richard A. Mack had been red-flagged ever since 1953 when Drew tried to raise a clamor against his nomination to the FCC because, as a member of the Florida Public Utilities Commission, Mack had been a stooge for the utility lobby. And we knew, from long pursuit of such matters, that the attorney-lobbyist Thurman Whiteside had a track record of gift-giving to regulatory officials. When I learned that Bernard Schwartz had received a complaint that Mack had pre-pledged his vote on Miami's Channel 10 to Whiteside's client, a complaint that was suspect in that it came from a disgruntled loser in the competition, it had for me the sound ring of truth, and when the subcommittee's information showed that thirty-three phone calls had passed from Mack to Whiteside, I was off and running.

Schwartz and his few dependable aides were hampered in their investigation not only by Commissioner Mack's refusal to account to the subcommittee for his gifts, and Chairman Harris' refusal to sub-poena the information, but by the insistence of subcommittee members that Schwartz act toward commissioners in an inoffensive, even deferential, manner. Schwartz planned, then, to move in on Mack by indirection, through patient voluntary interviews with people close to the Channel 10 affair. I feared that as word of these interviews got back to Mack and Whiteside they would, forewarned, get the bugs out of their subterfuges and do away with any eradicable evidence. I had learned that Whiteside controlled a trust fund and I was half satisfied he was using this as a funnel for payments to Mack, but I had no proof. So I called Mack, assuming Whiteside to be the smarter of the two, and tried to con the truth out of him before he could get his defenses straight. After giving him the nerve-jangling news that I was Jack Anderson of Drew Pearson's office, I bluffed: "Commissioner, I have an accountant who is prepared to testify that Whiteside has paid you money from the Grant Foster trust. I'd like to hear your side of it."

There was a moment of dead air as Mack fell for the bait and groped for a way to reconcile the irreconcilable. "Those were only loans," he ventured, not seeming to realize that even in sweetening up the trans-actions, he was admitting to the impermissible offense—taking money under any guise from an attorney in the Channel 10 case. That he was lying about the "loans" was confirmed when I asked how he had repaid them and he used the standard bribe-takers dodge that they were repaid in cash. In trying to parry my educated guesses and explain away checks

from Whiteside which I claimed to have before me, Mack got himself
in deeper and deeper, admitting at one point that perhaps not all of
the money from Whiteside was loans and at another that Whiteside
may have "forgiven" some of the loans.

After hanging up the phone, I felt that alternation of triumph and
guilt that often accompanies an investigative breakthrough. I had
brought off a coup that would redound to my advantage—and to the
public's in that, for one thing, the commission probe could not now
be easily squelched. But Richard Mack, only a few minutes before a
person of prominence, a success at home and in the world, was henceforth a man marked for disgrace, ouster, trial, the eclipse of hope, all
the private ravages that attend public ruin. He seemed an unsinister
sort of dodger, so uncalculating or witless that he had given himself
away. A life, perhaps more than one life, was to be eviscerated—all over
a few thousand dollars, taken for some pressing need perhaps, in return
for shifting a piece of public boodle from one gang of self-promoters
to another.

I told Shacklette and Schwartz what Mack had confessed to, and I
suggested they get to him while he was still scrambled, for the publication of my story would surely concentrate his mind. They did, equipped
with hidden recording gear, and Mack repeated his indiscretions.

Beginning in January 1958, as the subcommittee majority moved,
with the baronial swagger of congressmen of a former day, to shut down
the Schwartz probe, our columns and broadcasts published exclusive
after exclusive, aimed at forcing it to explore the full scandal of the
Eisenhower commissions. Through story after story—of Chairman
Doerfer's fake billings and grabbings for industry gratuities, of Mack's
acceptance of money from Whiteside, of the hidden strangulation by
Oren Harris of the subcommittee's powers to probe, of the secret
contents of the "Schwartz memorandum" which had reported to the
subcommittee widespread misconduct throughout the regulatory commissions and had proposed in vain a public airing of it—we again and
again forced into public view matters the subcommittee majority
thought it had safely buried. By itself, the "Washington Merry-Go-
Round" could keep the door from being slammed shut, but couldn't
blast it wide open. What was needed was for the entire big-time press
to jump in on the FCC scandals, but with the exceptions of Clark
Mollenhoff and one or two other working reporters, the press hung
back, and for a reason darker than the diffidence toward investigative

journalism that was thick in that era: 182 of the 497 television stations operating in 1958 were owned by newspapers, an ownership dependent on the favor of the FCC/White House/congressional axis our stories were offending.

The *Progressive* magazine explored this angle in an April 1958 article by Miles McMillin:

> Pearson continued to dispatch excerpts from the suppressed report [the Schwartz memo] . . . But the rest of the press, including the Washington *Post,* which dropped out after firing one shot, brooded in silence . . . The wire services . . . kept a stony silence through the Pearson chirping.
>
> The indifference of the press to the suppressed Moulder Committee report for the week that Pearson was running excerpts was rooted in something more serious than innocence or ignorance . . . 12 newspapers sold television and radio properties in 1957 for a return of $40 million.

The *Progressive* went on to point out that our stories were being censored out in some areas, citing the example of the Washington *Post*–owned radio station WTOP: "Drew Pearson's broadcast on that station was censored to remove the references to Chairman Doerfer's padding of expense accounts and acceptance of favors from the broadcasting industry."

The *Progressive* had illuminated problems—failure to pick up, and outright censorship—that were by no means limited to our stories about the Eisenhower regulatory commissions, problems which Drew used complex stratagems to counteract. One of the reasons why he hammered away on the same story, feeding it out a yard at a time, column after column and broadcast after broadcast, had to do with his psyching of the press at large. He believed that in each of the respectable news organizations the sight of a legitimate exposé struggling to be born would touch off an internecine struggle between the real newspeople, who would want to jump in, and the time servers and businessmen, who would have a half-dozen sober arguments for staying out. In time, if our story refused to die, the newspeople would gain the upper hand in at least one of the great organizations. When that happened, the front of establishment silence would be broken and the rest of the quality papers, in which the same battle was being fought out, would then join in with a vengeance. So it proved now. On January 23 the New York *Times* featured a page-one story on the Schwartz memorandum, and published almost the entire text. We had already published the guts of the memo but the *Times* entry made the story henceforth unignorable.*

Chairman Harris went to Speaker Rayburn, as their stone wall began to crumble, for a reassessment and emerged with a policy that vindicated another of Drew's axioms: there comes a time when politicians will suddenly jettison their second love—the special interests that finance them—in order to protect their first love—their political status and survival. Rayburn directed Harris, as Schwartz later recounted, "to go ahead full steam [with the FCC investigation], as the prestige of the House of Representatives was now at stake." Having previously blocked public hearings on the Doerfer and Mack affairs, the subcommittee now reversed itself and held them, under a brighter spotlight than would have shone before. Having been exposed as the castrator of the oversight subcommittee, Oren Harris now had to play the crusading investigator by staging truly convincing hearings.

But there is a methodology to defusing a hot investigation, just as there is one for averting it, and the able Arkansan, even as he donned his interrogator's livery, was moving to limit the damage and regain control of events. Just as he liquidated his sweetheart interest in KRBB-TV now that it was exposed, so he permitted hearings into what already had been essentially revealed, hearings through which Doerfer was disgraced and ultimately forced to resign, and Mack was ruined, ousted and indicted. But as he partially satisfied the demand for action, thereby letting the reformist pressure spend itself, he was all the while maneuvering to get rid of Schwartz and get control of his accumulated files before it could be gotten across to the public that the Mack and Doerfer derelictions were not episodic but represented a systemic corruption of the regulatory structure that extended to the White House itself. There were two elements to the case Harris was contriving against Schwartz, one for the public, one for the Congress: a trumped-up accusation that Schwartz had mishandled subcommittee travel funds to his own advantage, and the fell charge that Schwartz was leaking information to the press—tantamount to treason in the eyes of most congressmen.

When Schwartz conferred with me about the pending kangaroo court, I gave him the kernel of my wisdom about dealing with errant

---

*Schwartz justified "releasing" the memo to the *Times* on the ground that someone else had already leaked it to us. He later wrote: "Key extracts from the text of the memorandum appeared in Drew Pearson's column. Only after this happened did I think of releasing a copy."

congressmen—that the congressional servant of the monied interests is, as was said of the Hun, either at your throat or at your feet, depending on whether you are timid or bold. Citing my hoary uprising at the Black Legion hearing and the tour de force of Howard Hughes, I urged the professor to shout defiance, to demand that his inquisitors take the oath and testify about *their* leaks. Who leaked the investigative plans to the commission malefactors? Who leaked the Schwartz memo to Drew Pearson's column?

At the subcommittee showdown on January 30, 1958, he did just that, and the subcommittee was tied in knots all day as member after member, ten in all, took the stand and swore to Almighty God that they were not secret agents of Drew Pearson. For the moment, Schwartz had turned their flank; the plot against him was stayed, and the subcommittee was so shamed by the day's proceedings that it ordered the transcript sealed and took extraordinary steps to keep it under lock and key. We roared with pleasure upon reading it.

For almost a fortnight Schwartz remained in business while the subcommittee majority regrouped for the resumption of hostilities. I had pipelines into the enemy camp and gave Schwartz daily progress reports on the gangplank his bosses were building for him. At the same time, with the painstaking but doomed diplomacy of an anxious heir who must risk alarming his sick uncle by pressing him to have his will drawn, I impressed upon Bernard that important as his personal survival was, in the likely event of his demise the survival of his files was equally important. This must be attended to before the gendarmes and locksmiths from the Sergeant-at-Arms Office suddenly appeared one morning to usher him out, secure his premises and impound his papers. I remember the dissolving of a great knot of tension when Schwartz, who had become a doughty battler indeed, told me that he had repeatedly foiled watchful eyes and had assembled in his apartment, under his wife's constant custody, a huge duplicate file containing photostats of all the essential documents.

On Friday, February 7, I got hold of firm information that on the following Monday, Oren Harris would convene the subcommittee to vote for Schwartz's dismissal. I immediately informed Schwartz and Drew.

Here was a situation that prompted Drew Pearson to act out the life role he most enjoyed, that of maximum politico—part intelligence sleuth, part commentator, part lobbyist, part propagandist, part conspirator, part caucus-master. The sun was most in its heaven when

Drew could make a damning discovery or hatch a pregnant idea, cajole a senator into making a speech about it, write the speech for him, enlist other senators to be on hand to praise the speech, sit in the press gallery to hear it delivered and praised, write a column celebrating it and its remarkable Senate reception, begin his agitations for Senate hearings, and personally call on the appropriate Cabinet member to advise him of the groundswell rising behind a movement he'd better get out in front of.

With sixty hours to turn around the anti-Schwartz putsch, Drew glowed in contemplation as he charted for us his favorite, and my least favorite, genre of weekend—skullduggerous days spent wrangling and plotting with politicians, sleepless nights devoted to churning out incendiary blurbs for delivery in the House or Senate. His plan was, first, to get the subcommittee vote on ousting Schwartz delayed until Monday afternoon so that phase two, a blitz of pro-Schwartz speeches in both Houses on Monday morning, could have its intended effect of putting a searchlight on the quiet mayhem Harris planned. The second-level approach was to try to stimulate personal interventions by powerful friends that could switch two subcommittee votes, changing the outcome from 7 to 4 against Schwartz to 6 to 5 in favor.

At Drew's urging, Morgan Moulder, the nominal subcommittee chairman, and John Moss, our most *simpático* ally, agreed to a strategy of dragging out the Monday session into the late afternoon. Drew noted in his mental black book that Moulder had to be talked into it, whereas Moss was "not reluctant." As the weekend progressed we tracked down dozens of traveling members of Congress and got many of them to pledge to help us and to get back to Washington in time to do so. We lined up five senators—Estes Kefauver, Wayne Morse, John Sparkman, Pat McNamara and John Carroll—to make speeches which we would write, and two more—Richard Neuberger and Joe Clark—to ask leading questions of the speakers and give the general impression of a Senate awakening to an outrage. On the House side, where only one-minute speeches were allowed, we got pledges from Harry Shepperd and Jack Shelley of California, Edith Green of Oregon, Frank Thompson of New Jersey, Stewart Udall of Arizona and Henry Reuss of Wisconsin. Eugene McCarthy was particularly helpful, promising to produce "a whole slew" of one-minute orators. The "Washington Merry-Go-Round" was to produce the diatribes and circulate them on Monday morning—the House speeches in a bundle to Congressman Shelley, who would distribute them at a caucus he was holding in his office at eleven o'clock, the Senate speeches personally to each Solon.

For helping in the speech writing I enlisted Schwartz himself—not only to lighten my own load but to hasten along his transformation to total comrade in arms. The professor, obviously relishing the opportunity to settle some scores anonymously, delivered three splendid orations to me, all of which were so laced with attacks on subcommittee members that Drew decided they were not usable—even our trusty speechmakers would not so abuse their colleagues, and under the House rules, could not if they would. But the good doctor's fighting edge was a tonic to us all.

Drew's concept of the ultimate goal of the entire investigation was visible in his ghosted tracts. Their recurring refrain was that Commissioners Mack and Doerfer and the others were just following the moral example set by Eisenhower and Nixon; Drew larded his efforts with our old lists of gifts Eisenhower had accepted for his Gettysburg farm from oilmen, and with examples of the favors Nixon had done for the contributors to the "Nixon fund." It was appropriate to Drew's ends that he called on the Democratic National Committee for research help on the speeches; Bill Welsh, the DNC research director, cooperated handsomely, getting his people in early on Monday morning and providing us with a collection of pious "clean as a hound's tooth" campaign bromides from Ike and Dick exalting morality in government and decrying cover-ups, first-rate embarrassments now to a GOP that had filled the regulatory commissions with political hacks and was out to suppress an investigation of them.

In the midst of these tendentious effusions, the personal intercession was not neglected. For example, relying on some strange bond he enjoyed with Senator Herman Talmadge of Georgia, Drew called the senator and asked his help in getting subcommittee member John Flynt, also of Georgia, to change sides and support Schwartz. "Hummon" allowed as to how he didn't have much influence with Flynt, but that he'd give it a fling. That success was unlikely did not deter Drew; in maximum politico-ing, you try everything.

As the House of Representatives opened for business on Monday, February 10, Drew was conspicuously present in the press gallery, not only to savor his handiwork but to remind congressmen that he was serious about their weekend promises to him. Speaker Rayburn must have sniffed a certain restiveness in his domain, for he presided in his august person, instead of Majority Leader John McCormack, whom

Drew had briefed and from whom he hoped, at the least, procedural neutrality. Rayburn quickly rang down the curtain on our drama by using one of his inevitable prerogatives and canceling the one-minute speech privilege for that day. Whereupon Drew moved over to his fall-back arena, the Senate chamber. There, where members are not so easily silenced, the show went on as planned. Erect and pugnacious, with the visage of an offended eagle, Wayne Morse, who could mount the heights of oratorical indignation every day of the month if neces- sary, led off with a blistering attack on the House cover-up, demanding that the Senate take on the regulatory investigation if the House continued to shirk its duty. The speech was to have important conse- quences, if not for its effect on the Congress, then for its impression on Bernard Schwartz. Senators Sparkman, McNamara, Carroll and Kefauver followed Morse, with Neuberger and Clark swelling the cho- rus of debate. Drew was well pleased; it was a big enough show to merit an immediate dispatch on the wires, which meant that over in the House, they were reading all about it on the news tickers.

Behind the closed door of the oversight subcommittee meeting room, our forces showed surprising strength for a few hours, and were carrying the day. In the first test of strength, Congressman Flynt switched to Schwartz's side, along with Charles A. Wolverton of New Jersey, giving him a 6-to-5 majority. But as the session wrangled through the afternoon and on into the evening, Schwartz lost ground by insisting that he not only survive, but survive in a meaningful way. He demanded for himself the right to hire and fire the staff, and for Chairman Moulder the normal power of a chairman to issue subpoenas. And he was impolitic enough to give the members a glimpse of the spirit with which the new powers would be wielded, declaiming with a rising fervor that marked him as a man who could never be trusted in the china shop of government's delicate arrangements with big business: "In a case such as this, if the laws are administered by men who are corrupt, dishonest, if the laws are administered by agencies under the thumb of the White House, if the laws are administered in agencies where votes are bought and sold, then the law becomes a façade."

At seven-thirty the guardians of the law fired Bernard Schwartz by a vote of 7 to 4. Morgan Moulder, who in the end had proved too honest to be Harris' puppet but too compromised to be a swashbuck- ling crusader, resigned his "chairmanship" in protest. Baron Shacklette and another subcommittee investigator had to cancel a scheduled flight to Boston, on which they were to check out a report of costly favors received by Sherman Adams from a textile mogul in trouble with the FTC. There was no need for this information now, for Schwartz's planned hearings into illicit White House interventions in the regulatory process were kaput.

With my inside sources ousted or neutralized, my thoughts flew to what was the last hope, Schwartz's secret files. If I could get hold of them, I could check out their tips, connections and innuendos myself, and I could hold them over Harris' head to prevent him from scuttling the probe. But Oren Harris was too foresighted an intriguer to be circumvented in such a manner. If he had underestimated the character of Schwartz in the past, he understood all too well the hold of his professional code and how it could now be invoked to snuff out any incipient rebellion. Moments after he severed Schwartz, Harris issued a subpoena ordering the former chief counsel to appear in the morning with all documents or copies of documents related to subcommittee work that were in his private possession. Harris knew that Schwartz, a man whose past and future were rooted in the strictest observance of legal tenets and procedures, would feel bound to honor that lawful command. The glowing career that stretched ahead of him in academe or government administration or corporate law would be forfeited if he now became a fugitive from a subpoena.

A telephone tip from a friend gave Schwartz a half-hour's warning that the U.S. marshals were on their way, and in that interim I phoned Schwartz's apartment as part of my regular keeping-in-touch routine; Mrs. Schwartz answered and told me of the impending subpoena and of the quandary it posed for her husband, both as a jailable citizen and a legal paragon. How could he not obey? My usual ready answer to this establishmentarian dilemma is "Turn yourself in to a higher authority, namely, the press—as stand-in for the American people," but since Schwartz would require a less simplistic rationale (though I to this day aver its correctness), I felt I must conjure up another authority for him to turn in to, another branch of government, perhaps. Why not deliver the files to the U.S. Senate before the House subpoena reached him? Thus we could preserve Bernard's decorum *and* his liberty, and keep the files in friendly hands to boot. I said I would try to recruit a suitable senator and call Schwartz back in a few minutes.

I called Drew, who instantly volunteered his closest Senate ally, Wayne Morse, a former law-school dean and administrative-law lion with a reputation for tough independence. Should we wait for Morse's agreement, I queried, before invoking his name in what was bound to be an uproarious rhubarb?

"No, every minute counts," Drew replied. "You produce the files, and I'll be responsible for producing Morse."

I phoned back to Schwartz's apartment but his line was busy. I kept calling. When at length I got through, it was to hear from Mrs. Schwartz that the resourceful Clark Mollenhoff—who was obviously watching developments even more closely than I—had appeared at the apartment with not only the same rationale as mine but with a candidate at the ready. Mollenhoff had talked Bernard into leaving with him for the Mayflower Hotel apartment of Senator John Williams of Delaware with, alas, his boxes of files!

Before my eyes passed eight months of patient nursing of the Schwartz investigation, disappearing down the drain. Damn Mollenhoff! Senator Williams was a corruption fighter of vigor and integrity, but there were two things wrong with him from the viewpoint of our cause and my participation in it: he was a Republican who was up for re-election, and he was Mollenhoff's man. When Williams found that the trail led to the White House, would he cooperate in the discrediting of his party in an election year? Would he be able to resist the various pressures the White House and the GOP would surely bring on him in his somewhat dubious posture as the holder of purloined files? I suspected that he would, but allowed myself to be persuaded that he would not. Then I cast about me for a way to convince Schwartz.

Since Schwartz and Mollenhoff and the files were already with Senator Williams, I had only one rather forlorn hope of reversing Mollenhoff's *fait accompli*. During my association with the Schwartzes I had noticed from time to time that Bernard was one of those wise men who pay instinctive heed to their wives. On the phone to Mrs. Schwartz I asked her if she had a *Congressional Directory*, knowing full well that she did. (I needed a prop to distract her from my obvious personal interest, if she stopped to think about it, in acing out Mollenhoff.) In my most ominous tone I suggested she look up the entry on Senator John Williams. She did "What is his party affiliation?" I asked, hoping she was unaware of Williams' above-party investigative reputation.

"Oh my God," she said. I briefly suggested a "worst possible case" scenario of backsliding by Williams while contrasting it with the unrivaled merit of our bulldog, Wayne Morse, the fellow who had defended Bernard on the Senate floor and had demanded a Senate investigation of the machinations against him. Then I asked her to phone Bernie and urge him to snatch back the files and flee to our offices, where I would meet him and take him to Morse.

A preposterous plan under any circumstance, and the more preposterous in that Clark Mollenhoff was not only one of the sharpest, most persuasive reporters around, he was also the biggest and most intimidating, a veritable giant in size and zeal. But in the realm of last resorts, the preposterous has its honored place.

Consider the scene unfolding at the Mayflower Hotel apartment of Senator Williams, while back at Schwartz's apartment building a throng of reporters and process servers are gathering in the lobby. It is about eleven o'clock. The Schwartz documents are strewn in piles all over Williams' floor. For more than an hour Schwartz has been leading the senator through the papers and their implications, with assists from Mollenhoff, who is agog at the near-prospect of co-possession of this trove and the headlines he may develop from it. The phone rings; it is for Schwartz, his wife calling. When he returns from the phone, there is a distance in his eyes that divides him from his audience, and in some agitation, he begins to snatch up his papers and repack them in the large "overseas case" and two cardboard cartons that eventually form the baggage of every document thief. Awkwardly he explains that he wants to show the papers to Senator Wayne Morse. Williams seems somewhat relieved to have this cup pass from him, which confirms Schwartz in his countermarch; Mollenhoff is appalled, but following the reporter's credo of staying with the documents until forcibly parted, he decamps with Schwartz, shouldering the overseas case. His disenchantment mounts as he learns that they are on their way not to Senator Morse, but to Drew Pearson's place, to pick up Jack Anderson; truly Schwartz has fallen among Samaritans.

When I arrived at Drew's on the chance our ruse might work, I was distressed to find that Drew had not yet contacted Morse. It would be soon enough, he felt, when and if the papers actually came into our hands. The arrival, through the murk, of Mollenhoff, Schwartz and their burdens sent Drew scurrying to the phone out of earshot; if the prickly Morse did not come to the phone at this hour, or did not fancy becoming a safehouse for controversial contraband, my coup would be in vain and a vindicated Mollenhoff would gain the reward of his tenacity and bear back the boxes to Williams. But Morse did come to the phone and Drew had gauged his man aright, for he readily assented.

Morse received us at his apartment, Mollenhoff still in tow, with a conspiratorial élan that Schwartz found a reassuring contrast to the apprehensiveness of Williams. By midnight the Oregon senator was putting on heartening displays of anger over what was in the files, and truculence against those House leaders who would cover it up. And so all the papers were left with Morse. Mollenhoff withdrew grudgingly but gracefully, accepting that I, not he, would momentarily be romping through the files he had lugged all over town. Schwartz went home to face the flashbulbs and process servers and, empty-handed, was "served" at thirty minutes after midnight. He immediately called Drew for help in retaining a prestige lawyer, as he told Drew, "an ex-senator, a man of Cabinet rank." For an hour or two Drew awakened a series of former Cabinet or White House figures, each of whom was, or claimed to be, otherwise occupied for the morrow. Schwartz finally agreed to settle for George Arnold, the son of the famed attorney Thurman Arnold; it helped that George was also Drew's son-in-law. Meanwhile I grabbed a few hours' sleep in preparation for tackling the files immediately for, though Senator Morse had sworn to Schwartz to protect them forever, I figured I had about twenty-four hours before Morse found his position untenable and turned back the files to their duly constituted owners.*

Racing through the Schwartz papers (while Schwartz's attorney George Arnold gained us extra hours through delaying tactics which postponed the revealing of their whereabouts), I scribbled down many an incriminating index of the favoritism-riddled conduct of the public business by the Eisenhower Administration: extralegal interventions by Thomas E. Dewey's law firm that swung the awards of airline routes and earned legal fees as high as $110,000 for Dewey; cooing correspondence about career opportunities in broadcasting between CBS President Frank Stanton and the son of FCC Chairman George McConnaughey; White House obstruction of a CAB crackdown on an airline client of Murray Chotiner, Vice President Nixon's campaign manager, allowing that client to reap two additional years of profits from illegal actions; no fewer than a dozen tainted-looking awards of television channels; a doubling of the price of gas to consumers awarded to the Olin Gas Co. by the Federal Power Commission, under Chairman Jerome K. Kuykendall, after a "hearing" at which the single witness was Olin Gas.

---

*As it happened, Morse held them a day and a half; Speaker Rayburn himself led the array of House dignitaries who negotiated with Morse for their return.

The most explosive possibility, however, resided in the scantiest set of leads, which indicated personal muscling in on Federal Trade Commission decisions by Sherman Adams and hinted at Adams' receipt of valuable commodities from the beneficiary of his interventions, a textile manufacturer named Bernard Goldfine. For years we had been sniffing evanescent whiffs of Adams' trail through the regulatory thickets; now we had a little something to go on.

Sherman Adams, by dint of his own administrative drive and Eisenhower's distaste for the nuts and bolts of government and politics, was considered by knowledgeable observers to be the most powerful unelected official in American history. He dominated Ike's White House; in function and authority he was Haldeman, Ehrlichman, Colson and Chapin all rolled into one. Reported the New York *Times:* "The legend, 'O.K.—S.A.' or 'No—S.A.' on a document carries almost as much weight throughout the Executive Branch as the President's signature."

A spare, crisp, craggy man, formerly the governor of New Hampshire, Adams wielded his power in an abrasive and self-righteous manner. Adjectives commonly used to describe him ran to "sharp" "cold," "tough," "brusque," "no-nonsense," "get-to-the-point." White House reporters nicknamed him "the Iceberg" and "the Abominable No-Man." Determined to impose upon the politicians under him at least the appearance of dignity and efficiency—a risky and quixotic goal for any political chief—he made war on smoking in the White House corridors, feet-on-the-desk informality and the backslapping, bottle-stashing, unbuttoned, grab-assing atmosphere beloved of politicos come into their kingdom. He was, moreover, an unforgiving martinet, quick to lop off the heads of those who slipped, and a bitter partisan forever harping on the corruptions of the Truman Administration, which Drew and I had come to regard as amateur night compared to the organized looting now under way. Adams was not only the de facto straw boss of the Eisenhower Administration but its most authentic symbol save for Ike himself. Expose him as a hypocrite, a bribe taker and a tax dodger, and a mighty blow would be struck at the clean-as-a-hound's-tooth façade that Richard Nixon was about to inherit. Thus he presented a magnificent opportunity to redeem at one last roll our blunted offensives of six years.

Two strands of information in the Schwartz papers kindled these grandiose speculations. First, there were intimations that an attorney at the Federal Trade Commission might be willing to talk about various instances of interference by Adams to stop enforcement of the law against a chronic violator named Bernard Goldfine. Second, there were unsubstantiated hints that Adams accepted favors from this same Goldfine on a continuing basis—suits, overcoats, liquor, furnishings, payment of hotel and resort bills—in other words, the patented list of goodies invariably snatched up by crooked politicians at all levels. How improbable it seemed that the austere, cheerless Adams, sitting at the right hand of the President of the United States, oozing morality and probity, would suffer the indignity, let alone the risk, of permitting himself to be indebted to a gross, indiscreet promoter like Goldfine for the clothes on his back, the liquor in his glass, the rug on his floor, the tabs for his weekends. Or, for the sake of such trinkets, to permit a predictable type like Goldfine to go around boasting, "I've got Sherman Adams in my pocket."* It couldn't be!

Had I not long had my nose rubbed in the ways of Homos politicus, I would have paid little heed to such unsupported charges, particularly against a person who had made as many enemies as Adams had, but as it was, I was conditioned to believe the worst without blinking and I began immediately, in mid-February, by contacting the attorney at the Federal Trade Commission.

Any government agency in which men connive to court the favor or dodge the obloquy of politicians is bound to be a spawning ground for one of the most valuable species in American life—the informer. The informer is our principal protection against the designs of public wrong-doers who have built massive walls to hide their activities. From Drew Pearson and my own improvisations, I had learned something of the art of cultivating informers. I had come to understand the psychology of one who has a dark secret and is teetering on the awful brink of disclosing it. His motive may be noble or base or just human; he may seek to protect the public from fraud, to advance a good cause, to discredit a rival or to avenge a personal grievance. To the reporter the motive should be secondary, except as it bears upon the validity of the information. The lonely informer fretting in his cubicle at the FTC was of the conscientious variety. He perceived a wrong that should be set right.

I learned from him that Adams had twice gotten the FTC to ease

---

*As he had, among others, to John Fox, publisher of the Boston *Post*, a one-time Goldfine enterprise.

up on its pursuit of Goldfine for putting false labels on the products of his textile plants. This could fairly be interpreted as suborning the law-enforcement process, especially so since after the first fix, Goldfine continued with the same violations, and Adams' second successful intervention was to squelch criminal proceedings for incorrigible misconduct. From another source I learned that Adams had actually arranged for a meeting between Goldfine and Eisenhower, a breach in Adams' no-nonsense pattern that revealed Goldfine's grip on him.

This would appear scandalous to the public, however, only if the second set of charges were true—that Adams was "on the take" from Goldfine; otherwise Adams could get away with the usual malfeasor's defense that he was just trying to see that justice was done for a harassed businessman and that he'd do the same for any American. All I had to go on here were rumors and tips, with no one willing to stand behind them; to verify them I must find eyewitnesses, get hold of hotel registers and payment records in Boston, New York and Plymouth, infiltrate Goldfine's inner circle, cozen tax agents who had access to Goldfine's returns, inspire confidences from rug merchants, tailors and liquor dealers. It would take many weeks, since I could not drop my other beats and responsibilities for daily output. This was a nagging weakness of the understaffed "Washington Merry-Go-Round," then and now; we could not, like a great newspaper or magazine, detach a reporter, or a team of reporters, to one story and have them work on it concentratedly for weeks until it was broken.

By May I had buttoned down the key ingredients of the Adams-Goldfine scandal. We knew that the story had the potential of inflicting a crushing blow on the Eisenhower White House. But we knew also that if astutely handled by the White House and played down by a cooperative press, it could be a mere two-day wonder. We decided not to go with all that we had up front, but to start off by revealing only fragments, in hopes that the White House would ensnare itself on false explanations which we could then explode, building up the story from week to week and providing time for the professional conflict within the big-time press to generate and crest; moreover, our stories would be couched as an attack on the Harris committee (as it was now popularly called) for covering up what we were revealing; only an official inquiry could force the admissions-under-oath from Adams and Goldfine that would finally vindicate our story, and our experience with the Doerfer and Mack cases had shown us what must be done to force such an investigation.

Drew was on a European trip, with the column left in my hands, when I fired the first salvo, on May 13, 1958. Charging that Congressman Harris had "instructed his investigators to lay off Adams," I presented the first installment of what was not being investigated:

Federal Trade Commission records show that Adams intervened to help textile tycoon Bernard Goldfine, who got into trouble with Uncle Sam for mislabeling wool products. After Adams poked his sharply chiseled nose into the case, Goldfine was excused from further investigation with the admonition not to violate the law again.

But in less than nine months he was caught pulling the same old tricks. This time the FTC attorney in the case, Charles Canavan, recommended criminal proceedings for "willful and deliberate flouting of the law."

Again Adams came to the rescue with a phone call to FTC Chairman Edward Howrey, asking him to see Goldfine. The textile baron and his son, Horst, showed up in Howrey's office on April 14, 1955, for a confidential conference. At the end of the meeting, Goldfine blurted: "Please get Sherman Adams on the phone for me."

Then, in front of FTC officials, he made a great show of his friendship with the assistant president.

"I'm over at the FTC," Goldfine boomed. "I have been treated very well over here. Thanks for arranging the appointment."

His friendship with Goldfine has been something of a mystery. It is known that Goldfine contributed to Adams' past political campaigns for governor and congressman in New Hampshire. Most of Adams' neat, gray suits are also made in Goldfine's mills.

Adams' unique position and holier-than-thou façade made him such big game that reporters pressed the White House for comment. The White House press operation fumbled the ball this time (or maybe it's just that when you have plenty of reserves, the other side's countermoves always turn out to be errors). Press Secretary Jim Hagerty tested the theory of executive privilege—that he could not discuss the contacts between Adams and his Administration colleagues which, under the Constitution, were privileged. When this was widely lampooned as an admission of guilt, Hagerty essayed the reverse tack of trivializing the matter—yes, Governor Adams had made three calls (we had missed one) to federal agencies on behalf of his old friend, Mr. Goldfine, but that was really just part of his job. "Adams would do the same for anyone." When the preposterousness of it—"the Abominable No-Man" posing as universal ombudsman—caused it to fall flat, the creative Hagerty, who had after all silenced greater tempests than this, opened up the civil-libertarian front and accused us of "trying to smear" Adams. Meanwhile, amid tokens of the President's esteem, the governor went about his business with the air of one who carries on his great obligations undistracted by the contumely from below.

But the story would not go away, in part because we were able to stoke the fire every few days with a new combustible—one we had held in reserve or a new one which, as always happens, our raising of the flag against Adams caused to come to us. During the next few weeks of May and June we periodically revived it with stories such as these:

- Goldfine paid for most of Adams' clothes.
- Goldfine paid a $2,000 hotel tab for Adams at Boston's Sheraton-Plaza, and other tabs elsewhere.
- Adams arranged a private meeting for Goldfine with President Eisenhower, a commodity for which senators had to wait months.
- Goldfine gave Adams an expensive vicuña coat.
- Adams used to have liquor hauled away by the stationwagonload from a storehouse in the rear of Goldfine's Boston residence.
- Adams had taken a number of Oriental rugs from Goldfine, one of them valued at $2,400.
- Goldfine had provided much of the furniture in Adams' home and had loaned him his airline credit card.

By the last week in May the prestige press—the New York *Times*, the New York *Herald Tribune*, the Washington *Post*, the St. Louis *Post-Dispatch*—had jumped into the story, and by mid-June the whole press pack was baying on the Adams trail. On June 14 we published our *pièce de résistance:* not only did Adams take a vicuña coat from Goldfine, *Eisenhower did, too.*

So well had design and events interlocked to gradually build these small transactions into a drama that this last item was a sure-fire front-page bombshell everywhere. We knew its proportions when Drew, arriving in Chicago to make a speech, was met at the airport by a photographer for the Chicago *American,* and on his arrival in mid-town, was deluged with calls for radio and television interviews.

The able Hagerty again played into our hands, which only shows that the most touted of defense mouthpieces is reduced to a bumbling charlatan when forced into confrontation with a fact. He kept rushing out denials of our charges in the obvious hope that we either could not prove our case or would not be heard above the din of his denials. This time, neither assumption worked. We produced a thank-you note from

Ike to Goldfine and wired other supporting data to all of our outlets so they would not be bluffed out. For example:

> When Hagerty went to Adams and asked him about the vicuña coat, Adams replied that the "old man" got one too. He even described it as a three-quarter-length coat. You will recall that Hagerty came back and told newsmen at the time that he couldn't comment. He continued to be evasive and on Monday, June 16, even when he received a direct question from the correspondent of the Manchester, (N.H.) *Union* as to whether Goldfine had "offered some suits to the President," Hagerty replied, "I have no knowledge of that."
>
> This, of course, was untrue. Hagerty had known the facts for three days. It was not until the next morning, June 17, that Hagerty, faced with my categoric statement that Ike had sent a letter to Goldfine thanking him for the coat and that the letter had been seen by others, finally admitted that at least some vicuña cloth had been received and accepted.

Hagerty's claim that Eisenhower had given the "vicuña material" to a friend, but couldn't remember who, was taken by most as an inexcusably weak ploy.

Now that Drew was being interviewed on the national media, he forbore to play the objective press statesman and instead used his every opportunity to trot out—yes—the long-peddled list of gifts Ike had accepted over the years from fat cats with a large stake in government decisions. Afraid that the Democrats would not seize the day, he badgered Democratic National Chairman Paul Butler to organize a campaign that by-passed Adams and stressed Eisenhower's and Nixon's culpability. Events would show his foresightedness.

Eisenhower lent himself to all this by an uncharacteristic bit of imprudence. Historically, he possessed in high degree the statesman's clear-headed fortitude in promptly disposing of those whose personal errors embarrass the Chief; normally, his order to one in Adams' position would have been to either clear himself immediately or resign. But Adams was so valuable to Ike's part-time presidency that the President was loath—for reasons of gratitude, loyalty and order in his household—to nip the scandal in the bud by banishing the offender. Ike, after all, would never again be running for office and was in a mood to put his day-to-day convenience higher than the temporary buffeting of a passing political squall. By coming down hard on Adams' side, he hoped to snuff out the story and rob it of the potential drama of a great one's impending fall. So he kept saying that his trust in Adams was unimpaired, that he liked and respected and trusted Adams and continued to have every confidence in him. He went beyond this, touchingly. "What Sherman Adams did was imprudent, but I *need* him."

Adams hung on, even when the Harris committee again succumbed to rising pressures and scheduled hearings. When Bernard Goldfine and his entourage came to Washington for them, my old collaborator Baron Shacklette, still chief investigator for the Harris committee, decided to attempt to eavesdrop on Goldfine's suite, and to tape-record whatever he could pick up on a microphone located on his own premises. The rationale was that Goldfine was reported to have hired private investigators to dig up discrediting information about members of the Harris committee (not too hard a task, I thought) and that it was necessary to be able to anticipate and counteract his moves. Shacklette arranged for rooms adjoining various Goldfine suites at the Sheraton-Carlton, set up the eavesdropping gear and invited me to join him to monitor the proceedings.

I fully encouraged this official snoopery and assisted with the clandestine arrangements. No ethical problem troubled me at the time. If a government agency, whether the FBI or a congressional committee, decided to bug someone and permitted me to cover the affair, I persuaded myself that it was the reporter's duty to gain access and to report the news. So I helped Shacklette in registering in the various rooms and took to checking in regularly with him and his electronic marvels. I would stay for about an hour at a time.

If the ethical objection to this course was obscure to me, its public relations pitfalls were soon borne home. Goldfine's attorneys, our old adversaries Roger Robb and Edward Bennett Williams, and his public relations man, Jack Lotto, well knew the mettle of their opposition and divined something suspicious going on in the adjoining room. It was my fortune to be on the premises one midnight when there came a loud rap-rapping on the door which persisted with such confident authority that I realized we could no longer play possum and persuaded Shacklette that the only thing to do was open up. We did, to find Lotto and a group of reporters he had summoned. Shacklette explained, with as matter-of-fact an air as he could, that since the Goldfine forces were investigating members of the Harris committee, he was keeping a counterwatch. I tried to maintain the detached mien of an observer, even when confronted with the embarrassment of being registered in that room under the false name of Elliott Brooks. (J. Edgar Hoover took immense delight from this; hereafter, new entries in my dossier were to be headed "Jack Anderson, a/k/a Elliott Brooks.")

I did not realize the trouble I was in until I learned in the morning that some of Drew's closest friends were urging him to suspend me so as to separate himself from the contretemps; instead, he issued to a clamorous press a paraphrase of Ike's statement on Sherman Adams: "Jack Anderson, of course, has been imprudent, but I need him."

Not everyone appreciated the humor, I myself the least. But some did. On that night's NBC news, David Brinkley, after describing the events at the Sheraton-Carlton, completely broke up when he came to Drew's "imprudent" statement; he tried a couple of times to recover himself and finish the account, but was unable to do so and the time slot ran out with Brinkley rolling in uncontrollable mirth—perhaps a "first" on network television news.

Goldfine's attorneys, naturally enough, tried to make this as large a diversion as possible from the events unfolding in the hearing room, where Goldfine was being impaled on his refusal to explain why he had kept $770,000 in uncashed cashier's and treasurer's checks for many years, some of it for as long as fifteen years, instead of depositing the money in accounts that drew interest. The suspicion was that he had allowed colluding politicians to use these checks as collateral for loans. Goldfine's secretary, Mildred Paperman, sought to expand the eavesdropping affair into a criminal matter (as eavesdropping was not) by charging that confidential papers had been stolen from her closet, Shacklette and I being the main suspects. Her charge got a grand jury convened but proved baseless; nothing came of it and the Sheraton-Carlton affair petered out.

It should have been clear by now that Drew would achieve his goal of cracking the shell of immunity that had for six years surrounded Ike; night-club comedians had begun to add vicuña jokes to their repertoires. Our revelation that Ike, too, was on Goldfine's gift list, and the transparently deceptive way the White House press office tried to deny it, ended all reasonable hope that Adams could ride out the storm without inflicting unacceptable damage on the Republican cause. It did not help that Goldfine refused to answer eighteen questions put by the Harris committee and faced inevitable indictment for contempt of Congress. But it was not clear to Eisenhower and Adams. Through a long, hot summer they refused to recognize the seeping erosion that was diminishing the standing of President and party. In September the Adams affair played a part in the Democratic wipe-out of Republicans

in elections in Maine, traditional GOP stronghold, and shortly thereafter Republican leaders began telling the New York *Times* that "party
pressure will force Adams' ouster." On September 22 Adams resigned,
still affirming that there was nothing wrong with the nation's second
highest official being kept by a much tarnished supplicant before federal agencies.

The resignation came too late to reverse the damage to Republican
candidates. In the November congressional elections the GOP suffered
a catastrophic defeat, resulting in the lop-sided Democratic majorities
in both House and Senate that have been the rule ever since.

There were a number of causes for that defeat, including Sputnik in
1957 and a sharp economic recession during the first half of 1958. The
role played by the Adams scandal in compounding the debacle was
assessed by Vice President Nixon in a post-mortem memorandum of
analysis for party strategists:

> Half of our loss was due to the fact that the issues ran against us from
> the time of the second term inauguration in 1957 until the campaign began
> . . . But just as soon as the good news that the recession was ending began
> to come out in July, there was another bad break—the Adams case. That
> kept us on the defensive so much that we couldn't play up the good news
> of improved economic conditions.
>
> Now, all the bad news was over by the first of October, but you can't
> undo in a month what had happened all this time.

Drew saw Nixon and his 1960 presidential bid as the big losers of
the 1958 elections. Huge Democratic congressional majorities would
ensure a stagnant, embattled look for the final two years of the Eisenhower Administration, and the loss of key governorships would cost
Nixon heavily in 1960 campaign resources.

But the unusual personal carnage of our year-long campaign was so
great as to taint our satisfaction in its success. Sherman Adams entered
a solitary exile from the world he had known which endures to this day;
he was saved from prosecution as a criminal only by the political
protection of President Eisenhower, and later President Kennedy, at
Eisenhower's personal request. Bernard Goldfine was ruined financially
and suffered a physical and mental breakdown that shortened his prison
term. Thurman Whiteside committed suicide. Richard Mack became
an alcoholic and ended up in a mental institution, too pathetic and
broken a figure to be prosecuted further.

The accumulation of these tragedies, to which I was a direct contributor, recalled the suicide of Forrestal, the self-destruction of Joe McCarthy, the jailing and ruining of J. Parnell Thomas and two other congressmen we had exposed for taking salary kickbacks—Walter Brehm and Ernest Bramblett. I was for a time enveloped in the mood of my early days with Drew when a successful story of mine had destroyed the lives of Sam Ripps and Joseph Mitchell, the Mobile, Alabama, pair exposed by me as embezzlers. Were these stories, some of them hinged on trivial amounts, worth the lives or sanity of people and the incalculable destruction wreaked upon their innocent families?

The two edges of the sword wielded by my calling were painfully apparent to me at such times. The events of 1958 had again proved the validity, in one sense, of our kind of muckraking: institutions will not reform themselves, and the nation dependent on them for equity will disintegrate, unless the wrongdoing of individual officeholders is exposed, arousing a public furor which forces compromised politicians to clean house. But every success of the investigative reporter means ruin for some human being who is typically weak rather than evil. Most of the time I am militantly convinced that the trade-off is necessary to maintain a free society. But there are seasons when it seems a close call.

12 · Kibitzing in Presidential Politics

Tₕₑ ₚₑᵣᵢₒ𝒹 that leads up to a presidential election, especially one that figures to be close, is for a political reporter the time of maximum stimulation and temptation. It is the time when public interest in political reporting reaches that high plateau normally reserved for sports news and sex crimes; when the leading figures of the land are most vulnerable to, and most benefited by, the press; when power at the highest level may change hands and when a news story, even an incorrect one, could tip the balance. The "Washington Merry-Go-Round" was particularly susceptible to presidential-year fever, for Drew Pearson was as much the political activist as the reporter. From the earliest phase of the nominating process he invariably served as part-time manager for one candidate, adviser to one or two others, and interested chronicler of the fortunes of the rest.

As the Eisenhower reign approached its constitutionally appointed end and politicians began positioning themselves for the change of regime in 1960, Drew surveyed the scene with anticipation. On the one hand, the last of his great *bêtes noires*, Richard Nixon, was likely to be the Republican standard-bearer, giving Drew that which energized him above all else—a menace to combat. On the other, the Democrats were fielding an unusually large group of credible hopefuls—Adlai Stevenson, John F. Kennedy, Estes Kefauver, Hubert Humphrey, Lyndon Johnson, Stuart Symington, Robert Meyner—among whom he could look forward to a long season of meddling and manipulating.

I approached the 1960 campaign with the hope that our involvement would be merely journalistic, and that Drew would not double as assistant campaign manager, go-between and speech writer for one of the candidates, with me as his ward heeler. We had played these roles in the 1952 and 1956 campaigns, in part because of his love for politicking, in part because of his attachment to the causes embraced in the campaigns of Estes Kefauver.

As no other candidate in those years, Kefauver stood for Populist reforms, for an end of boss-ruled conventions, for the growth of primaries, for a top-to-bottom structural reform of the secretive, insulated, elder-dominated processes of Congress, for a break-up of the cynical alliances between urban pols and mobsters and between Northern liberals and Southern race-baiters under the Democratic tent, and for a brass-knuckles assault on big-business monopolies and their price-fixing. Sixteen years before Eugene McCarthy's campaign of 1968, Estes Kefauver challenged and *defeated* a sitting President in the New Hampshire primary, hastened if not forced that President's withdrawal from the race, and went on to sweep the primary states, only to be blocked by the organization-ruled, nonprimary delegations, which were still numerically dominant in 1952 but whose legitimacy was fatally wounded by Kefauver.

I, too, had been swept up in the Kefauver campaigns and had co-authored, with Fred Blumenthal of our staff, a campaign-year biography of Kefauver in 1956. But Kefauver was not to be a serious factor in 1960, and not having the yen to play politics that Drew had, I hoped for a campaign season as a detached reporter rather than as a co-conspirator. But it was not to be.

As early as the beginning of 1958, Drew was trying to sift through the large Democratic field, pick his candidate to oppose Nixon and get mobilized behind him. He was attracted to Hubert Humphrey. Humphrey was the best campaigner of the lot, he would say, the brightest idea man, the truest fighter for the underprivileged, the boldest visionary on matters of peace and war; his only fault, Drew felt—and it could be a disabling one—was an incapacity for priority-setting and administrative toughness. "He's a wonderful guy, with wonderful ideas, but not much organization; he tends to run off in all directions."

With typical self-confidence, Drew was ready to help "Hubert" overcome this lack. In January 1958 he wrote to Humphrey with a view to setting up a meeting to discuss ways and means of organizing and raising money and getting the jump on the others, but Humphrey, perhaps with a firmer grasp on journalistic propriety than Drew, did not answer his letter. Attributing this to the mal-organization he was endeavoring to overcome, Drew was not offended and invited Humphrey to his home for breakfast in April.

"I talked to Hubert about the idea of running for President. I told him that . . . if the Democrats rowed too much among themselves they would lose. I also pointed out that . . . it's time for the liberals to get together on a real candidate. It seemed to me he was the best qualified."* Humphrey was "eloquent and alarmed" about the state of the world but noncommittal about his candidacy, then or in the months to come. In March 1959 Jim Rowe, who was working with Humphrey after his first loyalty, Lyndon Johnson, refused to declare himself, called on Drew, briefed him on the nascent Humphrey presidential campaign and asked him to support Humphrey in his column and broadcasts the way he had boosted Kefauver in the past. Drew noted in his diary: "I told him that last year I had told Humphrey I would like to talk to him about his candidacy, but that I had never heard from him again and figured that either he didn't take himself seriously or didn't take me seriously. 'Oh, that's typically Hubert,' said Jim."† This compounded Drew's central misgiving, which concerned Humphrey's state of organization, not his own vanity. Drew began to help the Humphrey cause but was never able to shake the feeling that it was a mom-and-pop affair going against the great chain stores and would fail because, despite Humphrey's superior gifts, he lacked the executive ability to marshal the campaign resources that could be his.

I was attracted to John Kennedy, and not just because of his much touted charm and grace—ornaments that ranked low on my list of presidential requisites. I was initially taken with Kennedy because I thought he had the sharpest, most incisive mind I had encountered, except possibly for Howard Hughes. Whenever I had business with Kennedy he would go straight and quick to the heart of each point at issue, with an impressive lack of fluff and jargon, and I would find myself out in the hall again amazed at how much ground we had

*Pearson Diaries (April 9, 1958), p. 453.
†Ibid. (March 25, 1959), p. 515.

covered in so short a time, and grateful to Kennedy for saving my time as well as his own. He gave me an impression of cheerful competence, of good intentions disciplined by reflection and ordered by a keen sense of what was practically possible.

But Drew was leery of Kennedy, so my admiration of him was to have little opportunity to surface in our columns. Kennedy was suspect to Drew on grounds the reverse of his misgivings about Humphrey. Kennedy was *too* organized; too deep in campaign resources; too tough-minded; in his back rooms Drew's mind's ear could pick up the hum of an efficiency that could be ruthless. If Humphrey was improvidently generous in his support of every remedy, Kennedy was too calculating in balancing his image to curry conservative favor, too cautious in writing off what could not be done.

Whenever the two met, Drew would be impressed by Kennedy's attractiveness and sophistication, but back in his office he would begin to worry about the influence of his domineering tycoon father and the way plutocratic money was greasing Kennedy's path. The closeness of the Kennedy clan to Joe McCarthy in his heyday was an important barometer to Drew, as was Jack's half-decade of weaseling on the McCarthy issue.

> I couldn't help but think as I talked to him that he was very much like his father. His dad was a warm-hearted liberal Irishman who did a fine job in the early days of the Roosevelt administration, then went sour, got bogged down with too much money and considered himself a law unto himself. Kennedy started as a fine Congressman and is still a good Senator. I told him as much. "I thought you were a wonderful Congressman when you first came here," I said, "but now that you are in the Senate, it seems to me you're wobbling . . ."*

In contrast to the uncertainty and diffidence of Humphrey, Kennedy mobilized early and, in good time, made a personal visit to Drew to ask his support for the presidential nomination, but Drew would not give it. He not only doubted Kennedy but underestimated him. He reported approvingly on the remarks at lunch of his old collaborator, Senator Tom Hennings:

> Tom summarized the Democratic candidates only as three: Stevenson, Hubert Humphrey and Lyndon Johnson. Lyndon he described as an opera-

Ibid. (January 14, 1958), p. 421.

tor, Humphrey as a man with real courage and ability, and Stevenson as a statesman.

We agreed that Symington hasn't any courage and that Jack Kennedy won't get anywhere, though he has done a pretty good job on the labor bill.*

Drew's first machination of the upcoming 1960 nomination campaign was to exploit its exigencies in order to extract a good deed out of a leading hopeful, Lyndon B. Johnson. Drew's relationship with the Senate Majority Leader, dating back a quarter century to the days when he was boosting Johnson's emergence as a comparatively progressive figure on the bleak Texas landscape, had proved durable but had its up-and-down phases. Johnson would grow philosophical about it by the time he became President: "I can always tell when I'm up or when I'm down, according to what Drew writes. When I'm down, Drew goes to my defense. When I am up, Drew takes a nick at me."

It was true that Drew would sometimes come to LBJ's defense when he thought he was in trouble, for he regarded him as too valuable a force behind many progressive causes to have him estranged from, or discredited by, the left. But in the main their rapport depended upon whether Johnson was pursuing his liberal impulses or heeding the constraints on him of the Texas and Senate political structures. Johnson talked turkey to Drew—another tie that bound—as at a Washington luncheon for Harry Truman in February 1958 when the Majority Leader approached Drew before the luncheon and lit into him for following a double standard where he was concerned:

> He shook hands cordially and we had quite a talk. He said that he agreed with the column this morning, adding that he didn't usually agree. . . . He made quite a little argument that both he and I had the same things in common, but that he had one disadvantage in that he had to represent the oil and gas people. "You forgive Hubert Humphrey when he champions the dairy people in Minnesota," said Lyndon. "You forgive Tom Hennings his faults. You forgive Kefauver his problems. But you don't forgive me mine."†

Drew conceded that there was some justice in this criticism and for a while went out of his way to praise LBJ's leadership, but by early 1959 relations were on the downside again, and in a pun on Johnson's name,

Ibid. (August 13, 1959), p. 544.
†*Ibid.* (February 25, 1958), p. 439.

Drew had begun to hang a contagious epithet on him, "Lyin' down Lyndon." As it began to catch on, it distressed Johnson even more than criticism usually did, for, in his courting of the next year's presidential nomination, he feared the mischief Drew could cause him in liberal and Northern circles just when he was counting on Drew to help improve his image there. Word came to us that the Leader wanted a nonaggression pact.

It was not the first such negotiation. In 1956, another down-period when the column was raking Johnson for having engineered an outrageous tax forgiveness for George Brown of the Texas-based Brown and Root Construction combine, Johnson had seized upon Drew's championship of Kefauver to offer a deal.

Kefauver made a great showing against Adlai Stevenson in the early 1956 primaries and our hopes were high. So Johnson sent an aide to Kefauver's campaign manager, Jiggs Donahue, with a bald-faced deal: if Drew Pearson would drop the Brown-Root mini-crusade, Lyndon would pledge to throw his weight to Kefauver at the convention. It was a vintage Johnsonian deal: he would get his end of it in the here and now, Drew would have to wait and trust for six months, during which Kefauver might either drop out or become the sure winner. But it was a Pearson deal, too: he had just about exhausted the tax story anyway. Stipulating that he remained free to write about Johnson in all other matters, he sent word to Johnson that he agreed.

He was bothered about it, and mooned around a bit, as if he had given up his maidenhead for England; he confided to his diary: " . . . I figured I might do that much for Estes. This is the first time I've ever made a deal like this, and I feel a little unhappy about it. With the Presidency of the United States at stake, maybe it's justified, maybe not—I don't know."*

As it turned out, Kefauver began to lose primaries and the day came when he asked Drew to act as his go-between with Adlai in arranging his withdrawal and the switch of his delegates to Stevenson. Johnson thus had gotten a free ride the last time around, but this time there was something that Drew wanted very badly, and that Johnson would have to deliver up front.

Admiral Lewis L. Strauss, the Atomic Energy Commission Chairman, had just been nominated by President Eisenhower as his next Secretary of Commerce. In Drew's view, Strauss was in the tradition

*Ibid. (April 16, 1956), p. 359.

of Forrestal—a Wall Street banker (Kuhn, Loeb) who, making a gift of himself to the public, had filled high offices by serving hard-line causes and catering to the big-business interest. Drew explained his particular motives for opposing Strauss to his biographer:

> Strauss had fallen for McCarthyism and staged a trial of Dr. Robert Oppenheimer, father of the A-bomb, which ended in Oppenheimer being purged from the government altogether. I went to bat vigorously for Oppenheimer during his trial and felt that it was only poetic justice that Strauss, the man who persecuted Oppenheimer, get his just deserts when he came up for Senate confirmation. I argued that Strauss had been mixed up in the Dixon-Yates conflict of interest case, had not told the truth in the Senate during this investigation and that any man who did not tell the truth to the Senate was not worthy of confirmation.*

Drew was appalled at the lack of opposition to Strauss in a Democratic Senate, almost losing his temper with John Kennedy after an unsuccessful attempt to recruit him: ". . . you fellows understand the hams and the deep freezes but you don't understand a $200 million Dixon-Yates deal—the worst conflict-of-interest case since Teapot Dome."†

Beyond this, for political reasons, in the larger sense, Drew wished to follow up the Adams ouster with a second rebuff to the Administration, one of equal magnitude. Eisenhower continued to dominate a Democratic Congress that seemed not to know what to do with its tremendous electoral mandate; a pitched battle over a Cabinet nomination would rouse the listless Democrats to fighting trim over more important issues.

Determined to ignite a movement of opposition to Strauss, and painfully aware of his many defeats in confirmation battles, he decided to parley with the one man who could carry off the defeat of Strauss. Lyndon Johnson's leadership—open or covert—of the anti-Strauss fight was to be Drew's price for another armistice. Since a pact of this character is not seemly made by the principals, but through the agency of some hind who can be disowned if things go awry, I was selected to take Drew's offer to Johnson.

Lyndon Johnson, with his intimidating bulk, his mobile and menacing facial expressions, his air of being preoccupied with annoying matters, was not an easy man to approach. But I watched for an appropriate

---

*Klurfeld, *op. cit.*, p. 246.
†*Pearson Diaries* (May 26, 1959), p. 527.

moment and bearded him alone one afternoon. Trying to summon an authoritative tone as he glared at me impatiently, stuck out his chin like Mussolini and fiddled with one of his ears, I said, "If you want to get Drew off your back, there's a way."

He stared at me balefully for a moment, through heavy-lidded eyes. "Who do I have to kill?" he said.

"Admiral Strauss."

"Oh, no. Oh, no. That's impossible."

I started to leave, and as I reached the door he sighed and then moaned, "Sure would like to get Drew off my back."

I paused at the door, eyebrows poised for bargaining.

"Tell Drew I'll see if I can work something out," he said.

Lyndon Johnson had sound reasons for not wishing to deplete his leadership capital and complicate his *modus vivendi* with the executive branch on a gambit that would cast him as a narrow partisan and seemed destined to fail anyway. No presidential nominee for a Cabinet post had been rejected by the Senate in almost half a century, so strong was the tradition that a President was entitled to his Cabinet choice unless some overpowering scandal or disability was discovered. Admiral Strauss (the military title was given him in honor of his contributions to the war effort as a civilian) had served five Presidents of both parties, had attained a Baruchian status, possessed an undoubted competence and was the choice of a President still popular in the country.

The only prospective gain to Johnson, aside from whatever value he placed on keeping Drew at bay, was a strengthening of his dwindling rapport with the restive liberal wing of the Senate, which could be achieved in other ways at less cost than the invidious drama of a high-level purge. However, without formally telling Drew he agreed to the deal, Johnson began quietly to encourage opposition to Strauss and to instruct Drew in what to do, and what not to do, in his lobbying, and Drew tentatively dropped all reference to "Lyin' Down Lyndon" and began to celebrate "Likeable Lyndon."

Johnson's first advice to Drew was not to complicate the task by getting his coterie of junior senator–collaborators initially identified with it. "He . . . says to get the top leaders in the [Commerce] committee pledged in the order of their importance from Magnuson [the chairman] down. After you've got the first three senior members, he said, the rest should be fairly easy. Don't go for the young fellows first, he said."*

Ibid. (March 2, 1959), p. 511.

Warren Magnuson's situation illustrated the difficulty of arousing opposition to Strauss in a body that had twice confirmed him for high office. When the Senate had considered Strauss's nomination to a second term on the Atomic Energy Commission in 1953, Senator Magnuson rose on the floor to give this unqualified endorsement: "I merely wish to say that I do not know of any finer statesman in the United States than is Lewis L. Strauss. He is my personal friend."

Strong words which would have to be eaten, and Drew would have been even more concerned about Chairman Magnuson had he known that when the President announced Strauss's current appointment, Magnuson had wired the Admiral from Seattle: "Congratulations on your new appointment. I hope this will be a resumption of our former pleasant relationship." Yet reassessments and reversals are the lifeblood of politics, and it was not beyond hope that Magnuson, Drew's long-time ally, could be persuaded.

Drew did as Johnson directed, and after calling on the top three committee members, he successfully pressed Magnuson, on the advice of Johnson and with the help of Clinton Anderson, the most widely influential anti-Strauss senator, to delay the confirmation hearings for two or three months in order to provide time for opposition to Strauss to build up. Later the meeting at which the anti-Strauss campaign was organized took place in Drew's home—a stag dinner for well-disposed members of the Commerce Committee on the night before the confirmation hearings were to begin. Lapping up the role of conspirator from the inside, Drew was guardedly pleased with the results:

> Magnuson, who has been wobbly, seemed to have been bolstered somewhat, though I still am worried about him. He has agreed, however, to appoint a subcommittee of about three men to investigate [Strauss] thoroughly. We even discussed who might be on the committee—probably McGee and Yarborough of Texas [two Strauss critics]. Yarborough was at the dinner and is an eager beaver. Maggie [Magnuson] also suggested Morton of Kentucky, Republican, because he is lazy.*

Months passed as opposition multiplied and as Strauss quite properly but in vain protested the unannounced filibuster against him. The issues which were most telling against Strauss were (1) the seeming personal arrogance of a bright and quick mind, undeferential toward

Ibid. (March 16, 1959), p. 513

the ponderosities of Senate jargon, and (2) an occasional lack of forth-
comingness in long years of dealing with Congress on sensitive subjects.
We sought to sharpen these negative images as the struggle built up
steam and became the top ongoing Washington news drama, and we
found a way to do so. When Strauss began to testify, I positioned
myself behind him where I could see the papers visible on the table in
front of him. I noticed, with a start, a file with the familiar look of an
FBI security summary. It was stamped "Top Secret" or "Confidential"
and its subject was Dr. David Inglis, chairman of the Federation of
American Scientists and a leading Strauss critic at the hearings.

This could be effectively tied in, I speculated, with the apparently
concerted effort under way by the Strauss side to discredit Dr. Inglis.
The implication I drew from the document in front of Strauss was that
he was abusing his entrée to Eisenhower security chiefs to dredge up
derogatory information about a citizen whose offense was to testify
before a Senate committee in opposition to Strauss—a bona-fide "dirty
trick."

This was the burden of our next column, and it sparked a minor
uproar. Strauss categorically denied that he had made inquiries or "ever
called anyone" about Inglis; Drew and I volunteered to corroborate our
charges to the committee and were called as witnesses. On the stand
I most adamantly stuck by my recollection of what I had seen, and
Strauss most adamantly denied it—a stand-off in the absence of objective proof. Drew pursued a more definitive tack. Reasoning that if
Strauss would call on the FBI for information about Inglis he would
also call on the AEC, from which he had only recently departed after
many years as chief, Drew tried one of his patented early-morning
phone calls—to the assistant to the new AEC Chairman. Oh, yes,
recalled the assistant, perhaps unaware in his pre-breakfast fog of the
controversy raging on Capitol Hill, Strauss had personally telephoned
the AEC for information about the life and background of David
Inglis. To this Drew testified, flatly contradicting Strauss's testimony
that he hadn't called anyone. To extricate himself, Strauss said that the
call to the AEC was made *after* Pearson's May 5 column appeared,
whereas his testimony was meant to apply to the prior period. But a
letter from the new AEC Chairman, John McCone, was introduced
showing that the date of the Strauss call about Inglis was April 20. This
had to be a damaging blow to Strauss; Bobby Baker, Lyndon Johnson's
nose-counter in the Senate, reported that the confirmation vote was
now a horse race, with about 50 votes on each side.

At this point Alfred Friendly, managing editor of the Washington *Post,* our premier outlet, called Drew to suggest not too subtly that we had written enough about Strauss. This was undoubtedly true, and of course, it was not the half of it. For several months we had been knee-deep in things that journalists should never do. Between the two of us, we had made lobbying visits to more than half the members of the Senate to argue against confirmation. We had written anti-Strauss speeches for more than a dozen senators, and when we found Senator Russell Long friendly but more interested at the moment in attacking Douglas Dillon, we wrote an anti-Dillon speech for him.

When a reporter asks a politician for a favor, even though it be a vote on the "right" side, there is an unspoken implication that someday there will be a favor in return, either in what we write in the column, or forgo to write. One senator did not leave the implication unspoken. Allen Frear of Delaware, home of DuPont, passed a message to Drew through Clinton Anderson that he might vote against Strauss if Drew would refrain from attacking Frear's special tax-avoidance legislation for DuPont; Drew did not respond to Frear, but nonetheless, we should never have been in a posture to receive such an offer.

Once we were fevered with the heat of classic politicking, few of its iniquities were to be forborne. One of my charges was to keep the wavering Senator Bob Bartlett, the Alaska Democrat, on the team. I would jaw faithfully with Bartlett and would report back to Drew that old Bob was firm. Then Drew picked up a rumor that Bartlett was wobbling, so I asked Clinton Anderson to shore him up, which he did, for a time. But then, more rumors of wobbling, and Drew glowered at me as though I were a precinct captain unable to deliver his neighborhood. Finally I got Bobby Baker to corner the rough-hewn but ambiguous Alaskan and pin him down, whereupon Bartlett reaffirmed his intention to vote against Strauss; we rested then—after declaring yourself to Bobby Baker, there was no turning back.

When Drew learned that former Defense Secretary and now master lobbyist Louis Johnson was planning to testify for Strauss and eulogize his role in ramrodding America toward development of the H-bomb ahead of Russia—testimony that would be especially effective coming from so highly placed a Democratic partisan and Defense insider as Johnson—Drew cast about for a way to gag his old anti-Forrestal co-intriguer. Deciding that Johnson could best be moved by business considerations, Drew called Cyrus Eaton, the radical industrialist, whose Chesapeake & Ohio Railroad was the largest business enterprise in Louis Johnson's home base of West Virginia. Within an hour or two Eaton called back to tell Drew: "I talked to Louis; there'll be no testimony for Strauss."

Since we were not beyond tampering with the jury and suborning witnesses, we surely would not stop at helping to pack the prosecution. When the make-up of the Commerce Committee's investigative unit on Strauss, first nominated at Drew's house, started to come unstuck as Yarborough, the designated chairman, began to get second thoughts about being in the middle of such a divisive battle, Drew jumped into action. He called Yarborough and gave him a pep talk, and got Clinton Anderson to twist his arm; then Drew called a group of Yarborough's key supporters back home—Texas liberals who were close to Drew— and got them to put pressure on Yarborough, who at length agreed to shoulder the solemn responsibility.

Lyndon Johnson never publicly owned to leading the anti-Strauss drive, but his fine hand was everywhere. No development was too small to escape his attention. When Senator Thomas Dodd, a first-year Democrat from Connecticut, tried to reserve floor time for a pro-Strauss speech, Johnson moved in on him, for he did not want any contagious demonstration that the Northern Democrat front against Strauss was not necessarily solid, especially from Dodd, an incendiary orator; moreover, Johnson wanted to keep Dodd publicly uncommitted and in reserve in case he needed his vote at the last moment. Johnson told Dodd that he wouldn't ask him to change his position on Strauss, but there was one little thing Dodd could do for him (and Dodd owed him a great deal): postpone his speech, and the announcement of his position for a few days—this wouldn't compromise his principles or hurt him with the Connecticut Jews—and it would help the weary Leader in his manifold tasks. Dodd agreed and for days carried his speech around in his coat pocket waiting for the green light.

As the day of the final vote drew near, the outcome was so close as to hang on one or two votes out of ninety-eight. And at least one vote was unstable, that of the Senate's only woman, Margaret Chase Smith of Maine. A Republican and an Eisenhower backer, she seemed a safe vote for Strauss, but she was also a woman scorned and this, thought Drew, created an opening for mischief. She had been scorned by Air Force General Emmett "Rosy" O'Donnell, a hard-drinking, indiscreet legend who had passed the word to the press that Mrs. Smith, in her position on the Armed Services Committee, was holding up a slew of Air Force promotions, including his own, because she was miffed at the

Air Force for having failed to make her the chief of its Woman's branch—the WAF.

Drew spied the raw material for a two-in-one victory here: persuade the Democrats to hold up O'Donnell's promotion (a worthy goal in itself to Drew, for "Rosy" was a MacArthur intimate who had urged the use of the A-bomb in Korea) as an offering to Mrs. Smith for her vote against Strauss.

Drew explored Mrs. Smith's interest in this arrangement somewhat delicately with Bill Lewis, her administrative assistant who lived under the same roof with the widow Smith and had an unusual degree of influence over her. The sacrificing of General O'Donnell was not brought forward as a tit-for-tat deal but rather as a fond gesture the Senate Democrats might make to create an ambience of reciprocity. The reaction from Lewis was positive and Drew went to the indispensable Clinton Anderson. Senator Anderson phoned Senator Henry "Scoop" Jackson, the key Senate figure in the O'Donnell confirmation proceedings, and Drew listened in some fascination at the laconic indirection with which the unscrupulous is prosecuted in the higher realms.

Anderson asked Jackson "not to push" the confirmation of O'Donnell, saying, "Mrs. Smith is very interested in this and she's also interested in something very close to me. We gave you a lot of help on Hanford [a great atomic installation in the state of Washington] and I would appreciate your holding this up." Jackson replied that come to think of it, he'd "probably be absent this week," so nothing would be moving on O'Donnell in the near future.*

Anderson said to Drew, as the vote neared, that "everything was in Lyndon's hands," signifying that we mere mortals had done as much as we could and the outcome now rested with the master. Just before getting on a plane for London, where he was a delegate to an international conference on the strengthening of NATO, Drew phoned Johnson and reviewed with him the status of the Margaret Smith–"Rosy" O'Donnell matter, a subject which definitely roused the interest of the phlegmatic wheeler-dealer from the Pedernales.

So it was that the continuation of the distinguished public career of Lewis L. Strauss, the judgment as to whether that career was, at its peak, to be crowned or forever blighted, hung upon the chaotic mercies of an incoherent maze of political biases, personal resentments, side deals, whims and trade-offs. On the level of issues, his fitness for the

Ibid. (May 26, 1959), p. 526.

Secretary of Commerce post was the least consideration, submerged in a referendum on the hoary decisions he had made in another arena—on the bomb, Oppenheimer, TVA. On a less respectable level, his future was hostage to a crazy quilt of considerations having little to do with him. He did not know why the Majority Leader was against him. He was losing votes for the sake of one senator's IOU to another, a lady's pique over a general's indiscretion, the subterranean pulls of factional herding. He was getting votes for reasons no more complimentary to the impact of his long career—because he was a Jew, because of Administration promises to deliver a dam or a sewer system somewhere, because of military jets that were speeding home from foreign travels those senators the party could count on.

It was about midnight on June 19, 1959, when the roll call on the confirmation of Lewis Strauss finally began. Senator Dodd had just concluded his long-delayed speech for Strauss, an impassioned appeal that, too late to have effect on senators, stirred the packed galleries to bursts of forbidden applause. As each senator cast his vote, anxious tabulators on both sides saw their estimate of a dead heat being confirmed—until, near the bottom of the roll, Senator Margaret Chase Smith's name was called and she voted against Strauss. Shock waves rippled through the chamber; it was over. Another senator who would have voted for Strauss if his vote was needed to make the difference left him now, and the final count was 49 to 46, against confirmation, with three not voting.

In his Strauss pact with Lyndon Johnson, Drew had not agreed to support Johnson for President, only to "lay off" him. But the months of collaboration during the confirmation battle restored his old-time regard for Johnson and impressed upon him anew his capacity as a political leader. "The liberals," he mused, "will always talk big, but nearly always lose either through faulty footwork or lack of determination. They don't go for the jugular. In the Strauss fight we worked with the conservatives and the moderates. The conservatives are far more efficient with their footwork and they fight to kill—provided they are genuinely on your side."*

He felt comfortable with Johnson, despite divergences, because Johnson, great dissembler though he was, seemed to reveal more of himself, seemed to get closer to the bone, than many of Drew's ideological soulmates. "Never get me into a fight like this again," Johnson

*__Ibid.__ (June 29, 1959), p. 536.

groused to Drew, complaining that the Strauss victory had soured his working relationship with Eisenhower.* Drew was delighted; that had been one of his objectives.

As the 1960 Democratic nomination quest shaped up into a primary contest between Kennedy and Humphrey, with Johnson hoping for a stand-off that would result in a convention stalemate and a turn to him, the "Washington Merry-Go-Round" was for Humphrey. But Drew was not surprised when Humphrey's gallant one-man show was out-gunned, outspent and outmaneuvered by the Kennedy machine. When Humphrey dropped out of the contest after losing the West Virginia primary, in which he was unconscionably smeared by the Kennedy forces as a draft dodger, Drew slowly moved to the support of Johnson. After a half-dozen fallings-out and rapprochements, he was satisfied as to Johnson's essential liberalism and of something equally important and incomparably scarcer—a leadership capacity that would ensure the adoption of a program of domestic reform that would rival FDR's.

Kennedy, so insubstantial compared to Johnson in the Majority Leader's domain of committee room and cloakroom, was clearly his master on the hustings, at the imagery game and in the garnering of delegates; his first ballot victory over Johnson in Los Angeles reminded Drew once again of how unamenable presidential-nomination politics was to his ministry.

But a general election, especially one as close as this one figured to be, was a different cow altogether; only John F. Kennedy now stood between Richard Nixon and the presidency, and the column ineluctably jumped into the fray on Kennedy's side, rounding on Nixon from day to day with our routine ammunition while searching for the reporter's desideratum—the exposé that would make a difference.

Drew had several times had his hands on stories which, properly staged, possessed the potential of turning presidential elections around; from trial and error he thought he knew what to look for, and if he found it, how to uncork it.

In the 1944 campaign (so the Pearson lorists told me, for it was before my time with Drew) he pieced together compelling evidence of Franklin Roosevelt's medical unfitness to serve a fourth term, but he suppressed his own story, for in his rankings, statecraft stood higher than journalism, and with the world to be restructured in the coming year, he preferred a dying Roosevelt to a robust Dewey.

*Ibid. (July 28, 1959), p. 541.

Twelve years later, in the campaign of 1956, Drew fished in deep medical waters again and came up with fascinating but not conclusive evidence that President Eisenhower had suffered a "mild relapse" of his heart ailment while electioneering. He could not be 100 percent sure because of the stone wall around Eisenhower, but this time Drew's political motor pushed him to publish—in the last week of the campaign. Jim Hagerty loosed all his artillery in denying the story, including having Ike enter Walter Reed Hospital for a day of tests, to emerge with the standard clean bill of health from medical experts. Drew stuck to his story but couldn't come up with anything to really make it stick; Hagerty whipped us badly this time, to the extent that even Drew referred to the story in later years as "the boo-boo."*

During the 1952 race, another possible election-decider (or self-incinerator) was within our grasp. In late summer, after the respective conventions had nominated tickets of Eisenhower-Nixon and Stevenson-Sparkman, we were at work on the story that a group of California businessmen had put up an $18,000 slush fund to supplement the salary of Senator Nixon. It could be a sensation, the more so because of the sanctimonious and overblown Ike-Nixon attack on the rather anemic corruption of the Truman Administration; but it could also be a three-day wonder. It needed time, Drew thought, time for the campaign to be further evolved and Nixon to emerge an inextricable part of it, time to button down the story beyond wriggling out and to trace the favors received from government by the various contributors to the Nixon fund—for *this* was the half of the story that could change the fund from a civic enterprise to a criminal conspiracy.

And so we burrowed quietly, but not so quietly that Nixon did not hear our scratching. With considerable care the vice-presidential nominee chose the threat best calculated to deter Drew, and the ambassador best suited to deliver it. William P. Rogers, the future Attorney General and Secretary of State, had been Drew's adviser and attorney through such hairy episodes as the Howser libel trial; now he was Nixon's campaign aide. Rogers called me from the Nixon campaign train in Montana to warn that if we went ahead with any revelation of a Nixon fund, Nixon would have no recourse but to retaliate by

---

*Nonpartisanship does not protect the reporter from presidential-year fever. I made a similarly spectacular mistake in 1972, at the expense of a ticket I favored, when I linked the medical problems of vice-presidential candidate Thomas Eagleton to alcoholism, based on reports I believed in but could not corroborate when sources refused to "go public"; so I retracted, to universal jeers.

discrediting Drew as a Communist operative; it was part of Rogers' role —perhaps keenly felt—to seem distressed about this needless danger to Drew and to caution that parrying Nixon on this charge, in the national spotlight of a presidential campaign, would be much harder than parrying the guerrilla attacks of Joe McCarthy, which almost had Drew on the floor as it was.

If anything could have made Drew more determined to bag Nixon than he already was, it was the blackmail threat transmitted by Rogers. When I reported the Rogers call to Drew, he replied firmly, "All right, I'll change the story. I'll make it stronger."

We were rapidly nailing down several accounts of Nixon official favors to fund donors. For example, he had intervened with the Justice Department in behalf of a $100,000 tax refund for the lawyer who set up the fund, Dana Smith; Nixon had again interceded for Smith, this time with the American ambassador in Cuba, to help Smith out of a jam occasioned by his failure to pay a $4,200 gambling debt at Havana's Club Sans Souci; again, two oilmen contributors, Tyler Woodward and William O. Anderson, who had been refused government permission to explore for oil on a military reservation, were now the beneficiaries of a Nixon bill to open up that reservation for exploration.

As it happened, however, two or three other news organizations were also digging away at the first half of this story, and while we were still tracking down what the Nixon donors got back, the saga of "Nixon's Secret Fund" erupted simultaneously at both ends of the country in the New York *Post* and the Los Angeles papers. But it was a case of premature exposure, as Nixon's classic escape quickly demonstrated. Had we been ready, as we soon were, with our stories about Nixon's reciprocal services, I doubt that the vice-presidential nominee would have been able to sell his Boy Scout version of the fund. But Richard Nixon had already won the battle of public opinion by the time we brought up our reserves.

Such might-have-beens, what aborted them, what could have saved them, were much on Drew's mind in the fall of 1960, as, in another presidential campaign with the one-chance-only brass ring whizzing toward us, we sighted upon a story that was pale compared to some that had misfired but, rightly managed, had color enough to convey the message.

The story revolved around a 1956 loan to the Nixon family, a loan which might be traceable to Howard Hughes and which, at first sighting, had the earmarks of a gift in the six-figure range. It was brought to my attention by the late James McInerney (he had been an Assistant Attorney General under Truman), who directed the clandestine investigative arm of the John F. Kennedy campaign. He supplied me with enough tantalizing tips to get our investigation off to a running start.

Fully assembled, the story boiled down as follows. With the approval of Richard Nixon, a bail-out loan of $205,000 was made by the Hughes Tool Company, represented by a stand-in for Hughes named Frank Waters, for the benefit of Nixon, Inc., which operated a small chain of restaurants featuring "Nixonburgers." The head of Nixon, Inc., was F. Donald Nixon, the candidate's brother. Richard Nixon was a stockholder. The purpose of the loan was to save Nixon, Inc., from impending bankruptcy; it was made to Hannah Nixon, mother of F. Donald and Richard, the only security being her corner lot in suburban Whittier, the site where she had brought up her children; the lot had been assessed at $13,000 and could be assumed to be worth about three times that. Two years after the loan, it was defaulted on.

We were certain of the facts. The question before us was whether there was in this transaction the necessary degree of scandal to justify exploding it in the midst of a presidential campaign. The reader may chortle over the unlikely spectacle of Drew Pearson, the hanging judge and Nixon archfoe, closeting himself to weigh the justice of loosing this attack, but consider that in addition to Drew's sense of propriety, there were compelling reasons for avoiding self-delusion: if no genuine scandal was involved, our column stood to suffer a serious compounding of the damage done in the last campaign by the Eisenhower "boo-boo;" and if the public did not perceive the story as legitimate, its effect would be to create sympathy and votes for Nixon, the more so given his genius for tear-inspiring self-defense.

There was a respectable scandal here; of that we were sure. Howard Hughes, the manipulative recluse known for his nonplatonic relationships with politicians, had several major interests pending before the Eisenhower Administration—from air routes to government contracts to legal disputes—at the time he was asked to make a sweetheart loan to the family of that Administration's number-two personage; if the conflict of interest concept meant anything, it meant that Richard Nixon and his immediate family should have eschewed even a legitimate loan from Hughes. But the loan was not legitimate. On the same security offered to Hughes, Don Nixon had been unable to borrow from traditional lending institutions even half the money he readily got from the tycoon. The subsequent default on the loan underlined its unbusinesslike nature; if the Hughes Tool Company had in fact taken possession of the Nixon lot, it recovered only a fourth of the principal and interest due, so that the transaction, in effect, amounted to a gift to the Nixons of between $125,000 and $175,000. Hughes was not known for charitable horse-trading, unless he had an ulterior motive. Moreover, the use of go-betweens to keep the name of Howard Hughes once removed, and then twice removed when a person named Philip Reiner was brought in to take over the trustee function of Frank Waters, showed an intention to hide a suspect transaction. Even the timing of the loan, in the weeks right after a triumphant re-election, a favored time—when incumbency is safe and no one is looking—for politicians to collect tainted "campaign" contributions, accept vicuña coats, and do other things they wouldn't do in the weeks *before* an election, was a giveaway that the participants knew all too well that the deal could not stand the clear light of day.

Our decision to publish having been made, the manner of publishing occupied Drew's deliberations. The story was less than compelling in its claim upon distracted public attention. The money, after all, hadn't gone to Richard Nixon. Many would praise Nixon for permitting his influence to be used to bail out not himself, but his brother. The only parties visibly despoiled were Howard Hughes and Hannah Nixon, whose widow's inheritance was gambled away by an improvident son. As a public offense it was nonlethal, hard to pin down, yet evocative of semisleeping perceptions of Nixon the sharpster, the corner-cutter, the huckster whose personal ethics were less than presidential.

Upon the pluses and minuses Drew brought to bear the experience painfully gained from high-stakes misfires in past presidential campaigns. It was a story easy to lose in the campaign maelstrom. If loosed too early, it would soon be forgotten in the hurly-burly of competing alarums; if held until too late, it could be discounted as a last-minute smear and might be killed altogether by editors grown leery of November First marvels.

Drew decided to publish just two weeks before the election, late enough to retain its impact till election day if it caught on, early enough to give the Nixon campaign ample time for rebuttal. We would open up with a full-throated charge to get attention, and with some of our proof, enough to ensure publication, but we would hold back critical items of proof to tempt the Nixon camp into the hope that we had only half the story and that if they were so disposed, they might yet lie their way out of it, at least for two weeks. If they opted for this course, we had them.

While we held the story and watched the clock tick, Nixon headquarters, which had gotten reports of our inquiries, decided on a bold move. Rather than wait for the bomb to go off and hope for a misfire, they would try to defuse it by means of a "backfire" news story fed to a sympathetic news organization that would not ask embarrassing questions, a story which gave an idealized version of the loan and alerted the press and the public to be wary of unscrupulous attempts that might be made to distort the innocent facts. If successful, this gambit would decrease the news value of our loan exposé, would confuse an already complicated matter for the public, and would constitute an unspoken warning to any editor about to run Pearson's story that the facts were in dispute, that due notice had been given and that a libel suit was a probability. But the "backfire" tactic was risky; it was an admission that there was smoke; our story, coming as a rebuttal to an official Nixon announcement, might have more news value and more editorial legitimacy than a gratuitous charge tossed from left field in the last inning of the campaign.

On October 24, sixteen days before the November 8 election, Nixon's "personal campaign manager," Robert Finch, later to be Secretary of Health, Education and Welfare, put out through the Scripps-Howard chain the following story: There had indeed been a loan of $205,000 but (1) Richard Nixon had absolutely nothing to do with it; (2) the loan came from a family friend, attorney Frank Waters, whose wife had gone to school with F. Donald's wife (a to-be-cherished specimen of Nixonia); and (3) that the property put up as security was worth between $200,000 and $300,000, so there could be no question of impropriety in the loan. The dread name of Howard Hughes was nowhere in evidence in this ordinary arrangement between old friends.

Two days later our story appeared. The $205,000, it charged, came from the Hughes Tool Company. Frank Waters "was actually acting for Howard Hughes with the approval and knowledge of the Vice President." The lot in Whittier offered as security "was worth $50,000 or $60,000 now but was worth less at the time of the loan." After the loan, Hughes's relations with various government agencies improved: "Trans World Airlines had been authorized to fly a new route to Miami; a Justice Department suit against the Hughes Tool Company was settled by a consent decree April 4, 1958; the Far East route of T.W.A. had been extended to Manila; the Hughes Aircraft Company had been awarded defense contracts and the Hughes Tool Company had received some business from the Civil Aeronautics Board that it had been unable to get previously." Drew was careful to state "Whether the improvement was connected with the loan is not known," but he followed up with the observation "There was no evidence that the Hughes loan was connected with any government favors given Hughes. But the reason for conflict of interest laws is because of this very fact—namely that it is difficult, if not impossible, to prove favoritism in high places. For that explicit reason, both the law and good ethics require that high government officials and those close to them have no financial interest in and accept no pecuniary favors from companies with problems before the government."

The absence from our article of key specifics that would show we knew the *entire* story apparently emboldened Nixon headquarters to hope it could bluff its way through: instead of waiting to see how widely our story would penetrate, Finch counterattacked instantly, which proved to be a mistake, for the Associated Press decided that the charge and countercharge aspect made it a big story and filed a lengthy dispatch on Pearson vs. Finch which was featured prominently in newspapers all over the country, including the New York *Times* and the Washington *Post.* Finch branded our story "an obvious political smear in the last two weeks of the campaign"; he repeated that the lender was Frank Waters and that there was "no basis for any claim that the money lent by Waters came from Hughes." Finch continued to float his inflated estimates of a house lot worth hundreds of thousands and to insist that Richard Nixon had nothing to do with the loan and didn't even know about it at the time.

Drew did not want the story to come to a head too quickly, so he turned the Nixon camp slowly on the spit. Referring mysteriously to correspondence in his possession between the attorney for Howard Hughes and a former law partner of Richard Nixon's, he issued a challenge: "I should be delighted to produce photostats of the secret deeds, transfers and other documents pertaining to the Howard Hughes loan, and show them on television with Don Nixon or Howard Hughes or Robert Finch present to deny them."

Now fearing the worst, the Nixon camp had to go into reverse gear and back off, a fatal shift once a dispute has reached the headline stage. Finch announced he could "not make a flat statement" on whether Hughes was the source of the loan "because I am not privy to the transaction." He said that the Nixon family was "getting all the documents together" and would make "full disclosure the first of next week." The telltale aura of culpability hovered over the sweating evasions of public relations men. Richard Nixon remained unavailable for comment. Howard Hughes, of course, could not be reached. Frank Waters continued to have no comment. Thus Drew's statements that "with his brother Don's finances becoming desperate, the Vice President asked his old friend Frank Waters, attorney for Howard Hughes, to help out" and that Waters "was actually acting for Hughes with the approval and knowledge of the Vice President" remained uncontradicted by the chief actors.* Their silence, and the folding of spokesman Finch, conveyed a sense of the sinister that the complicated facts themselves might not have. The announcement that "the Nixon family" was to be suddenly thrust out front to do the talking from now on seemed to presage that there remained no defense but bathos.

And so it was to be. In Monday's papers, F. Donald led off with several weepy paragraphs about how Drew Pearson, in order to smear his brother, was forcing F. Donald and his wife and daughters and mother to relive those dark days of financial embarrassment they had struggled so bravely to get behind them; then he admitted that the loan came from the Hughes Tool Company and that his "old friend" Frank Waters was acting as the trustee for Hughes, whom F. Donald had never met; his mother's lot had been deeded over to Hughes, he said, and he claimed it was worth $228,000.

Now in possession of the high ground, we fired the salvos we had been saving up. We quoted a dissent from Mrs. F. Donald Nixon to the official explanation that the loan came through the good offices of Frank Waters because of the family friendship dating back to the school days of the respective wives. The only factual thing about that, she said, was that long ago she had been in school with the future Mrs. Waters, but "Frank Waters never helped us out at all. We barely know the man. There is nothing to that at all."

We produced an affidavit relative to the claims of Finch and Don Nixon that the Whittier lot was worth variously $200,000 or $300,000 or $228,000, and was thus legitimate security for the loan. The affidavit was that of Hannah Nixon, made to the Los Angeles County Recorder

---

*With good reason. ". . . Noah Dietrich, executive vice president of the Hughes Tool Company, eventually told how he visited Richard Nixon before he paid the money in a circuitous fashion to Donald. Though Hughes had already approved the loan, Dietrich warned the Vice President it would become known sooner or later and cause a scandal. Nixon, he said, responded stiffly: 'Mr. Dietrich, I have to put my relatives ahead of my career.' "—Pilat, *op. cit.*, p. 294.

of Deeds on January 8, 1957, one month after the loan, and it stated that the total property left her by her recently deceased husband, including the Whittier lot, "did not then exceed the sum of approximately $100,000."

We further cited correspondence showing that neither Hannah Nixon nor any other individual was held personally liable for the Hughes loan in the wording of the agreement, and we revealed that Hannah Nixon was still, in November 1960, listed as the owner of the Whittier lot in the records of the Los Angeles County Recorder, a fact confirmed by Anthony Lewis in the New York *Times*. It may well be that Hannah Nixon, after the default, had come forward to assume responsibility for the family's good name, and that her property had found its way into the Hughes empire in a way not tracked by the Los Angeles County Recorder; but what was at issue was the character of the loan on December 10, 1956, not Hannah Nixon's self-sacrificing attempt to partially fumigate it later on.

Henceforth the Nixon camp hunkered down on its past statements and retreated into silence. Altogether there had been six separate stories down the neck-and-neck homestretch of the campaign, most of them carried or recapitulated in most newspapers.

Kennedy's victory over Nixon was so razor-thin as to become an automatic hostage to various debatable claims as to what made the final difference: the stealing of votes for Kennedy in Chicago; the knee injury to Nixon, getting out of a car, which put his campaign off schedule; the poor pancake make-up on Nixon, which caused him to "lose" the first debate on television though he "won" it on radio, etc. One of these putative tide-turners was the Hughes loan story. It is not for me to push the claim, but it is appropriate to note evidence that both the Kennedy and Nixon high commands took it seriously. Right after the election Kennedy's campaign manager, brother Robert, in discussing the decisive factors, said that Nixon "had been hurt by a story of an alleged loan from Howard Hughes to Donald Nixon." When a panel of Nixon strategists was asked to assess Kennedy's statement, as reported in the New York *Times* of November 13, Robert Finch snapped, "I think that's a despicable comment."

Despicable or not, there are ample reports that Nixon himself blamed his defeat on the Hughes loan stories. So durable was that conviction that in describing the Nixon White House of twelve years later, John Dean, H. R. Haldeman and others have alluded to the persistent belief that, in Dean's words, "the 'Hughes loan' scandal had cost Richard Nixon the 1960 election to John F. Kennedy."

For eight years following the Kennedy-Nixon election, Drew took satisfaction from the notion that, whichever of his objectives in life had gone awry, he had at least had a hand in keeping down Richard Nixon. But suddenly there he was again, revived, rehabilitated and leading Hubert Humphrey in the polls as decision day approached in the presidential campaign of 1968, which was to be Drew's last.

We upheld Humphrey, of course, and smote Nixon with standard fare about how the big special interests represented by his New York law firm would be in the saddle if the Republicans won. Then, in the midst of the campaign, Drew got hold of another story that might have the potential to turn around a close election. He learned that Dr. Arnold Hutschnecker, a New York psychiatrist who described himself as a "specialist in psychosomatic medicine," had secretly treated Nixon for a year in the mid-1960s. Drew pursued the matter and got impeccable confirmation that the treatments had indeed taken place. Dr. Hutschnecker could not be expected to reveal confidences about Nixon's condition, and would be in violation of his code if he did. On the contrary, he could be expected, like all previous doctors of presidential-level patients, to minimize the implications of Nixon's problem, whatever it was, and he did. But the very fact that Nixon had been under the care of a psychiatrist, whatever the official explanation, would probably galvanize the sleeping concern of many that Nixon had emotional problems—concern fed by the uptightness of the man, the scene of him weeping on Senator Knowland's shoulder at the Nixon fund denouement in 1952, the disturbed "You won't have Nixon to kick around anymore" outburst at the press after his 1962 defeat in California, the reports from inside his current campaign that he was being carefully paced to prevent any further unravelings under strain.

But Drew held off. Was he again waiting for the optimum time? As Humphrey closed the gap and another presidential campaign roared into its last days "too close to call," that time would seem to have arrived. But Drew would not run the story—even the bare fact, without background music—that Nixon had been under Dr. Hutschnecker's care, certainly a legitimate story. He seemed torn by concerns that a few years before would not have finally inhibited him: that, however sanitized our account, Nixon would be victimized by the public's ignorant fear of things psychiatric; that he, Pearson, would be responsible for another acrimonious upheaval at a crucial moment; that, on the heels of his 1956 and 1960 campaign missiles, he would be thought incorrigibly partisan and venal. So he did not use the story; only when the campaign was over did he reveal its details, in a low-key way, during a luncheon talk to reporters. A comparative mellowness had come to Drew Pearson in his seventieth year.

During the first months of the Nixon Administration, the column was uncharacteristically observant of the honeymoon tradition, after its fashion. At the six-month mark, Drew called his staff together to discuss whether or not the time had come to call off the truce and go on the attack. Most of us favored opening up. But Drew decided to give President Nixon more time to reveal his direction. "Nixon was working for his ambition until he became President," he said. "Now he is working for the history books."

It was to be Drew's last staff conference.

Afterthought

IN HIS seventy-first year the seeming eternal surge of purposeful energy, restless but disciplined to a steady hum, suddenly slackened from a weariness that was to him unaccountable and unacceptable, and in a few weeks he was gone. "His passionate voice is stifled," said President Johnson. "The nation will feel the silence."

The immediate cause of death, on September 1, 1969, was a heart attack; the ultimate cause was a refusal to heed the warnings that he cease his striving. Two days before, he had told me he was ready to resume his regular writing schedule; he had a bunch of columns all thought out in his head.

The opening lines of the Washington *Post*'s farewell, written by Chalmers Roberts, summed things up about as well as three sentences could: "Drew Pearson was a muckraker with a Quaker conscience. In print he sounded fierce; in life he was gentle, even courtly. For thirty-eight years he did more than any man to keep the national capital honest."

Two months before his death, in giving an interview to the *Nation* magazine, he had defined the journalistic purpose that remained after all the dreams of youth had either vanished or been fulfilled. "My chief motive is to try to make the government a little cleaner, a little more efficient and I would say also, in foreign affairs, to try to work for peace."

His last years with the column were as eventful as the first. On the Washington front, they were enlivened by long-running exposés which led to the expulsion from the House of Representatives of Adam Clayton Powell, for exceeding even the Congress' tolerance of high private living at public expense, and to the censure by the Senate of Thomas J. Dodd, for high private living on political contributions; these were landmark scandals, as it turned out, in that they finally, after almost two centuries, forced the enactment in each house of the first halting ethical standards and enforcement machinery. On the larger field of world peace Drew consummated, in his sixties, the kind of grand gesture to which his youthful visions had always inclined him by three times going halfway around the world to act as self-injected intermediary between Nikita Khrushchev and the American people.

This was the quintessential Pearson, the idealistic visionary behind the scandalmonger's mask, willing to gamble at one throw, if the stakes were high enough, the public image and public access he so assiduously cultivated and protected; when I reflect on Drew's life and its lessons, I am drawn to this episode.

From the latter days of the Eisenhower Administration, when Khrushchev broke off the Paris Peace Conference, through the Kennedy-era crises over Berlin and Cuba-based missiles and into the Johnson reign, the Russian dictator was viewed by most Americans as a menace somewhat akin to Hitler, a reckless, vulgar and brutal missile-rattler who kept the world on the edge of nuclear war. Drew, who had studied his moves with all the hope of a Quaker and who had talked with him at the United Nations in 1959, saw him in a different light—as an innovative ruler walking a tightrope, trying to partially de-Stalinize Russia, reduce the size of its armed forces, reform its grotesquely overcentralized economy, raise living standards and move from a near-war footing to a less confrontative competition by nonmilitary means with the West, but to do all this he must at the same time keep off balance the Communist old guard, which resisted any departure from the old priorities and rigidities, by talking tough to the West, and on some sensitive matters, by acting tough. Khrushchev's dilemma was, in Drew's analysis, that to succeed in pulling his old guard with him toward change, he needed some gestures from the West that he could hail at home as victories, but his pugnacious image made it dangerous politics for a U.S. President to appear to accommodate him. Drew's self-confidence and his belief in the power of open communication were such that he hoped he could influence Khrushchev to stop fouling his American image with tough-guy poses, could explain to him both the peaceful intentions and the political realities of America, and could serve as both an unofficial forum for stating Khrushchev's underlying views to the American people and an informal avenue for signals to our officialdom. Moreover, Drew was alert to a historic split developing between Russian and Chinese Communism which, ending the era of a single world Communist front, opened up opportunities for new diplomatic overtures, and he wanted to probe the degree of that split.

And so in 1961, 1963 and 1964 Drew conferred with Nikita Khrushchev, twice at his vacation home in the Crimea and then in Egypt, where Khrushchev was dedicating the Aswan Dam. These meetings involved a series of marathon interviews, some of them lasting up to four hours. Between sessions the two swam together in the Black Sea, the squat Khrushchev paddling around cradled in a rubber tire, the tall Pearson, a relentless swimmer, showing off his best moves. Out of the interviews came briefings, delivered personally to Presidents Kennedy and Johnson and other officials, and of course a series of news dispatches that were sensational journalistic coups but severe public relations hazards, in that Drew was portraying a sometimes congenial, progressive, peace-tending Khrushchev, by Kremlin standards, and letting Khrushchev state his case in the interviews with a minimum of editorial heckling.

I warned Drew that the timing was wrong, as it invariably was; that the public, just after being warned by President Kennedy to build air-raid shelters because a confrontation loomed over Berlin, or after being scared to death by Russian missiles in Cuba, was not in a mood to look upon Khrushchev as any kind of reformer or to sympathize with his domestic problems. I cautioned that the public would reject any talk of a Sino-Soviet split and our hard-liners would attack the concept as "a trick to sap our eternal vigilance," and I predicted that boycotts, cancellations and the old charge of "Communist agent" would be revived against us. But Drew would not be deterred either by bad timing or by organized reprisals, and his articles ran as planned, causing an anti-Pearson furor but also planting seeds here and there that later prompted Chalmers Roberts to credit him with "dabbling in East-West *détente* long before it became fashionable."

The Khrushchev episodes illustrated the pre-eminent qualities in

Drew Pearson that advancing age would not diminish: the journalistic imagination and boldness, the surging hope born of idealism, and the toughness and courage to act on his better impulses in the worst weather. The memory of those qualities was the heritage he left to those who knew him and his work.

He did not give me any considerable instruction in the practical techniques of newspapering—which is what I had thought I would learn from him—but he took infinite pains to inculcate his convictions on the moral objectives of the newspaper column and the just society: to champion the cause of the voiceless instead of the dominant, the dissenter as well as the organization, the helpless as against their exploiters, the small enterprise over the octopus, the public's right to know and control rather than the official's prerogative to conceal and manipulate. During the years that I have been on my own, when I have tended to stray from that standard, I always see Drew shaking his professorial head in gentle reproof.

As the preceding pages show, his tactics violated many of the canons of conventional journalism, in the main because, as almost the only voice in his field, he had to stunt and overdramatize and oft-repeat to fill the void left by the failure of the establishment press to live up to its watchdog responsibilities. His view of the larger role of the press has been vindicated in the decade since his death by the growth of investigative, muckraking journalism to its present fashionability. The would-be informer of today has a bewildering array of outlets to turn to, and even enjoys special protection under the civil service laws.

I objected frequently, and am not yet reconciled to, his subordination of the rules of journalism to "larger" considerations—his mixing of reporting with political activism, his getting into bed with what he judged the lesser offender in order to get help in bagging the greater, his occasional use of deduction to carry on from where investigative fact left off. Yet, even here, the experience of our time may bring him out right.

Our world is being vandalized and poisoned piece by piece by tidy specialists who scrupulously obey the codes of their narrow professions but claim no responsibility to larger realms—chemists whose wonders foul the air and the seas; economists whose rules speed the racing materialistic change that is obliterating social mores with catastrophic effect; agri-scientists who would poison and destroy the land tomorrow so that it might yield a bigger crop today; lawyers who endlessly complicate their procedures while justice languishes; politicians who, in the name of getting the most for their districts, bankrupt the common-wealth. Drew Pearson tried to see the world whole and to subject his speciality to that ordered vision. I am cautious enough to fear the superimposing on journalism of larger designs but I am not wise enough to dare condemn it.

On the morning of the day he died, he was lifted up by thoughts of the morrow's return to his office on 29th Street. He was preparing a column on the state of medical care, which, of late, he had perforce been observing close up. His adopted son, Tyler, took him driving on an inspection tour of his beloved Potomac farm, his favorite pastime. He stopped at the beanpatch, looking forward to a chat with a hired hand about that which is ultimately important—sunlight, water, soil, insects. Then he pitched forward, struggling for breath, and in an hour his journey was over. A fortnight before, he had said to a friend, "We've got to live a long time. We've got so much to do."

Index

About the Authors

JACK ANDERSON was born in Long Beach, California, but brought up in Salt Lake City, Utah. He served as a Mormon missionary between 1941 and 1943, and the rest of the war years briefly as a cadet officer in the merchant marine, and then as a civilian war correspondent. When he was sought by his draft board in 1946, he was with a band of Chinese guerrillas behind Japanese lines; he was inducted and assigned to the Shanghai edition of *Stars and Stripes*.

Mr. Anderson joined Drew Pearson's staff on 1947 and took over the "Washington Merry-Go-Round" when Pearson died in 1969. The column now appears in nearly a thousand newspapers both here and abroad. Mr. Anderson is also the Washington Bureau chief for *Parade* magazine, and he appears daily on the ABC *Good Morning America* program as well as on the Mutual Radio Network. Winner of the Pulitzer Prize for National Reporting in 1972, he is the author of several best-selling books, including *The Anderson Papers*. He lives in Maryland with his wife; they have nine children and three grandchildren.

JAMES BOYD is the author of *Above the Law: The Rise and Fall of Senator Thomas J. Dodd*, and the co-author of *In the Name of Profit: Profiles in Corporate Irresponsibility*. His articles have appeared in *Harper's*, the *New York Times Magazine*, *Washington Monthly* and other publications. Formerly a U.S. Senate aide and executive director of the Fund for Investigative Reporting, he was born in Portland, Maine, and now lives in Etlan, Virginia.